Tying
Emergers

Jim Schollmeyer
and
Ted Leeson

Tying Emergers

Jim Schollmeyer
and
Ted Leeson

Frank
Amato
PORTLAND

Acknowledgements

We'd like to thank all the tyers whose work appears in these pages. A book such as this relies on the cooperation and good will of a rather large number of people, and fortunately, we've never found these qualities particularly difficult to come by among fly tyers. They are compulsively helpful, and we are most grateful for it.

We are particularly indebted to Hans Weilenmann who, in addition to contributing patterns to this book, generously allowed us to borrow from his published materials, and to pillage his wonderful archives of tyers and flies. Thanks as well to Ian Moutter for his kind permission to present ideas and patterns from his book on Paraloop patterns. We are grateful to Howard Cole and Mike Mercer, gifted fly designers and tyers, for going the extra mile. Thanks to two fly-tying authorities with very different areas of expertise—Dr. Andrew Herd and Wayne Luallen—for many kindnesses and for their enlightening correspondence about emergers,

emerger patterns, and fly tying in general. It was a privilege, during the course of this book, to exchange tying ideas with the late Andrija Urban of Macedonia, one of the region's most respected tyers, who generously shared with us many of his patterns and techniques; we will miss his inventive imagination and devotion to the craft. And thanks to Bruce Salzburg who took an interest in this project from the start and pointed us in many useful directions.

A number of tyers went out of their way to furnish patterns, flies, materials, information about their designs, and clarification of their tying techniques. We're grateful to Andy Burk, Paul Dieter, Chip Drozenski, Thomas C. Duncan, Sr., Oliver Edwards, Joe Evans, Richardt Jensen, Vladimir Markov, Darrel Martin, Tomaz Modic, John Mundinger, Denny Rickards, Shane Stalcup, Henk Verhaar, Martin Westbeek, and Steven Williams, for help above and beyond the call.

All inquiries should be addressed to:
Frank Amato Publications, Inc.
P.O. Box 82112
Portland, Oregon 97282
503-653-8108
www.amatobooks.com

Photography: Jim Schollmeyer
Book production: Tony Amato/Jerry Hutchinson

Softbound ISBN: 1-57188-306-1   Hardbound ISBN: 1-57188-307-X
Softbound UPC: 0-81127-00140-8   Hardbound UPC: 0-81127-00141-5
Hardbound Limited ISBN: 1-57188-320-7
Hardbound Limited UPC: 0-81127-00154-5

Printed in Singapore

1 3 5 7 9 10 8 6 4 2

TABLE OF CONTENTS

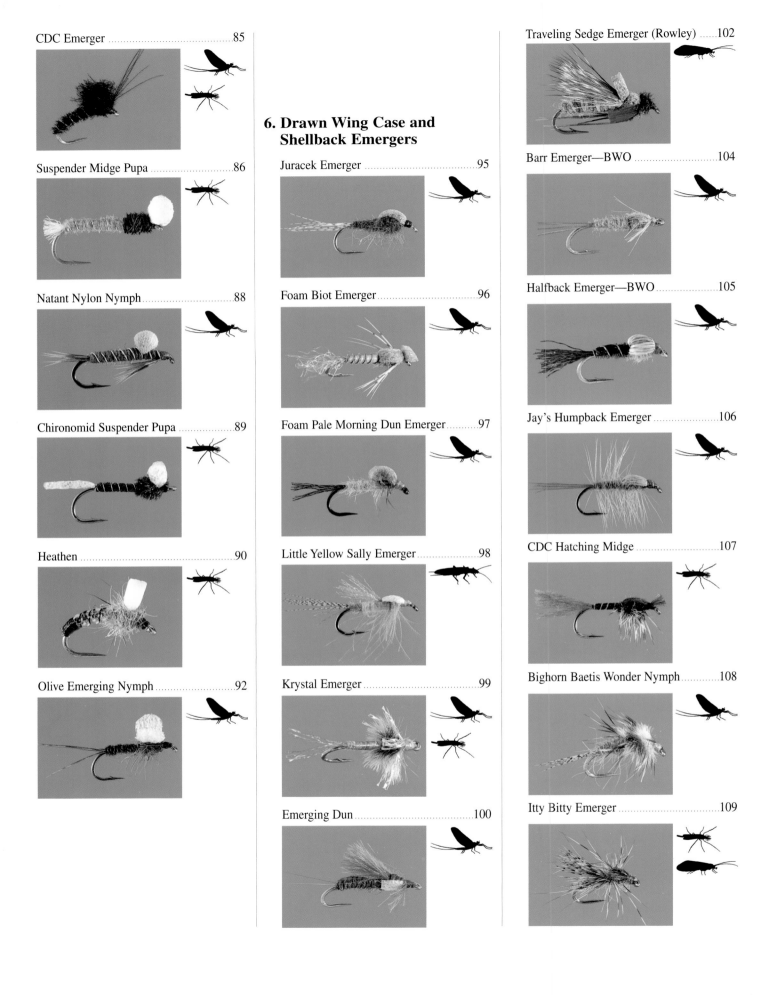

6. Drawn Wing Case and Shellback Emergers

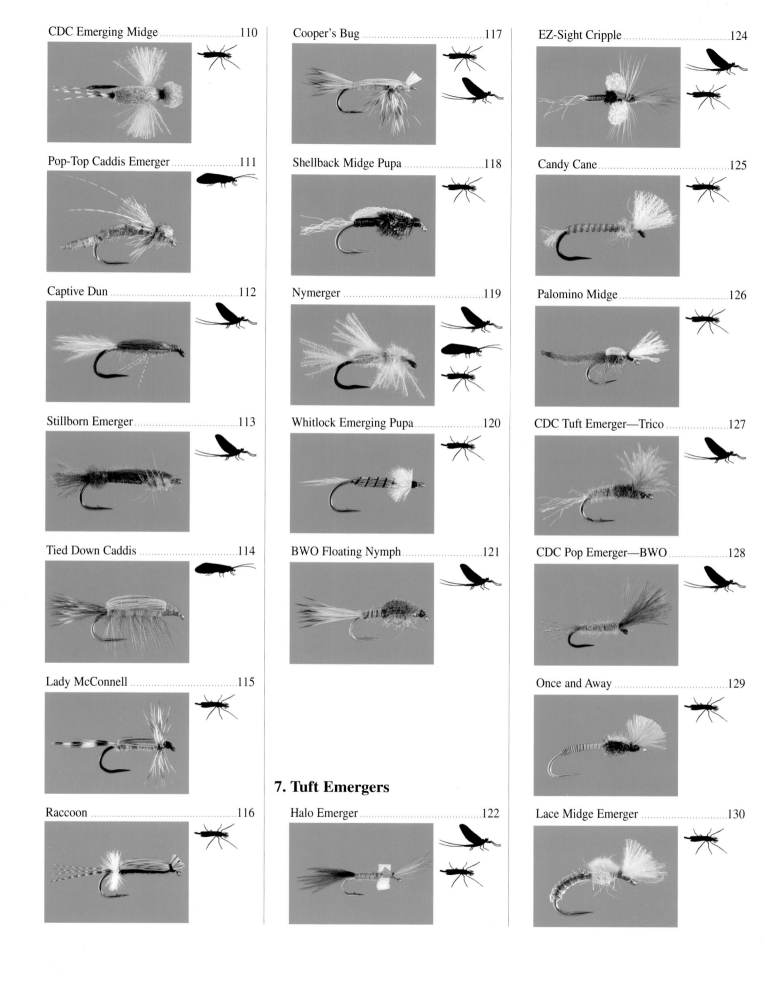

7. Tuft Emergers

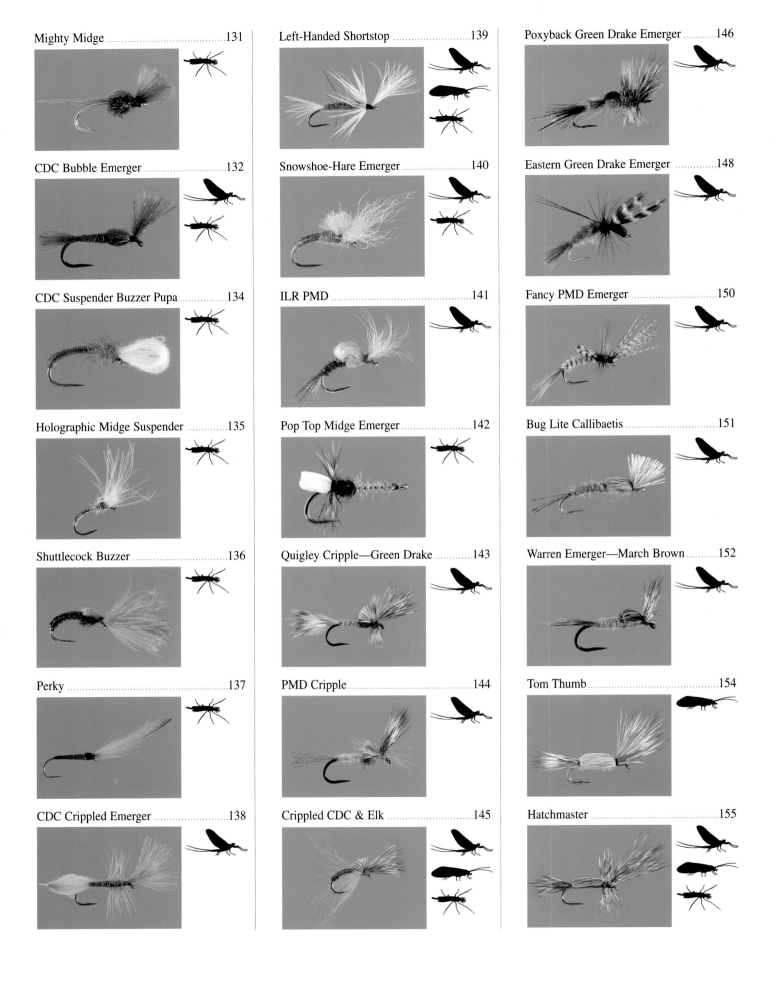

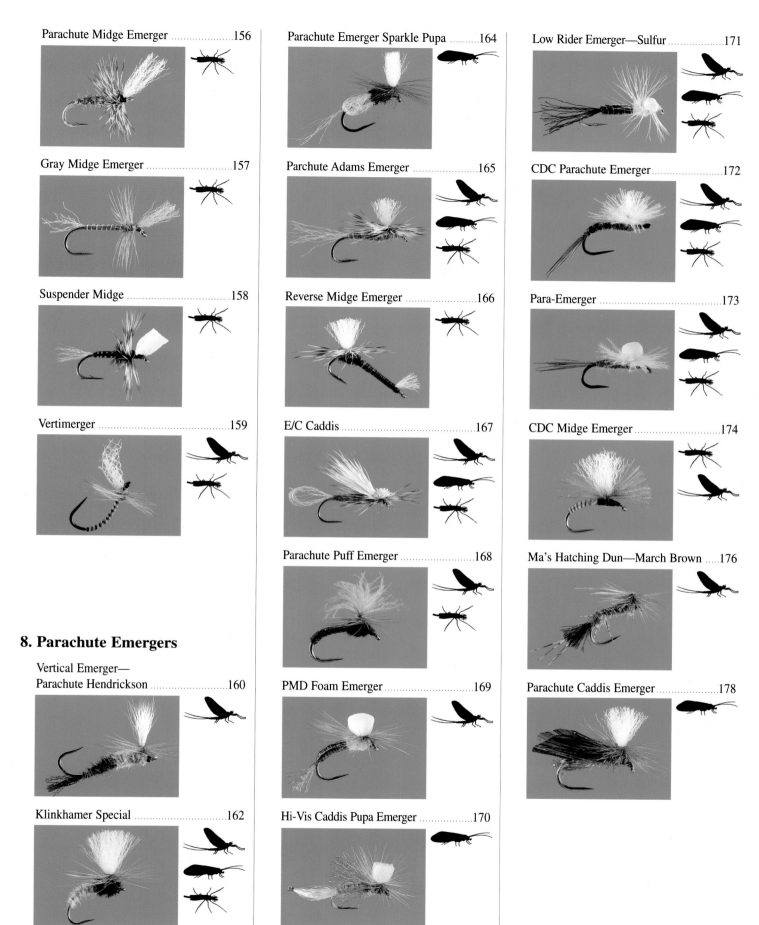

8. Parachute Emergers

9. Parasol and Umbrella Emergers

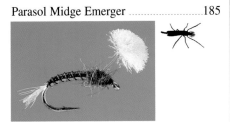

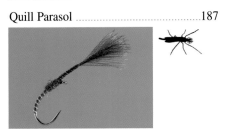

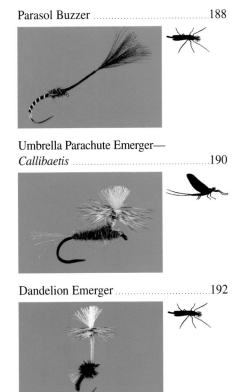

10. Paraloop Emergers

11. Collar Hackle and Herl Collar Emergers

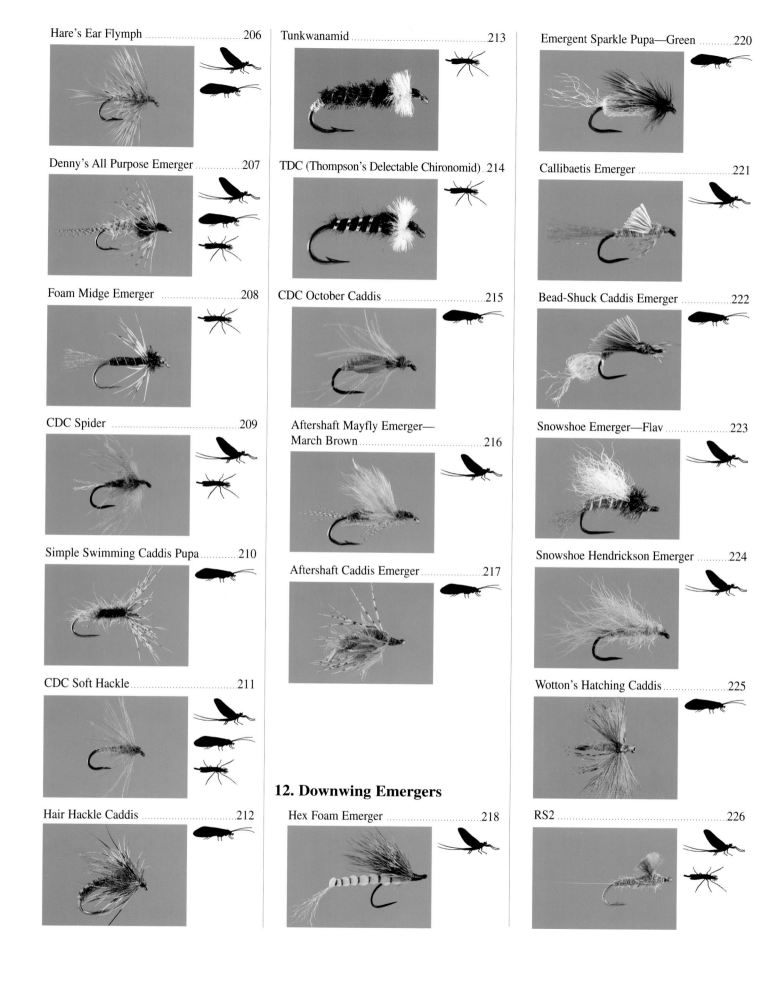

12. Downwing Emergers

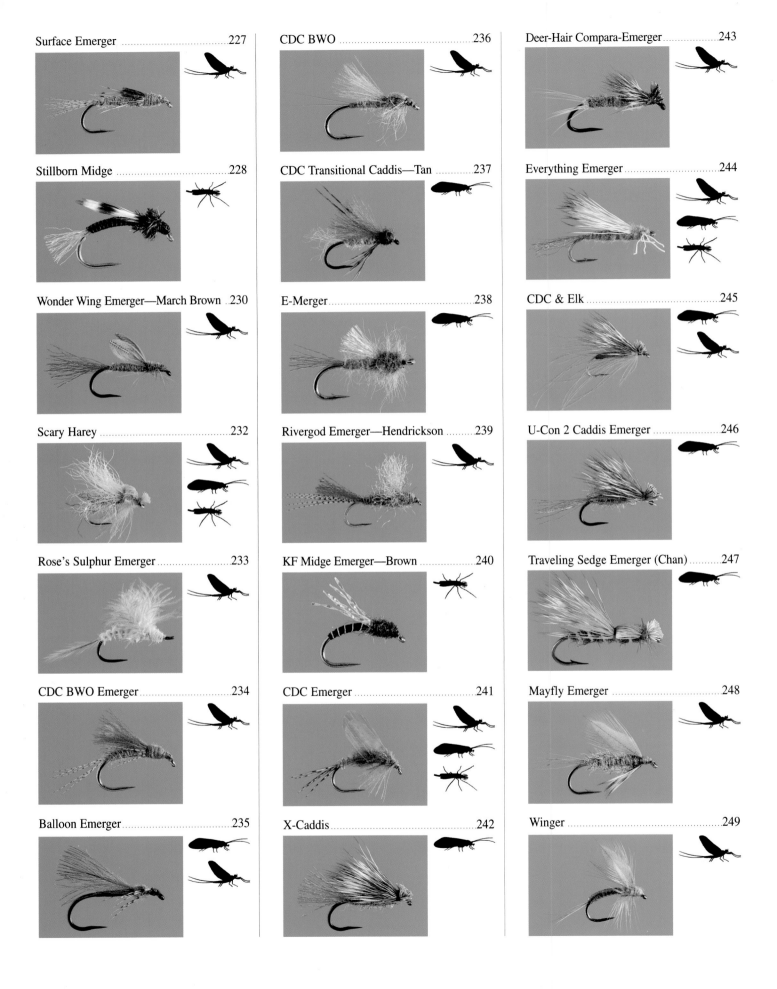

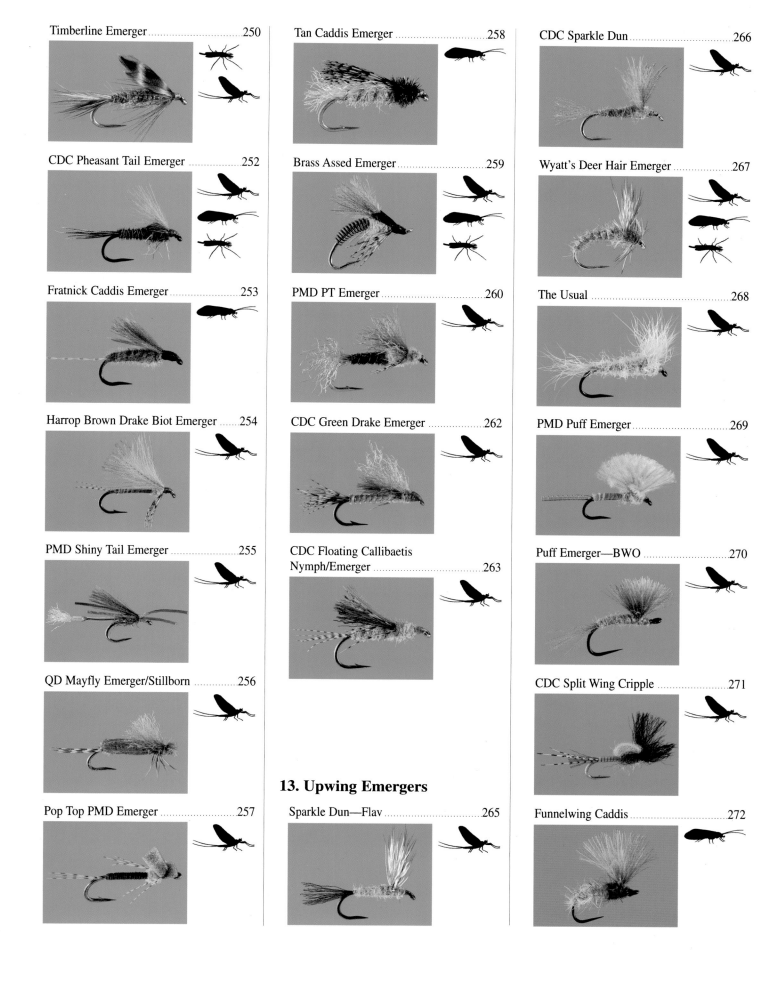

13. Upwing Emergers

14. Loopwing Emergers

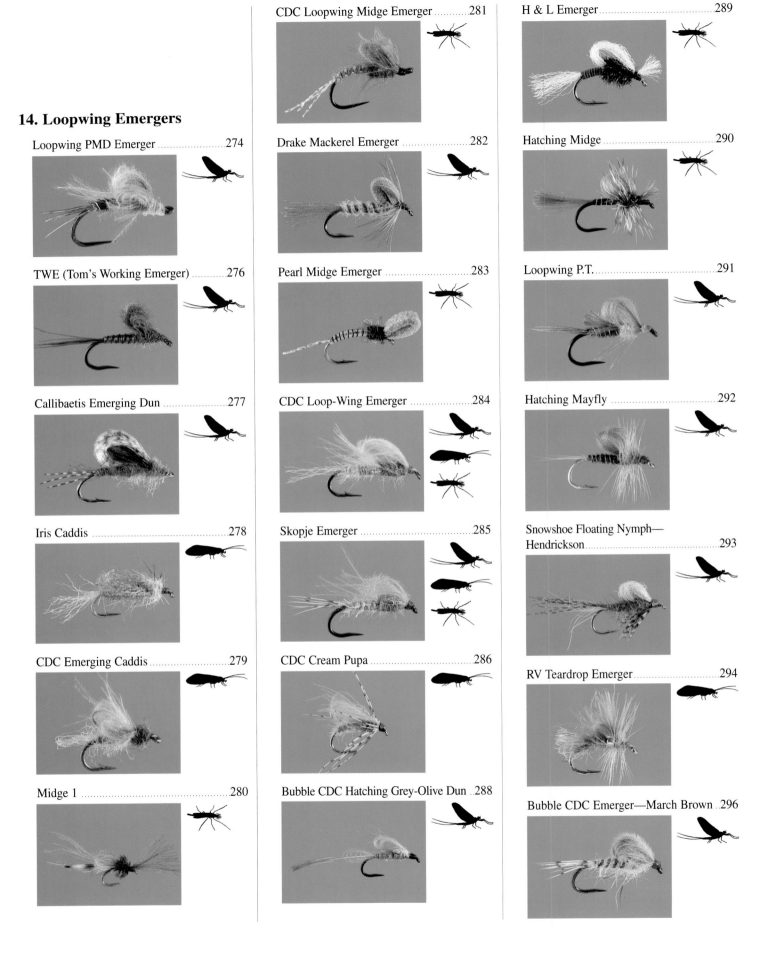

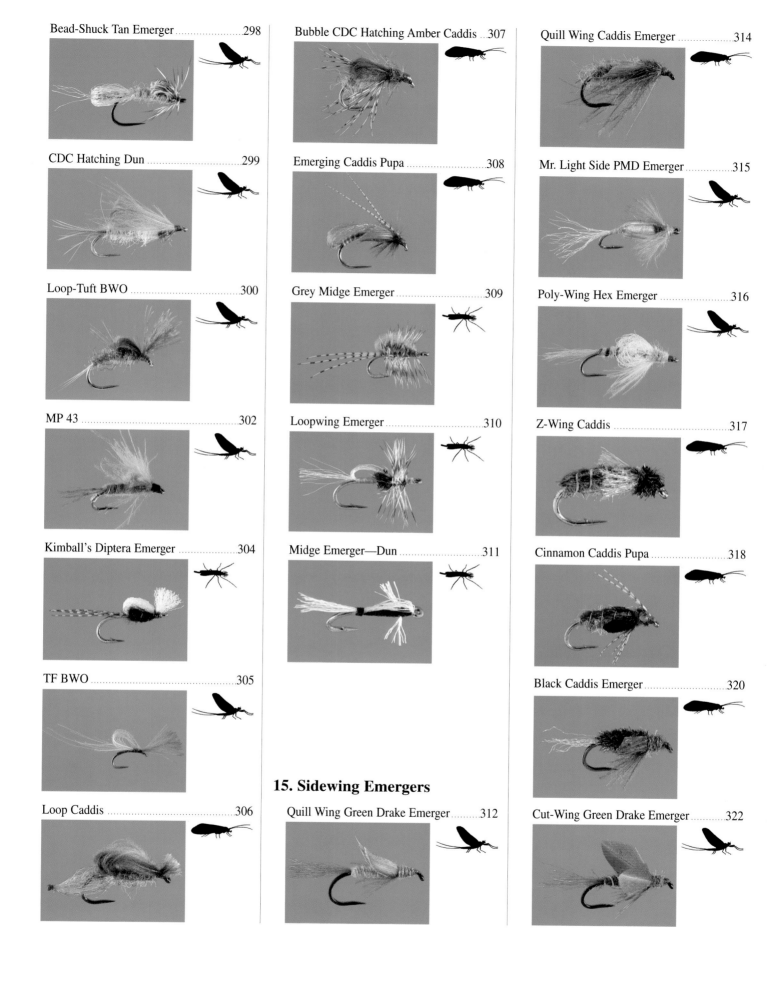

15. Sidewing Emergers

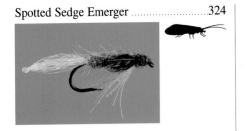

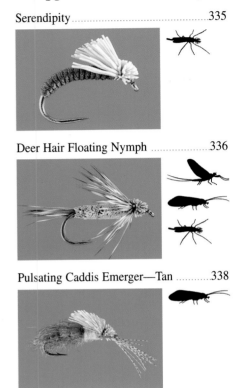
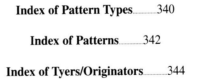

Introduction

The transformation of an insect from an aquatic form to a terrestrial one is an event both humble and dramatic. It is a small-potatoes spectacle that happens a million times a day in nature, yet each metamorphosis is so complex and so complete that it never fails to astonish. The great majority of insects important to trout anglers undergo such a change. And while not all families of insects, or even species within a family, accomplish this change in quite the same way, the specifics of emergence can be divided into three general categories:

First, the nymphs or pupae of some insects crawl out of the water onto stones or vegetation, where they complete their transformation into the adult terrestrial form. Certain species of caddisflies and mayflies, and nearly all species of stoneflies, behave in this way, and the emergent forms of these insects are generally unimportant to fishermen.

Second, some mayflies and caddisflies shed their nymphal skins or pupal shucks under water and swim or float to the surface as adult insects. These species are significant to anglers and can be fished with emerger patterns presented anywhere in the water column.

Third, a great many species of mayflies and caddisflies, and nearly all midges, emerge as the nymphal or pupal insect swims, wriggles, floats, or otherwise rises to the surface and crawls from its shuck onto the platform of the surface film. The crumpled wings unfold and dry as the adult insect waits to fly off. Insects that exhibit this particular mechanism of transformation are so important to fly-fishers that they are virtually synonymous with "emergers" in the angler's vocabulary.

Emerging insects have always been important to trout—and so by extension to fishermen—though until comparatively recent times, anglers failed to appreciate that significance largely because the phenomenon of emergence itself went unrecognized. Certainly in the long course of fly-fishing history, individual fishermen here and there observed aquatic insect transformation and perhaps took note of its specifics even though they may not have understood the complete life cycle of the creature. But as Dr. Andrew Herd notes in *The Fly*, his fascinating account of the origin and development of fly-fishing, ". . . even in the middle of the nineteenth century, the majority of anglers still laboured under the peculiar misconception that the flies they saw on the surface of the water had fallen there from above." Odd, even incredible, as it may seem that the metamorphosis of aquatic insects went unremarked for centuries in the literature of angling, what we might call "emerger-style" fishing may actually have been one of the earliest forms of fly-angling practiced. Dr. Herd observes, "Having watched people fish with hazel rods and horsehair lines in the Balkans [where Dr. Herd argues persuasively that fly-fishing may have originated], and reading between the lines of the older angling accounts, I am pretty certain that fishermen have known the importance of fishing in the film and just under it since time began. They may not have had a word for what they were trying to imitate, and they may have thought that flies fell on the water from above, but their method was good—even in the seventeenth century they knew their best chance was when the fly was fishing in that shallow surface layer."

From our perspective now, looking back, it seems reasonable to think that once the life cycles of trout-stream insects were understood, anglers would be keen to take advantage of this information, enlarge their repertoire of artificial flies, and improve their chances on the water. But for various reasons—perhaps the conceptual dominance of the dry fly foremost among them—the headway made in emerger fishing was largely sidelong and indirect, a byproduct of other fishing approaches and types of fly patterns. And only in perhaps the last half century or so has the specific imitation of this part of the insect life cycle become a deliberate and conscious concern of fishermen and "emergers" become a recognizable category in fly tying.

We suspect that this growing interest in tying and fishing emergers has a number of intersecting causes, but it can probably be traced most directly to a general increase in awareness among fishermen of the importance of entomology, and to its corollary technical approach—matching the hatch—both of which first reached a wide angling audience in the work of Ernest Schiewbert. Though at first a principle applied chiefly to duplicating the size, color, and silhouette of insect species, hatch-matching was soon broadened to encompass imitating stages in the life cycles of insects. A number of fishermen undertook more systematic field studies in which the particularities of emergence were more closely observed and anatomized. Anglers such as Dave Whitlock, Fred Arbona, Mike Lawson, Gary Borger, Al Caucci, Bob Nastasi, Gary LaFontaine, René Harrop, and particularly Doug Swisher and Carl Richards—whose books *Selective Trout* and *Emergers* are still indispensable reading—began translating their field observations into new fly designs and fishing techniques. At the same time, a growing number of anglers, heavier fishing pressure, and (we would argue) the rise of tailwater fisheries all encouraged new fly designs that would deceive increasingly angler-savvy populations of trout. Finally, within the last two decades or so, the avenues for disseminating information to fly-fishermen have increased as well—more books, more magazines, and most recently, Internet communication, which has made the exchange of fishing and tying ideas both rapid and international. The net result is that "emergers" have entered the vocabulary and the fly boxes of a great number of anglers, though by no means all of them.

Emerger Patterns

For many fly-fishermen, particularly those new to the sport, emerger patterns are sometimes a source of some confusion—understandably since, as an artificial fly type, "emerger" is the most wide ranging and amorphous of pattern categories. There's a good reason for this—emergers combine approaches to representation that are customarily held separate. Generally speaking, we might say that the successful representation of an aquatic food form has two parts—its appearance and its behavior. The tyer seeks to replicate the appearance of one stage in the life of an aquatic insect—a caddis larva, for instance, or a midge pupa, or a mayfly spinner. The angler is responsible for imitating the behavior of the organism—the dead-drift of a nymph caught in the current or a mayfly dun on the surface, the skittering of an egg-laying caddis, the darting movement of a baitfish or damselfly nymph. But the creature we call an "emerger" does not represent a fixed stage in the life cycle of an insect in the way that a nymph or spinner does. Emergence is a dynamic phase, an ongoing process, a transition from one identifiable stage to another. That is, emergence is itself a behavior, and it puts the tyer in a challenging and rather unusual position—not that of imitating a fixed and recognizable form of the insect, but rather of representing a process.

An artificial fly, of course, cannot represent an ongoing process, the continually changing appearance of the insect. It can only freeze that process at one point in time, and this constraint goes a long way toward explaining why "emerger" as a fly-tying category is so varied and ill-defined. An artificial fly may represent a point very early in the transformation, which gives rise to emerger patterns that look a good deal like nymphs and are generally designed to ride just below the surface. Or a tyer may imitate a point at which the insect begins to emerge from the nymphal or pupal skin and produce one of the many "halfway" patterns that sit in the surface film and contain features of both the aquatic and terrestrial stages of the insect. Or a tyer might freeze the process of emergence at a point very late in time, when the insect is almost fully emerged, and produce a pattern that is almost indistinguishable from an adult insect sitting on the surface film. The metamorphosis of the insect is so dramatic, and the life forms at the start and finish of the process so different in appearance, that there's little wonder why individual emerger patterns representing the same insect often bear little resemblance to one another.

The problem of drawing boundaries around the fly-tying category of emergers is further compounded by the fact that emergence behavior can be replicated by the fisherman using patterns that we typically assign to a different fly category. That is to say, some patterns, nymphs for instance, can be *fished* as emergers; we may dead-drift, say, a Hare's Ear, and then let it swing and bring it to the surface, as in a "Leisenring lift." We often conclude that trout we catch this way "took" the fly for an emerger. The conclusion may or may not be accurate, but it does complicate the question, "What is an emerger pattern?"

In writing this book we had, of necessity, to make some decisions about the matter; to include every fly pattern that might be fished or taken as an emerger would quite literally be an endless task. So we have restricted the emerger patterns in this book to those that ride just underneath, in, or on the surface film to imitate insects whose emergence is imminent, in process, or nearly finished. And for our purposes, the category "emergers" also includes floating-nymph patterns, typically intended to represent insects on the verge of hatching, as well as cripple and stillborn imitations, designed to represent imperfectly or incompletely emerged insects. (Many of the patterns in this book, of course, particularly those in Chapter 4, Bubble Brushed-Sheath Emergers, can in fact be successfully fished deeper in the water column—and routinely are—either by weighting the fly or the leader.) But even with the limits we set, the process of selecting flies from an abundance of patterns was no small task.

About This Book

We used two basic guidelines in choosing the 217 flies that appear in this book. First, we simply wanted to present a broad assortment of patterns—some familiar standards, some quite new—that are effective in fishing mayfly, caddis, and midge hatches. Second, we wished to illustrate a wide range of emerger designs and styles along with the various materials that can be used to dress them. The logic of the first criterion, we trust, is self-evident; the rationale for the second may be less obvious. Our own time at the vise, probably like that of most tyers, is divided among dressing proven patterns, modifying existing designs, and trying out our own ideas. Thus while we enjoy using pattern books of all kinds, we particularly appreciate those that are geared as much toward presenting ideas in fly design as they are specific patterns. So our aim in this book is really twofold: to present step-by-step tying sequences for specific, useful patterns; and to give tyers a reservoir of ideas and approaches for designing emergers that best accord with their perceptions of hatching insects, with their tastes in fly patterns, and with their styles of tying.

To further this second goal, we've broken with the more traditional formats that either present patterns alphabetically or organize them by insect type—midge, caddis, mayfly. These approaches certainly have their merits, and we have provided an alphabetical index of fly patterns at the end of the book, as well as an index of pattern types that assigns the flies in this book to specific insect categories. To this same end, each recipe is accompanied by one or more silhouette icons that indicate the type or types of insects for which the pattern is designed:

mayfly   caddis

midge   stonefly

But to be consistent with our purpose of producing a kind of "idea book" for tying emergers, we've chosen to arrange the patterns here by fly "style"—a method that we are the first to admit may introduce as many problems as it solves, since the notion of "fly style" itself does not always suggest clear and unambiguous distinctions. But here is how we approached it.

Most tyers, we think, tend to regard fly patterns as belonging to style categories; a dry fly, for instance, may be a parachute pattern, or a collar-hackle pattern, or a downwing design, and so on. Our categories are often based on somewhat loose and inconsistent principles; sometimes they are based on materials (clipped deer-hair patterns, for instance, or quill body patterns). Sometimes they are based on tying techniques, such as palmer hackle or woven body patterns. But often the style category is based on some predominant feature of the natural insect, a feature in fact that is so conspicuous and important that we regard it as a "trigger" for the trout's feeding instinct; in mayfly duns, it may be upright wings or an extended body, in nymphs a flashback wing case, and so on. That is, we establish our categories based on what we see as the most "distinctive" feature of the fly, both the natural and our imitation.

Emergers and emerger patterns might be seen as having two predominant components or triggers: the nymphal or pupal skin, often as a trailing shuck; and the distended wing case, the wing buds, or the thorax and wings themselves emerging from the nymphal skin. These are the most distinctive features of an emerger and typically the ones tyers expend the greatest energy and ingenuity in replicating.

We've organized the chapters in this book primarily around the second of these two components, that is, according to approaches for representing the enlarged thorax, wing buds, emerging and emerged wings or thorax. Not only are these significant representational features of artificial flies, but they quite often have a significant architectural or structural role in positioning the fly on, in, or under the surface film. Thus there are chapters devoted to "dubbing pod and suspender emergers," "loopwing emergers," and so on. A number of patterns, unfortunately, do not neatly fit into these categories, and we have placed them in chapters that, we hope, correspond to other obvious tying styles, such as "parachute emergers" or "clipped deer-hair emergers." Even so, classifying individual patterns is not without its problems. Some fly designs fit equally well into more than one category. For instance, the Quigley Cripple, a popular emerger-style pattern, might logically be placed in either Chapter 1, Collar Hackle Emergers, or Chapter 7, Tuft Emergers, since it has both of these components. The Quigley, and some of its variations, are in fact placed in the chapter devoted to tuft emergers, since the tuft-like wing projecting over the hook eye seems to us a more distinctive characteristic of the pattern than the hackle. There are many such judgment calls in these pages, and we have tried to use simple, basic tying principles and common sense in assigning patterns to specific chapters. No organizational system is perfect, and this one is perhaps significantly less perfect than many, but we hope that its benefits compensate for its drawbacks.

The virtue of this arrangement, we think, is that it groups together flies that are generally similar in appearance, allowing tyers to become acquainted with variations of a basic design, the way in which that design is incorporated into imitations of specific insects, and the range of materials that might be used to dress the fly style. This approach to organization also groups together flies that involve a similar tying technique and, in many instances, shows how different tyers employ different methods to achieve similar results. Finally, taken together, the chapters represent the various options in emerger design that we hope will be useful to tyers who wish to create their own patterns. In order to present these options in a simple, comparative format, as well as to help locate specific flies, we've included a chapter-by-chapter pictorial table of contents that provides thumbnail images of all the patterns in the book.

Emerger shucks, the second distinctive component of the category, are illustrated in patterns throughout the book, but again, as a convenience to tyers who wish to design their own patterns, we've included a separate chapter, Shucks and Bubble Sheaths, that presents a variety of dressing styles for this component. Our hope is that with the shuck designs presented in Chapter 3, and the enlarged thorax/wing bud/emerging wing designs presented in the other chapters, tyers will be well supplied with options for embodying their own ideas about emergers.

Instructional tying sequences, like the ones contained in this book, always involve tradeoffs. Practiced tyers familiar with common tying techniques require only basic guidelines for constructing a pattern; experience fills in many of the blanks. Beginning tyers, on the other hand, profit from expanded, detailed instructions that illustrate relatively fundamental tying methods. We've tried to accommodate less-experienced tyers by including Chapter 2, Basic Tying Techniques, that presents in detail some of the methods used frequently in the book. These techniques are cross-referenced in italic type as they are needed in specific tying sequences, and the tyer can refer as necessary to Chapter 2 for more detailed instructions about the particular tying procedure that is called for. This approach, while admittedly a little cumbersome, prevents a great deal of unnecessary duplication of elementary fly-tying instructions, streamlines the sequences for easier use by experienced tyers, and ultimately allows more space for additional patterns.

At the risk of stating the obvious, there is one final point we'd like to emphasize about the patterns in this book. While all the flies are pictured as specific patterns, it is perhaps best to regard them as designs that can be altered in size and color to match a variety of hatches. The highly popular Sparkle Dun, for instance, can be tied to imitate blue-winged olives, pale morning duns, March browns, and a number of other mayfly species. But it seemed to us pointlessly redundant to include all these variations once the basic design was set forth. The Sparkle Dun pictured in this book represents an emerging *flavilinea*; tyers who wish to dress the pattern for a different hatch, PMDs for instance, can find information about appropriate sizes and colors by consulting the many other PMD emerger designs in these pages. Thus the flies pictured in this book can be seen as both endpoints and starting points, both guides to tying specific patterns and points of departure for modification, experimentation, and invention.

Chapter 1: Emerger Design and Materials

Emerger patterns, in a sense, straddle a line between sub-surface and floating flies. This line is in part a figurative one—a representational border between aquatic and terrestrial forms, since emergers represent a transition between the two and often incorporate anatomical components of both. The approaches to this kind of representation are, of course, the subject of the fly-tying sequences in this book. In another sense, emerger patterns straddle a very literal line, one defined by the surface film. Where nymph and pupa patterns are positioned below the surface, and adults on top of it, emerger patterns often lie in the surface film, or partly above it and partly below. The particular position of an emerger in the water is, as with all trout flies, a combination of fly design and materials, which are the subjects of this chapter.

EMERGER DESIGN

From what might be called an "architectural" standpoint, the vast majority of emerger patterns can be divided into one of two types: "flush-floating emergers"—those that are designed to ride horizontally with the body of the fly flush against the surface film; and "descending-body emergers"—those that are designed to have all, or some portion, of the abdomen angling down, or curving, or hanging below the surface film. We draw this distinction because the constraints of these two emerger designs come into play for tyers who wish to alter the patterns in this book—either by changing particular components, or by substituting materials or hooks on a pattern—or for tyers who wish to design their own emergers. In both cases, tying a fly that properly positions itself on the water is a matter of coordinating the fly style, hook style, and materials, and so a brief look at each of these two emerger types is in order.

Flush-Floating Emergers

Emerger patterns of this type sit horizontally on, in, or just under the surface film and often represent an insect in a later stage of emergence, though there are certainly exceptions here, such as some types of floating nymphs. This emerger style is often (though not always) tied on a straight-shank hook, with a trailing shuck, a body of a color that imitates the adult insect, and the wings or wing buds of an emerging adult. In some cases, such as the popular Sparkle Dun, emergers of this type are, except for the shuck, almost indistinguishable from patterns used to represent the adult insect.

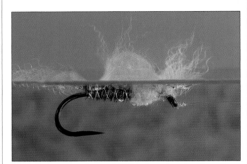

This Loopwing PMD is typical of a flush-floating emerger design.

To sit horizontally, the fly must be supported on the film both fore and aft. Ordinarily, the front of the fly is supported by wings, wing buds, or a wing case fashioned from some buoyant material—deer hair, CDC, foam, poly yarn—or by a parachute or collar hackle. The rear of the fly is supported by an abdomen tied from a buoyant material or a water-repellent one—poly dubbing or other dubbing treated with floatant—and by a fiber or feather shuck. Flies tied with an abdomen material that has no inherent floatation, such as quill or biot, are supported at the rear primarily by the shuck material.

This combination of design and materials is probably familiar to most tyers, since it is the same one that underlies the construction of most dry flies. And at the risk of belaboring the obvious, we mention it here primarily as a reminder to tyers who are designing their own patterns or substituting materials on the patterns in this book that body and shuck materials on this style of emerger should be chosen to promote floatation in the rear of the fly, and dense, non-buoyant materials such as vinyl cord or wire, should be avoided. To change the abdomen material, for instance, from dubbing to peacock quill may also require an alteration in the shuck if the fly is to ride horizontally on the water.

This, of course, is the theory. In actual fishing, broken or turbulent water or waterlogged materials may cause the fly to sink partially or completely, and it might still catch fish perfectly well. But in creating or altering emerger patterns, it still seems worthwhile to choose combinations of materials that preserve the original rationale of the design.

Descending-Body Emergers

Of the two basic emerger designs, the descending-body type appears to be the more recent style. It is, in any case, a design that is increasing in popularity, in part we think because of the wider range and availability of hook styles suited to the purpose. On descending-body emergers, part or all of the fly abdomen (and sometimes the thorax as well) angles or curves or hangs below the surface, suspended there by wings or float pod or parachute hackle or some other floating component on the pattern. Typically, this style represents the emergent portion of the fly above the surface film, partially withdrawn from the nymphal body and shuck which are below the waterline. As specific as this stage of emergence might sound, the patterns representing it show a wide latitude—

from the "suspender pod" type emergers that represent the enlarged thorax of nymph just prior to emergence or the wings and thorax just beginning to break through the nymphal skin, to patterns in which the components above the water represent an almost fully hatched insect and the descending portion of the hook primarily suggests an empty nymphal or pupal shuck.

This Klinkhamer Special is typical of descending-body emergers.

Straight-shank hooks can also be used for descending-body emergers, such as the Gray Midge Emerger shown here. Using a collar hackle that rests horizontally on the surface film to support a straight shank hanging vertically downward may in fact represent one of the first approaches to the descending-body design.

A variety of hook styles can be used for this design, and perhaps the most popular are scud hooks since the curved hook naturally places some part of the shank beneath the surface film, regardless of where the floating component of the fly is dressed. But curved swimming-nymph hooks are sometimes used as well and account for some of the more unusual emerger patterns, such as Harold McMillan's Vertical Emerger.

Our experience tying and fishing descending-body emergers has suggested a few basic guidelines for producing and preparing a pattern that will sit properly on the water.

* Dress the shuck with materials that will readily penetrate the surface tension and sink beneath the film. For shucks, Antron, Darlon, Z-Lon, and webby hackle barbs, which sink readily, are preferable to materials that tend to float a fly, such as poly yarn or CDC.

* Dress the abdomen with non-buoyant or denser materials—floss, flexible floss, tying thread, vinyl cord or tubing, biot, peacock quill, hackle stem, wire, and so on. If using dubbing for the abdomen, twist the dubbing tightly to produce a smooth body; a rough, spikey dubbing tends to trap the body in the surface film. If the abdomen does not sink, the fly will sit on the film, often on its side.

* Treat only the floating portion of the fly—wings, hackle, tuft, and so on—with floatant. Conversely, if the abdomen is dubbed, squeeze a little stream water or saliva into the dubbing, or apply a drop of wetting agent (such as one of the commercial fly-sink treatments) to help get the body below the surface.

* Finally, tying the fly to the tippet with a loop knot rather than some form of clinch knot helps position the fly properly on the water, since the hook eye can move freely along the loop as the rear portion of the hook sinks. This is particularly true on small flies, where even a light tippet can be stiff enough to hold the hook horizontally along the surface film, which defeats the purpose of the descending-body design.

Again, this is the theory. A descending-body emerger, resting entirely on the surface film, lying on its side, may well catch trout. But if one chooses to dress this style of fly in the first place, it seems only reasonable to coordinate materials and prepare the fly for fishing in ways that observes the logic of the design, regardless of how the matter plays out in the end.

HOOK CHARACTERISTICS AND DESIGNATIONS

Because emerger patterns, like emergers themselves, fall into that middle ground between the nymphal or pupal form of the insect and the adult form, tyers draw on an unusually wide range of hook styles in constructing their imitations. In a great many cases, hook style is a matter of individual preference—we all have our favorites—but in some instances, such as the descending-body design, performance is more closely tied to hook characteristics. And in general, at least some small attention to hook style can help maximize the effectiveness of a fly.

As most tyers have learned, there is no real uniformity among hook manufacturers in the characteristics of a given hook type and size. A #16 standard dry-fly hook from one manufacturer may well differ in shank length, wire diameter, and gap size from a second manufacturer's hook of the same designation. While this can be confusing and sometimes frustrating for a tyer, in our experience these discrepancies are, for the most part anyway, small enough so that different brands of the same hook style can be substituted for one another with no real violence to the finished fly. In the pattern recipes shown in this book, we've preserved whenever possible the originator's specified hook style. But in some cases, particularly in some European patterns, the preferred the hook style is not readily available in the U.S., and in other cases, specific hook models have been discontinued by the manufacturer. In both instances, we've substituted a hook with the same general characteristics.

Here's a brief a breakdown of those relevant characteristics, the designations used by manufacturers to describe them, and the functions that those characteristics serve in emerger design.

Shank Length

Though there is no consistency among various manufacturers, each individual manufacturer specifies shank lengths in relation to a specific set of hooks in its line—usually, the standard dry-fly hooks. These become a kind of default gauge against which other shank lengths are measured. Hooks with long shanks are designated "XL" (extra long), and the amount of extra length is specified by a number. A #14 1XL hook, for instance, has a shank length "one times longer" than the standard #14 hook; that is, it's a #14 hook with a shank as long as a standard #12 hook. A #14 2XL hook has shank length as a long as a standard #10 hook, and so on. Short-shank are designated "XS" according to the same principle. A #14 1XS hook has a shank length equal to that of a standard #16; a #14 2XS has the shank length of a standard #18, and so on.

Hooks with standard shank lengths are the most widely used for mayfly, caddis, and midge emergers for the simple, if somewhat circular reason, that they have become standards—so much so, in fact, that fishermen use hook sizes to identify insect sizes; we speak of a "#16 pale morning dun emerger" or a "#20 midge emerger," and the hooks referred to are standard shank lengths.

Hooks with extra-long shanks are used for tying emergers in a couple of different cases, but for the same reason in each. Extra-long hooks enable a tyer to imitate larger species or dress longer emerger patterns without incurring the extra weight that would come from using a standard shank. One might, for instance, dress identical *Hexagenia* emerger patterns on a #12 IXL hook or a #10 standard hook; the

shank lengths are the same. But the #10 hook would have a thicker hook wire and larger bend, both of which add weight and could diminish floatation on a sparsely dressed pattern. In some emerger designs, part or all of the nymphal shuck is dressed on the hook shank, usually with dubbing. In this case, the shank must be long enough to accommodate part or all of both the shuck and the adult body; a standard hook could be used, but again, weight is a consideration in some designs, and so tyers often choose an XL hook

Hook Wire

As with shank length, hook wires are designated in relation to a standard wire, again usually the manufacturer's standard dry-fly hooks. Hooks made of a thinner wire than the standard are designated as "XF" (extra fine), and the deviation from the standard is specified by a number. Thus the wire in a #14 1XF hook is as thin as the wire on a standard #16; a #14 2XF has the same wire diameter as a standard #18. Conversely, hooks made of wire thicker than the standard are designated "XH" (extra heavy) or sometimes "X-Stout." A #14 1XH hook has the same wire thickness the same as a standard #12 hook; a #14 2XH has the same as wire diameter as a standard #10.

Since the vast majority of emergers are tied to float in or on the surface film, a great many tyers use standard-wire hooks for their patterns, since standard wire diameters are designed for floating flies.

Fine-wire hooks, as one might expect, are often used on sparsely dressed patterns, where a minimal amount of material may not adequately support a heavier wire. Some tyers, however, routinely dress virtually all their emergers in the middle range of sizes—about #12 to #18—on fine-wire hooks, arguing that patterns float better, that thinner wires penetrate a trout's mouth more easily, and that the

loss in strength from a lighter wire is not a significant matter. Most tyers also prefer fine wire on scud hooks. Generally, these hooks have extra-short shanks, which means that the hook wire is actually sized for a larger hook. A fine-wire scud hook eliminates the extra weight without, in our experience, any real compromise in strength.

Heavy-wire hooks are most often used in dressing emergers fished more than a few inches below the surface, or flies dressed heavily to float the extra wire weight or suspend it just beneath the film. Probably the most common use of heavy-wire hook in tying emergers is in the smaller sizes, from #18 or #20 on up. As Darrel Martin has shown in his book *Micropatterns*, on very small hooks of standard or fine wire, even a fine tippet can exert enough force to "spring open" the hook, bending the spear far enough to release a fish, or in extreme cases, breaking a hook altogether. That is, on some hook brands and designs, even a light tippet can exceed the holding power of the hook. So many tyers go to XH hooks in the small sizes to ensure that the hook has sufficient strength to hold a fish; they argue, rightly in our experience, that as hook size gets smaller, wire diameter has less effect on how well a hook floats or sinks. Tiny hooks are so light, even in XH designations, that even the small amount of materials used to dress such hooks are usually sufficient to float them.

Hook Gap

Hook gap (or gape) is the perpendicular distance between the hook point and the shank, and it is roughly a measure of the "capture space" or width of the "bite" that a hook provides. As noted before, hook gap becomes a concern to fishermen only in smaller hook sizes, where the bite of the gap can be narrow enough to make holding fish a problem. On some fly designs, certain components—a wide thorax or a collar hackle, for instance—that occupy space below the shank can obstruct the gap and effectively narrow it even further. The most common recourse among tyers concerned with this problem is to use a larger hook with an extra-short shank; a #16 2XS hook, for instance, offers a shank length appropriate to a size 20 imitation, but gives the gap of standard #16 hook.

Some hook models are designated as having extra-wide gaps, though for the most part, these larger gaps are by-products of the hook shape, as explained in the section below on "Scud Hooks."

Hook Eye

Hooks ordinarily used in tying trout flies have one of three eye styles. The "turned-down eye" (usually designated TDE) is the most common and has an eye that is angled downward about 30-45 degrees from the shank. The "turned-up eye" (TUE) is angled upward from the shank about the same amount. The "ring eye" (RE), sometimes called "straight eye" is unbent and lies on the axis of the hook shank.

Much has been written and debated about the hooking properties of these various eye styles, considering angles of applied force, leverage from the hook shank, torque, and so on. Though a good deal of heat has been generated by these discussions, they have in the end, we think, produced precious little light. Investigations into the mechanics of hooking involve assumptions about the relative positions of angler, fly, and fish; the distance between them; about the way a fish actually takes a fly; and so many other variables that the analyses finally correspond to only a small fraction of the circumstances encountered in actual fishing. Even when these theoretical assumptions are granted, there is still some disagreement in interpreting the results. Suffice it to say that fishermen successfully use hooks with all three eye

styles and, as a practical matter, choose hook styles based primarily on other characteristics such as shank length, wire diameter, and so on, rather than eye style.

The one possible exception is with very small hooks, where a turned-down eye might intrude into the space below the shank, reducing the size of an already narrow gap. But such interference is only a problem on very slender-bodied flies. On most patterns, some component—usually the thorax—intrudes into the gap farther than a turned-down eye does, and is the more significant obstruction. Going to a ring-eye or turned-up eye will not widen the gap size.

HOOK STYLES

Hook style, as we're using the term, refers to the shape of the hook, and in dressing emerger patterns tyers employ three basic types that range from general-purpose to specialty hooks.

Straight-Shank Hooks

Straight-shank hooks are the standard in tying trout flies of almost any kind, and they are used on virtually all flush-floating emerger patterns. (Along with traditional straight-shank hooks, we include in this category hooks with a shallow bend at the rear of the shank, such as the TMC 200R, the Daiichi 1270, the Dai-Riki 270 and similar hooks; or those with a very slight bend along the length of the shank, such as the TMC 2302, Daiichi 1260, Dai-Riki 280, and so on. Flies tied on these hook styles rest on or in the surface film in a manner that far more closely resembles flies tied on straight-shank hooks than patterns tied on scud hooks.) We looked at many hundreds of emerger patterns, if not more, in compiling this book, and there is little doubt in our minds that a standard, straight-shank dry-fly hook is the single most widely used style in emerger tying.

The popularity of straight-shank hooks probably has less to do with their actual shape than with the fact that they are readily available, serve multiple purposes in fly tying, and perhaps most importantly, offer tyers the broadest selection of shank lengths and wire diameters, from extra-short/extra-fine to extra-long/extra-heavy.

Scud Hooks

There is no uniform definition of a scud hook, and designs vary, sometimes significantly, from one manufacturer to another. We consider this category to contain any hook that is curved over more than 50% of its length from behind the hook eye to the rearmost point of the bend (with the exception of the swimming-nymph hooks described below). Our definition may, in one sense, be arbitrary, but it does have the practical benefit of including virtually all the hooks used in tying descending-body emergers, which is the principal reason for differentiating them from other hook styles in the first place.

Not all that many years ago, scud hooks were something of a specialty item for tyers. Formed of heavy, curved wire, they were originally designed to give a lifelike, flexed profile to subsurface patterns such as scuds, sowbugs, cress bugs, and caddis pupae that were (rightly or wrongly) perceived as having a more pronounced curve in the body than other aquatic food forms. Tyers gradually appropriated the hook style for other types of imitations—particularly emergers—and many manufacturers began offering scud hooks in standard- and light-wire versions better suited to floating patterns. Which of these two developments was the cause and which the effect is not altogether clear. But as matters stand now, tyers have a fairly wide range of options in choosing scud hooks.

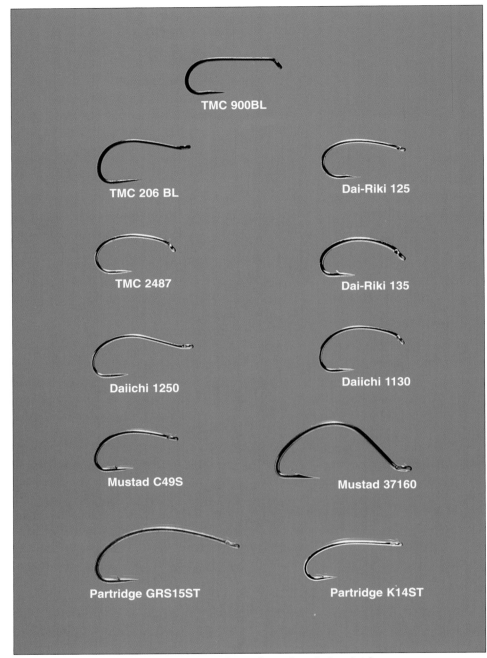

Shown here are a variety of scud-style hooks from different manufacturers. All of the hooks are size 14. (The TMC 900BL at the top is a standard #14 dry-fly hook included for reference.)

length of a standard straight-shank hook of the same size from the same manufacturer.

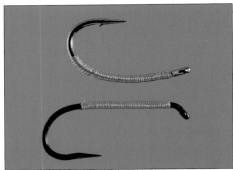

For example, the effective length of the shank on a #14 TMC 900BL (a standard-shank dry-fly hook) is very nearly the same as the effective shank length on a #14 TMC 2488 (a scud hook with a 2X short shank), as shown here. The thread wraps indicate effective shank length. Thus a tyer who wishes to dress a descending-body emerger to match a hatch of #14 March browns (that is, a hatch in which the length of the adult mayfly corresponds to a #14 hook), can choose a #14 scud hook with some confidence that the effective shank length will correspond to the size of the natural, even though the hook itself is described as having an extra-short shank.

These direct translations in size, of course, hold only for hooks from a given manufacturer, and even then only sometimes. As always, though, the tyer's best guide is to choose a hook with an effective shank length that approximates the size of the natural, regardless of the designated size of the hook.

Scud hooks can be divided into two rough categories: those on which the shank forms a continuous curve from the back of the eye to the base of the bend, and those on which the shank is straight for a short length behind the hook eye. Some tyers prefer hooks with a straight shank behind the eye so that the forward portion of the fly rides flush in the film, and some find this style of hook to be marginally easier to tie on. Others prefer the more symmetrical continuous-curve style. In our experience, once tying

As is probably clear from the photo above, differences in hook sizing among manufacturers that appear as relatively small inconsistencies in straight-shank hooks occasionally descend to the level of capriciousness where scud hooks are concerned. One rough consistency is that most scud hooks are designated as having extra-short shanks, a description that does correspond, sometimes usefully, to a practical reality in fly tying. Typically the body of a fly dressed on a scud hook extends much farther down the bend than the body on a straight-shank hook. Thus while the scud-hook shank may be extra short, the "effective length" of the shank, that is, the length of shank on which materials are applied, is often fairly close to the materials are applied, it is often difficult to determine the precise profile of the hook beneath; both hook styles position themselves on the water in much the same way, and we've noticed no difference in how they are received by the fish.

One minor annoyance that tyers experience in dressing scud hooks is positioning the thread at the rearmost point of the body which, as we've noted, is often well down the bend at a point where the hook shank is nearly vertical. The weight of the bobbin causes the thread to slip downward past the mounting for the body material, often right to the jaw tips—a particular nuisance when multiple materials, body, ribbing, and so on, must be mounted before the thread can be advanced up the shank.

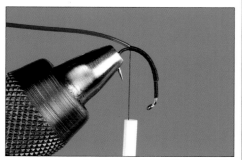

Tyers with standard vises have little recourse but to reposition the hook in the jaws so that the bend of the hook is uppermost.

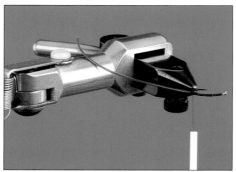

Tyers with rotary vises can solve this problem by turning the jaws 90 degrees, so that the entire hook lies in a horizontal plane; the thread will stay in position while materials are mounted, and body and ribbing materials can in fact be dressed with the hook in this position.

Swimming-Nymph Hooks

As the name suggests, this relatively new hook style was designed to imitate the curved or undulating body of swimming nymphs. Though a form of curved-shank hook, it is in a sense the opposite of a scud hook—the shank is bent away from, not toward, the hook point, and such hooks have extra-long shanks rather than extra-short ones. A small number of patterns in this book, both descending-body and flush-floating types, incorporate this hook style into their designs. But for the most part, in the world of emerger patterns, the swimming-nymph hook has remained a minor player.

There are a couple of possible reasons. First, versions of this hook style seem to come and go among manufacturers, which tends to discourage much experimentation with it among tyers. Second, some manufacturers furnish this hook only in relatively large sizes (which is more consistent with its purposes as a nymph hook). Tiemco, to take one example, offers the style only in #14 and larger, which is oversize for representing many of the major insect hatches in North America, particularly considering the hook sports an extra-long shank. (We've attempted to produce swimming-nymph hooks in smaller sizes by reshaping extra-long straight-shank hooks, bending them with pliers. It can be done, but, as you might expect, it is tedious work.) Some anglers have reported that hooking and holding fish on this swimming-nymph style is less reliable than on other designs. We see no obvious reason that this should be the case, and in our own, admittedly limited, experience with this hook style we've not had this problem. It is certainly possible, though, that particular fly designs may reduce the hooking capabilities of this style by obstructing or intruding fly components into the hook gap.

Still, the swimming-nymph hook is undeniably one of the more intriguing styles in fly tying, and it may well

yield further interesting approaches to emerger design.

MATERIALS

There is no single fly-tying material used exclusively for dressing emergers, and patterns draw freely on materials traditionally used for both floating and subsurface flies. There are a two materials, however—CDC and snowshoe hare's foot—used repeatedly on patterns throughout this book that may be less familiar to tyers than some standard materials or that may show enough variance in their characteristics that a few words about their properties and selection are in order.

CDC

Most tyers are by now at least distantly acquainted with CDC feathers, a material long used by European tyers that has become popular in North America only in the last decade or so. CDC feathers are found on waterfowl, where they surround a small oil gland at the rear of the bird's back, just ahead of the tail, and they assist the bird in distributing the oil that waterproofs and conditions the body and wing plumage.

CDC feathers are highly useful in tying for a variety of reasons. First and foremost is the structure of the feather. The non-interlocking feather barbs are more widely spaced than in most other feathers, and this fern-like array of barbs maximizes the contact area of the dense, curly barbules with the surface of the water. The barbules themselves, corkscrew in shape, trap small air bubbles that help float the fly and that scatter and reflect light in a way that seems to enhance a pattern's appeal to trout. Natural, undyed feathers retain some of the gland oil—so much so that feathers taken directly from a wild bird may require blotting prior to tying—and this oil helps preserve the waterproofness of the feather, making it ideal for use on floating patterns. (Dyed CDC is often stripped of oil to accept the dye, though in our opinion, the oil is secondary to feather structure in accounting for floatation.) The barbs are quite soft, supple, and mobile, giving a lifelike movement to patterns both on and in the water, and CDC is being used increasingly often in subsurface flies as well as floating ones. The fluffy barbs give the impression of volume even when relatively little material is used, as in winging a fly for instance, and the barbs are fairly compressible, which allows tying in or tying off the material with little bulk on the hook shank.

Depending on the source of the feathers, natural CDC runs from light gray to dark gray to a medium or dark brownish-gray and, in some cases, white or cream. It is also sold in a range of dyed colors as well, though here the tyer must exercise some caution. For reasons we don't pretend to understand, shades of dyed dun— which one might reasonably expect to run from light to dark tones of gray or bluish-gray—often end up the most peculiar shades of pale lavender, purplish-blue, or even a dirty powder-blue. And in our experience, buying dyed-dun CDC, sight unseen, is as often as not a disappointment. Other dyed colors, however, seem to run reasonably true.

The best material we've used comes from wild birds, and if you number a waterfowl hunter among your acquaintances, it is certainly worth taking steps to secure his or her goodwill; the CDC that might come your way will not only be of high quality, but also contain a more useful range of feather types, as explained below, than you typically get in packaged material. But the CDC marketed to tyers will serve perfectly well in tying flies, offers a greater range of colors, and is certainly easier to obtain.

In many pattern recipes, the material required for a specific component may merely be listed as "CDC," which in some respects is about as

specific and helpful as if the recipe simply called for "hackle." Like hackle, CDC feathers differ in their characteristics, though not as dramatically and for a different reason. Where hackle varies in the properties of its barbs, from soft and webby to stiff and smooth, CDC varies in its conformation, that is, the shape and proportions of the feather itself. Tyers that have experienced problems or poor results in tying CDC may in fact have been using a particular type of feather that was ill-suited to the purpose— understandably, since no one had ever bothered to draw useful distinctions among feather types.

Fortunately, this is no longer the case. Well-known fly-tying authority Hans Weilenmann of the Netherlands, recently devised and published a short, simple, and useful taxonomy of CDC feathers and has generously allowed us to reproduce his ideas here.

Weilenmann divides CDC feathers into the following four categories:

The Type I feather pictured here, Weilenmann notes, resembles a partridge body feather. It has a relatively short stem and slightly rounded tip. Because the barbs on the upper half or so of the feather reach quite nearly to the tip, the Type I feather is useful in wrapping bodies, provided they are relatively short. Weilenmann prefers this feather for his CDC & Elk pattern, since the barbs at the base of the feather that are too short to reach the tip form the trailing filaments on the fly when the feather is wrapped. We use this type on occasion for winging flies, since a substantial number of barbs extend to the tip of the feather where they contribute to the wing profile.

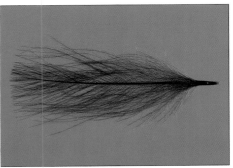

This Type 2 feather is markedly different in conformation—thin-stemmed, narrow, with most of the barbs extending to the feather tip which, Weilenmann notes, is squared off and brushlike. This is, in our estimation, the most versatile type of CDC feather. The long barbs that reach the tip make it useful in wrapping bodies, tying wings and wingposts, forming loop wings and tufts, and particularly in applications that require longer feather length.

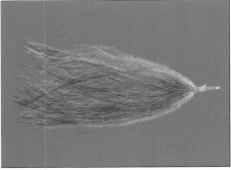

The Type 3 feather pictured is the nipple plume. It grows nearest the oil gland and is characterized by almost a complete absence of a feather stem; the barbs grow from a small bulb-like structure at the base, much like a feather duster. Virtually all the barbs are of uniform length, and the barbules appear denser, longer, and fuller than on other types of CDC feathers; we find this combination of characteristics make an ideal feather for winging, puff-type emergers, wing posts, and emerging wing buds. It is also useful in tying trailing shucks. The absence of a quill makes for a compressible fiber bundle that ties in with little bulk. The one limitation with Type 3 feathers is size; feather length varies with the species of bird, but Type 3 feathers are typically short and not always suited to larger patterns, though this depends on the specific application.

The Type 4 feather shown here has a relatively long stem with shorter barbs. Weilenmann notes that René Harrop uses this type of feather on his Transitional Caddis pattern. The relatively uniform barb length make this feather suitable for patterns that require a few turns of CDC wrapped as a collar hackle, for use in CDC dubbing loops, and for applications that require stripped CDC barbs.

This system of classification, of course, does not describe every CDC feather. Like all natural materials, CDC varies, and some feathers fall between two types. But it nonetheless draws useful general distinctions for the tyer.

If you obtain your feathers directly, from domestic or wild waterfowl, you will end up with an assortment of all the feather types noted above. Feathers purchased from a fly shop are more limited in range. Type 3 feathers, packaged and sold separately as "puffs" or "oiler puffs," are readily obtainable. Other packaged CDC feathers, even those labeled "select," contain very few Type 1 or 2 feathers, and frequently contain none at all. It isn't clear why this should be the case, particularly since feathers we have acquired from European sources show a greater range of feather types. But CDC feathers from domestic fly shops will quite probably be Type 4.

If you tie with packaged CDC, all is hardly lost. Type 4 feathers can be used in virtually all applications that call for Type 1 or Type 2. In some cases, such as tying downwing, upwing, or tuft style emergers—where the tip of the feather forms the

fly component—it may be necessary to use more than one Type 4 feather to obtain the desired density of barbs. When making this substitution, we often find it helpful to choose the largest Type 4 feathers we can find and snip away the very tip of the feather; the finished component on the fly contains no feather stem, incorporating more of the useful material into the fly while reducing bulk on the shank. The result may not be quite as tidy as you'd achieve with an ideal feather, but the fly will be eminently fishable. In other applications, such as wrapped bodies or loop wings, the effect of substituting a Type 4 feather usually amounts to some short, stray barbs splaying outward from the wing or body, and on emerger patterns, these fibers may in fact help reproduce the somewhat unruly and disorganized appearance of a hatching insect. Finally, in many CDC applications, stripped barbs can be substituted for whole feathers. This method is more time-consuming and, in the tyer's eyes, the results may not be as neat and trim as using a single feather; but tying stripped barbs is not at all difficult, and it is a practical way of getting the most out of your material. The upshot is that Type 4 feathers, while sometimes less convenient from the tying standpoint, still make effective patterns.

Snowshoe Hare's Foot

Snowshoe hare's foot was first brought to the attention of most tyers by Fran Betters, who dressed his pattern, The Usual, entirely of this material. While The Usual has been popular, at least regionally, for a couple of decades, the use of snowshoe hare's foot never appears to have extended much beyond this application until only recently. Within the last five years or so, there has been a renewed and rather widespread interest in the material, and snowshoe hare's foot, which for a long time was virtually unobtainable by tyers in most parts of the country, is now quite readily available. The reasons for this

increasing popularity aren't altogether clear; no single, prominent pattern using the material appears to have sparked the resurgent interest, nor since Betters designed The Usual has any particularly influential tyer championed its use. While still a very distant second in popularity to CDC as a material for dressing emergers, there is no question that its use is on the rise. In researching patterns for this book, we found dozens and dozens of flies from tyers in various regions of the country that incorporate snowshoe hare's foot in one way or another.

The characteristics of the material suit it well to emerger patterns. Though the claims to the waterproofness of snowshoe hare seem to us perhaps a bit overstated, there is no question that, as natural furs go, it is exceptional in this respect. It has a subtle sheen and a natural translucence, particularly when used as dubbing. The best fur is slightly crinkled—a bit like calf tail, but much finer and softer in texture—and its crinkliness gives the impression of volume, in a wing for instance, even when smaller amounts of material are used. On the most useable part of the foot, the hair grows to a uniform length, which means that no stacking or aligning of the hair tips is needed. And the hair itself ties in easily and generally behaves itself on the hook shank. Natural colors run from a dirty cream to light gray, and a small number of dyed colors—primarily duns—are available.

The fur on a snowshoe hare's foot varies rather dramatically from toe to heel; some is useful and easy to work, some is not. And these differences are compounded by some significant variations exhibited by individual hare's feet, perhaps arising from the geographic region of origin, the age of the animal, and the season of harvest. Still, it's possible to talk, at least in general terms, about the types and characteristics of hair on the foot and where it is located.

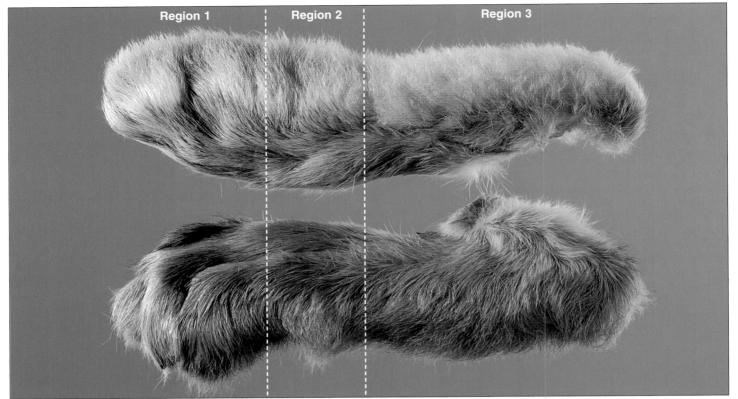

Shown here are two representative snowshoe hare's feet—a natural version at the top and a dyed-dun sample at the bottom. The feet are shown here in profile, and only the hair on the "sole" of the foot is used on the patterns in this book. It's useful in tying to consider the foot as being divided into three regions, based on the characteristics of the hair, as shown here.

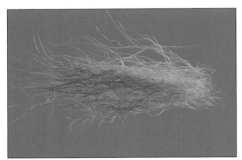

Region 1. The hair in this region may occupy from ⅙ to ⅓ the length of the foot. It is generally the longest hair on the foot, but coarse and stiff in texture, and relatively incompressible in tying; there is typically no underfur in this area. On some hare's feet, this hair may lend itself to tailing dry flies because of its length and stiffness. But it is highly inconsistent; the hair tips are often broken, and even hair that is intact can be so curved at the tip as to make it useless.

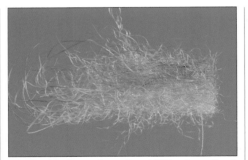

Region 2. Covering about ⅓ the length of the foot, the hair in this region forms a transition of sorts between the stiff, coarse hair at the toe and the softer, finer hair toward the heel. The fur from this region often, but not always, contains hairs of mixed lengths and of three general types. The longest of these resemble the hair in Region 1, but the fibers are typically smoother and finer in texture. Occasionally, this longer hair has intact tips and can be used in tying—mixed in as it occurs naturally with a pinch of fur clipped from this region. Often, though, the tips are quite curved—as is the case with the sample shown here—and many tyers find it unsatisfactory.

The second type of fur is very much like that of Region 3—fine, soft, and crinkled in texture—and is quite satisfactory material. This hair from Region 2 is often the longest high-quality material on the foot, and we tend to reserve it for applications that require longer fibers—upwings, downwings, or loopwing/tuft combinations—and particularly for tying on larger hooks.

The third type of hair is shorter and finer. One might be tempted to call it "underfur," though unlike the underfur on most animals (including the rest of the rabbit), these shorter hairs do not form the dense, distinct, and well-defined "layer" of hair that is normally associated with underfur. Rather, the lengths of this shorter fur are more random, and it does not grow as densely.

As noted, there are sometimes significant differences among feet from different animals. Some that we have seen contain little useable hair in this region—mostly stiff, coarse fibers; other feet hold an abundance of good material. But typically, a tyer using hair from this region will snip off a bundle of hair, pinch it at the base, and pull out the fibers that are excessively long, or very stiff, or curved, producing a bundle in which the hair tips are reasonably even.

Then the hair tips are pinched, and the shorter fibers are preened from the base, much as you would clean out underfur; this is valuable as dubbing material and reserved for the purpose. The resulting bundle will contain hair that varies a bit in length but is reasonably well-aligned, and it's useful for winging and tailing, though the texture may suit it best to larger hooks.

Region 3. This is the prime stuff, occupying from ⅗ to ⅚ the length of the foot. It is fine, soft, crinkly, densely packed on the skin, and nicely translucent. This section of the foot ordinarily contains few, if any, of the short "underfur" type hairs, and most of the fur here grows to quite nearly a uniform length—a great convenience to the tyer since the hair requires virtually no alignment before mounting. A pinch of this hair clipped from the skin has a distinct "springy" feel, and when pinched tightly at the base, it will fan outward and produce, as we've said, a bundle with the appearance of volume and bulk even though it may contain only a modest amount of material. If you take care not to use too much material, the hair ties in nicely, with little bulk.

The fur that runs lengthwise down the middle of Region 3 is the best of the best, primarily because it is the longest. As you move outward toward the edges of the foot and the end of the heel, the hair becomes shorter; though there is no loss in quality, it becomes somewhat more difficult to handle these fibers and they may be suited only to small hooks. At the very edge of the "sole," this hair meets the stiffer, glossier fur that curves down the side of the foot from the top. As is probably obvious, the quantity of high-quality hair on a foot is not large; the sole itself is narrow, and the central band of long hair is narrower still; care in handling fur will help maximize the amount obtained from each foot.

We have never, incidentally, seen a pattern that called for hair from the top of the foot. In type and texture, this fur most closely resembles fur from a hare's mask—stiff, relatively short, glossy fibers, over a layer of short underfur. This material might well be used for the same applications as hare's mask dubbing, though on natural feet, it is generally much lighter in color.

Tips On Using Snowshoe Hare's Foot

*Though the hair itself ties quite nicely, separating out and clipping individual bundles of hair can be a bit frustrating—particularly on a new, unused foot—primarily because a rabbit's foot is not a terribly convenient format. Unlike a patch of deer hair on a flat hide, for instance, the foot is curved from side to side; the bones make it quite inflexible; the fur is not terribly long and grows densely, which makes isolating a bundle of the desired size a bit cumbersome. All in all, the foot can be clumsy to handle when trying to grab a pinch of fur of the proper size and clip it at the same time.

One solution is to begin from the edge of the foot. Trim away the hair that grows downward from the top of the foot, exposing the edge of the hair on the sole. In Region 3, you may need to trim away the short hair that grows at the edge of the sole as well in order to reach hair of sufficient length; reserve this short fur for dubbing. But you will then get unobstructed access to the base of the fur closer to the center of the foot, and snipping off the right amount of material is easier. Clip the hair as close to the skin as possible,

since longer hair is more useful and easier to handle when tying.

*No matter how carefully you clip the hair, there will always be stray fibers that splay from the edges of your fingertips, or stray hairs that come from clipping more fur than you've pinched in your fingers, or short hairs preened from the base of a bundle, or hair that simply sheds from the foot. Save this material for dubbing. The quantity of prime material is fairly small, and clipping off the best stuff for dubbing seems an inefficient use of material.

*When dubbing with snowshoe hare's foot, choose a thread color that is consistent with your representational purposes, and dub thinly. One of the virtues of the material is its translucence when wet, which allows the thread color to show through.

*When buying snowshoe hare's foot, look for the largest feet; these generally contain the most and longest hair. Longer hair is more versatile than shorter fibers, since it can be used on both large and small hooks; all things being equal, choose feet with the longest hair in Region 3. Look for feet on which Region 1 is smallest, since this is the least useful material.

Chapter 2: Basic Tying Techniques

This chapter presents detailed instructions for some of the tying procedures that are used repeatedly throughout this book. We've collected them here to avoid an unnecessary repetition of material in the tying sequences themselves; when one of the methods here appears in the instructions for a particular pattern, the method is cross-referenced to the page number in this chapter for easy reference. (The one exception is the technique for whip finishing, which is not cross-referenced since it appears in every single tying sequence.) Though seasoned tyers may learn a tip or two in this chapter, the instructions here are provided primarily for less-experienced tyers who may not yet have encountered a particular technique or who are unsure exactly how a specific procedure is accomplished.

The tying techniques here are presented alphabetically.

Align and Strip

This procedure is used to align the tips of feather barbs and gather them into a bundle for shucks, tails, legs, wing cases, or other fly components. The method can be used with any type of feather—hackle, flank, body. CDC feathers however—which often have sparse, irregular barbs—are more easily handled using the method shown in *stripping CDC barbs,* (p. 40), when larger bundles of bundles of barbs are needed.

Step 1: Select a feather, such as the hen hackle shown here. Strip away all the fuzzy, or short, or crooked barbs at the base of the stem; the lowermost barbs remaining on the quill should be well formed and of uniform length. Preen the barbs, from tip to butt, so that they stand outward from the stem at right angles.

Step 2: With your right fingers, pinch the desired number of barbs close to the feather stem. On many feathers, simply

preening the barbs perpendicular to the stem will align the tips. If the tips are not aligned, however, use your left fingers to pull the pinched barbs as a group toward the tip or butt of the feather—whichever direction will bring the tips into alignment.

Step 3: Pinch the aligned tips in your left fingertips. You can pull the barbs toward the feather butt, stripping the bundle from the stem, though the necessary force sometimes pulls the tips out of alignment. Many tyers prefer to clip the barbs from the stem, as shown here.

Step 4: Use your right fingertips to pinch the barbs at the base and consolidate them into a bundle.

Biot Body—Fringed

Some emergers are tied with biots in such a way that the fly body is ribbed with a fringe-like structure on edge of the biot. Other patterns are tied with a *smooth biot body* (p. 31). The difference is in the mounting orientation of the biot.

Step 1: Peel a biot from a biot strip by pulling it against the direction of natural growth. Note the indentation or notch on one side of the biot, as shown here. This notch is used as an orientation guide in mounting.

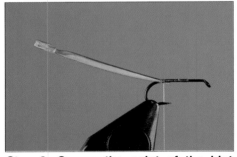

Step 2: Secure the point of the biot against the near side of the shank, directly over the rearmost tailing wrap or, if no tail or shuck is used, at the rearmost point of the body. The notch in the biot should face upward, as shown.

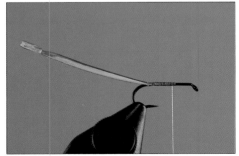

Step 3: Use a *flattened thread* (p. 37) to wrap forward, binding down the point of

the biot and creating a smooth, uniform underbody. A biot is quite thin, and any irregularities in the thread foundation will be visible in the finished body.

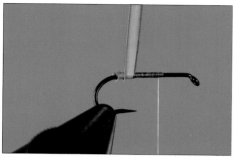

Step 4: Clip the butt end of the biot in a pair of hackle pliers, and wrap forward. The turns of material should be edge-to-edge, not overlapping, so that the fringe raised on each wrap is visible.

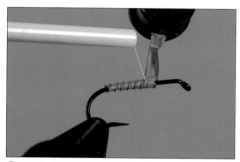

Step 5: When the body is complete, tie off the biot by taking a complete turn of thread under light tension around the biot. After one complete wrap, apply pressure on the thread to snug the wrap around all sides of the biot evenly and prevent slipping. Then take additional tight thread wraps to secure the biot, and clip the excess.

Biot Body—Smooth

Some emergers are tied with biots in such a way that the fly body is smooth with a distinct segmented appearance. Other patterns are tied with a *fringed biot body* (p. 30). The difference is in the mounting orientation of the biot.

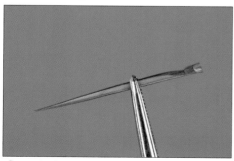

Step 1: Peel a biot from a biot strip by

pulling it against the direction of natural growth. Note the indentation or notch on one side of the biot, as shown here. This notch is used as an orientation guide in mounting.

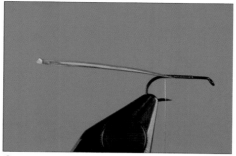

Step 2: Secure the point of the biot against the near side of the shank, directly over the rearmost tailing wrap or, if no tail or shuck is used, at the rearmost point of the body. The notch in the biot should face downward, as shown.

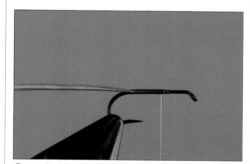

Step 3: Use a *flattened thread* (p. 37) to wrap forward, binding down the point of the biot and creating a smooth, uniform underbody. A biot is quite thin, and any irregularities in the thread foundation will be visible in the finished body.

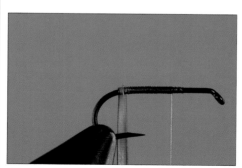

Step 4: Clip the butt end of the biot in a pair of hackle pliers, and take one turn of the biot over the rearmost thread wrap. Notice that the leading edge of the biot has a fringe of hairlike barbules.

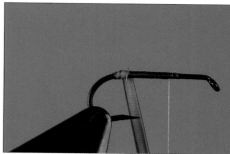

Step 5: Take a second wrap of the biot, slightly overlapping the previous one so that the fringe of barbules on the first wrap is covered by the rear edge of the biot on the second wrap.

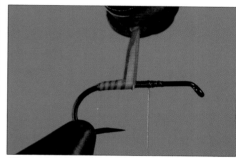

Step 6: Continue wrapping forward, always making certain that the rear edge of the biot overlaps and covers the fringe left from the previous wrap and forms a smooth body.

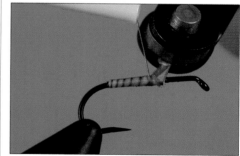

Step 7: When the body is complete, tie off the biot by taking a complete turn of thread under light tension around the biot. After one complete wrap, apply pressure on the thread to snug the wrap around all sides of the biot evenly and prevent slipping. Take additional tight thread wraps to secure the biot, and clip the excess.

CDC Dubbing Loop

Some of the patterns in this book require CDC barbs spun in a dubbing loop. While the methods for forming the loop and spinning the material are identical to those used when hair or dubbing fibers are put in the loop, handling the material is somewhat different, and so we are presenting the CDC loop as a separate method. Tyers use a number of different methods for preparing and handling the material. We show two of them in the following sequence.

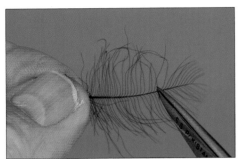

Step 1: Prepare the CDC feather by stripping away the very short fuzzy fibers at the base of the stem. Hold the feather by the tip, and preen the barbs toward the base so that they project outward, perpendicular to the feather stem. Then clip away the very tip of the feather; these very short barbs at the tip sometimes pose an obstacle in mounting and trimming the feather.

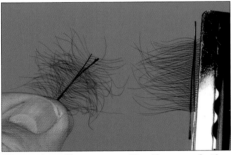

Step 1a: Some applications of the CDC dubbing loop, such as parachute hackling, are best undertaken with a denser loop that incorporates more CDC barbs. In this case, two feathers can be mounted in the loop simultaneously. Select two CDC feathers that are similar in size and conformation. Prepare them as shown in Step 1. Stack the feathers, one atop the other, tip to butt, as shown on the left. Some tyers prefer to stack feathers so that the curvatures match, as we've done here, finding the feathers easier to handle this way; others prefer to stack the feathers with curvatures opposing. Carefully clip the section of barbs on the right side of the feather

into a paper clamp, as shown at the right. Starting on the right side of the feather like this simplifies trimming away the stem for a right-handed tyer. (The use of a paper clamp here is certainly not restricted to mounting multiple feathers. Some tyers find even a single feather easier to handle this way.)

Step 2: Form a dubbing loop with the thread as shown in *dubbing loop*, Steps 1-3, (p. 35). Insert your left index finger in the base of the loop to hold the loop threads apart. Then hang a dubbing hook, dubbing twister, or dubbing whorl from the bottom of the loop, beneath your index finger. Hanging the tool like this keeps it handy when it comes time to spin the loop.

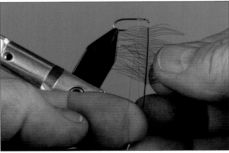

Step 3: If desired, wax one of the loop threads. Waxing the thread helps grip the CDC fibers in the loop and prevents them from shifting when the feather is trimmed and the loop closed. But some tyers like to manipulate the CDC barbs once they are trapped in the loop— arranging them in a more uniform distribution, for instance—and a waxed thread inhibits movement of the barbs inside the threads.

Insert the barbs on the left side of the feather into the loop so that the feather stem is positioned to the right of the loop threads. This simplifies trimming for a right-handed tyer. Insert the barbs through the loop the desired distance. The length of the barbs that project beyond the loop threads will determine

the length of fibers once the loop is spun, and this length can be adjusted to produce barbs that are proportional to the hook size you are using. Here, we've inserted the barbs to the maximum extent to produce long fibers; note, however, that there must be sufficient space, at least ⅛" or so, between the loop threads and the hackle to allow for trimming with scissors.

The technique for mounting feathers held in a paper clamp is identical to what is shown here.

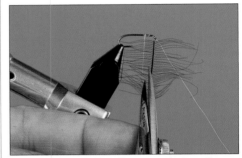

Step 4: Carefully slip your index finger from the loop. At the same time, use your left thumb and middle finger to pinch the loop threads against the tip of the dubbing hook or twister. Pull slightly downward on the threads to hold the CDC barbs as firmly as possible. With a scissors, carefully trim the barbs from the feather stem.

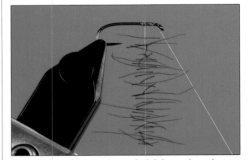

Step 5: Spin the dubbing hook or twister, clockwise when viewed from above, to trap and flare the feather barbs. The CDC dubbing loop is now ready to be wrapped.

Clip, Clean, and Stack

This procedure is used to prepare hollow hairs, such as deer or elk, for use as tails, wings, wing cases, bodies, or shellbacks.

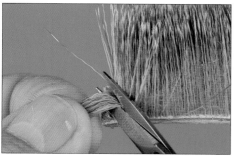

Step 1: Use your left fingers to pinch a clump of hair of the desired size and fold it away from the rest of the hair on the hide. Clip the hairs at the base, close to the hide.

Step 2: Grasp the hairs close to the tips, and pull out the soft, crinkled underfur and any short hairs.

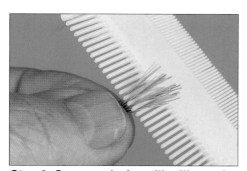

Step 3: Some underfur will still remain. To remove it, use a fine-toothed comb, such as the flea comb shown here, to comb out the remaining underfur. For some tying applications, the hair is now ready for use. But many procedures require that the hair tips be aligned, as shown in the following steps.

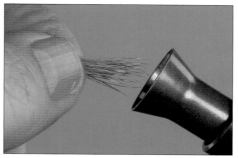

Step 4: Insert the bundle of hair, tips first, into the barrel of a hair stacker.

Step 5: Hold the hair stacker as shown, making sure that your forefinger completely covers the barrel opening. Tap the bottom of the stacker sharply against a table top 3 or 4 times. Coarse hair or large bundles may require additional taps.

Step 6: To consolidate the bundle inside the stacker—particularly if a small amount of hair is used—tilt the stacker at a 45-degree angle, as shown, and tap a few more times.

Step 7: Hold the stacker horizontally, with the barrel in your right hand. With the left hand, slide the base from the barrel.

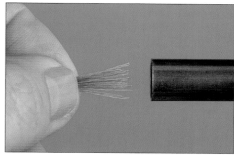

Step 8: Carefully grasp the exposed tips in your left finger, and remove the hair from the barrel.

Step 9: Transfer the bundle to your right fingers, and it is ready to mount.

Counter-Rib

Where conventional ribbing involves wrapping the rib material in the same direction as the body material (that is, clockwise when viewed from the hook eye), a counter-rib is wrapped in a direction opposite of the body material (that is, counter-clockwise when viewed from the hook eye). Counter-ribbing is used to make the rib material more distinct or conspicuous, or to reinforce fragile body materials such as peacock quill, feather barbs, or herl.

Step 1: After the tail or shuck is secured and any body material is tied in, the rib

material is mounted. Then the fly body is formed and tied off. To counter-rib the body, the ribbing material is raised above the shank, brought toward tyer, then under the shank and around the far side to the top.

Step 2: Continue spiraling the rib material over the body material.

Step 3: When the front of the body is reached, the rib material is tied off. As you tie off, put tension on the rib material. The pressure of the tie-off wraps pushes against the wrapping direction of the ribbing and will tend to loosen it unless you maintain tension.

Direct Dubbing

This simple technique—frequently employed for fashioning the body, thorax, and sometimes head of a fly—involves twisting loose fibers around a thread core to make a yarn that is wrapped around the shank. Some tyers prefer a waxed thread for dubbing; wax makes the dubbing fibers adhere to the thread and provides some grip during spinning. But wax also makes the fingertips sticky, which can be a nuisance when handling other materials afterward. Most soft, fine-textured dubbings—fine or superfine poly, soft furs, fine Antron—can be dubbed without wax, though moistening the fingers, with a damp sponge kept on the bench or (if

you're not finicky about such things) a bit of saliva, gives a little grip when spinning the fibers. Coarse fibers, such as hare's ear or synthetic seal substitutes, are easier to spin on a waxed thread.

Many synthetic dubbings consist of very long filaments, which can be a bit unruly when dubbing, and on small patterns they make the precise application of dubbing to the thread difficult. To simplify matters, simply separate out a clump of dubbing fibers, and randomly cut through the clump a few times with scissors to shorten the fibers.

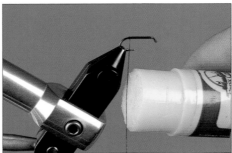

Step 1: Position the tying thread a few thread-wraps ahead of where the fly body begins. Leave about 3" of tying thread between the bobbin and shank. If necessary, spin the bobbin for a *flattened thread* (p. 37); it is more difficult to apply dubbing to a tightly twisted thread. If a waxed thread is desired, take one pass of the wax along the length of the tying thread. A thin film is all that's required. If small clumps of wax appear along the thread, smooth them out with your fingers.

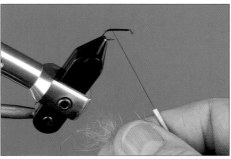

Step 2: Hold the bobbin in the palm of your right hand and a clump of dubbing fibers in your right fingertips.

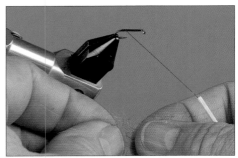

Step 3: With your left fingertips, tease out a loose, sparse pinch of dubbing. Loose fibers spin more readily.

Step 4: With the right hand, put a very slight tension on the bobbin. Take a small pinch of the teased dubbing fibers, and hold them against the back of the tying thread, near the hook shank, with your left forefinger tip. Don't use too much material. Thick clumps of dubbing spin poorly and often produce a badly shaped body. If a thicker body is needed, build it up from layers of dubbed thread rather than trying to spin a thick yarn. Or use a *dubbing loop* (p. 35), which allows more material to be applied at once.

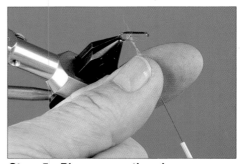

Step 5: Place your thumb over your forefinger and pinch the dubbing fibers tightly. Maintaining the pinch, slide your thumb against your forefinger to roll the dubbing and twist it onto the thread. Spin the dubbing in one direction only, not back and forth. If the dubbing is not twisted tightly enough, reposition your

fingers, and repeat this step until the fibers are twisted into a yarn on the thread. You can spin the dubbing in either direction—but not both—though twisting the dubbing clockwise when viewed from above follows the direction of thread twist and will keep the dubbing strand tighter when wrapping it around the hook shank.

Step 6: Repeat Steps 4 and 5, placing a second pinch dubbing directly below the first, then twisting it onto the thread in the same direction as the first pinch. There should be no gaps in the spun dubbing; it should appear as a continuous, uniform yarn on the thread. If a thin spot appears, spin a very small amount of dubbing on the thread to fill it in.

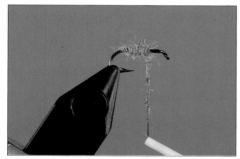

Step 7: Continue adding and spinning dubbing until enough of the thread is covered to form the body, though generally speaking, dub only 2"-3" inches of thread at a time. Long lengths of dubbed thread are cumbersome to handle. For larger flies, dub a couple of inches of thread, wrap it, then begin dubbing the thread again.

When a sufficient amount of thread is covered, wrap the dubbing around the shank in tight, adjacent turns. If a thin spot appears in the body, take another turn of dubbing over it. If excess dubbing remains on the thread when the body is complete, pull it from the thread.

Some patterns call for tapered dubbed bodies. Tapering the body can be accomplished in a couple of ways. The first is to dub the thread sparsely to make a yarn of uniform diameter. Then wrap the body, taking additional wraps of dubbing over the portions of the body that are thicker, building the taper by dubbing back and forth to form layers. The second method is to vary the amount of dubbing applied to the thread to form a tapered yarn, as shown above left. Gradually increasing the amount of dubbing applied down the length of the thread will produce the tapered body shown above right, typical of a mayfly abdomen.

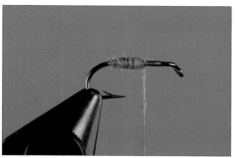

To produce a tight, compact body with a well-defined silhouette, use soft or fine-textured dubbing, sparsely applied, and spun very tightly on the thread.

To produce a rougher, shaggier body, use a coarser dubbing with longer fibers, and spin it more loosely on the thread.

Dubbing Loop

Dubbing loops are probably used most often to form the two "extreme" types of fly bodies that are difficult to form with the direct dubbing method—that is, very tight bodies with a distinctly segmented appearance, on the one hand, and very loose, shaggy bodies on the other. But the technique is quite versatile and can also be used to form CDC bodies and hackles, legs, and collars.

After a material is placed in the dubbing loop, the loop threads are spun to form a yarn. A rather wide variety of tools for this purpose are commercially available—dubbing hooks, dubbing spinners, dubbing whorls. An acceptable substitute can be made by bending a large paper clip or 6" length of wire into the shape of a shepherd's crook, or by using an ordinary crochet hook.

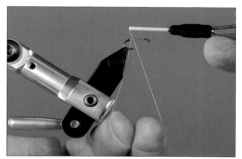

Step 1: Position the tying thread a short distance ahead of where you wish the dubbing loop to begin. Strip off about 8" of thread from the bobbin. Pass the thread around the first two fingers of the left hand to form a loop. Then bring the thread back to the shank as shown.

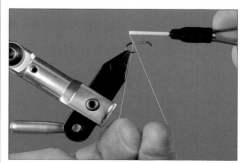

Step 2: Keep your fingers in the loop. Wrap the tying thread around the

shank, binding down both threads rearward, and stopping at the point where
you want the dubbing loop to begin.

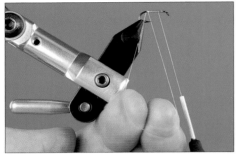

Step 3: Wrap the tying thread forward to
the point on the shank where you will
tie off the loop—in this case, at the front
of the abdomen.

Step 4: Apply a bit of wax to one of the
loop threads. Hold a clump of dubbing
between your left thumb and forefinger. With the right fingers, tease out a
sparse pinch of dubbing, and touch
the dubbing to the waxed thread near
the point of the loop. The wax will hold
it in place.

Step 5: Repeat Step 4, applying additional pinches of dubbing to the thread.

Step 6: When sufficient dubbing is
applied, catch the base of the loop with
a dubbing hook or twister.

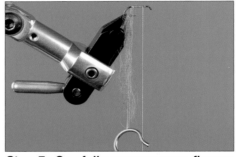

Step 7: Carefully remove your fingers
while pulling on the dubbing hook to
close the loop threads.

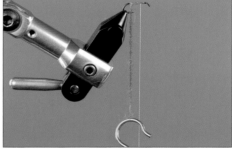

Step 8: Spin the dubbing hook (clockwise when viewed from above) to
twist the loop threads and dubbing
into a yarn. Twist tightly, but be aware
that there is a point of diminishing
returns—when twisting tighter will
not produce a noticeable difference
in the yarn and the risk of twisting to
the breaking point of the thread
increases.

Step 9: Wrap the dubbing around the
shank until the tie-off point is reached.
Tie off and clip the excess as you would
any other material.

A dubbing loop formed as shown in
the preceding sequence will form a
spikey, rough body, particularly if
long-fibered or coarse-textured dubbing is used. To produce a smoother,
distinctly segmented body, combine
direct dubbing with a dubbing loop.

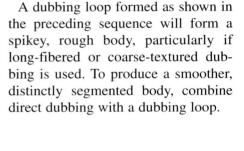

Step 1a: First, dub a length of thread as
explained in *direct dubbing*, Steps 1-6,
(p. 34).

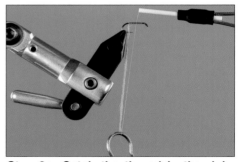

Step 2a: Catch the thread in the dubbing hook at the base of the dubbed
strand, and double the thread back on
itself, as shown.

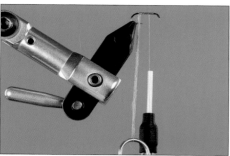

Step 3a: Finish forming the dubbing loop as shown in the preceding sequence, Steps 2-3, by binding both ends of the loop to the hook shank. Advance the thread to the tie-off point.

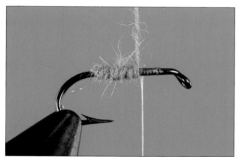

Step 4a: Twist the dubbing loop into a tight yarn, and wrap the dubbing forward.

Flattened Thread

As you wrap during tying—mounting, securing, and tying off materials—the thread accumulates twist, one twist for each wrap taken. But some tying operations, such as forming underbodies, are best accomplished with an untwisted, flat thread, which lies neater on the shank.

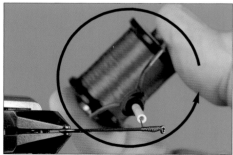

Step 1: To flatten the tying thread, simply spin the bobbin, counterclockwise when viewed from above. Observe where the tying thread meets the hook shank (we're using floss here to give a better view). When the thread is completely untwisted, it will flatten and spread slightly. The degree of flatness

depends a good deal on the type of thread used. Some threads are almost flosslike in their structure and will flatten almost completely; other threads have bonded filaments and flatten less.

Horizontal-Mount Parachute Hackle

Most of the parachute patterns in this book use a hackle that is mounted on the shank in a horizontal orientation. It's worth noting, however, that the *vertical-mount* method (p. 42) is equally satisfactory for these same patterns, and some tyers prefer it. Wrapping the hackle is the same with either mount. Tyers vary a good deal in the specifics of mounting hackle horizontally. The technique shown below is a fairly simple, workmanlike method. The hackle in this sequence is mounted for wrapping in a clockwise direction.

Step 1: *Prepare a hackle feather* (p. 39). The portion of the stem stripped of hackle barbs must be long enough to secure to the hook shank and spiral up the wing post—a bare section of quill about equal in length to the hook shank is usually sufficient. Position the tying thread 4-5 thread-wraps ahead of the wing post.

Hold the feather as shown, angling rearward and up at a 45-degree angle, with the stem crossing the base of the wing post on the near side of the hook shank. Most tyers prefer that the front, or glossy side, of the feather faces upward. Note the bare feather stem left between the rear of the wing post and the lowermost barbs on the hackle. This bare section must be long enough to spiral up to the top of thread foundation on the post. A length of bare quill about 2-3 times the diameter of the wing post is usually sufficient. It is better to have too much bare stem rather than too little.

Step 2: Hold the feather in position and wrap rearward over the feather stem, binding it to the upper part of the near side of the shank.

Step 3: When you reach the front of the wing post, angle the thread rearward, and take 2 tight wraps over the stem directly behind the wing post, as shown. Clip the excess feather stem. The feather should be positioned as shown, pointing to the rear, angling upward, with the front of the feather facing up. Some feathers may twist a bit during mounting so that the front of the feather does not face directly upward. This is not a matter of great consequence, since you can compensate for the twist as you spiral the stem up the post and bring the feather into proper position for wrapping.

Mounting Collar Hackle

Tyers have devised many methods for mounting a hackle feather that is wrapped as a collar. The technique shown here is one of the simpler ones.

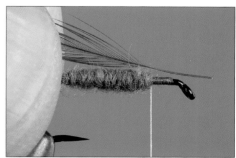

Step 1: *Prepare a hackle feather* (p. 39). Position the tying thread at the hackle-mounting point. Hold the

feather horizontally, tip to the rear, with the back or dull side of the feather facing you. The feather can be positioned against the near side of the shank, atop the shank, or anywhere between these two positions. On some patterns, other components of the fly may dictate where the hackle can be mounted. On a pattern with wings, for instance, the wings pose an obstacle to mounting the hackle atop the shank, so it must be positioned somewhere on the near side, as shown here. The exact mounting location is not extremely important since wrapping the hackle is the same regardless of where the feather is secured.

Step 2: Hold the feather in position and take a wrap of *flattened thread* (p. 37) around the hackle stem. Note the small length of bare quill between the lowermost hackle barbs and the thread wrap. Leaving this short length of stem assists in the proper positioning of the feather for wrapping. This bare stem is about 3 thread-wraps in length.

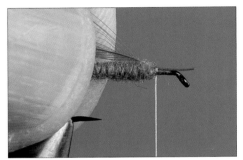

Step 3: Keep the thread flat, and wrap forward, securing the stem to the shank and laying as smooth and uniform a thread foundation as possible. A smooth thread base helps to produce a neatly wrapped hackle with no splayed barbs. Bind the step with 5 or 6 wraps, and clip the excess. Take another wrap or two over the exposed quill butt to smooth out the thread foundation.

Palmering Hackle

A palmered hackle is essentially a collar hackle that is spiraled over the abdomen or thorax of the fly, or both, with uniform gaps left between the wraps. The distance between the wraps of hackle may vary with the particular pattern or the location of the hackle on the fly; generally, a palmered hackle over the abdomen is wrapped in a more open spiral; on a thorax, the wraps are placed closer together. The photos of specific patterns are the best guide.

Step 1: The technique for palmering hackle used on the patterns in this book is identical to the method shown in *wrapping dry-fly hackle* (p. 44), except that the hackle feather is not held vertically during wrapping, but angled slightly toward the hook eye to produce the open spiral.

Pinch Wrap

This basic technique is used to secure materials to the shank without disturbing their mounting position. It is particularly helpful when mounting very limp or soft materials—feather barbs, yarn fibers, or hair, for instance—which are easily pushed out of position or alignment by the thread pressure used in wrapping.

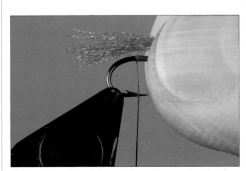

Step 1: Position the thread at the mounting point. If the material is to be mounted to its finished length, size it against the hook shank, as shown here with the Antron yarn used for a shuck.

Step 2: While holding the material in place with the right fingers, transfer it to the left fingers so that the left fingertips pinch both the material and the hook shank at the mounting point. Using a *flattened thread* (p. 37), raise the thread over the near side of the shank, and slip it between your thumb and the hook shank.

Step 3: Form a small loop above the shank. Without closing the loop, slip the thread between your forefinger and the far side of the shank. If you have difficulty forming the loop, the thread may not be sufficiently flattened. A twisted thread will tend to curl up on itself, or furl, and resist forming a loop.

Step 4: Pinch the loop threads tightly against the sides of the hook shank, and pull directly downward on the bobbin to tighten the loop over the material.

Step 5: Form a second loop just like first, and tighten it. Check the position of the material; small adjustments can be made at this point.

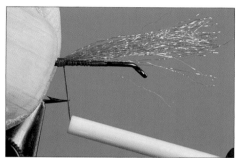

Step 6: When the material is satisfactorily positioned, form a third loop just like the first two, and tighten it. Then slide your left fingers rearward, and add additional tight wraps to finish securing the material.

Prepare A Hackle Feather

Most of the patterns in this book that incorporate hackle—whether wet-fly or dry-fly, collar style or parachute—use a feather tied in at the butt end and wrapped by the tip. The first step is selecting a feather of the proper size.

Most hackled dry flies are tied with feathers that have a barb length of 1 ½ times the hook gap. To check barb length, bend the feather around the hook shank as shown. The barbs should extend above the hook point a distance equal to ½ the hook gap. Hackles used on wet flies vary far more

in length; the barbs may be as short as ½ the hook gap or as long as 2 ½ times the hook gap. The best guide here is to gauge the barb length from the photograph of the fly.

Preparing a dry-fly hackle is largely a matter of minimizing "webbiness" in the feather. The web appears as a tapering, shadowlike band on either side of the feather stem; on the feather shown at the left, the web is visible as an inverted "V" along the lower half of the hackle stem. The best-quality dry-fly hackle has little or no web, and preparing the feather is simply matter of stripping away the fluffy barbs at the base of the stem. On feathers that have some webbiness, locate the point on the stem where the webby portion of the barbs is no more than ¼ of the total barb length. That is, the lowermost barbs on the prepared hackle, shown at the right, have web that extends only ¼ the distance to the barb tip.

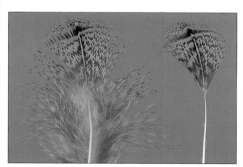

Web is desirable in a wet-fly hackle. The limiting factor in many wet-fly hackles is the stem thickness. A partridge feather is shown at the left. To prepare the feather, first strip away the fuzzy barbs at the base, along with any thin, irregular, or very short barbs directly above the fuzzy barbs. Observe the feather stem. If it is thick, strip away additional barbs until you reach a point where the feather stem is sufficiently thin and flexible to wrap around the shank, as shown at the right.

Side-Mounted Legs

Legs of this style can be made of a variety of materials, but most of the patterns in this book incorporate legs made of feather barbs, as shown in the following sequence. Typically they are mounted directly ahead of the thorax, though the method for dressing them is the same regardless of where they are placed.

Step 1: Position the tying thread at the leg-mounting point. *Align and strip* (p. 30) a bundle of feather barbs. The number of barbs varies from tyer to tyer, but typically the bundle is sparse, perhaps 3-6 barbs. With the right fingers, pinch the bundle at the mounting point. Leg length varies as well, but it is commonly about one hook-gap, as shown here.

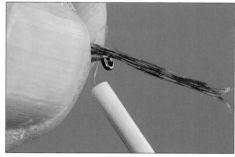

Step 2: With the left fingers, pinch the bundle by the tips so that the left fingertips are positioned at the mounting point. Position the bundle against the far side of the hook shank. (Note: if you are tying on a rotary vise, rotate the jaws 90 degrees so that the far side of the shank is now on top; it will simplify mounting.) Use a *pinch wrap* (p. 38) to secure the legs to the shank, as shown in this top view.

Step 3: When the pinch wrap is tightened, check the leg position. The fibers should be secured to the far side of the shank and splayed outward by the thorax. If some fibers have strayed to the bottom of the shank, you can twist them back into position. When the legs are properly positioned, secure them with 2 tight wraps.

Step 4: Repeat Steps 3 and 4 to mount an equal number of fibers against the near side of the shank. Check the leg length to make sure it is equal to the length of the first bundle of fibers. If not, pull gently on the butts or tips to make the two bundles symmetrical, as shown here from the top. When the fibers on the near side of the shank are correctly positioned, secure both bundles with a few tight thread wraps.

Step 5: Clip the excess feather butts close to the shank, and bind with thread. Side-mounted legs are often the final component on the fly, in which case the trimmed butts can be covered with thread as you *whip finish* (p. 43) the head of the fly.

Stripping CDC Barbs

Small bundles of CDC barbs—for trailing shucks, legs, or throat hackle—are most easily prepared by using the method shown in *align and strip* (p. 30). "Aligning" CDC barbs, however, is frequently a concept without much meaning, since CDC barbs are rarely of uniform length. When a bundle of CDC fibers of uniform length is required, tyers typically clip or break the tips of the barbs to make the bundle even.

When a larger bundle of fibers is required, two or more feathers are stacked for stripping since the barb count on CDC feathers is low; moreover, the barbs themselves are a bit limp and unruly, and minimizing the handling of fibers helps keep them under control. When a large bundle is needed, or you are working with small feathers, it's often best to strip 2 or 3 feathers simultaneously, as shown below, mount the barbs on the hook, and then gather and mount more barbs as needed. Though any type of CDC feather can be used, the Type 4 feather (see "CDC," p. 27) is most often employed since it has limited applications in other types of CDC tying.

Step 1: Select two or more CDC feathers, and strip away any fuzzy or excessively short barbs at the butt end of the stem. Stack the two feathers so that the curvatures match. Hold the tips of the feathers in the fingertips, and use the left hand to preen the barbs from tip to butt to stand them perpendicular to the stem.

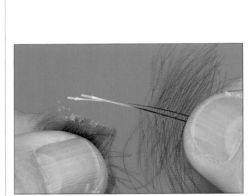

Step 2: With the left fingers, grasp a section of barbs on both feathers, and pull them toward the butt end of the feather to strip them away.

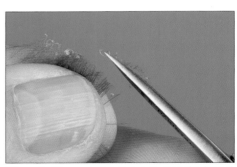

Step 3: Turn the feathers over. While holding the bundle of barbs in the left fingers, carefully slip another section of barbs between the fingers, atop the first section or adjacent to it. Strip this section away.

Step 4: If more barbs are needed and the feather is long enough, repeat Steps 2 and 3, stripping the remaining barbs from the feather. If bits of feather stem adhere to the butts of the barbs, you can trim these away now, as shown here, though in some applications, the barbs can be mounted on the hook and the butts clipped afterward.

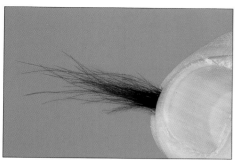

Step 5: Pinch the butts of all the fibers in your right fingertips, and the bundle is ready to be mounted.

Throat Hackle

Throat hackle is often used to simulate legs on an emerger pattern; it is ordinarily tied directly ahead of the thorax, as the last component on the pattern. Though throat hackle can be dressed from a variety of materials, the patterns in this book all employ feathers, as shown in the following sequence.

Step 1: Position the tying thread at the hackle-mounting point. *Align and strip* (p. 30) the desired number of feather barbs, and gather them into a bundle. Pinch the bundle in the fingertips at the mounting point—usually the point that will produce a hackle that reaches to the hook point, as shown here, though the length can vary with specific patterns.

Step 2: Hold the fibers beneath the hook, parallel to the shank, and pinch

them with the left hand so that the left fingertips reach to the mounting point. Note that the upper half of the left fingertips pinches the hook shank; the lower half pinches the feather barbs. (Note: if using a rotary vise, simply turn the jaws 180 degrees so that the underside of the shank is on top. The hackle can then be mounted with a simple *pinch wrap*, p. 38.)

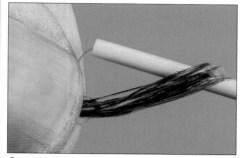

Step 3: The fibers are mounted with a pinch wrap formed underneath the hook shank. Form a loop of thread beneath the shank. Slip the thread between the left thumb and the hook shank. Then raise the bobbin above the shank, as shown.

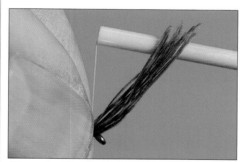

Step 4: Pinch the fibers and thread tightly in the fingertips, and pull straight upward on the bobbin to tighten the thread and seat the fibers against the shank.

Step 5: Check the hackle. If it is satisfactorily positioned, pinch it again in the left fingers and secure with additional tight wraps toward the hook eye.

If some of the fibers have moved around shank, twist them into position, and secure with a few tight wraps.

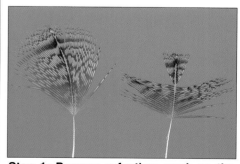

Step 6: If greater flare in the hackle is desired, wrap the thread rearward, forcing the fibers against the front of the fly body, which will cause them to spread outward.

Step 7: When the hackle is properly positioned, clip the excess fiber butts. Bind the butts with thread wraps or, if the hackle is the last component on the fly, with a *whip finish* (p. 43).

Tip-Mounted Hackle

Mounting a wet-fly hackle by the tip eliminates the problem of wrapping the thick, bulky stems often found on feathers such as partridge and grouse.

Step 1: Prepare a feather, such as the partridge hackle shown on the left, by first stripping away the fluffy barbs at the base of the stem. Then preen the barbs below the tip to stand perpendicular to the stem, as shown on the right.

The uppermost barbs that are preened outward are sized to the hook—usually of a length to reach the hook point, though this can vary from pattern to pattern.

Step 2: Position the thread at the hackle-mounting point. Place the feather atop the shank, with the front, or most distinctly marked side, facing downward. Mount the feather by taking a thread wrap over the bare quill between the feather tip and preened barbs. Wrap rearward, securing the tip of the feather.

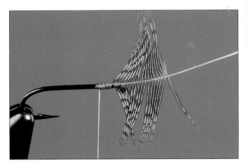

Step 3: Clip the feather tip and bind with thread.

Twisted Thread

Some tying operations that require building bulk—forming thread bumps to elevate wings, for instance—are best accomplished with a twisted thread.

To twist the tying thread, simply spin the bobbin, clockwise when viewed from above. Observe where the tying thread meets the hook shank (we're using floss

here for a better view). When the thread is twisted, it will appear cord-like and round in cross-section. Since twist accumulates naturally during tying, add additional twist carefully. Excessive twist weakens the thread, and overtwisting by spinning the bobbin can even break it.

Vertical-Mount Parachute Hackle

Some of the parachute patterns in this book call specifically for this method of mounting hackle, but it can be used on virtually all parachute patterns. While it is slightly more involved than the *horizontal-mount* (p. 37), some tyers find the feather easier to wrap when mounted vertically and the resulting hackle to be neater, since the feather stem is bound to the wing post and forms a smooth wrapping foundation.

Step 1: After the wing post is mounted, use a *flattened thread* (p. 37) to form a thread foundation on the post by wrapping up the post the desired distance. The post should be just tall enough to allow for the necessary number of hackle wraps.

Hold a *prepared hackle feather* (p. 39) vertically against the post, as shown. The back, or dull side, of the feather should face you, and the lowermost hackle barbs should be located just above the top of the thread foundation.

Step 2: Take a horizontal wrap around the feather stem, binding it against the

topmost thread wrap on the post. Note that a small section of bare quill is left between the thread wrap and the lowermost hackle barbs. This bare section simplifies positioning the feather when it comes time to wrap the hackle.

Step 3: Continue wrapping down the thread post, securing the feather stem, and laying a smooth foundation as you wrap.

Step 4: When you reach the base of the wing post, bend the feather stem toward the hook bend, and secure it to the shank with additional wraps. Note that the stem can be bound toward the hook eye instead; some patterns may have components already dressed behind the wing post. But when possible, most tyers prefer to place the stem rearward to avoid building excessive bulk behind the hook eye.

Step 5: When the stem is securely fastened, clip the excess and cover the exposed stem with a wrap or two of thread.

Whip Finish

The whip finish is a knot used to secure the thread when the fly is complete. It is usually, but not always, placed behind the eye of the hook. Tyers disagree, sometimes vehemently, about whether the whip finish is best formed by hand or with a whip-finishing tool. Both methods give the same result, and both are shown below.

Hand Whip Finish

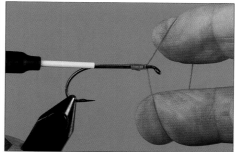

Step 1: Strip about 6" of thread from the bobbin. (We're using wire here for better visibility.) With the back of your right hand facing you, wrap the thread around the first two fingers of your right hand.

Step 2: Raise your hand above the hook shank so that your palm points downward. Draw the bobbin rearward so that the bobbin thread is above the hook shank and parallel to it. The bobbin thread is now behind the mounted thread. Spread your right fingers slightly so that the mounted thread is positioned vertically, perpendicular to the bobbin thread.

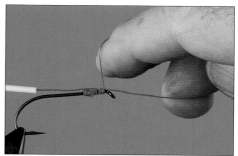

Step 3: Lower the bobbin thread to the hook shank. Rotate your wrist so that your palm faces you; as you rotate, use the index finger to guide the vertical strand around the shank, trapping the bobbin thread against the hook shank.

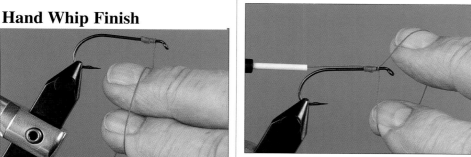

Step 4: While maintaining tension on the loop with your fingers, rotate your wrist so that the back of your hand faces you, letting your fingers slide inside the stationary loop. No thread is wrapped here; this merely repositions the hand and fingers.

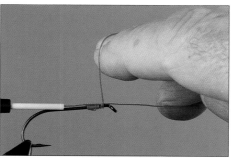

Step 5: Raise your fingers above the hook shank, with your palm facing down. The bobbin thread is now bound to the shank with one complete wrap of the vertical thread. Your hands are now in the same position as shown in Step 2.

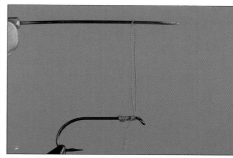

Step 6: Repeat Steps 4-6 three or four more times, placing each subsequent wrap ahead of the last one.

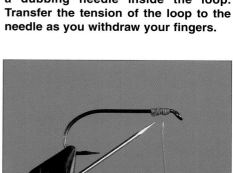

Step 7: After the last thread wrap, let the bobbin hang. With your left hand, place a dubbing needle inside the loop. Transfer the tension of the loop to the needle as you withdraw your fingers.

Step 8: With your right hand, pull downward on the bobbin to close the loop, using the needle to guide the closing the loop to the desired position. When the needle touches the shank, remove it; tighten the thread and clip it close to the shank.

Whip-Finish Tool

Some tyers find a whip-finish tool simpler to master than the hand whip finish. Tools of many different designs are available. The one pictured in the following sequence is an orbiting whip finisher made by Matarelli, which we find one of the easier styles to use. Wire is used instead of thread in the following demonstration for better visibility.

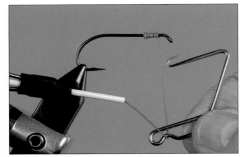

Step 1: Pinch the whip finisher above the handle sleeve to prevent the tool from rotating. Position the tool, as shown, in front of the hanging bobbin thread. With the left hand, raise the bobbin and catch the thread in the guide notch.

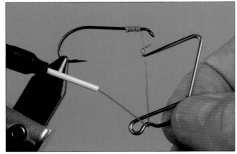

Step 2: Catch the vertical thread in the tool hook. The point of the hook is behind the thread.

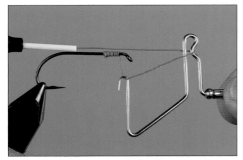

Step 3: Slide your right fingers downward, and hold the tool by the handle sleeve. Keep tension on the bobbin with your left hand. Raise the bobbin and lay the bobbin thread along the top of the hook shank. The handle will remain stationary, but the tool head will spin to the position shown.

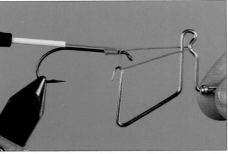

Step 4: While holding only the handle sleeve, use a cranking motion to rotate the tool clockwise (when viewed from the hook eye) one turn. As you turn the tool, the guide notch should remain in line with the hook eye, while the wire elbow below the point orbits around the shank, guiding the placement of the thread against the shank.

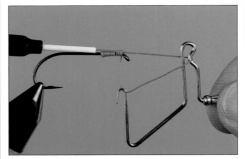

Step 5: Repeat Step 4 four more times. If the vertical thread grows too short, rock the tool back and forth to draw more thread from the bobbin.

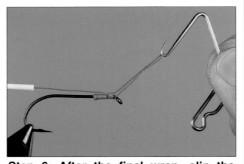

Step 6: After the final wrap, slip the thread from the guide notch. Pull on the bobbin to tighten the thread, while using the hook to guide the thread into position. Unhook the tool when it touches the shank. Pull on the bobbin to seat the knot, and clip the thread close to the shank.

Wrapping Dry-Fly Hackle

Dry-fly hackle is typically wrapped so that the barbs radiate outward perpendicular to the shank. Most tyers strive

to dress a dry-fly hackle that has no barbs that are splayed or bound down beneath the hackle quill.

Step 1: *Prepare a hackle feather* **(p. 39) and mount as shown in** *mounting collar hackle* **(p. 37). On some fly patterns, additional components may be dressed ahead of the mounted hackle feather. When mounting and tying off these components, take care to keep the thread foundation smooth, with no bumps or ledges. When it is time to wrap the hackle, position the tying thread at the base of the mounted hackle. Use a** *flattened thread* **(p. 37) to wrap forward toward the hook eye, laying a smooth foundation over the hackle stem, shank, and any bound-down tags of other materials. A smooth foundation is the first step in neatly wrapping hackle. Position the thread a few wraps ahead of the hackle tie-off point.**

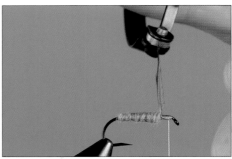

Step 2: Clip the tip of the feather in a pair of hackle pliers so that the pliers are in line with the feather, not crosswise to it. Insert your index finger in the loop of the pliers (you'll have to rotate the pliers about a quarter-turn), and draw the feather away from you, to the far side of the shank so that the front, or glossy, side of the feather faces the hook bend. The feather barbs nearest the hook shank should be vertical, not parallel to the tying bench.

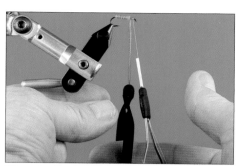

Step 3: Begin wrapping the feather by orbiting the index finger around the hook shank. The pliers will slide around your finger as you wrap. Note the index finger is kept parallel to the hook shank at all times. When your finger is directly beneath the shank, the hanging thread will obstruct further wrapping. Note here the left fingers ready to hold the pliers momentarily.

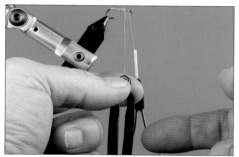

Step 4: Transfer the hackle pliers to the left hand. Don't wrap further, just hold the pliers until you can reposition your right hand in front of the tying thread, as shown here.

Step 5: Insert your index finger into the loop, and resume wrapping. Each wrap of hackle touches, but does not overlap, the previous one. If the hackle barbs begin to splay, the feather stem is twisting. Unwrap the splayed portion and wrap again, this time slightly repositioning the feather stem on the shank. A small change in placement of the wrap will sometimes cure the problem. If the barbs continue to splay, use your fingers or hackle pliers to twist the feather in a direction opposite the splay. The goal here is to produce a nicely perpendicular hackle, as shown.

Step 6: When the tie-off point is reached, unwrap the thread so that there no wraps on the shank ahead of the hackle. The thread should appear to be coming off the shank directly beneath the last wrap of the feather. With the right fingers, hold the feather vertically above the shank. With your left fingers, hold the tying thread vertically and angled slightly rearward so that the thread crosses the feather stem at the hook shank.

Step 7: Put tension on the thread with the left hand. With the right hand, unwrap the hackle a quarter-turn, so that it is pointing directly toward you. This will flare the feather barbs on one side of the stem. Slip the tying thread between the flared barbs, over the top of the shank, and to the far side, trapping the feather stem against the hook.

Step 8: Once the feather is trapped against the shank, unclip the hackle pliers, and use your right hand to add a few additional tight wraps over the first one.

Step 9: Clip the excess feather tip and bind it down with thread. Typically, the hackle is the last component to be dressed, and the clipped end of the feather can be covered with thread as the *whip finish* (p. 43) is formed.

Wrapping Feather-Barb Bodies

Some of the patterns call for bodies made of wrapped feather barbs, primarily pheasant-tail fibers. Fibers like this can be twisted and wrapped to produce a segmented body, but virtually all the patterns in this book call for flat-wrapped bodies, as shown in the following sequence. The vast majority of these patterns also use a *counter-rib* (p. 33) to reinforce the fragile feather barbs. Pattern recipes that don't specify a rib can often profit from one nonetheless—a piece wire or, if you wish the rib to remain inconspicuous, a fine tying thread of a color to match the body.

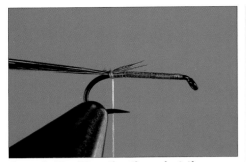

Step 1: Position the thread at the rearmost point of the body. *Align and strip* (p. 30) the desired number of feather barbs, such as the pheasant tail used here. Mount them as a group by the tips, taking the first wrap about ⅛" back from the very tips, as shown here. Mounting barbs by the extreme tip end can cause breakage during wrapping.

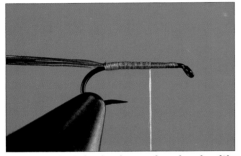

Step 2: Bind the barbs to the shank with smooth, even wraps to produce a uniform underbody. Wrap the thread about 3 or 4 wraps beyond the frontmost point of the body.

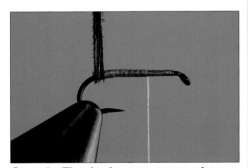

Step 3: The barbs are wrapped as a group. Try to keep the barbs side-by-side and flat, as though you are wrapping a length of ribbon. This approach maximizes the body length that can be obtained with the barbs.

Step 4: When you reach the tying thread, tie off the barbs as a group, and wrap back toward the hook bend a few turns to the frontmost point of the body. Overwrapping the very front of the barbs like this hides the small inconsistencies that sometimes occur when tying off a flat section of fibers. When the barbs are secure and the thread is positioned at the front of the body, clip the excess.

Wrapping Parachute Hackle

A well-tied parachute hackle has barbs that radiate horizontally outward from the parachute post, with no splayed or trapped barbs. The first key to neat parachute hackling is to lay a smooth and uniform thread foundation over the base of the parachute post where the hackle will be wrapped. An irregular foundation will cause the hackle stem to twist and splay the barbs.

Step 1: *Prepare a hackle feather* (p. 39) and mount it as shown in *horizontal-mount parachute hackle* (p. 37). Clip the feather tip in a pair of hackle pliers so that the pliers are in line with (not crosswise to) the feather stem. Rotate the hackle pliers a quarter turn, and insert your index finger downward into the loop of the pliers. Spiral the bare feather stem to the top of the thread foundation. You can spiral the stem in either direction as long as the direction that you choose does not fold the hackle stem

back on itself, levering the stem against the mounting wraps, which can break the feather. Here, we're wrapping clockwise when viewed from the top. When the hackle reaches the top of the foundation, the feather barbs should lie in a horizontal plane, parallel to the tying bench, as shown. (Note: if you've mounted the hackle with a vertical mount, simply clip the tip in a pair of hackle pliers, and draw the hackle downward to a horizontal position. When you begin to wrap the hackle, as in the next step, you can wrap in either direction.)

Step 2: When you reach the top of the thread post, begin taking a wrap around the top of the post; the feather barbs should begin to flare outward, as shown in this top view. You'll need to keep just enough outward tension on the feather to keep the hackle pliers from sliding downward off your finger. If the wing post wiggles excessively under this tension, pinch the tip of the post with your left fingers and support the post as you wrap.

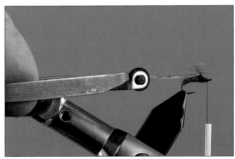

Step 3: Continue wrapping by orbiting your hand around the wing post, letting the hackle pliers slide smoothly around your index finger as you wrap. Each wrap goes beneath the previous one; that is, the wing post is hackled from the top down. Again, if you wish, support the wing post with your left fingers as you wrap, momentarily releasing it to let the hackle pliers pass. Once you get a few wraps completed, the wing post will probably prove rigid enough that it no longer needs support.

Step 4: As you complete the last, lowermost wrap at the bottom of the post, draw the feather tip toward the hook eye and angle it downward. Raise the tying thread vertically so that it crosses the feather stem, as shown.

Step 5: Pull the feather stem toward you, bending it against the tying thread, as shown. This will flare the barbs on one side of the feather. With your left hand, bring the thread to the far side of the shank. As you come over the top of the shank, angle the thread toward the hook eye. Keep the bobbin tip low so that the thread passes under the wrapped hackle, and sneak the thread between the flared hackle barbs so that the thread traps the hackle stem against the shank.

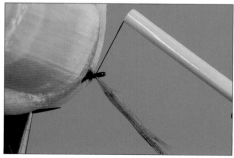

Step 6: Take one or two more thread wraps directly over the first one, and then release the feather from the pliers. With the left fingers, gently preen back the barbs that extend over the hook eye, and take another tight wrap of the thread. Then clip the tip of the feather.

Step 7: Take a couple of tight thread wraps over the clipped end of the feather, then *whip finish* (p. 43) the fly.

Wrapping Quill Bodies

When tyers speak of "quill" bodies, they are generally referring to one of two materials: a hackle feather stripped of its barbs, or a strand of peacock herl stripped of its fuzzy flue (which, technically speaking, is a barb stripped of its barbules). The method for wrapping both of these materials is virtually identical, as shown in the sequence below, but the preparation differs slightly for each as illustrated in the following photos.

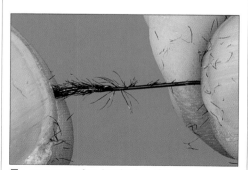

To remove the barbules from peacock herl, use your thumbnail to scrape away the iridescent fuzz from the quill. Work from the tip of the quill to the butt, and take several passes under light pressure; scraping too energetically will break the quill.

You can also strip peacock quill by using a coarse ink eraser, again working from tip to butt with repeated light strokes.

To prepare a hackle feather for a quill body, hold the feather near the tip. Pinch the lowermost barbs on the feather, and pull them toward the feather butt to strip them off. Repeat, working up the quill toward the tip. Then strip the barbs from the other side of the quill.

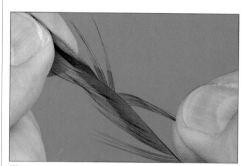

One of the keys to attractive quill bodies is a smooth underbody over which to wrap the material. Peacock quills are quite flat and tie in with very little bulk. Hackle quills, however, are oval in cross-section and can produce a bump or ridge in the underbody. To eliminate this bulk, lay the quill against a table, and rub the side of your scissors down the last half-inch or so of the quill. Apply pressure to flatten the stem.

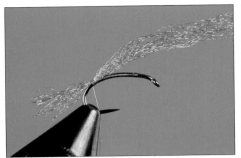

Step 1: As noted, one of the keys to a good quill body is a smooth underbody. If tails or a trailing shuck are used on the pattern, use a *flattened thread* (p. 37) to mount the material with only 2 or 3 tight wraps, as shown on the Antron shuck here. Do not bind or clip the excess material.

Step 2: There are many ways to mount the quill. The approach shown here positions the quill for easy wrapping. Position the thread over the rearmost thread wrap securing the tail or shuck. Mount the quill atop the shank at angle, as shown. Use 2 or 3 tight wraps. If using a stripped hackle stem, the first mounting wrap should be taken over the uppermost point of the flattened stem. Do not clip the excess.

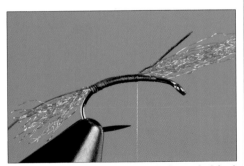

Step 3: Using a flattened thread, bind the excess quill and the tag ends of any tail, shuck, or rib material to the top of the shank, keeping this thread foundation as smooth as possible. Bind the tags forward to the front end of the quill body.

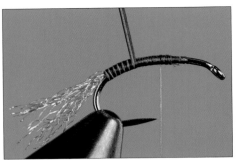

Step 4: Trim the excess materials. The first wrap of the quill should cover the rearmost thread wrap. Then wrap the quill forward, placing the wraps of materials snugly against one another. When using peacock quill, avoid overlapping the edges of the material as you wrap; the segmentation effect will be diminished or lost.

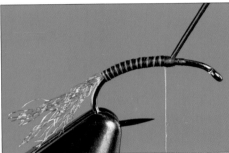

Step 5: Wrap forward to the tie-off point. Take one complete, snug wrap over the quill and around the hook shank. Then pull the thread to tighten the wrap. Tying off like this will help prevent the material from shifting under thread pressure. When this first wrap is complete, take additional tight wraps forward to secure the quill.

Wrapping Single-Herl Collars

The thorax or head on some emergers is formed by wrapping a single strand of herl, usually peacock or ostrich, to form a narrow, bandlike collar. Single-strand collars are quite often used on smaller patterns to avoid bulk. Longer or thicker thoraxes or collars, particularly those on larger hooks, are usually formed by *wrapping twisted-herl collars* (p. 49).

Step 1: Position the tying thread at the rearmost point of the collar. Clip a herl from the feather stem, and observe the cut end as shown above left. The tiny barbules that make the fuzzy part of the herl are not centered on the quill, but rather, they grow outward from one edge of the quill—the edge that faces you when you look at the front of the herl strand, as shown above right. The "bare edge" of the quill faces the rear of the feather.

Step 2: With your thumbnail, strip away the fuzzy barbules from lowermost ¼" of the herl strand. Mount the herl atop the shank so that the edge containing the barbules (the front of the herl) faces you; the "bare edge" of the quill faces the far side of the shank. Note that a small section of bare quill is left between the first mounting wrap and the lowermost barbules. This section helps align the quill neatly for wrapping. Bind the quill to the collar tie-off point, forming a smooth underbody. Clip the excess.

Step 3: Draw the herl away from you, to the far side of the shank. The fuzzy edge of the herl, the front of the strand,

should face the hook bend. Begin wrapping the herl. Adjacent wraps overlap so that the fuzzy edge of the herl on one wrap is laid atop the "bare edge" of the quill from the previous wrap. This ensures a dense, full collar.

Step 4: You can promote a very full collar by using the left fingers to preen back the barbules from the previous wraps as you take additional turns of the herl—much like the technique used to wrap a dense chenille body or a wet-fly hackle. When the tie-off point is reached, bind down the herl strand, clip the excess, and secure with a few thread wraps.

Wrapping Twisted-Herl Collars

Twisted herl makes a thorax or collar that is more substantial and better suited to cover longer lengths of hook shank than the method shown in *wrapping single-herl collars* (p. 48). Twisting also improves the durability of the collar, particularly if the optional thread core, shown in the sequence below, is used. This thread core is not specifically mentioned in any of the patterns in this book, but it is a widely used approach among tyers and is recommended.

Step 1: Position the tying thread at the rearmost point of the collar. Clip the desired number of herl strands and

align the tips. Clip off the top ¼" or so of the herl tips; these are fragile and tend to break when wrapping.

Step 2: Mount the herls as a bundle about ⅛" back from tip. Bind down the excess, wrapping toward the hook eye and forming a smooth underbody. Position the thread at the tie-off point for the collar.

Optional: To improve the durability of the collar, mount a 4" length of tying thread, shown here in red, along with the herl.

Step 3: Gather and gently draw downward all the herl strands (and the piece of tying thread, if used). Try to put an even tension on all the strands. Clip them in a pair of hackle pliers. The E-Z Hook type pictured here works especially well, since it simplifies twisting the herl.

Step 4: Twist the herl clockwise when viewed from above. The tips of the strands next to the hook shank will begin to twist first.

Step 5: When a short length of the herl, about ½" or so, is twisted to a fuzzy, chenille-like rope, take a wrap around the shank. Don't attempt to spin the entire length of the herl all at once. The twist is tightest near the shank, and trying to spin a longer length of herl may cause it to break.

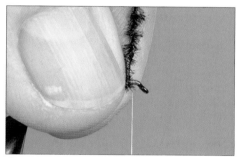

Step 6: Repeat Step 5, spinning and wrapping the herl, until the desired amount of hook shank is covered. You can encourage a full, brushy collar by using the left fingers to stroke back the barbs on the preceding wraps as you take additional turns of material.

Step 7: When the frontmost point of the collar is reached, tie off the herls, clip the excess, and bind down the exposed butts.

Wrapping Wet-Fly Hackle

Wet-fly hackle is generally mounted and wrapped so that the feather barbs curve toward the rear of the fly. Unlike dry-fly hackle, which helps support the fly on the water, wet-fly hackle usually has no structural function; it is typically used to imitate the legs of the natural insect and so is sparsely dressed.

Step 1: Position the tying thread at the hackle-mounting point, and *prepare a hackle feather* (p. 39). Mount the feather as shown in *mounting collar hackle* (p. 37). When the feather is mounted, advance the thread to the hook eye.
Clip the tip of the feather in a pair of hackle pliers so that the pliers are in line with the feather stem, not gripping it crosswise. Slip your index finger in the pliers loop and raise the pliers vertically above the shank so that the front, or most distinctly marked side of the feather, faces the hook eye. Use your left fingers to preen back all the feather barbs toward the rear of the hook.

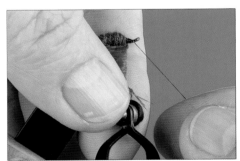

Step 2: While holding the barbs, wrap the hackle around the far side of the shank to the bottom of the hook. With your left thumb and middle finger, reach below the vise head and momentarily hold the hackle pliers as you reposition your right hand in front of the tying thread. Here, the right fingers are in front of the thread, ready to take the pliers and resume wrapping.

Step 3: Insert your right forefinger into the pliers loop, and continue wrapping. As you bring the feather up the near side of the shank, reposition your left hand and use your left fingers to preen back the barbs again. Wet-fly hackle lacks the stiffness of dry-fly hackle, and preening the feather like this as you wrap helps avoid trapping barbs beneath the feather stem.

Step 4: Repeat Steps 2 and 3, wrapping the hackle in touching, but not overlapping wraps, always stroking the barbs rearward as you wind, until the desired number of wraps are taken. When the last wrap is taken, raise the hackle pliers vertically above the shank, and unwind the tying thread until it abuts the last wrap of hackle.

Step 5: With your left hand, take two or three tight wraps around the feather.

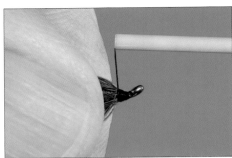

Step 6: Clip the feather tip and bind it down with a few tight wraps. If the hackle is satisfactory, *whip finish* (p. 43) the fly. If you wish the barbs to slant farther toward the rear of the hook, use your left fingers to draw all the barbs rearward. Then take a few thread wraps toward the rear of the fly, over the frontmost wrap of hackle, to force the barbs back.

Step 7: Here the barbs have been slanted slightly rearward and the head of the fly whip finished.

Chapter 3: Trailing Shucks and Bubble Sheaths

Though the imitation of an emerging insect can be approached in a number of ways—representing its position in the water column, for example, or the bulge of an emerging thorax, as we noted earlier—one of the chief aims of a great many emerger patterns is to suggest the nymphal or pupal skin. Representations of this component generally take one of two forms—trailing shucks or bubble sheaths.

TRAILING SHUCKS

On mayfly, midge, and some caddis patterns, tyers look to replicate the discarded or partially discarded skin of the aquatic form of the insect that is left empty as the adult fly wriggles and pulls free at the surface of the water. Typically, the nymphal or pupal skin splits longitudinally at the top of the thorax, and the adult insect emerges from this opening. The thorax portion of a hatching insect, then, is really where the action takes place; it's the "business end" of the emerger. As the adult insect withdraws its body, the abdomen of the nymphal skin is vacated, and this empty abdominal husk is suspended in or below the surface film. It appears to trail behind the hatching adult, and tyers most often represent this portion of the emerging fly with a "trailing shuck" or simply "shuck," as most tyers call it. In a few patterns, other portions of the nymphal skin—the thorax portion, for instance—are represented. But because the thorax area is a "busy" part of the hatching insect, the distinction between the features of the adult and nymphal or pupal forms is not always clear; and because the abdomen is generally the longest and most conspicuous part of the insect, tyers focus most often on imitating this rear portion of the empty skin.

The trailing shuck of an insect is an interesting feature; water fills the empty skin and preserves in remarkably faithful detail the structures of the original nymph or pupa—the abdominal segments, the tails, even gill structures if they are present. It is also very thin and so quite flexible. But what is most conspicuous—to the human observer at least—is the slightly glossy translucence of the empty skin. Shuck colors run from almost clear; to slightly milky; to a pale, translucent version of the original nymphal or pupal coloration. Viewed from beneath, backlit by the sky, the shuck appears slightly shiny from the diffused and scattered light.

In designing and tying trailing shucks, tyers have sought to replicate one or more of these features: sheen, translucence, tint, mobility, a three-dimensional hollow structure, and even anatomical features such as segmentation and tails. The relative importance given these characteristics depends, of course, on the experience and taste of individual tyers—what they consider the significant feature of the shuck that triggers a strike and whether simplicity of design and ease of tying rank high or low on their list of priorities.

The trailing shuck on an artificial fly is arguably one of the two components that define an emerger pattern and make it what it is (the other, as we've noted, is the emerging wings or body). This chapter contains a variety of trailing shuck styles, from the simplest to the more elaborate designs. In a few instances, these tying sequences provide more detailed instructions for some of the shucks used on flies that appear in subsequent chapters. But the main purpose here is to provide a selection of trailing-shuck styles for tyers who wish to design their own emerger patterns. Virtually all of the trailing shucks pictured can be used on any of the fly styles shown in this book, allowing tyers to customize basic emerger designs in a way that best accommodates their ideas about effective patterns.

Simple Shuck

The most basic of shuck styles uses a single strand of synthetic or natural material mounted at the tailing point. Typically, trailing shucks are intended to represent the abdominal portion of the discarded skin, and so they are often sized to be equal in length to the abdomen dressed on the shank. But there is a great deal of latitude here; some tyers prefer a shorter shuck, others a longer, though they are rarely dressed to be more than one shank-length long.

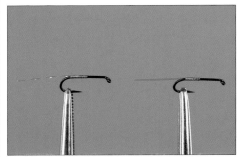

The most commonly used synthetic materials for simple shucks are Krystal Flash, shown on the left, and a strand of pearlescent tinsel (or Flashabou), shown on the right. Because Krystal Flash is rather thin, it is ordinarily used on small patterns, such as midge emergers. Pearlescent tinsel is available in a variety of widths and can be used on a larger range of hook sizes; it has the added advantage of being quite mobile in the water.

Other synthetics, however, can certainly be used, and we've seen patterns incorporating trailing shucks formed of flexible floss, rubber leg material, and even a thin strand of vinyl cord such as V-Rib or D-Rib.

To tie the shuck, simply secure the material atop the shank at the tailing point with a *pinch wrap* (p. 38). Secure with additional tight wraps and clip the excess.

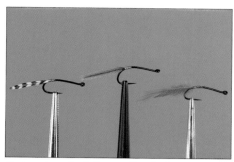

Natural materials, particularly feathers, are also widely used for simple trailing shucks. A narrow hackle tip, such as the grizzly feather shown at the left, can be used for a shuck on midge emergers; dun and grizzly dun are sometimes used as well. The single barbs of some feathers are sometimes tied as shucks. Shown here are ostrich herl (middle) and pheasant afterfeather trimmed to a taper (right). These latter two materials are easy to tie and have a lifelike mobility in the water, but they are quite fragile.

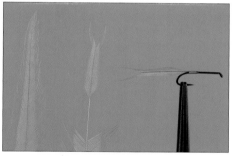

For mayfly emergers, a trimmed hen or rooster hackle makes a credible shuck, as shown on the right. Select a feather on which the barbs near the tip are the right length for tails on the hook size being used, as shown on the left. Snip away the feather tip, then trim barbs at a taper, close to the stem, leaving a few barbs on either side of the tip for tails, as shown in the middle. Strip away the lower barbs to produce a shuck of the desired length. Then mount the shuck with a pinch wrap at the tailing point, as shown on the right. This shuck style somewhat resembles the *drawn-feather shuck* (p. 53), but is more durable.

Reverse CDC Shuck

We first saw this shuck style used by Vladimir Markov, though other tyers may well have discovered it on their own. Unlike a simple CDC shuck, which is mounted with the feather tip

rearward, this approach mounts the feather in the reverse direction, with the butt of the stem rearward. It produces a tapered, hollow-looking, slightly ballooned shuck. Since the CDC gives significant floatation at the rear of the fly, the style is best used on patterns that float flush in the film rather than those with bodies that descend below the surface. The key to the style is selecting the right feather. The CDC feather should have barbs of uniform length, and the lowermost barbs must be slightly longer than the finished shuck length. The best feathers for the purpose are Type 3 "puff" feathers, as shown in the following sequence, which are suitable for hooks up to about #12. Type 1 or Type 2 CDC feathers can also be used.

Step 1: Position the thread at the tailing point. Hold the feather atop the shank with the stem butt pointing rearward. Take one wrap of the thread over the bare feather stem, directly behind the lowermost barbs.

Step 2: With the right hand, put downward tension on the bobbin. With the left fingertips, grasp the butt end of the stem and pull rearward, drawing the feather beneath the thread wrap. Pull the feather stem until it extends beyond the thread wrap the desired distance, usually about one shank-length. At this point, you can simply secure the feather

with additional tight thread wraps, and then clip and bind the excess. If you wish to produce a more "balloon-like" shuck, proceed to Step 3.

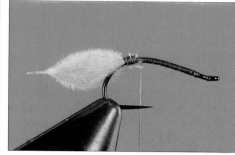

Step 3: To produce a more billowed shuck with the impression of greater volume, lift the bobbin very slightly with the right hand to reduce thread tension. The thread should not be slack; there should be slight tension on it. With the left fingers, push the butt of the feather stem back toward the hook eye very slightly. This will slide some of the interior barbs (or the feather stem if using a Type 1 or Type 2 feather) back under the thread wrap; the exterior barbs will not slide but instead balloon outward. When the desired degree of fullness in the shuck is reached, secure the feather with additional wraps; clip and bind the excess.

Drawn-Feather Shuck

Though this tying technique has been used for some time as a way of creating extended-body dry flies, Doug Swisher and Carl Richards, in their book *Emergers*, explored its use as trailing shuck on mayfly emerger patterns. The method produces a graceful, delicate, tailed shuck with the suggestion of segmentation. Most tyers use large neck hackle or saddle hackle, either rooster or hen, to form this type of shuck, though other feathers such as wood duck or mallard flank can also be used. The only real requirement is barbs of sufficient length. Perhaps the biggest drawback to this shuck is durability; it is, as it appears, rather fragile.

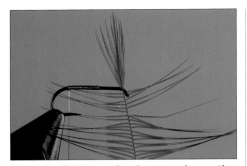

Step 1: Select a feather, such as the saddle hackle shown here. The feather is a bit easier to handle if the fuzzy barbs at the base are stripped away. Beginning a short distance below the tip, preen the barbs outward to stand perpendicular to the stem. The topmost barbs that are preened outward must be about 1 ½ times as long as the length of finished shuck (not including the tail length). Mount the tying thread; use a *flattened thread* (p. 37) to form a foundation at the tailing point, and position the thread a few wraps ahead of the rearmost wrap.

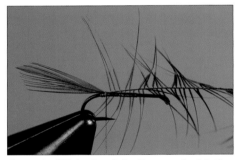

Step 2: With the left fingers hold the feather by the tip and place it atop the shank. Take one wrap of the thread around the feather stem between the rearward-pointing tip and the preened back barbs.

Step 3: With the right hand, put a slight downward tension on the bobbin. With the left fingers, pull the feather tip rearward, sliding it beneath the thread wrap. If the feather wants to drag the tying thread along with it, raise the bobbin vertically and angle it toward the hook eye; then use the right hand to put

enough counter-tension on the thread to hold it in position as you slide the feather rearward.

Slide the feather far enough out to produce a shuck of the desired length. If a thin, compact shuck is desired, simply secure the feather to the top of the shank with additional tight wraps. Then clip and bind the excess, and form the tail as shown in Step 5. If a wider shuck with a more segmented appearance is desired, proceed to Step 4.

Step 4: To make a fuller shuck, put a slight tension on the bobbin with the left hand. With the right hand, carefully pull the butt end of the feather toward the hook eye. The feather stem will slide beneath the thread wraps, while the barbs bulge out on either side to form a wider trailing shuck. When the feather reaches the desired shape, bind down and clip the feather stem.

Step 5: Clip away the stem at the tip of the feather, leaving a few barbs on either side to form the tails.

Pulled CDC Shuck

Serbian tyer Andrija Urban takes this somewhat unusual approach to forming drawn-feather shucks from CDC. The tubing used in the technique helps control the limp feather barbs during tying; it can be fashioned from a short length of wire insulation, tubing sold at hobby shops, or even a strip of rolled and taped paper.

Step 1: Insert the butt of the feather into the tubing, and draw it through until only the feather tip projects from one end.

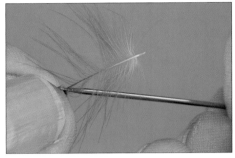

Step 2: Pinch the tubing in the left fingers, making sure that you pinch the tip of the feather as well. Use a dubbing needle to pull the barbs on the exposed side of feather stem back through the tubing, freeing them.

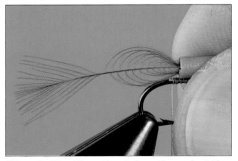

Step 3: Hold the tubing in the right fingers. With the left fingers, pull the feather tip to form the abdomen of the shuck. Continue pulling the feather until the shuck is the desired length, usually about one shank length.

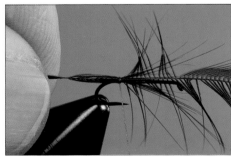

Step 4: Position the tying thread at the tail-mounting point. Hold the tubing atop the shank so that the left end of the tubing is above the tying thread.

Step 5: Secure the CDC feather flat atop the shank. Trap the feather first with a soft wrap of thread, then add tight wraps moving toward the hook eye.

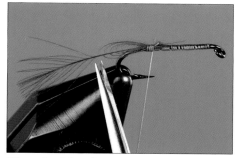

Step 6: Clip the excess feather. The shuck can be left as shown here for mayfly emergers, or the feather tip can be trimmed away where the scissors are positioned for an untailed caddis shuck.

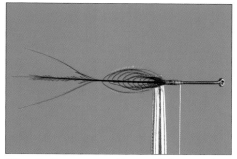

Step 7: On some patterns, Urban makes a three-fiber tail by clipping away the barbs at the feather tip, trimming them close to the stem, until only a single fiber remains on either side, as shown in this top view. The center tail is formed from the trimmed feather stem.

Bundled-Fiber Shuck

We'd hazard a guess, without much risk, that bundled-fiber shucks are currently the most widely used style in tying emergers. And with good reason—they are easy to tie and durable, and with the appropriate selection of materials, they can reproduce the sheen, translucence, and color of the nymphal skin.

Both natural and synthetic materials can be used, but synthetics are probably the more popular of the two. And of these, Antron and Z-Lon are the first choice of many tyers. The light-reflecting properties of these materials are well-known, and they are available in a wide range of colors. But poly yarn can also be used, particularly on flies designed to ride with body flush against the surface, as the yarn assists in floatation. And in fact, we have seen patterns using bundled Krystal Flash; strands of highly reflective dubbing, such as Ice Dubbing; various types of synthetic hair designed for saltwater patterns; and indeed just about every kind of stranded fiber used in fly tying. Regardless of the material, the dressing technique is the same.

Aside from shuck length, as noted in "Simple Shuck," tyers differ somewhat on two other elements pertaining bundled shucks. The first is the density of the bundle, that is, how many fibers it contains. Certainly there is no rule that specifies the amount of material that should be used, and patterns with thick shucks and those with sparse ones both catch fish. Thick shucks, of course, present a more substantial and well-defined profile to the trout, and a dense shuck tied of reflective material is quite shimmery in the water. But thick shucks tie in with greater bulk and can increase the finished body diameter on slender-bodied flies, such as midges, to unnatural proportions. The greater numbers of fibers also reduces translucence and with more flexible materials can reduce mobility in the water as well. A sparser bundle of material ties in more neatly but creates a shuck with the overall impression of lower volume and a less distinct appearance. In the end, as with much in fly tying, it is a matter of taste. For what it's worth, we offer a couple of observations on shuck density that may be useful. When using materials with a crinkled texture, such as "kinky" Z-Lon (which also comes in straight "standard" version) or snowshoe hare's foot, fewer fibers are needed since the crinkly texture gives the impression of greater volume. We feel the same is true of CDC barbs; their fluffiness gives the illusion of bulk.

Antron is enormously popular for tying trailing shucks, and its availability in different forms gives tyers some latitude in selecting a material appropriate to the purpose. Spooled Antron is the most convenient to use, and a strand of spooled yarn can be split lengthwise to produce a sparse bundle or one sized to smaller hooks. But spooled Antron is a fairly coarse, relatively straight material. Tyers who desire a more crinkled fiber and a finer texture, particularly for smaller patterns, might look to two other forms of Antron that are somewhat underutilized in tying trailing shucks. Multiply carded Antron yarn has much thinner fibers that produce a wispy shuck with excellent mobility in the water. Antron dubbing—the type spun into long filaments, not the chopped form often sold as "touch dubbing"—also has a fine texture and is moderately crinkled as well. (One form of this dubbing, for instance, is sold under the name "Sparkle Blend.") Tying trailing shucks with both of these materials is explained below.

Aside from shuck density, the other option in tying bundled-fiber shucks is the shape of the shuck, that is, whether the fibers are of uniform or random lengths. Tyers, as always, have differing opinions, though there's no doubt that both approaches are effective. Uniform shucks, usually clipped to length after mounting, are perhaps marginally easier to tie, and the squared off end may more accurately suggest the silhouette of most caddis species, which have blunter, blockier abdomens, and of midges which have abdomens of relatively constant diameter. Bundles with fibers of random length produce a more tapered shuck that is generally sparser in appearance and may better suggest the tapered abdomens of most mayfly species. Practically speaking, the differences in the two styles may ultimately be small, but both approaches are shown below.

Step 1a: Some bundled-fiber shuck materials profit from a little preparation before mounting. Single-ply materials composed of very thin filaments— spooled Antron, Z-Lon, poly yarn—can be combed out prior to mounting to form a shuck that is fuller in appearance without using an excessively thick bundle of material. This same preparation is useful when it is necessary to split a bundle of fibers lengthwise for the shuck on a smaller pattern.

Cut a length of material, such as the spooled Antron shown here, 2 or 3 inches long. Run a fine-toothed comb several times through one end of the material to separate and untangle the fibers. Reverse the strand and comb through the other end. If necessary, divide the strand lengthwise with a dubbing needle, as shown here, to produce a smaller bundle of fibers proportionate to the hook size.

Step 1b: Mounting a bundled-fiber shuck is quite simple. Secure the material atop the shank at the desired point using a firm *pinch wrap* (p. 38). Hold the material in place with the left fingers, and take 3 or 4 additional wraps toward the hook eye, binding the material to the shank. If using a thicker bundle of

fibers, such as the Z-Lon shown here, angle cut the butt end and then bind down the fibers. For a shuck with uniform fibers, clip the shuck to the desired length.

Step 2a: To form a tapered shuck from materials such as poly yarn, Z-Lon, or the spooled Antron shown here, prepare the material by combing a strand as explained in Step 1a. If necessary, split the strand lengthwise to produce a fiber bundle of the appropriate thickness.

Hold the material in the right fingers. With the left fingers, grasp about half the fibers and pull them out short distance so that the tips are no longer aligned. Then pull a few of the long fibers out a short distance to produce a bundle that is roughly tapered.

Step 2b: Mount the shuck as explained in Step 1b. Note that when the tag of yarn is trimmed, the unclipped end still has fibers of random lengths; this end can be used as a shuck on the next fly.

The approach shown in the previous photo may leave a small hump of bound-down shuck material at the rear of the fly. This rarely causes a problem with dubbed bodies, since the wraps of dubbing can compensate for any unevenness in the underbody. With certain body materials, however—hackle or peacock quill, feather barbs such as pheasant-tail fibers, biots, floss, stretch floss, vinyl cord or tubing—this

unevenness can cause a tying problem or result in a poorly formed abdomen. The solution is to incorporate the tag end of the shuck material, along with tags of body and ribbing materials, into the underbody. Two approaches are shown below.

Step 3a: If the trailing shuck is the first component to be tied in, secure the shuck material atop the shank with a *pinch wrap* (p. 38), leaving a tag that extends to the eye of the hook. Take one or two additional tight wraps toward the hook eye. Return the thread to the rearmost wrap. Mount the body material—we're using V-Rib here—and any ribbing material. Leave tags that extend to the hook eye on both body and ribbing materials.

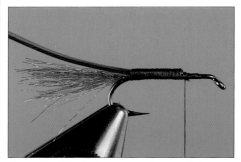

Step 3b: Bind the tags of material, as a group, to the top of the shank, using a *flattened thread* (p. 37) to form a smooth underbody. Clip the excess materials at the frontmost point of the abdomen. Trim the shuck to length. The body can now be wrapped easily over this smooth foundation.

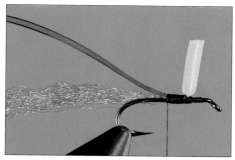

Step 4a: If the first component of the pattern is dressed on the forward portion of the shank, such as the foam parachute post shown here, mount the shuck, body, and rib materials at the front of the abdomen.

Step 4b: Use a *flattened thread* (p. 37) to bind the materials as a group atop the shank. When the tailing point is reached, reverse direction and wrap the thread back to the front of the abdomen, forming a smooth underbody. Then clip the shuck to length. The body can now be wrapped and ribbed.

Step 5a: Multi-ply yarns, such as Antron or other types of "sparkle yarns," have a finer texture than the spooled variety, making them well suited to smaller patterns. To prepare this material for a trailing shuck, first cut a 2"-3" length, and separate the plies.

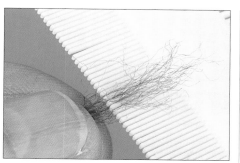

Step 5b: Grasp one ply of yarn by the very end, and lay it against the top of your thigh. With a fine-toothed comb, brush several times through strand to separate and untangle the filaments. (Note: If a denser shuck is desired, hold two plies side-by-side and comb them out together). The filaments in multi-ply yarns are actually shorter strands of material twisted into a cord. As you comb, some of these filaments will pull out, and the combed strand will be tapered.

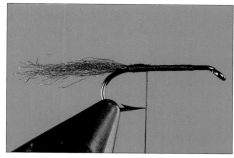

Step 5c: The shuck is mounted as explained in Step 1a. Here we've formed a tapered shuck, but the ply of yarn can be mounted longer than is required for the pattern, and then clipped to length if a blunter shuck shape is desired.

Step 6a: To form a shuck from long-fibered Antron dubbing, hold a pinch of dubbing in the left fingers. With the right fingers, grasp some of the fibers and pull them a short distance, tapering the bundle.

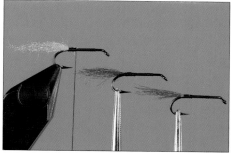

Step 6b: The bundle is mounted as explained in Step 1b. A tapered shuck is shown here on the left, but the bundle can be mounted longer than necessary and trimmed to length if desired.

Shown here are the shucks formed from the 3 different types of Antron— Antron dubbing (left), multi-ply Antron yarn (middle), spooled Antron (right).

Other materials made of multiple filaments can be employed for bundled-fiber shucks and can give some interesting effects. Braided mylar tubing can suggest the crumpled or twisted shuck of an emerging insect. Cut a length of the tubing, such as the pearl Diamond Braid shown at the right. Tease out one or two strands from the end of tubing and pull them out to unravel the braid, as shown in the middle. Mount a section of the unraveled braid for a shuck, as shown on the left.

Feather barbs from partridge, hen and rooster hackle, woodduck flank, mallard flank, and other plumage are sometimes used to dress trailing shucks, though more often they form tails on patterns that resemble the nymphal stage of an insect—such as floating nymphs. Admittedly, it is not always entirely clear on some patterns if fibers at the tailing position are intended to represent nymphal tails or trailing shucks. And perhaps it does not matter in the end. The trout probably don't draw this distinction, and the tying technique is the same regardless.

Marabou and CDC, however, are perhaps the most commonly used feather barbs to dress bundled-fiber trailing shucks. Both are flexible and mobile in the water, and CDC in particular is well-known for its capacity to trap small air bubbles that may scatter light in much the same way as the shuck on a natural.

Burned Teardrop Shuck

This version of a bundled-fiber shuck was designed by Carl Richards and Bob Braendle and is used on a number of caddis emerger patterns in their book *Caddis Super Hatches*. Melting the end of the fibers produces a hollow, balloon-like shuck that holds its shape in the water. Richards and Braendle use Z-Lon for the shuck material, as shown in the following sequence, but spooled Antron and poly yarn can be used as well.

Two approaches to the teardrop shuck are shown below. The first is the method used by Richards and Braendle and is best suited when the shuck encloses a portion of the dubbed abdomen. The second method shown is best used when the shuck does not enclose any of the body, but is tied in at the tailing point as a conventional trailing shuck. Forming the shuck separately makes it easier to control the shuck length on the finished fly, and several shucks can be fashioned in advance and tied in as needed.

Step 1a: Position the tying thread at the rearmost point of the body. Use the *direct dubbing* method (p. 34) to dub the rear portion of the abdomen. Position the thread directly in front of the dubbing.

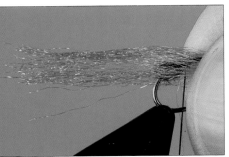

Step 1b: Cut a length of Z-Lon about 1" long and comb out the ends to separate the fibers. If necessary, split the Z-Lon lengthwise to produce a strand with fewer fibers for smaller hooks. Position the strand against the top of the shank. With your fingertips, work the fibers down around the sides of the shank so that they are evenly distributed around the shank.

Step 1c: With the left fingers, pinch the fibers around the dubbing; with the right hand, secure the fibers directly in front of the dubbing with several tight thread wraps. Clip and bind the excess Z-Lon

Step 1d: Take 6" length of tying thread; we're using red thread for better visibility; ordinarily the thread color would match the shuck color. With the thread, tie a loose knot around the Z-Lon fibers, just at the rear of the body. The best knot is an ordinary overhand knot in which the tag is passed through the loop twice—in just the same way you'd tie a surgeon's knot. Tighten the knot just enough to lightly consolidate the fibers.

Step 1e: Pull the tags of the tying thread to slide the knot rearward along the Z-Lon. Pull the knot tight, binding the fibers together to form a shuck of the desired length. Clip the tag end of the fibers to within ⅛" of the knot.

Step 1f: Use a lighter or a hot-tip tool to melt the Z-Lon tag and fuse the fibers together. Melt the fibers just to the base of knot; don't burn the tying thread. Clip the tag ends of thread close to the knot.

Step 2a: If the teardrop shuck does not enclose any of the body, you can form the shuck in advance.

Cut a length of Z-Lon about 1" long. Run a fine-toothed comb through both ends to separate the fibers. If necessary, split the Z-Lon lengthwise to produce a strand with fewer fibers for smaller hooks. Cut a 6" length of tying thread, and tie a surgeon's knot near one end of the Z-Lon strand. When the knot is secure, trim the short end of the Z-Lon to make a tag that extends beyond the knot about ⅛".

Step 2b: Use a lighter or a hot-tip tool to melt the Z-Lon tag and fuse the fibers together. Melt the fibers just to the base of knot; don't burn the tying thread.

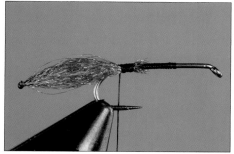

Step 2c: Trim the ends of the tying thread close to the knot. The completed shuck is mounted at the tailing point using a *pinch wrap* (p. 38).

Knotted Teardrop Shuck

This simplified version of a teardrop shuck is fashioned by casting an over-hand knot in the shuck material. Continuous-filament materials—spooled Antron, Z-Lon, or poly yarn—are better suited to this technique than are strands made from random-length filaments, such as Antron or poly dubbing or multi-ply yarns. Knotted shucks work particularly well with sparser bundles of material.

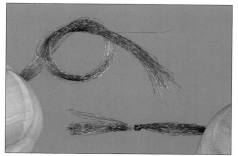

Step 1: Cut a strand of material, such as the spooled Antron shown here, about 2" long; lengths much shorter are difficult to knot. If necessary, split the material lengthwise to pro-duce a strand with fewer fibers for smaller hooks. Tie a simple overhand knot in the strand, as shown on top. Tighten the knot firmly, as shown on the bottom.

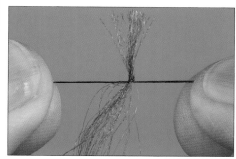

Step 2: With the fingertips of both hands, grasp a few filaments from the long end of the strand, and pull them firmly outward. Repeat a couple times, grasping and pulling new filaments each time. This procedure helps seat the knot tightly and helps distribute the filaments radially to produce a more uniform teardrop shape.

Step 3: Run a fine-toothed comb once or twice through the long end of the strand to separate the fibers. Mount the fibers at the tailing point using a *pinch wrap* (p. 38) to form a shuck of the desired length. Clip and bind the excess. To make an untailed shuck—on a caddis emerger, for instance—simply trim away all the fibers behind the knot,

and apply a small drop of head cement to the knot itself, as shown on the left. To make tailed shuck for a mayfly emerger, trim away most of the fibers behind the knot, leaving a few for tails, as shown at the right. Trim the tails to length, and apply a drop of the cement to the knot.

Cored Teardrop Shuck

A teardrop shuck can be tied around a core of a stiffer material to give the impression of greater density in the interior of the shuck. Though this style of trailing shuck is not particularly mobile in the water, the core does help preserve the shape of the surrounding bubble. The bubble portion of the shuck is most easily tied with Z-Lon or Antron yarn; Antron in dubbing form is more difficult to handle in this method. The most practical core mate-rial is round or oval mylar tinsel that is woven around a thread core; it is stiff enough to provide some rigidity when tying. Woven mylars without a core, such as Diamond Braid and similar materials, can also be used, and these produce a softer silhouette inside the bubble portion of the shuck. Gluing the wraps at the tail of shuck is crucial for durability.

Step 1: Position the tying thread at the rearmost point of the body. Cut a length of Antron or Z-Lon about 2" long. Use a fine-toothed comb to comb through both ends of the yarn to separate the filaments. If necessary, split the strand lengthwise to produce a bundle that is half the desired density of the finished shuck. Secure the middle of the bundle atop the shank at the tailing point. Take 4 or 5 tight thread wraps toward the hook eye.

Step 2: Cut a length of core material about 2" long; we're using a woven green mylar tinsel. Mount the core atop the frontmost thread wrap securing the yarn; the tag of the core material should extend to the midpoint of the hook shank. Take tight thread wraps toward the hook bend, stopping at the rearmost wrap used to mount the yarn.

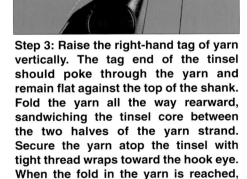

Step 3: Raise the right-hand tag of yarn vertically. The tag end of the tinsel should poke through the yarn and remain flat against the top of the shank. Fold the yarn all the way rearward, sandwiching the tinsel core between the two halves of the yarn strand. Secure the yarn atop the tinsel with tight thread wraps toward the hook eye. When the fold in the yarn is reached, continue wrapping forward, binding the tinsel tag to the top of the shank.

At this point, you can dress the remainder of the fly pattern and finish the shuck as the last tying operation. Or you can form the shuck now, as we're doing here.

Step 4: With the left fingers, preen the shuck fibers toward the end of the tinsel, smoothing them so that they surround the core evenly. With a separate piece of thread (we're using red thread for better visibility; normally, the thread color would match the shuck color), tie a loose knot around the shuck fibers next to the hook bend. The best knot is an ordinary overhand knot in which the tag passes through the loop twice—just as you'd tie a surgeon's knot.

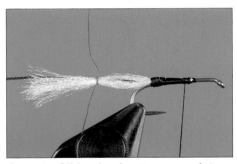

Step 5: Slide the knot rearward to a point that produces a shuck of the desired length, and tighten the knot. The resulting shuck bubble will hug the core tightly. If you want a more balloon-like bubble, proceed to Step 6. If this more compact shuck fits the fly design, proceed to Step 8.

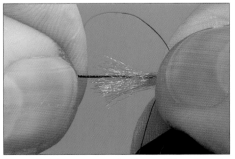

Step 6: For a more balloon-like shuck, grasp the tinsel core in the left fingers and put tension on it. With the right fingers, pinch the shuck fibers and the knot that secures them, and slide them toward the hook bend very slightly.

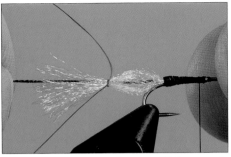

Step 7: The shuck fibers will bow outward, as shown.

Step 8: When the bubble is satisfactorily formed, tie one or two more surgeon's knots directly atop the first, and tighten securely. When the knots are secure, clip the excess thread. Clip the end of the shuck to within 1⁄16" of the thread wraps. Apply a drop of head cement or liquid (not gel) cyanoacrylate glue, such as Super Glue, to the thread wraps. Apply a second drop to the rear tip of the shuck.

Loop Shuck

This simple variation of a bundled-fiber shuck is formed from a loop of synthetic fibers—Z-Lon, poly yarn, Krystal Flash and other twisted mylar materials, even a few strands of pearl Flashabou or fine mylar tinsel, and Antron. Though any form of Antron can be used, the technique is best suited to the continuous-filament type that is most often sold on spools. This technique produces a blunt, teardrop-shaped trailing shuck that gives the impression of a nymphal skin with some volume, and so it's typically used in caddis patterns.

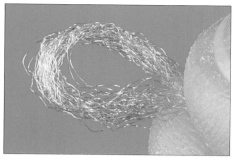

Step 1: Cut a length of shuck material about 2" long. We're using spooled Antron here. Use a fine-toothed comb to comb out both ends of the strand, separating and untangling the fibers. If necessary, use a dubbing needle to split the bundle of fibers lengthwise to produce a strand that is half the desired density of the finished shuck. Fold the strand in half, pinching it with the right fingers to form a loop.

Step 2: Position the loop atop the hook shank to produce a shuck that is about one hook-gap in length. Typically, loop shucks are dressed somewhat shorter than other bundled-fiber shucks.

Step 3: Pinch the loop in position with the left fingers, and secure it atop the shank with tight thread wraps. Clip and bind the excess.

Furled Shuck

Furled yarns, long used by tyers for dressing extended bodies, have recently become popular for tying trailing shucks. Ian Moutter, for instance (see Chapter 10, "Paraloop Emergers") favors them on a great many of his designs. Furled shucks are easy to tie, quite durable, give an impression of segmentation in the nymphal skin, and can be fashioned from many materials—synthetic yarns such as Antron, Z-Lon, and poly; from twisted mylars such as Krystal Flash; synthetic hairs; and even from dubbed threads.

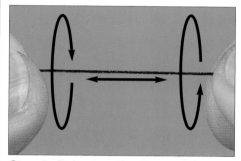

Step 1: Cut a length of material about 3" long; we're using spooled Antron here. Hold the strand between thumb and forefinger of each hand, and pull slightly to put tension on the strand. Roll the material between the fingertips of each hand, in opposite directions, to twist the strand.

Step 2: Relax the tension by moving your fingertips together. The strand will twist up on itself, or furl. If the strand doesn't furl, repeat Step 1, but twist the strand more tightly. If the strand furls up in several places, repeat Step 1, but relax the twist a little. Each material, or quantity of material, takes a little experimentation to the determine the optimum tightness of the twist.

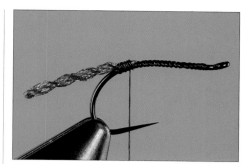

Step 3: Pinch the furled strand in the left fingers, and mount it atop the shank using a *pinch wrap* (p. 38). Clip and bind the excess.

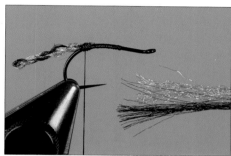

You can produce variegated or multi-color shucks by stacking strands of different colors, as shown on the right. The strands are treated as a single bundle when furling. In forming multi-color shucks like this, it's best to use strands of the same material in different colors rather than combining different materials. Each material takes twist differently and furls at a different rate. While combining materials is possible in a limited number of cases, the results are most often unsatisfactory.

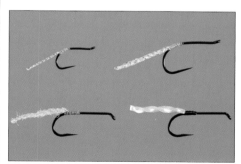

Almost any stranded material can be furled. For small flies, a single strand of pearl Krystal Flash can be furled for a shuck, as shown in the upper left. On larger hooks, a bundle of Krystal Flash can be furled, as shown on the upper right. The shuck at the lower left was formed from a thread dubbed with cream Antron dubbing, then furled and tied in. At the lower right is a shuck furled from a strand of stretch floss.

Twisted Furled Shuck

This version of the furled shuck, devised by Wayne Luallen and Ralph Cutter for caddis emergers, forms an elongated, bubble-like shuck that is characteristic of the natural insect. The loop at the end captures a bubble of air to give a more lifelike appearance. The limiting factor in this technique is the texture of the material. Coarser materials, such as spooled Antron and some poly yarns, are too stiff to consolidate during twisting and taper poorly. Finer-textured materials—Micro Zelon used in the following sequence; Antron dubbing, multi-ply Antron yarn, separated and combed as explained in *bundled-fiber shuck*," Step 5a-5b, (p. 57); and some of the very fine poly yarns—give the best results.

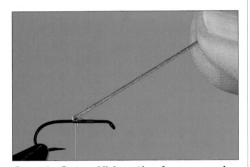

Step 1: Cut a 3" length of yarn—we're using Micro Zelon here—that is half the thickness of the density desired in the finished shuck. Secure one end of the yarn at midshank. With the right fingers, twist the yarn a moderate amount—a bit of experimentation is required to produce the right amount of twist.

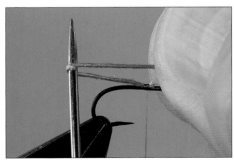

Step 2: Maintaining the twist, fold the strand around a dubbing needle as shown. The point of the fold will become the rear end of the shuck, so adjust the position of the needle to obtain the desired shuck length.

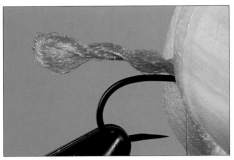

Step 3: Pinch the free end of the strand against the original mounting point of the yarn. Remove the needle. The shuck will furl up on itself, as shown.

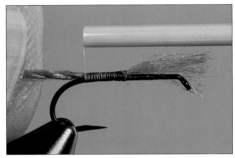

Step 4: Secure the free end of the yarn at the original mounting point. With the left fingers, twist the shuck in the direction that tightens the furl; this is the opposite direction from which you originally twisted the yarn. While holding the twist, wrap rearward to the tailing point.

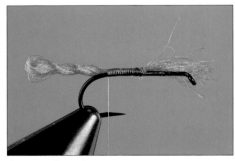

Step 5: Clip the excess yarn.

Combination Shuck

Tyer A.K. Best, in his book *Production Fly Tying*, advocates the use of a synthetic bundled-fiber shuck in conjunction with dry-fly hackle barbs in a combination that represents both the trailing shuck and the tails on an adult. This design provides some floatation for the fly and is best suited to flush-riding mayfly patterns that sit with the body in the surface film.

Step 1: Mount a bundled-fiber shuck about ½ the hook gap in length, using one of the methods shown in *bundled-fiber shucks*, (p. 55). Clip and bind down the excess material, and position the thread at the rearmost thread wrap.

Step 2: *Align and strip* (p. 30) a bundle of dry-fly hackle barbs, and mount them atop the shank with 2 tight thread wraps to form a tail one shank-length long.

Step 3: Maintain tension on the bobbin by pulling downward. With the left fingers, elevate the tail fibers (not the shuck fibers) upward at a 45-degree angle. Take 3 or 4 more tight turns, moving toward the hook eye.

Step 4: Clip and bind down the excess tail fibers.

Tailed Shuck

Russian tyer Vladimir Markov designed this shuck as the nymphal skin portion of a dubbed shuck (see *Markov shuck*, p. 64), but it can be used to represent a tailed trailing shuck on any standard mayfly emerger pattern. Any type of Antron— spooled, multi-ply, or dubbing—can be used to form the nymphal skin, as can Z-Lon, or even poly yarn on patterns designed to float flush in the film. The tails can be formed from mallard or woodduck flank, partridge or hen hackle, or even barred hairs such as woodchuck or squirrel.

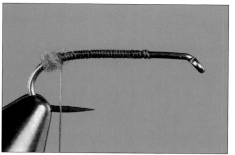

Step 1: Position the thread at the tailing point. Use the *direct dubbing* method (p. 34) to form a small ball of dubbing.

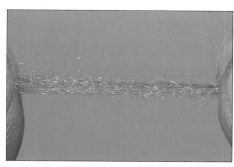

Step 2: Pull a pinch of material from a clump of long-fibered Antron dubbing. With the fingers of both hands, pull on the dubbing to elongate it. The skein of material should be half the density desired in the finished shuck and about 2" long.

Step 3: Mount the middle of the skein atop the shank, directly ahead of the dubbing ball. Trim the rear end to a length about equal to ½ the shank length.

Step 4: *Align and strip* (p. 30) 3-5 mallard flank fibers (or other desired tailing material). Mount them atop the shank directly ahead of the dubbing ball to form tails about twice the length of the trimmed Antron. Clip the excess feather, and bind down the butts with one or two thread wraps. Leave the thread positioned at this point.

Step 5: Fold the tag of Antron rearward over the top of the shank. Wrap the thread rearward to the front of the dubbing ball, binding the Antron as you go. The tail fibers should be sandwiched between the lower and upper halves of the Antron shuck. With the left fingers, elevate the top half of the Antron, and clip it to the same length as the lower half.

Step 6: When the Antron is trimmed to length, run a dubbing needle, if necessary, through the Antron to untangle and distribute the fibers so that they enclose the tails.

Transitional Shuck

A transitional shuck—a term we're using for want of a better one—is an unusual solution to the problem of representing an emerging insect. Where a standard representation usually has two components—a trailing shuck that imitates the shed nymphal skin, and the body of the emerged adult insect—a transitional shuck has 3 parts. The first is a relatively standard trailing shuck, though usually shorter than is dressed on a conventional emerger, that represents an empty part of the nymphal skin. Second is a dubbed portion of the hook shank which suggests either the remainder of the abandoned shuck, or a portion of the nymphal skin from which the adult is still emerging. Lastly is the body of the emerging adult insect, which may dubbed or dressed from another material, and is generally a different color than the nymphal portion of the fly. A transitional shuck, in a sense, represents the partially "telescoped" bodies of the nymphal skin and the adult.

This style is perhaps most strongly associated with tyer Harold McMillan and his Vertical Emerger design (p. 160), but has also been used by Russian tyer Vladimir Markov in his Ma's Hatching Dun (p. 176) and Serbian tyer Andrija

Urban's CDC Hatching Surface Dun (p. 299). Given that the basic approach is fairly obvious—to dress both the "nymphal" portion of the emerging insect (or at least part of it) and the adult portion on the hook shank itself—it is a little puzzling that this style is not seen more often because it presents some advantages. It is easy to dress, allows for a wide latitude in color and, perhaps more importantly, the texture of the dubbing used to represent the nymphal portion of the emerger; and it is quite durable.

One possible reason that this style has not caught on more widely is that it's frequently dressed on extra-long hooks—both McMillan and Urban, for instance, employ swimming-nymph hooks—and the resulting flies may appear unnaturally over-sized to tyers who dress more conventional emerger designs. Most tyers are accustomed to interpreting, almost automatically, the dubbed portion of a hook shank as the overall body length of the insect. Hence transitional-shuck emergers look too long. But it must remembered that dubbing at the rear of the hook should be viewed as part of the shuck rather than the adult body. When seen in this way, the patterns appear in more normal proportion.

Transitional-shuck styles can be as basic as a simple two-tone body dressed on the shank or as complex as some of Andrija Urban's patterns that incorporate not only tails, but a shuck abdomen, a shuck thorax, an adult abdomen, and an adult thorax—each of a different color dubbing. Particular approaches to this shuck style can be seen in the tying sequences for the patterns noted above. As indicated, these tyers favor extra-long hook shanks, but this type of shuck can be dressed on a scud hook as well, finding the extra shank length need by locating the tailing point well around the hook bend.

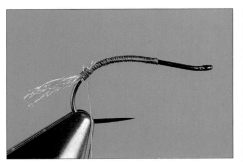

Step 1: Position the thread at the tailing point, and using one of the techniques shown in *bundled-fiber shucks* (p. 55), secure a bundle of fibers to make a trailing shuck that is equal in length to about ⅓ the distance from the tailing point to the hook eye. Clip and bind the excess.

Step 2: Use the *direct dubbing* method (p. 34) to dub a tapered abdomen equal in length to the trailing shuck. If the body of the emerging adult is to be ribbed, mount the ribbing directly ahead of the dubbed abdomen.

Step 3: Dub a tapered abdomen for the adult fly that extends from the front of the "nymphal" abdomen about ½ to ⅔ the distance to the hook eye. Rib the fly; tie off and clip the ribbing. The emerger wings and thorax, or other components, can now be dressed.

Many variations of the transitional shuck are possible. The fly on the left has a trailing shuck tied from Antron dubbing. The nymphal body at the rear of the hook is tied using a *dubbing loop* (p. 35) formed of wire. Rabbit hair, both underfur and guard hairs, are placed crosswise in the loop, which is then spun tightly and wrapped around the shank. The resulting brushlike body has been trimmed flat on the top and bottom, and then tapered on the sides to form the wedge-like silhouette of a March brown nymph, with the suggestion of abdominal gills. While tyers that use the transitional-shuck style tend to form the body of the adult insect from dubbing, the fly on the right suggests how other body materials—hackle quill, in this case—can be used.

Markov Shuck

We first saw this shuck design on patterns tied by Vladimir Markov. It is one of the more elaborate transitional-shuck designs that incorporates feather barbs to represent the nymphal tails, Antron to represent the vacated skin of the nymphal abdomen, dubbing to represent the nymphal thorax; and feather barbs to represent the nymphal legs. Though it may sound somewhat complicated, the tying operations are simple and produce an interesting and realistic imitation that can be adapted to many mayfly emerger styles. Markov favors a long-shank hook, such as the TMC 200R shown in the following sequence.

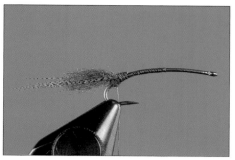

Step 1: Position the thread slightly down the bend of the hook, and dress a trailing shuck as explained in *tailed shuck*, Steps 1-6, (p. 63).

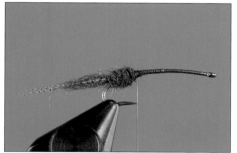

Step 2: Use the *direct dubbing* method (p. 34) to dub a stout nymphal thorax just about as long as the Antron portion of the trailing shuck.

Step 3: Use the technique show in *side-mounted legs* (p. 39) to mount 3 feather barbs (mallard, wood duck, partridge, or other) on each side of the shank, directly ahead of the nymphal thorax. Size the legs to about the same length as the hook gap. If ribbing is to be used on the portion of the fly representing the adult abdomen, mount it now.

Step 4: Form a slim abdomen that extends about ⅔ the distance from the nymphal thorax to the hook eye. We're using dubbing here, but almost any body material can be employed. If ribbing is used, wrap it forward; tie off and clip it in front of the abdomen.

Bead Shuck

Glass beads are a relatively new material for fly tyers, and though typically used to form the body of a fly pattern, they have some advantages when used to dress a trailing shuck. Beads are available in a wide variety of colors, and translucent beads—from clear, to milky white, to lightly tinted shades of olive, amber, brown, orange, and gray—are particularly well-suited to imitating the almost transparent nymphal skin. When beads are strung, they suggest the segmentation still visible in the trailing shuck. And they add weight at the rear of the fly and help position descending-body emergers properly, with the shuck below the surface film.

Perhaps the biggest drawback to beads is that they can be tedious to handle and string on a core, particularly in very small sizes, and shucks formed from beads are generally fussier and more time-consuming to tie than other types.

The bead shuck shown in this sequence is perhaps the most involved of all, as it is enclosed in bubble sheath, which complicates the tying. But it is an effective design for both mayflies and caddis.

Choosing beads of the right size is necessary for a shuck that is properly proportioned to the hook shank. The beads of choice are called "seed beads"—the type that is nearly spherical, but flattened on the ends. Larger sizes are available from fly or craft shops, but smaller sizes must be obtained from bead suppliers. A search on the World Wide Web will turn up a number of possibilities (try, for instance, www.beadcats.com). Seed beads are sized like fly-tying hooks, by number, and the larger the number, the smaller the bead. Coincidentally, if conveniently, the bead sizes used for trailing shucks are very nearly the same as the hook size, as shown in the chart below. (Note: these recommended bead/hook combinations are only for trailing shucks, not bodies. The bead holes will be too small to fit on the hook shanks.) The other components used to form this shuck are a monofilament core and Antron yarn. We prefer using multiply Antron yarn, usually a four-strand type sold on cards, because of its finer texture. Separate the yarn into individual plies, and use a single ply or portion of one as shown on the chart below.

Hook Size	Bead Size	Number of Beads	Mono Core	Yarn
#12	#14	4	5X	1 ply
#14	#16	4	5X	1 ply
#16	#18	3	6X	⅔ ply
#18	#20	4	6X	½ ply
#20	#22	3	6X	⅓ ply

The values on the chart are just a guide; more beads can be used for a longer shuck, and more or less yarn to produce a denser or sparser bubble sheath. Proper proportions should always be the principal guide.

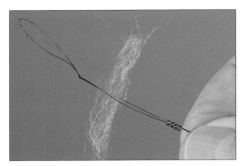

Step 1: Take 6" length of tippet material, and double it over. (We've darkened the tippet material for better visibility; for actual tying, clear or lightly tinted material is used.) Tie a double overhand knot in the loop end, as shown. Thread the appropriate number of beads over both tags of the loop. Cut a 3" length of Antron yarn, and run a dubbing needle a few times through both ends to separate and untangle the fibers. Center the yarn between the strands of mono, below the knot and above the beads, as shown.

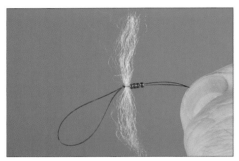

Step 2: When the yarn is positioned, slide the beads up against the yarn and seat them firmly against the knot.

Step 3: Lay a thread foundation over the rear ⅓ of the hook shank, and position the tying thread at the tailing point. If using a scud hook, you may find mounting the bead shuck to be easier if the hook is positioned in the vise as shown in the photo. Mount both mono tags of the shuck atop the shank using 3 or 4 thread wraps under only moderate tension. Pull the tags, sliding the mono under the thread wraps and snugging the beads against the hook

shank. Grasp the mono loop in the left fingers to help maintain the position of the beads, and then pull the mono tag to seat the beads tightly against the shank. Then bind the mono tags tightly to the shank, and clip the excess.

Step 4: If you wish the bead shuck to be separate from the body, proceed to Step 5 to form the bubble sheath. We often dress this shuck so that the sheath encloses part of the fly body to represent part of the adult abdomen still inside the nymphal skin. To tie this style, use the *direct dubbing* method (p. 34) to dub the rear portion of the abdomen, about ⅓ the distance to the hook eye.

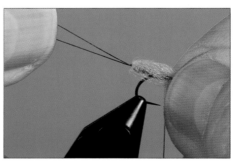

Step 5: In the left fingers, grasp the mono loop. With the right fingers, pull the Antron fibers forward, completely encircling the beads and the dubbed portion of the body (if you have dressed this component). You may need to stroke the Antron forward a few times to produce a smooth, uniform capsule; use the left fingers to provide a counter-tension on the loop while drawing the Antron forward. Don't pull the Antron tight against the beads, but rather, let it balloon out a bit to form a bubble.

Step 6: When the bubble sheath is satisfactorily formed, use the left hand to take a firm wrap of thread around the Antron, directly ahead of the dubbing. Then secure the Antron with additional tight wraps, and clip the excess. Clip the mono loop at the rear of the shuck, leaving mono tags for tails on a mayfly emerger, as shown here, or clipping them away completely for a caddis emerger.

Simple Bead Shuck

This version of the bead shuck omits the bubble sheath shown in the preceding sequence, which simplifies tying. The combinations of bead sizes with hook sizes are the same as those listed in the chart under *bead shuck*, (p. 65). In this variation, though, only one strand of monofilament passes through bead hole, so heavier tippet sizes can be used. Heavier monofilament also increases durability; some experimentation is necessary here, but as a starting point, try a tippet material 2 or 3 sizes larger than is listed in the chart in the previous sequence. Some interesting effects can be produced by combining bead colors with different colors of monofilament, either factory tinted or colored with a waterproof marker. This shuck style can be tied with tails, as show below, for use on mayfly emergers, or without tails for caddis and midges.

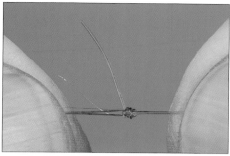

Step 1: Cut a 2" length of Z-Lon or spooled Antron, and separate out a sparse bundle of about 10 or 15 fibers. You don't need this much to form the tail, but you need a bundle of sufficient strength to seat the clinch knot properly. Cut a 6" length of tippet material, and use it to tie a clinch knot around the sparse bundle of fibers. Seat the clinch knot tightly by pulling the fiber bundle in one hand and the mono in the other.

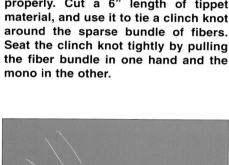

Step 2: Clip the tag of mono close to the knot. Trim away most of the tailing fibers by clipping close to the clinch knot, leaving short stubs—about 1/16" long—to ensure that the knot doesn't slip. Leave a few fibers long for the tails, and trim them to the appropriate length. (Note: to form a shuck for caddis or midge emergers, which lack tails, simply trim away all the tailing fibers.)

Step 3: Thread the desired number of beads onto the mono, and slide them up to the knot.

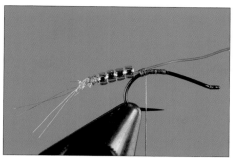

Step 4: Lay a thread foundation over the rear 1/3 of the hook shank, and position the tying thread at the tailing point. Mount the mono atop the shank using 3 or 4 thread wraps under only moderate tension. Pull the tag, sliding the mono under the thread wraps just until the beads abut the hook shank. Then bind the mono tag tightly to the shank, and clip the excess.

Step 5: When starting to dub the abdomen of the fly, use a thinly dubbed thread and the *direct dubbing* method (p. 34), and take one or two turns of dubbing around the bare monofilament between the beads and the rearmost mounting wrap. These turns of dubbing will cover the mono core and make a smooth transition between the trailing shuck and the body.

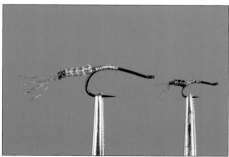

Shown here are a few of the options available in constructing simple bead shucks. The fly on the left uses clear beads over a core of reddish-brown Maxima tippet material; a lower-bulk mount is achieved by squeezing the mono flat with a pair of pliers after the beads are strung. Shucks like this can be practical even on small hooks. The fly on the right uses #20 amber seed beads over Maxima tippet and is mounted on a #22 hook.

Glass Tail Shuck

Mike Mercer designed this extended-body style for his series of Glass Tail Caddis Emergers, but it works well as a trailing shuck. It is one of the simplest bead shucks to tie, at least in the larger sizes. The Kevlar thread core can be quite tedious to thread through very small bead holes because of the limpness of the thread. For small beads, fine mono tippet material, which is a bit stiffer, is easier to work with, though it is not as durable as Kevlar. Though devised for caddis emergers, this shuck, in the appropriate sizes, can be used for midge and mayfly emergers as well.

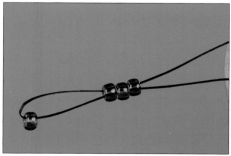

Step 1: Cut a 4" length of Kevlar thread, and string one bead, placing it in the middle of the thread. Thread both tags of the Kevlar through additional beads, the number depending on the desired length of the shuck.

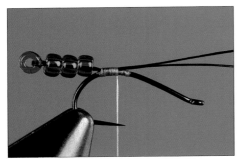

Step 2: Lay a thread foundation over the rear ⅓ of the hook shank, and position the tying thread at the tailing point. Mount both Kevlar tags atop the shank using 3 or 4 thread wraps under only moderate tension. Pull the tags, sliding the Kevlar under the thread wraps and snugging the beads against the hook shank. Then bind the Kevlar tags tightly to the shank with 3 or 4 more thread wraps.

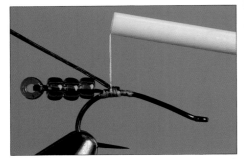

Step 3: Fold the Kevlar tags rearward atop the shank. Wrap back over them with additional tight wraps. Then clip and bind the excess.

Scintilla Bead Shuck

This approach to tying trailing shucks comes from Henry Hoffman, who uses Scintilla beads for forming shucks on caddis emerger patterns. The weight of the bead makes it most practical for the descending-body style, and the beads have an iridescent translucence. The biggest drawback is that, currently, the beads are only available in one size, suitable for about a #14 hook. Hoffman ties his shucks with feather-barbs tails, as shown below. Almost any webby feather barbs are suitable—partridge, mallard or woodduck flank, or mottled hen, which is used in the following demonstration. If synthetic fibers are used for the tail, a simpler method of dressing this shuck style is explained in the photo after the tying sequence.

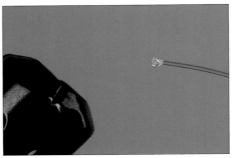

Step 1: Cut a 6" length of 20-pound monofilament. Use a lighter to melt the end into a ball.

Step 2: *Align and strip* (p. 30) a bundle of feather barbs. Pinch the barbs against the monofilament so that the barb tips extend the desired distance beyond the melted ball; on Henry Hoffman's patterns, the tail is about one hook-gap in length. Gently roll the barbs and mono between your fingertips to distribute the feather barbs around the outside of the monofilament. The distribution doesn't need to be exact; thread pressure when binding the barbs to the mono will help spread them evenly around.

Step 3: Slip the tag of the bobbin thread between your left thumb and forefinger so that it is pinched together with the feather barbs. With your right hand, take a few tight wraps directly ahead of the left fingertips, binding the barbs to the mono directly behind the melted ball, and at the same time locking down the tag of tying thread. The procedure here is identical to mounting the tying thread on the hook shank. Use thread

pressure to distribute the barbs as uniformly as possible around the core of monofilament. Then build up a button of thread directly behind the melted ball to prevent the tail from slipping inside the bead when it is mounted.

Step 4: When the barbs are secured, take a few half hitches behind the mono ball. You may find this easiest if you pull about 8" of thread from the bobbin and then clip it free, rather than trying to form the half-hitches using the bobbin. When the half-hitches are secure, clip both thread tags, and trim the butts of the barbs close to the thread wraps. Insert the free end of the mono through a Scintilla bead. Put a drop of a gel-type cyanoacrylate glue, such as Super Glue, behind the clipped butts of the feather barbs. Then pull the mono through the bead, seating the bead firmly against the base of the tail.

Step 5: Position the tying thread at the rearmost point of the body. Mount the mono atop the shank with tight thread wraps; clip and bind the excess mono.

Tying this shuck style is considerably simpler if synthetic fibers such as Z-Lon or Antron are used as a tailing material. The procedure is identical to the one described in *simple bead shuck*, (p. 66). Since the clinch knot tied in this technique prevents the bead from slipping off the end of the monofilament, the knot must be large enough. For a Scintilla bead, a mono diameter of. 015" (or roughly 30 pound) is about right.

Tubing Shuck

We first saw this approach used to form an extended mayfly body on Joseph F. Burket's PMD Shiny Tail Emerger, (p. 255), but it is equally useful in tying shiny, translucent trailing shucks. Since the tubing gives buoyancy to the rear of the fly, this shuck design is better suited to flush-floating emergers than the descending-body style. Vinyl tubing is available in a clear version and in a variety of colors, and the selection of different diameters make the material practical on a wide range of hook sizes. Burket uses copper wire for the core material, but gold, silver or colored wires can be used as can clear or tinted tippet material, particularly the fluorocarbon type, which is more durable than nylon.

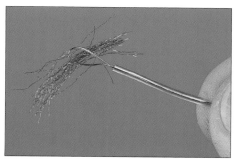

Step 1: Cut a 1" length of tailing material—we're using spooled Antron here—and comb through both ends with a fine-toothed comb. Split the strand lengthwise to produce a sparser bundle of fibers. The thickness of the bundle depends upon the inside diameter of the tubing, and a bit of experimentation will be necessary to determine the optimum amount of material to form the tail. Fold a 4" length of fine copper wire around the center of the tailing material. Then insert both ends of the wire through a 1" length of vinyl tubing.

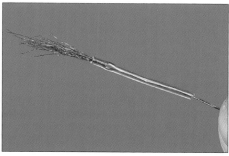

Step 2: Pull the ends of the wire to draw the tailing material just a short distance inside the tubing.

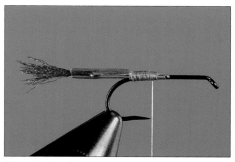

Step 3: Position the thread at the tailing point. Mount the shuck assembly atop the shank with several tight thread wraps. Make certain that the tubing, not just the wire, is secured to the shank. Clip and bind the excess. Trim the tail material to length, about one hook-gap. If a sparser tail is desired, trim away the tailing fibers until the desired number remain.

BUBBLE SHEATHS

Bubble sheaths, as a component on caddis pupa and emerger imitations, were introduced to fly tyers by Gary LaFontaine in his groundbreaking book, *Caddisflies*. In underwater observations, LaFontaine took note of the sparkle produced by a caddis pupa ascending through the water to hatch. He explains: "When a caddisfly pupa emerges it fills a transparent sheath around its body with air bubbles. These globules of air shimmer and sparkle as they reflect sunlight, creating a highly visible triggering characteristic. This sparkle is the key to imitating the emergent caddisflies." To replicate this shimmery shuck, LaFontaine incorporated in his emerger patterns a bubble sheath of reflective Antron, which has subsequently become one of the most popular synthetic fly-tying materials in use.

Antron Bubble

This style of bubble sheath, devised by Gary LaFontaine, is certainly one of the most widely employed in tying caddis pupa and emergers. Spooled Antron or the multi-ply version work best, though with care, this style of sheath can also be fashioned from long-fibered Antron dubbing.

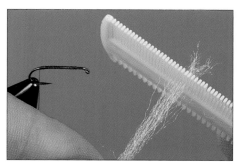

Step 1: Lay a thread foundation on the shank, and position the thread at the rearmost point of the body. Cut a 2" length of Antron yarn, and use a fine-toothed comb to comb out both ends of the strand to separate the fibers. If necessary, split the strand lengthwise to produce a sparse bundle for smaller hooks.

Step 2: Mount the strand on the far side of the shank.

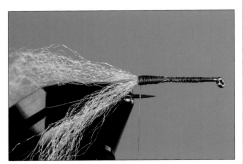

Step 3: Cut a second strand of Antron, comb it out, and mount it on the near side of the shank, directly opposite the first strand, as shown in this top view.

Step 4: Form the body over the rear ⅘ of the hook shank. We're using dubbing here, but other body materials can be used.

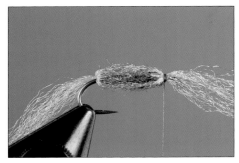

Step 5: Draw the strand on the near side forward over the near side of the shank. Keep the fibers separated and distributed around the side of the shank. Secure with 2 thread wraps directly ahead of the body material. Do not trim the excess.

Step 6: Repeat Step 5 with the strand on the far side. Use a dubbing needle to distribute the fibers uniformly around the body and pull them outward to form a bubble-like capsule surrounding the body.

Step 7: When the bubble is properly formed, secure both strands with additional tight thread wraps at the front of the body. Clip the excess Antron. At the front of the bubble, cut a few fibers, close to the thread wraps, from the sides and top and preen them rearward, as shown.

Quick and Dirty Bubble Sheath

Bob Braendle designed this sheath style for use on his Quick and Dirty Emerger in *Caddis Super Hatches*. Though similar to the LaFontaine style of sheath, it is easier to tie since it requires only one strand of sheath material, which is then pulled tight over a thick thorax to form a bubble-like capsule over the abdomen. Braendle uses Z-Lon for this pattern, though spooled or multi-ply Antron yarn can also be used.

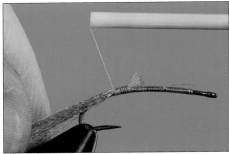

Step 1: Position the tying thread about ⅔ of a shank-length behind the hook eye. Cut a strand of Z-Lon about 2" long. Use a fine-toothed comb to comb out both ends of the strand to separate the fibers. If necessary split the strand lengthwise to produce a sparser bundle for smaller hooks. Mount the strand atop the shank. Wrap rearward to secure the strand. As you wrap, pull the strand to the rear and angle it downward. This will help distribute the fibers around the perimeter of the shank.

Step 2: Continue wrapping to a point just around the hook bend, as shown. Form the abdomen of the fly; we've used the tying thread, wrapped forward, for the abdomen, but other materials can be used. The only requirement is that the abdomen be kept very slender to allow the formation of the bubble. Use the *direct dubbing* method (p. 34) to dub a thorax at least twice the diameter of the abdomen.

Step 3: Comb the strand one more time to separate fibers. Draw the fibers forward to form a uniform capsule that is drawn snugly against the thorax.

Step 4: Secure the fibers in front of the thorax, then clip and bind the excess.

Half-Bubble Sheath

We've seen this approach from a number of tyers, most notably Howard Cole who uses it on his U-Con 2 Caddis Emerger (p. 246). This roughly hemispherical sheath helps float the fly and presents an unobstructed view of the fly body. Spooled or multi-ply Antron yarn or Z-Lon can be used.

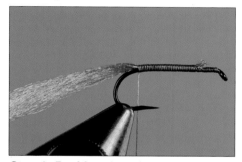

Step 1: Position the tying thread about ¼ of a shank-length behind the hook eye. Cut a 2" length of Antron or Z-Lon, and use a fine-toothed comb to comb out both ends of the strand. If necessary, split the strand lengthwise to produce a sparser bundle for smaller hooks. Mount the strand and wrap back to the rearmost point of the body, securing the strand to the top of the shank.

Step 2: At this point, form the body; we're using dubbing here, but other materials can be employed. Finish the body ¼ of a shank-length behind the hook eye. Position the thread at the front of the body.

Step 3: Pull the strand tightly along the top of the shank, and with the right fingers, pinch it against the hook eye.

Step 4: Now push the right fingers rearward to the front of the body; the fibers will balloon outward around the top half of the shank.

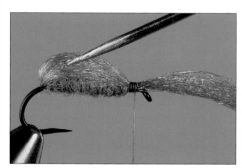

Step 5: Hold the fibers in position. With the left fingers, pinch the capsule against the body. With the right hand, take two firm, but not tight wraps directly ahead of the body material. Examine the sheath; if the fibers are not distributed fairly uniformly over the top half of the shank, use a dubbing needle to redistribute them.

Step 6: When the half-bubble is satisfactorily formed, secure the fibers tightly at the front of the body and clip the excess. Here is a bottom view of a properly formed sheath—open underneath and slightly heart-shaped.

Brushed-Body Sheath

This simple technique simultaneously forms the body and sheath on a caddis emerger. Though not a true bubble, like the ones formed in the three previous techniques, a brushed body produces a capsule-like appearance, and caddis emergers dressed with this method are undeniably effective. The one limitation here is that the sheath must be the same color as the body. (To form a sheath of a different color, see *dubbing-loop sheath*, p. 72.) "The technique shown below relies on a dubbing with long fibers rather than short, chopped ones. Antron dubbing or sparkly synthetics such as SLF dubbing are ideal.

Step 1: Position the thread at the rearmost point of the body. Use the *direct dubbing* method (p. 34) to dub the abdomen of the fly. Do not twist the dubbing too tightly; brushing the body is simpler if the abdomen is dubbed roughly.

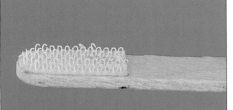

Step 2: The body can be brushed with a commercially available dubbing teaser, but a simple, homemade type works just as well and won't cut tying thread the way some metal teasers will. Here, we've mounted the "hook" side of a piece of adhesive-backed Velcro to a Popsicle stick.

Dubbing-Loop Sheath

This technique produces a bubble sheath very similar in appearance to the one shown in the preceding sequence, *brushed-body sheath*, p. 71. But because the sheath is formed independently of the body, the sheath and body colors can be different, or the sheath applied over a body material other than dubbing. You can give a more pronounced ribbed appearance to the abdomen by forming the dubbing loop in Step 1 from a separate piece of tying thread of the desired ribbing color.

Step 3: Twist the dubbing loop tightly, and wrap forward over the abdomen in an open spiral, as though palmering hackle. Tie off the dubbing loop directly ahead of the abdomen, and clip the excess.

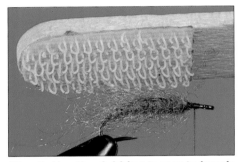

Step 3: Use the dubbing teaser to brush the body from front to rear. Work all the way around the shank, pulling dubbing fibers from the body to make a flowing sheath around the abdomen. The aim here is to brush enough fibers to make a translucent haze around the body.

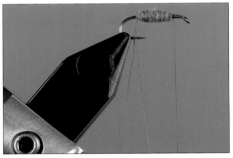

Step 1: Position the tying thread at the rearmost point of the body. Form a *dubbing loop* (p. 35) from the tying thread, or tie in a separate loop of thread of the desired color. Form the abdomen of the fly; we're using dubbing here, but other materials can be used.

Step 4: Use a dubbing teaser (see *brushed-body sheath*, Step 2, p. 72) to brush the dubbing loop fibers rearward. Work around the hook shank to form a flowing, uniform capsule.

Step 4: Trim away any excess fibers to produce a capsule-like shape around the abdomen.

Step 2: Take a generous pinch of long-fibered dubbing of the desired type. Tease the dubbing into a sparse, elongated skein, and cut the skein into 1" lengths. Wax one thread of the dubbing loop, and place the lengths of dubbing crosswise on the thread. They will adhere to the wax. The dubbing should be sparsely distributed along the thread.

Step 5: Trim the excess fibers to form a capsule-like sheath around the abdomen.

Chapter 4: Bubble and Brushed-Sheath Emergers

Flies of this style are tied to represent caddis pupae that have emerged from their pupal cases and are ready for transformation into the adult form. To assist in its ascent to the surface, the pupa generates a film of buoyant gas between the pupal skin and the body of the insect. This gas gives the pupa a glistening appearance in the water, and the patterns in this chapter illustrate approaches to representing the shimmer of the pupa by using reflective materials, such as Antron, or glossy translucent ones such as synthetic films or beads.

Although this type of imitation can be fished anywhere in the water column, the patterns as shown in the tying sequences are designed primarily for fishing in or just under the film. Even dressed with floatant, however, most of these tend to sit very low in the water and hence are not highly visible to the angler; we often tie them as droppers off the bend of a high-floating dry fly such as a Deer Hair or Elk Hair Caddis. The dry fly functions as both a strike indicator and as a means of tracking the drift or drag of the pupa. But these patterns work equally well when they are fished deep, either by adding weight, such as lead wire, to the hook shank, or weight to the leader.

Brushed Antron Pupa

Originator: Jim Schollmeyer
Hook: TMC 206BL, or other fine-wire scud hook, #10-#18
Thread: Brown 6/0
Bubble sheath: Tan or cream Antron dubbing
Abdomen: Green Jelly Rope or Larva Lace
Legs: Natural CDC fibers
Wing: Brown Antron yarn
Head: Dark brown dubbing

Brushed dubbing is a simple solution to the problem of imitating the pupal caddis skin. The bubble-sheath dubbing should consist of relatively long fibers rather than filaments that have been cut or chopped since they must have enough length to form a flowing capsule when brushed. This is also an effective pattern when tied with a brown body.

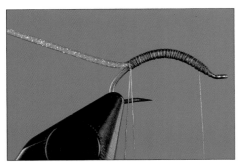

Step 1: Attach the thread, and secure the abdomen material a short distance behind the hook eye. Bind the material to the rearmost point of the body, forming a smooth underbody as you go. Form a *dubbing loop,* Steps 1-3, (p. 35) at the rearmost thread wrap and position the thread ¼ of a shank length behind the eye.

Step 2: Wrap the abdomen material forward in an open spiral over the rear ⅔ of the hook shank. Tie off.

Step 3: Insert the dubbing into the dubbing loop, and twist tightly as explained in *dubbing loop,* Steps 4-8, (p. 36).

Step 4: Wrap the dubbing material forward, placing it in the gaps between the body material. Tie off the dubbing loop directly in front of the abdomen.

Step 5: Use a dubbing teaser (we're using the "hook" part of Velcro material here) to brush out the dubbing to form a smooth, flowing capsule around the abdomen.

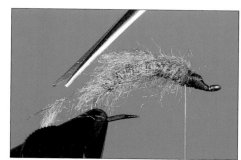

Step 6: Clip the fibers to form a tapered sheath around the abdomen, as shown here.

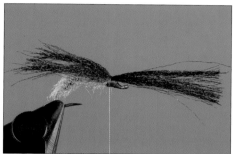

Step 7: Mount a strand of Antron yarn atop the shank and slightly to the near side. Mount a second strand atop the shank and slightly to the far side.

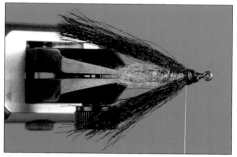

Step 8: Here's a top view, showing the placement and spread of the Antron wings.

Step 9: Lift both wings simultaneously, and position the scissors parallel to the tying bench to trim the wings at an angle. The trimmed wings should extend just to the rear of the abdomen.

Step 10: Gather a bundle of CDC fibers as shown in *stripping CDC barbs,* (p. 40). Using the method shown in *throat hackle* (p. 41), mount the bundle beneath the shank to form legs that extend just beyond the hook bend.

Step 11: Use the *direct dubbing* method (p. 34) to form the thorax. Whip finish the fly.

Step 12: Shown here is a front view of the finished fly.

Deep Sparkle Pupa

Originator: Gary LaFontaine
Hook: Mustad 94840 or other standard dry-fly hook, #10-#18
Thread: Black 8/0
Bubble shuck: Cream Antron yarn
Body: Green Antron dubbing
Legs: Brown hen hackle fibers
Head: Brown marabou herls (or brown dubbing)

Gary LaFontaine devised the Antron bubble shuck to reproduce the distinctive sparkle of a caddis pupa, and the Deep Sparkle Pupa is one of the most widely used and effective patterns in imitating emerging caddis. Orange, tan, and gray bodies are productive, and we tie a version with a black Antron bubble shuck to imitate the small, dark *Amiocentrus* caddis.

Step 1: Use the technique shown in *Antron bubble*, Steps 1-3, (p. 70) to prepare and mount two yarn strands to form the bubble. Use the *direct dubbing* method (p. 34) to dub the underbody, stopping about ¼ of a shank-length behind the hook eye.

Step 2: Form the bubble sheath as shown in *Antron bubble*, Steps 3-6 (p. 70).

Step 3: Use the steps shown in *side-mounted legs* (p. 39) to mount a small bundle of hen hackle fibers on each side of the shank.

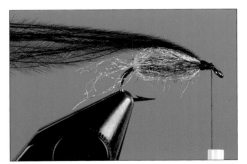

Step 4: Secure 4-8 brown marabou herls at the rearmost thread wrap used to mount the leg fibers. Position the tying thread behind the hook eye.

Step 5: Use the method shown in *wrapping twisted-herl collars* (p. 49) to form the head of the fly. Secure the herls behind the hook eye. Clip the excess and whip finish.

CDC Bubble Sparkle Pupa

Originator: Jim Schollmeyer
Hook: TMC 900BL, or equivalent dry-fly hook, #12-#14
Thread: Brown 8/0
Bubble sheath: Tan Antron yarn
Overbody/wing: Two Type 1 dark dun CDC feathers
Body: 3 strands green Krystal Flash
Legs: CDC feather tips
Head: Brown dubbing

The CDC on this version of the Sparkle Pupa suggests the trailing shuck, legs, and darker wings of an emerging adult while giving some floatation to the fly. We've seen versions of this design that use black CDC on small patterns for fishing emergences of the small, dark-wing caddis that figure prominently on many trout streams.

Step 1: Attach the thread and position it at the rearmost point of the body. Mount two lengths of Antron yarn as explained in *Antron bubble*, Steps 1-3, (p. 69-70). Position the thread atop the rearmost thread wrap.

Step 2: Stack the 2 CDC feathers so that the tips are aligned and curvatures match. Mount them atop the shank so that the tips extend rearward 1 ½ shank-lengths. Clip and bind the excess. Mount 3 strands of Krystal Flash atop the CDC. Clip and bind the excess.

Step 3: Position the thread ¼ of a shank-length behind the hook eye. Wrap the Krystal Flash forward as though it were one strand; tie off and clip. Draw the Antron yarns forward smoothly over the sides and bottom of the shank, and pinch them against the hook eye.

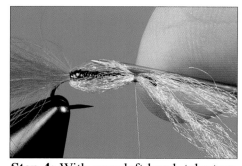

Step 4: With your left hand, take two snug, but not tight, wraps over the yarn directly ahead of the body. With a dubbing needle, raise the yarn fibers to create a uniform bubble around the sides and bottom of the shank. When the bubble is formed, secure the yarn tightly; clip and bind the excess.

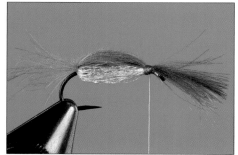

Step 5: Draw the CDC feathers forward, forming a bubble over the top of the shank that matches the shape and contour of the Antron. Allow some of the CDC fibers to escape and preen them rearward to form a trailing shuck. Secure the feathers in front of the body, but do not clip the excess.

Step 6: Clip the stems from the two feather tips. Draw half the CDC fibers along each side of the shank, and wrap back over the base with the thread to slant them rearward, as shown. Use the *direct dubbing* method (p. 34) to form the head of the fly, and then whip finish.

Henry's Lake Caddis

Originator: Marvin Nolte
Hook: TMC 200R, or other 2-4XL curved or straight-shank
    hook, #8
Thread: Light brown 6/0
Body: Tan SLF dubbing
Sheath: Woodduck flank
Hackle: Partridge
Head: Dark brown SLF dubbing

Marvin Nolte notes that this pattern is based on a method of binding the hackle at the rear of the fly that comes from an old French mayfly pattern, the Andelle.

Step 1: Mount the thread at the rear of the hook, leaving a 6" tag of thread untrimmed. Use the *direct dubbing* method (p. 34) to dub a body over the rear ⅖ of the hook shank.

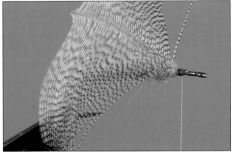

Step 2: Choose a woodduck flank feather with barbs about 1 ½ shank-lengths long. Prepare and mount the feather as shown in *tip-mounted hackle* (p. 41).

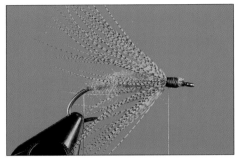

Step 3: Take 3 or 4 turns of the feather and tie it off as explained in *wrapping wet-fly hackle* (p. 50).

Step 4: Preen the feather barbs rearward so that they hug the body tightly, and pinch them beyond the hook bend. Then push the barbs forward so that they balloon out evenly around the body, as shown. Using the 6" tag of thread, secure the barbs directly behind the body; tie off the thread with two half-hitches, and clip the excess.

Step 5: Prepare and mount the partridge feather as shown in *tip-mounted hackle* (p. 41).

Step 6: Take 2-3 turns of the partridge feather and tie it off as shown in *wrapping wet-fly hackle*. Preen the partridge barbs rearward, and dub the head of the fly, taking a few wraps over the base of the barbs to slant them toward the hook bend. Whip finish the fly; apply head cement to the tie-off wraps at both ends of the fly.

Scintillator Pupa

Originator: Ken Ligas
Hook: TMC 101, or other ring-eye dry-fly hook, #14 to #16
Thread: Yellow 6/0
Underbody: Gold Scintilla or Antron dubbing
Bubble shuck: 3x6mm oval Scintillator bead, or other football-shaped iridescent bead of similar size
Legs: Partridge hackle
Head: Ostrich herl

Ken Ligas uses an iridescent clear plastic bead to produce the reflective bubble shuck on this emerging caddis pattern. Treated with powder-type floatant, it can be fished in the film. Colors can be varied to match a variety of natural caddis. Scintillator beads are available only in the size noted, but a search through a craft or bead store may turn up oval beads proportioned to other hook sizes.

Step 1: Mount the thread and position it at the tailing point. Use the *direct dubbing* method (p. 34) to build up a bump of dubbing large enough in diameter to prevent the bead from sliding rearward. Then dub a thin underbody, stopping about ¼ of shank-length behind the hook eye.

Step 2: When the underbody is complete, secure the thread with 3 half-hitches or a whip finish at the front of the underbody. Clip the thread. Slide the bead over the hook eye, and seat it firmly against the dubbing bump. Then reattach the thread in front of the bead.

Step 3: Using the procedure explained in *tip-mounted hackle* (p. 41), prepare and mount a partridge feather directly in front of the bead.

Step 4: Take 1 or 2 wraps of hackle as explained in *wrapping wet-fly hackle* (p. 50). Tie off the hackle, building a tapered bump of tying thread large enough to prevent the bead from sliding forward. Return the thread to the front of the hackle.

Step 5: Mount a strand of herl in front of the hackle, and bring the tying thread forward to a point just behind the hook eye.

Step 6: Using the procedure explained in *wrapping single-herl collars* (p. 48), form the head of the fly. Tie off and clip the herl. Whip finish.

S.L.F. Caddis

Originator: Davy Wotton
Hook: TMC 2487BL, or equivalent light-wire scud hook,
#8-#14
Thread: Pale yellow 6/0
Abdomen: Olive (#11) SLF dubbing
Sheath: Zing Wing material
Legs: Brown rooster hackle
Thorax: Rust brown (#37) SLF dubbing
Antennae: Woodduck flank fibers

A variety of materials can be used to form the sheath on this pattern—clear Swiss straw, Scintilla wing material, or virtually any translucent film. Orange, olive, and tan are all good colors. To appreciate this imitation, you must tie one up and observe it underwater; the wing film becomes more translucent and the body color and silhouette inside the film become quite visible and lifelike.

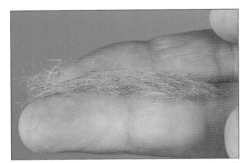

Step 1: Tease out a sparse mat of abdomen dubbing about 2" long and ½" wide, as shown. Set the dubbing aside.

Step 2: Mount the thread and position it at the tailing point. Form a *dubbing loop* (p. 35) about 3" long. Position the tying thread ⅓ the shank-length behind the hook eye. Carefully insert the mat of dubbing in the loop.

Step 3: Twist the dubbing loop tightly.

Step 4: Form the abdomen over the rear ⅔ of the shank. Bind and clip the excess dubbing loop if any remains.

Step 5: Cut a piece of sheath material about 1 ½ hook-gaps in width. Round the rear edge as shown.

Step 6: Place the sheath over the abdomen. The material should be wide enough to roll down and enclose the sides of the abdomen. The rear edge should project a short distance beyond the hook bend. Secure the material directly in front of the abdomen.

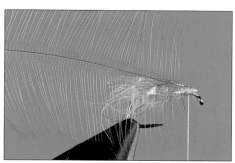

Step 7: Using the procedure explained in *tip-mounted hackle* (p. 41), prepare and mount the hackle feather.

Step 8: Take 2-4 wraps of the feather as shown in *wrapping wet-fly hackle* (p. 50). Tie off and clip the excess.

Step 9: Use the *direct dubbing* method (p. 34) to dub a thorax just short of the hook eye.

Step 10: Mount two woodduck fibers extending over the hook eye about one hook-length.

Step 11: Draw one fiber down each side of the body, and take a few wraps over the folded base of the fibers to hold them in this position, as shown in this top view. Form the head of the fly and whip finish.

Chapter 5: Float Pod and Suspender Emergers

The patterns in this chapter incorporate a buoyant, often ball-like component in the thorax area that suspends the fly just beneath the surface film and may suggest the enlarged thorax or emerging thorax or wings of a hatching insect. Dubbing pods use a ball of dubbing material for this component, which is a particularly useful approach on smaller patterns because of its simplicity. In tying the pod, first choose a material that resists water absorption, such as poly dubbing or CDC. And second, don't compress the dubbing too tightly; a compact, but not tight, dubbing pod will trap air that assists floatation.

Charles Brooks refined the pod by enclosing it in nylon mesh to improve durability; the nylon sheath does build bulk, and so it's not ordinarily used on very small patterns. British anglers John Goddard and Brian Clarke took the idea one step further by substituting polystyrene foam for the dubbing; though a bit more involved to tie, this type of pod is considerably more buoyant. When less brittle, more flexible foams became common in fly tying, tyers such as Phil Camera dispensed with the nylon sheath altogether and used a simple foam post.

Suspender-style flies suggest an insect just prior to, or in the early phase of, emergence, and the fly itself is generally tied in colors that represent the nymphal or pupal form of the insect.

Floating Nymph—BWO

Originator: Mike Lawson
Hook: TMC 100 or 101, or equivalent dry-fly hook, #18-#22
Thread: Olive 8/0
Tail: Light blue dun hackle fibers
Rib: Olive 6/0 thread
Abdomen: Blue-wing olive Superfine dubbing
Dubbing pod: Light gray poly dubbing
Thorax: Same as abdomen
Legs: Light blue dun hackle fibers

This simple, but highly versatile, technique is probably underutilized by tyers. The dubbing ball positions the fly body flush in the surface film, making this design particularly well-suited to the flat water found on spring creeks and tailwaters. Sizes and colors can be varied to match many mayfly hatches.

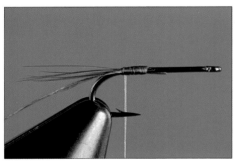

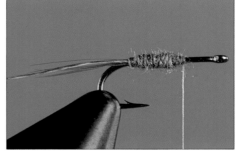

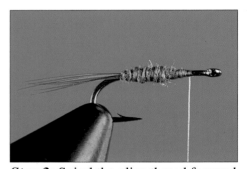

Step 1: Attach the thread and position it at the rear of the shank. *Align and strip* (p. 30) a sparse bundle of hackle fibers and mount them atop the shank to form a tail one shank-length long. Clip and bind the excess. Mount a length of olive thread for ribbing directly atop the tail-mounting wraps.

Step 2: Use the *direct dubbing* method (p. 34) to form a slightly tapered abdomen, stopping at the midpoint of the shank.

Step 3: Spiral the olive thread forward to rib the abdomen. Tie off and clip the thread. Advance the tying thread to the winging point, about halfway between the front of the abdomen and the hook eye.

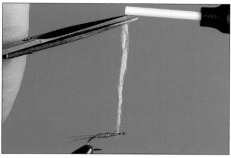

Step 4: Firmly, but not tightly, dub a short length of thread. Apply the dubbing in the slight teardrop shape shown here. Hold the dubbed thread vertically, and position a pair of scissors as shown. Holding the scissor blades about 45 degrees off the horizontal will prevent cutting the thread.

Step 5: Maintaining the angle on scissor blades, carefully slide the blades down the thread to compress the dubbing into a ball atop the shank.

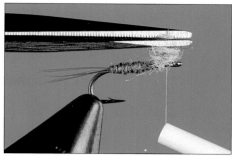

Step 6: Wrap the thread around the rear blade of the scissors, beneath the shank, and pull the bobbin directly toward you.

Step 7: Maintaining a firm, but not heavy, tension on the thread, carefully withdraw the scissor blades and snug the ball of dubbing against the top of the shank

Step 8: Take a few horizontal thread wraps around the base of the dubbing pod. Consolidating it slightly like this makes dubbing the thorax easier.

Step 9: With a dubbed thread, build up the rear of the thorax to its full size. Take a couple of crisscross wraps of dubbing beneath the pod to cover the exposed thread wraps, but do not build up the thorax to full size ahead of the dubbing pod.

Step 10: Using the method shown in *side-mounted legs* (p. 39), mount legs ahead of the thorax on both sides of the shank, as shown in this top view. Clip the excess fibers.

Step 11: Use a thinly dubbed thread to build up the thorax ahead of the pod to its full size. Wrap the dubbed thread back over the legs slightly to make the thorax of uniform size and to slant the leg fibers rearward. Whip finish and clip the thread.

Parachute Floating Nymph—Brown

Originator: Gary Borger
Hook: TMC 900BL, or equivalent dry-fly hook, #10-#22
Thread: Brown 8/0
Tail: Medium dun hackle barbs
Abdomen: Reddish brown dubbing fur and sparkle yarn, mixed
Dubbing pod: Gray fur and sparkle yarn, mixed
Hackle: Medium dun hackle barbs

Gary Borger's variation of the simple dubbing pod offers some distinct advantages. The parachute hackle gives the fly more lateral stability—it is less likely to land on its side and more suitable for rougher currents. The hackle also breaks up and scatters light in the surface film, an impression produced by many emerging flies.

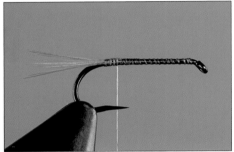

Step 1: Secure the thread and wrap it to the tailing point. *Align and strip* (p. 30) a sparse bundle of hackle fibers. Mount them atop the shank to form a tail about one shank-length long.

Step 2: Use the *direct dubbing* method (p. 34) to dub a slightly tapered abdomen.

Step 3: Form a dubbing pod as explained in Floating Nymph—BWO, Steps 4-8, (p. 83). Take a few additional horizontal wraps of thread around the base of the dubbing pod to form a foundation for the parachute hackle.

Step 4: *Prepare a hackle feather* (p. 39) and mount it using the method shown in *horizontal-mount parachute hackle* (p. 37).

Step 5: Dub the thorax, and position the thread behind the hook eye.

Step 6: Take 2-3 wraps of hackle and secure the feather as shown in *wrapping parachute hackle* (p. 46). Form the head of the fly and whip finish.

CDC Emerger

Originator: Theo Bakelaar
Hook: TMC 2487, or other light-wire scud hook, #14-#24
Thread: Black 8/0
Abdomen: Dyed black pheasant-tail fibers
Ribbing: Fine copper wire
Dubbing pod: Black CDC dubbing
Antennae: Black CDC fibers

Dutch tyer Theo Bakelaar devised this innovative use of CDC to make a buoyant dubbing pod. This is a good, all-purpose emerger design that, in appropriate sizes and colors, can serve as a midge or mayfly emerger. As with all CDC patterns, this one should not be treated with floatant.

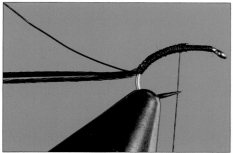

Step 1: Attach the thread and wrap it to the rearmost point of the body. Mount 2-4 pheasant-tail fibers. Mount the ribbing directly atop the rearmost thread wrap. Wrap forward with a *flattened thread* (p. 37) to produce a smooth foundation for the body, and position the thread just past the midpoint of the shank.

Step 2: Wrap the pheasant-tail fibers forward using the method shown in *wrapping feather-barb bodies* (p. 45). Tie off the fibers just past the midpoint of the shank, and clip the excess.

Step 3: *Counter-rib* (p. 33) the abdomen. Tie off the ribbing at the front of the abdomen. Lay a thread foundation over the thorax area, and position the thread at the center of this foundation.

Step 4: Form a dubbing pod as explained in Floating Nymph—BWO, Steps 4-8 (p. 83). Do not twist the CDC dubbing too tightly. You want a firmly consolidated, but not densely compressed, dubbing pod.

Step 5: Gather a small bundle of CDC fibers as shown in *stripping CDC barbs* (p. 40), and mount them, butt ends forward, behind the hook eye. Wrap the thread rearward toward the base of the dubbing pod, butting the CDC fibers against the dubbing pod and elevating the fibers to a vertical position. Clip and bind the excess, forming the fly head. Whip finish the fly.

Suspender Midge Pupa

Originator: John Goddard and Brian Clarke
Hook: TMC 900BL or equivalent dry-fly hook, #10-#18
Thread: Olive 8/0
Tag: White Z-Lon
Abdomen: Olive Antron dubbing
Rib: Fine silver wire
Thorax: Dyed olive pheasant-tail fibers
Suspender pod: Foam ball wrapped in nylon stocking mesh

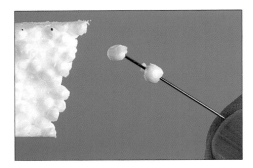

The most convenient material to form the suspender pod is expanded polystyrene, which is often used as a packing material for home electronic equipment. Break a block of this material, and you can see that it's composed of foam balls of various sizes. With a little care you can separate the individual balls and choose one proportioned to the hook size.

Step 1: Attach the thread and position it behind the hook eye a distance equal to the diameter of the foam ball. Stick the foam ball on a dubbing needle, and place the ball in the center of a small square of nylon stocking material.

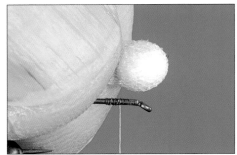

Step 2: Pull the nylon material firmly around the ball, and withdraw the dubbing needle. Twist the nylon around the base of the ball to make a close-fitting sheath.

Step 3: Mount the pod assembly at the tying thread location. Take a couple of wraps forward to tighten the nylon around the ball; then wrap the thread rearward to secure the nylon firmly to the shank.

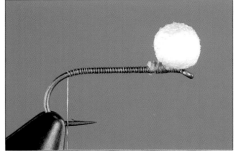

Step 4: Clip the excess nylon, and bind down the tag. Wrap the thread rearward, and position it at the tailing point, as shown.

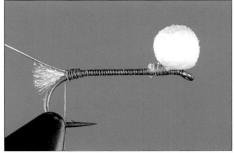

Step 5: Mount the Z-Lon tag, and clip it to about ½ the hook gap in length. Mount the ribbing material over the rearmost wraps securing the tag.

Step 6: Use the *direct dubbing* method (p. 34) to dub a slender abdomen.

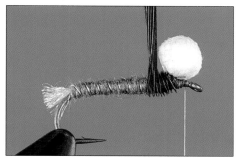

Step 7: *Counter-rib* (p. 33) the wire over the abdomen; tie off the ribbing and clip. Secure 6-8 pheasant-tail fibers at the rear base of the suspender pod. Position the tying thread at the front base of the pod.

Step 8: Using the technique shown in *wrapping feather-barb bodies* (p. 45), wrap the pheasant-tail fibers back to the front of the abdomen.

Step 9: Reverse direction and wrap the pheasant-tail forward. The double layer of pheasant-tail fibers will produce a slightly thickened thorax that is characteristic of the natural. Take the last wrap of pheasant tail just ahead of the suspender pod. Tie off and clip the excess. Form the head of the fly and whip finish.

Natant Nylon Nymph

Originator: Charles Brooks
Hook: 2XL dry-fly hook, #8-#18
Thread: Brown 8/0
Tail: Mottled brown hen hackle
Body: Brown wool yarn
Ribbing: Gold wire
Suspender pod: Ball of tan poly dubbing wrapped in nylon
    stocking mesh
Legs: Mottled brown hen hackle

Though this design lacks the buoyancy of the Goddard/Clarke Suspender Midge Pupa (p. 86), it is easy to tie with readily available materials. Like all Charles Brooks patterns, this is a simple, no-nonsense fly that catches trout. It can be adapted to match a variety of mayfly species.

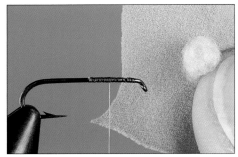

Step 1: Wrap a thread foundation over the front half of the hook shank, and position the thread ¼ of shank-length behind the eye. Roll a pinch of poly dubbing between thumb and forefinger to produce a firm, but not tightly compressed, ball about ½ the hook gap in diameter. Center the ball in a square of nylon stocking material.

Step 2: Draw the stocking material around the dubbing to form a pouch. Don't compress the dubbing too tightly inside the nylon or the buoyancy of the suspender pod will be reduced. Mount the suspender pod as shown in Suspender Midge Pupa, Steps 3-4, p. 86. Wrap the thread to the tailing point.

Step 3: *Align and strip* (p. 30) a bundle of hackle fibers. Mount them atop the shank to form a tail about one hook-gap in length. Secure the ribbing atop the tail-mounting wraps. Tie in a length of wool yarn atop the rib-mounting wraps.

Step 4: Twist the yarn tightly (clockwise when viewed from above), and wrap forward to produce a segmented body. Wrap the yarn to the rear base of the nylon, then under the pod, and continue wrapping ahead of the pod. Stop about 6-7 thread-wraps' distance behind the hook eye. Tie off and clip the yarn.

Step 5: *Counter-rib* (p. 33) the entire length of the body. Secure and clip the ribbing at the front of the yarn.

Step 6: Mount the legs as explained in *throat hackle* (p. 41). Bind and clip the excess. Form the head of the fly and whip finish.

Chironomid Suspender Pupa

Originator: Doug Jorgensen
Hook: TMC 101, Mustad 94859, or other ring-eye dry-fly hook, #12-#20
Thread: Black 6/0
Tail: Ethafoam strip
Body: Ethafoam strip colored black with waterproof pen
Ribbing: Fine gold wire
Thorax: Peacock herl
Post: Ethafoam strip

This standard midge emerger can be tied in a variety of colors and is relatively easy to tie in very small sizes. Foam, fore and aft, positions the fly horizontally in the surface film.

Step 1: Attach the thread behind the hook eye. Cut a strip of thin Ethafoam about twice the length of the hook shank and about ¼ to ⅓ the hook gap in width. Secure one end of the foam behind the hook eye, as shown.

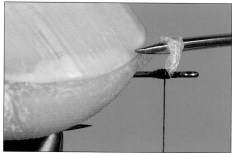

Step 2: Fold the foam strip over a dubbing needle held perpendicular to the shank to form the post. The height of the post should be about ½ the hook gap.

Step 3: Bind the excess foam tightly to the top of the shank, forming a smooth underbody, until the tailing point is reached. Clip the tag of foam to form a tail about one hook-gap long. Over the rearmost thread wraps, mount the ribbing, and then a strip of foam colored black for the abdomen.

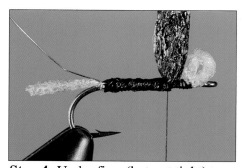

Step 4: Under firm (but not tight) tension, wrap the abdomen strip forward over the rear ⅔ of the shank. Tie off and clip the excess.

Step 5: *Counter-rib* (p. 33) the wire to the front of the abdomen. At the front of the abdomen, mount 2-4 strands of peacock herl.

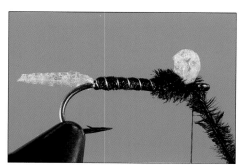

Step 6: Using the method explained in *wrapping twisted-herl collars* (p. 49), form the thorax. Take the last wrap of herl ahead of the foam post. Tie off and clip. Form the head of the fly and whip finish.

Heathen

Originator: Phil Camera
Hook: TMC 2487, or other light-wire scud hook, #16-#20
Thread: Black 8/0
Underbody: One strand pearl Krystal Flash
Overbody: Gray (#08) Larva Lace
Post: White closed-cell foam strip
Thorax: Coarse hare's ear dubbing

Various colors can be produced in this pattern by using different combinations of Krystal Flash underbody and Larva Lace tubing. Durability is a strong point in this fly.

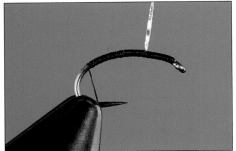

Step 1: Mount the thread near the hook eye, and wrap ⅓ of a shank-length toward the bend. Mount a strand of Krystal Flash, binding the tag end of the material toward the hook eye. Lift the strand of Krystal Flash, and with a *flattened thread* (p. 37), wrap back to the rearmost point of the body, forming a smooth underbody.

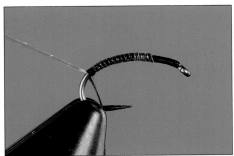

Step 2: Wrap the Krystal Flash back to the tying thread, forming a smooth body over the thread foundation. Tie off the Krystal Flash and clip the excess.

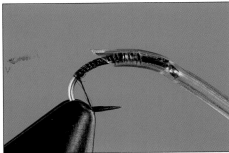

Step 3: Cut a short length of Larva Lace tubing, and trim the end at an angle to form a point. Slip the tubing over the hook eye until it covers about ½ the shank.

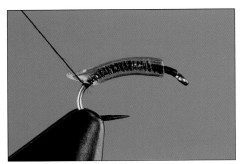

Step 4: Clip the end of the tubing even with the hook eye. Push the tubing to the rearmost point of the body. The point trimmed at the end of the tubing should be positioned atop the hook shank and should extend just beyond the tying thread.

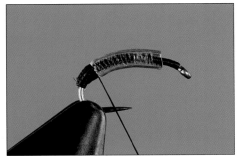

Step 5: Bind down the point of the tubing; then wrap the thread toward the hook eye just enough to bind down the end of the tubing all the way around the shank. The wraps securing the tubing should taper to a point at the rear.

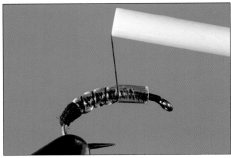

Step 6: Spiral the thread forward evenly to rib the body. Apply just enough thread tension to squeeze the tubing beneath into slightly bulging body segments.

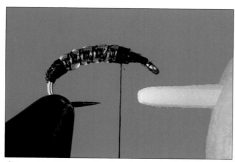

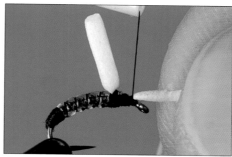

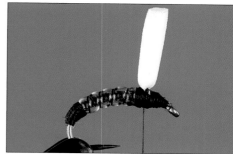

Step 7: When the body is fully ribbed, secure the front end of the tubing with additional wraps, and position the thread ⅓ of a shank-length behind the eye. Cut a strip of foam, square in cross-section, about ⅓ the width of the hook gap.

Step 8: Bind the foam to the top of the shank. Start with firm, but not excessively tight wraps. Then wrap toward the hook eye, using progressively tighter wraps.

Step 9: Pull the tag to stretch the foam tightly, then clip and bind the excess. Wrap the thread rearward, pushing the foam post against the front edge of the abdomen. If the foam is not positioned vertically at this point, take a few thread wraps at the rear of the foam, building a thread bump to stand the post upright.

Step 10: Use the *direct dubbing* method (p. 34) to dub a thorax behind and in front of the post. Form the head of the fly and whip finish. Clip the post to about ½ the hook-gap in height.

Olive Emerging Nymph

Originator: Richardt Jensen
Hook: TMC 100, or equivalent dry-fly hook, #14-#16
Thread: Black 8/0
Tail: 2 pheasant-tail fibers
Abdomen: Pheasant-tail fibers
Thorax: Brown hare's ear dubbing
Wing: 1mm Ethafoam
Wing case: Pheasant-tail fibers

This elegant emerger, from Richardt Jensen of Denmark, has foam wing buds protruding from a split wing case. Despite its appearance, it is a fairly easy fly to dress and can be modified to imitate many mayfly species.

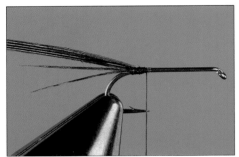

Step 1: Attach the tying thread and position it at the tailing point. Mount two pheasant-tail fibers, flaring them slightly, to form tails one shank-length long. Clip and bind the excess. Secure 3 or 4 pheasant-tail fibers atop the tail-mounting wraps.

Step 2: Advance the thread to the mid-point of the shank. Wrap the pheasant-tail fibers as explained in *wrapping feather-barb bodies* (p. 45) to form an abdomen over the rear half of the hook shank.

Step 3: Mount 6 pheasant-tail fibers for the wing case at the front of the abdomen.

Step 4: Using the method shown in *dubbing loop*, Steps 1-2, (p. 35), form a 2" loop of tying thread directly atop the mounting wraps for the wing case material.

Step 5: Use the *direct dubbing* method (p. 34) to dub a thorax slightly larger in diameter than the abdomen. Position the tying thread a short distance behind the hook eye.

Step 6: Cut a strip of foam about as long as the hook shank and half as wide. Fold the foam in half crosswise and trim both ends simultaneously to the rounded shape shown. It may help to hold the foam in a hackle pliers while trimming. Here, the wings are shown trimmed and unfolded.

Step 7: Fold the wings around the thread loop from underneath.

Step 8: Fold the thread loop down along the top of the shank, trapping the wings atop the thorax. With the tying thread, take two firm, but not tight, wraps over the thread loop behind the hook eye.

Step 9: Pull the loop straight out from the hook eye to seat the wings firmly against the top of the thorax. Then take additional tight wraps to bind the loop threads behind the hook eye. Clip the excess loop of thread

Step 10: Take 3 of the pheasant-tail fibers and fold them forward across the base of the wing on the near side of the shank. Secure the fibers behind the hook eye with 2 tight thread wraps.

Step 11: Repeat Step 9, drawing three fibers forward across the base of the wing on the far side. Secure them with thread. Clip and bind down the excess pheasant tail. Whip finish the fly. Here is a view of the finished fly from the front.

Chapter 6: Drawn Wing Case and Shellback Emergers

Flies of this design use material mounted atop the shank and drawn forward over the thorax (drawn wing case patterns) or pulled over the entire length of the body (shellback designs). Drawn wing cases, and to a lesser extent shellbacks, are familiar components on a great many nymph patterns. In emergers, however, the wing case or shellback is sometimes exaggerated to suggest an emerging insect, and it is often the principal component giving buoyancy to the fly.

The resemblance of these emergers to traditional nymph designs rightly suggests that these patterns are generally tied to represent the nymphal or pupal insect just prior to emergence, and many of them might reasonably be assigned to that loosely defined category "floating nymphs." These flies tend to ride quite low in the water and as a result are often difficult to see; fishing them as a dropper as behind a more visible dry fly is often the best solution.

It is a short step from forming an ordinary wing case to forming one in which the excess case material is left untrimmed to form a tuft over the hook eye. Indeed, a large number of patterns take precisely that approach. We have grouped flies of this design in Chapter 7, Tuft Emergers, since the tuft is quite often the more conspicuous component in representing the emerging insect and generally provides most of the floatation in the pattern.

Juracek Emerger

Originator: John Juracek and Craig Mathews
Hook: TMC 100, or equivalent dry-fly hook, #16-#18
Thread: Brown 8/0
Tail: Mallard flank fibers
Body: Sparse dark dubbing
Wing case: Dark gray foam

The use of a foam wing case makes this floating nymph one of the simplest approaches to tying emerging mayflies. The foam can be colored with a black marker, or black foam used, to imitate the darkened wing pads on a nymph that is ready to hatch. This one is tough to see on all but the very flattest waters.

Step 1: Secure the thread and wrap back to the tailing point. Mount a sparse bundle of mallard flank fibers that extend rearward about the length of the hook shank. Clip and bind the excess.

Step 2: Apply dubbing sparsely to the thread, and dub a slightly tapered abdomen over the rear half of the hook shank.

Step 3: Cut a strip of foam about ¾ of a shank-length in width. Secure the foam at the front of the abdomen, as shown. Begin with very firm, but not excessively tight, thread wraps at the front of the abdomen, and make the wraps tighter as you wrap toward the hook eye. Clip, and bind the excess.

Step 4: Dub a thorax about twice the thickness of the abdomen. Use a dubbing needle to tease out some fibers for legs.

Step 5: Fold the foam strip forward over the thorax. Use firm, but not tight, pressure. Secure the foam a short distance behind the hook eye.

Step 6: For a neat head, stretch the foam out beyond the hook eye, then clip the tag. Bind down the excess and form the head of the fly. Whip finish.

Foam Biot Emerger

Originator: Bill Black
Hook: Daiichi 1100, or equivalent dry-fly, #14-#22
Thread: Gray 8/0
Shuck: Gray Sparkle Yarn
Rib: Same as tying thread
Body: Gray goose biot
Thorax: Gray Fine & Dry dubbing
Wing case: Gray closed-cell foam
Legs: Light partridge hackle fibers

This basic design can be easily modified by changing the abdomen, thorax, and wing case colors; using CDC for the legs; and leaving a longer tag of foam at the head, which can improve the visibility of the pattern on the water.

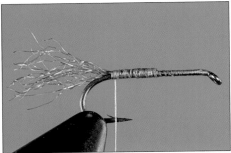

Step 1: Attach the tread and wrap to the tailing point. Secure the Sparkle Yarn to make a shuck about one shank-length long.

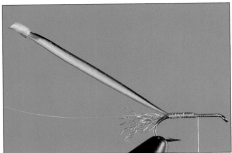

Step 2: Secure the ribbing material directly atop the rearmost thread wraps. Mount the biot atop the ribbing as shown in *biot body—fringed* (p. 30).

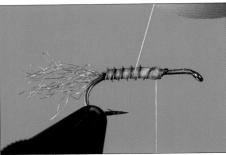

Step 3: Wrap the biot forward over the rear half of the shank; bind and clip the excess. Rib the abdomen by wrapping the ribbing thread over the smooth part of the biot abdomen, taking care not to bind down the fringes.

Step 4: Tie off and clip the ribbing. Mount a strip of foam about ½ the hook gap in width for the wing case; clip and bind the excess. Use the *direct dubbing* method (p. 34) to dub the thorax as shown, and position the tying thread at the front of the thorax.

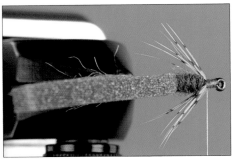

Step 5: Using the method explained in *side-mounted legs* (p. 39), secure a small bundle of partridge hackle fibers on either side of the shank, a short distance behind the eye, as shown in this top view. Clip and bind the fiber butts.

Step 6: Fold the foam forward and tie it off behind the hook eye. Whip finish beneath foam, around the hook shank only. Clip the foam to leave a small stub at the head.

Foam Pale Morning Dun Emerger

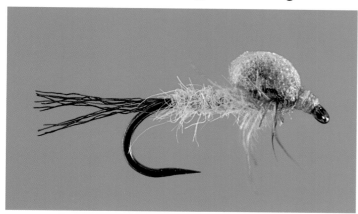

Originator: Craig Mathews and John Juracek
Hook: Standard dry fly, #16-#18
Thread: Yellow 8/0
Shuck: Brown Z-Lon
Abdomen: Orange-yellow beaver or rabbit fur
Hackle: Dun starling hackle
Wing case: Gray closed-cell foam

The pronounced hump in the wing case incorporates more buoyant material into this pattern for better floatation than is achieved by drawing the foam tight over the thorax. The height of the wing case can be varied to suit the tyer's taste; in extreme versions, it becomes almost a foam loopwing.

Step 1: Attach the thread at the tailing point, and mount the shuck fibers to extend rearward one shank-length. Tightly dub about 1" of the thread. Then form a dubbing loop as shown in *dubbing loop*, Steps 1-3, (p. 35). Advance the tying thread to the mid-point of the shank.

Step 2: Twist the loop tightly and wrap forward to produce a segmented abdomen over the rear half of the hook shank. When you reach the tying thread, secure the dubbing loop and clip the excess.

Step 3: Mount a strip of foam about ⅔ of a hook-gap in width at the front of the abdomen. *Prepare a hackle* (p. 39) and secure it ahead of the foam as shown in *mounting collar hackle* (p. 37).

Step 4: Take 3-4 wraps of hackle and tie off the feather as explained in *wrapping wet-fly hackle* (p. 50).

Step 5: Clip the hackle on the top and bottom, leaving only the fibers projecting out from the sides, as shown in this front view. Position the tying thread a short distance behind the hook eye.

Step 6: Fold the foam forward, but do not pull it tightly over the thorax. Leave a slight hump as shown here. Secure the foam behind the eye. Stretch the foam tag, clip it, then bind down the excess. Whip finish.

Little Yellow Sally Emerger

Originator: Howard Cole
Hook: TMC 5212, or other fine-wire 2XL hook, #12-#16
Thread: Tan 8/0
Undertail: Amber Z-Lon
Tail: Woodduck flank fibers
Abdomen: ⅓ fluorescent orange dubbing; ⅔ creamy
   yellow dubbing
Wing: Dun Z-Lon
Thorax: Creamy yellow dubbing
Hackle: Light dun CDC
Wing case: Thin Ethafoam

This is an usual pattern—the only stonefly emerger in this book. Howard Cole notes, "Many fishermen don't realize that these little stoneflies can emerge in the water and not necessarily on land, like their bigger brothers and sisters. A very effective pattern when *Isoperla* are present."

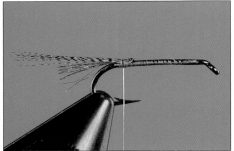

Step 1: Position the tying thread at the tail-mounting point. Secure a sparse bundle of Z-Lon and clip to one hook-gap in length. Secure a bundle of woodduck flank fibers over the Z-Lon to make a tail one shank-length long. Clip and bind the butts of both materials.

Step 2: Use the *direct dubbing* method (p. 34) to dub a slender tag of orange dubbing over the rear ⅕ of the hook shank. Dub the next ⅔ of the shank with the yellow dubbing, keeping the abdomen slender.

Step 3: Secure a bundle of dun Z-Lon directly ahead of the abdomen, and clip to make a wing that extends to the tail-mounting point. Clip and bind the excess. Cut a strip of Ethafoam about one hook-gap wide. Mount it directly ahead of the Z-Lon.

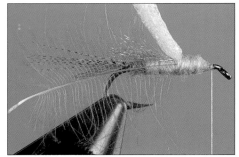

Step 4: Using the technique shown in *tip-mounted hackle* (p. 41), prepare and mount a CDC feather directly ahead of the foam. Dub a thorax slightly larger in diameter than the abdomen, ending about 6-7 thread-wraps' distance behind the hook eye.

Step 5: Using the method shown in *palmering hackle* (p. 38), spiral the CDC feather over the thorax. Tie off and clip directly in front of the thorax.

Step 6: Draw the uppermost CDC fibers to either side of the shank, and fold the foam forward through the gap in the CDC barbs. Secure the foam behind the hook eye. Clip the excess and whip finish.

Krystal Emerger

Originator: Rick Murphy
Hook: TMC 100, or equivalent dry-fly hook, #18-#24
Thread: Gray 14/0
Shuck: Rust Antron
Abdomen: BWO turkey or goose biot
Thorax: Gray ostrich herl
Wing case: Pearl Krystal Flash

In small sizes (#22-#24) this pattern works well during both midge and *Baetis* emergences; larger sizes are effective for PMDs. Rick Murphy finds black or peacock Krystal Flash and olive or tan ostrich herl to be useful alternative colors.

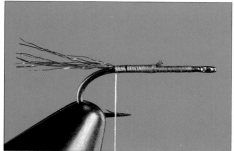

Step 1: Attach the thread and position it at the midpoint of the shank. Secure a sparse bundle of Antron, and wrap rearward, binding the Antron atop the shank and forming a smooth underbody. Stop at the tailing point, and clip the Antron to one shank-length.

Step 2: Mount and wrap a biot as explained in *biot body—smooth* (p. 31) to form an abdomen over the rear half of the shank. Tie off and clip the biot at the midpoint of the shank.

Step 3: Mount 4-6 strands of Krystal Flash directly ahead of the abdomen. Tie off and clip the excess. Mount a strand of ostrich herl directly ahead of the Krystal Flash.

Step 4: Wrap the herl forward as shown in *wrapping single-herl collars* (p. 48). Tie off and clip the herl about 4 thread-wraps' distance behind the hook eye.

Step 5: Draw the Krystal Flash over the top of the herl, forming a smooth wing case. Tie off the strands directly ahead of the thorax, but do not clip the excess.

Step 6: Draw half the Krystal Flash strands rearward along the far side of the shank, and the other half along the near side. Pinch them in the left fingers. Take a few thread wraps back over the base of the Krystal Flash to angle the legs rearward. Whip finish and clip the legs to one hook-gap in length.

Emerging Dun

Originator: Oliver Edwards
Hook: Partridge K14ST, or other 2XL or 3XL curved hook, #16-#20
Thread: Brown 12/0 or Danville Spider Web
Tail: Brown Micro Fibbets
Abdomen: Brown Antron yarn
Wing case: Ethafoam
Wings: Two or three Type 1 or Type 2 natural CDC feathers
Thorax: Same as abdomen

Foam and CDC give this Oliver Edwards design both good floatation and a low profile. It is one of the more involved patterns in this book to dress, but the results are a pleasing combination of realism and "bugginess." Sizes and colors can be modified to match a variety of mayfly hatches.

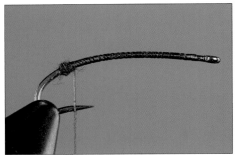

Step 1: Mount the tying thread and position it just around the hook bend. Use the *direct dubbing* method (p. 34) to apply a very small amount of dubbing, and wrap it tightly to form a small ball at the tailing point.

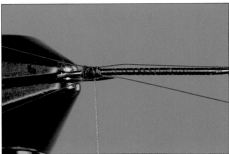

Step 2: Mount a Micro Fibett on the near side of the side shank to form a tail about ½ the shank length. Mount a second fiber on the far side to form a split tail, as shown in this top view. Bind and clip the butts.

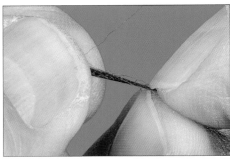

Step 3: Cut a length of Antron yarn. If using a multi-ply yarn, split it lengthwise so that you have only 1 or 2 plies. Repeatedly scrape one end with your thumbnail to "shave down" the yarn and taper it.

Step 4: Secure the yarn, and use the thread to form a tapered underbody over the rear half of the hook shank.

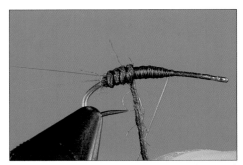

Step 5: Twist the yarn tightly and begin wrapping the abdomen. You may need to pause every few wraps and re-twist the yarn to form distinct abdominal segments.

Step 6: Continue wrapping to the front of the underbody. Tie off, but *do not* clip the yarn. Cut a strip of Ethafoam about ⅓ the hook gap in width. Mount the foam directly ahead of the abdomen on the near side of the shank.

Step 7: Cut a second strip of foam, and mount it on the far side, as shown in this top view.

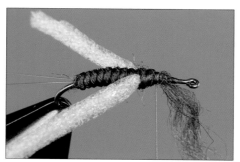

Step 8: Clip the tags of foam, and wrap the tying thread about ⅓ the distance to the hook eye. Twist the yarn again, and take two wraps forward, covering the mounting wraps securing the foam. Tie off the yarn, but again, *do not* clip it.

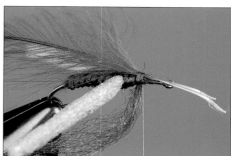

Step 9: Align the tips of the CDC feathers, and strip the lower barbs so that the feather tips are about 1 ½ times the length of the shank. Mount them as a group, stems side-by-side atop the shank, directly in front of the yarn wraps. Use only two moderately tight wraps. The edge of the yarn should prop the feathers up and rearward.

Step 10: Grasp the CDC butts and gently pull them forward over the hook eye, sliding the feathers beneath the thread wraps. Pull until the feather tips form wings about ¾ the shank length. Then bind them down securely, but *do not* clip the butts.

Step 11: Advance the tying thread half the distance to the hook eye. Twist the yarn again, and take two more wraps. Secure the yarn tightly, and clip the excess.

Step 12: Fold the foam strips forward, keeping them on the sides of the hook shank. Bind the strips directly atop the wraps used to secure the yarn in the previous step. Clip the foam tags.

Step 13: Clip away the central quills and barbs from the CDC feathers, but leave 4-5 barbs on each side unclipped. Notice the scissors here have captured the center of the CDC bundle, but a few barbs on each side run beneath the scissors, and won't be clipped.

Step 14: Now trim the barbs you left in the previous step to be about equal in length to the foam wing case, as shown in this top view.

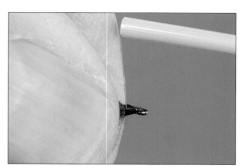

Step 15: Draw the bundle of CDC barbs rearward along either side of the hook shank, and secure them in this position with a few thread wraps, simultaneously forming the head of the fly. Whip finish.

Traveling Sedge Emerger (Rowley)

Originator: Philip Rowley
Hook: 2XL dry fly, #10-#16
Thread: Black 6/0
Underbody: Poly yarn (any color)
Body: Olive-brown Antron dubbing
Ribbing: Yellow or lime-green Super Floss
Wing: Deer or elk hair
Thorax: Olive-brown Antron dubbing
Wing case: Brown closed-cell foam
Legs: Hen pheasant fibers
Wing pads: Brown raffia or Swiss straw
Head: Peacock herl

British Columbia tyer and stillwater devotee Phil Rowley uses deer hair and foam to suggest wings emerging from the wing case on this caddis pattern. Colors of the natural insect vary, with shades of green and olive being the most common.

Step 1: Attach the thread and wrap to the rear of the shank. Mount the ribbing material. Mount the poly yarn, and wrap it forward over the rear ⅔ of the shank to form a smooth underbody. Clip the excess.

Step 2: Use the *direct dubbing* method (p. 34) to dub the abdomen over the underbody.

Step 3: Spiral the ribbing to the front of the abdomen. Bind down and clip the excess.

Step 4: *Clip, clean, and stack* (p. 32) a clump of deer or elk hair. Mount it at the front of the abdomen so that the tips extend to the rearmost point of the body.

Step 5: Clip and tightly bind the hair butts.

Step 6: Cut a strip of foam about ⅔ the width of the hook gap. Mount the foam over the wing butts, leaving a short tag extending to the rear, as shown.

Step 7: Fold the foam back and dub the thorax to a point about 6-8 thread wraps' distance behind the hook eye.

Step 8: Tie an overhand knot in each of 6 pheasant-tail fibers, as shown.

Step 9: Grasp the pheasant-tail fibers as a bundle, with the tip ends aligned. Mount them beneath the shank as explained in *throat hackle* (p. 41). Clip and bind the excess.

Step 10: Cut a strip of Swiss straw or raffia about ⅓ the hook gap in width. Fold the strip in half lengthwise.

Step 11: Position the folded wing pad against the near side of the shank, extending rearward about ⅓ of a shank-length, and angled down about 45 degrees. Secure the wing to the side of the shank.

Step 12: Repeat Step 11 to mount a wing pad on the far side of the shank. Then fold the foam wing case forward, and secure it just ahead of the wing pads.

Step 13: Mount 2-3 strands of peacock herl ahead of the wing case, and using the method shown in *wrapping twisted-herl collars* (p. 49), form a small head on the fly. Clip and bind the excess. Whip finish.

Barr Emerger—BWO

Originator: John Barr
Hook: TMC 101, or other ring-eye dry-fly hook, #16-#22
Thread: Dun 8/0
Tail: Stiff brown hackle fibers
Abdomen: Fine olive dubbing
Thorax: Fine dun dubbing
Wing case: Dun hackle fibers
Legs: Dun hackle fibers from wing case

This slender, minimalist design is effective and easy to tie, but it incorporates no naturally buoyant material. Treated with floatant, it rides flush in the film; with no floatant it sits under the film. In either case, it is not easy to spot on the water, and using it as a dropper off a dry fly is the easiest way to detect strikes.

Step 1: Attach the thread and wrap to the tailing point. Mount a bundle of hackle fibers. Clip them to the length of about one hook-gap. Use the *direct dubbing* method (p. 34) to dub a sparse, slightly tapered abdomen over the rear ⅔ of the shank.

Step 2: Mount a bundle of hackle fibers at the butt end, directly ahead of the abdomen.

Step 3: Dub a thorax slightly thicker than the abdomen, leaving room behind the hook eye to tie down the wingcase fibers.

Step 4: Pull the wingcase fibers forward, and secure them at the front of the thorax.

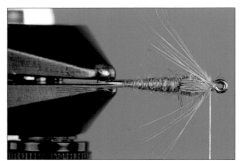

Step 5: With a dubbing needle, divide the fiber tips into two equal bundles. Pull one bundle to near side of the shank and one to the far side. Pinch them against the sides of the shank, and take a few thread wraps over the folded ends of the fibers to hold them in position, as shown in this top view.

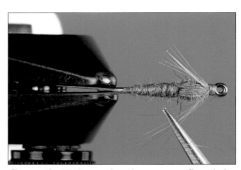

Step 6: When the legs are fixed in position, clip them to a length of about one hook-gap. Form the head of the fly and whip finish.

Halfback Emerger—BWO

Originator: Mike Lawson
Hook: TMC 100, or equivalent dry-fly hook, #18-#20
Thread: Olive 8/0
Shuck: Brown Z-Lon
Rib: Fine copper wire
Abdomen: Pheasant-tail fibers
Wing case: Natural gray deer hair
Thorax: Superfine olive dubbing

This design can be modified to match a number of smaller mayfly species. The key in tying is not to draw the wingcase fibers forward too tightly or you will collapse the hollow hairs that give buoyancy to the pattern. This is a simple and highly productive flat-water fly.

Step 1: Attach the thread and position it at tailing point. Tie in the ribbing wire and, directly atop it, 6-8 pheasant–tail fibers. Wrap the pheasant fibers to form an abdomen over the rear half of the shank as explained in *wrapping feather-barb bodies* (p. 45). Clip and bind the excess.

Step 2: Tie in the Z-Lon at the front of the abdomen. Clip the excess.

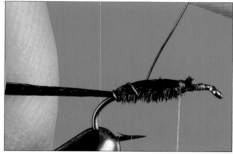

Step 3: With the left fingers, pull the Z-Lon over the top of the abdomen and hold firmly. With the right fingers, *counter-rib* (p. 33) the wire, binding the Z-Lon to the top of the abdomen. Tie off and clip the ribbing at the front of the abdomen.

Step 4: Clip the Z-Lon shuck to the length of the hook shank. *Clip, clean, and stack* (p. 32) a bundle of deer hair. Mount it at the front of the abdomen with the tips extending rearward.

Step 5: Use the *direct dubbing* method (p. 34) to dub a thorax slightly larger in diameter than the abdomen.

Step 6: Draw the deer hair forward as uniformly as possible. Secure the hair at the front of the abdomen. Then clip the excess and bind down. Form the head of the fly and whip finish.

Jay's Humpback Emerger

Originator: Jay Buchner
Hook: Mustad 94845, or other standard dry-fly hook, #14-#22
Thread: Brown 8/0
Tail: Brown hackle fibers
Body: Olive-brown fine dubbing (or tying thread on smaller sizes)
Hackle: Dun or grizzly dyed dun
Wing case: Natural gray deer hair

The palmer hackle along the entire length of the body makes this an atypical emerger design, but you can't argue with the results. Sizes and colors can be varied, but it is particularly good in smaller sizes.

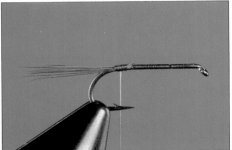

Step 1: Attach the thread and wrap to the tailing point. Secure a bundle of hackle fibers to make a tail that extends about one hook-gap beyond the bend. Clip the excess.

Step 2: *Prepare a hackle feather* (p. 39) and mount it as explained in *mounting collar hackle* (p. 37). Advance the thread to the midpoint of the shank.

Step 3: *Clip, clean, and stack* (p. 32) a bundle of deer hair. Mount the hair atop the midpoint of the shank, leaving the tips as long as possible for easier handling in Step 6. Trim the butts and wrap with thread. Return the thread to the tailing point.

Step 4: Use the *direct dubbing* method (p. 34) to dub a slender, slightly tapered abdomen. Continue dubbing past the deer hair, taking a crisscross wrap under the shank beneath the hair to cover the thread wraps. Finish dubbing about ¼ of a shank-length behind the eye.

Step 5: Spiral the hackle forward, as explained in *palmering hackle* (p. 38), over the entire dubbed length of the shank. Secure the feather in front of the dubbing.

Step 6: Pull the deer hair forward over the top and sides of the shank, as shown. Secure tightly with thread. Then clip the excess and bind with thread. Whip finish the fly.

CDC Hatching Midge

Originator: Randall Kaufmann
Hook: TMC 100, or equivalent dry-fly hook, #14-#20
Thread: Black 8/0
Shuck: Type 1 or Type 2 dark dun CDC feather
Rib: White thread
Abdomen: Black thread
Wing case: One or two Type 1, Type 2 or Type 4 dark dun CDC feathers
Thorax: Peacock herl
Hackle: Grizzly

This is one of the first American midge designs we remember that used CDC as a material. With adjustments in color, this pattern makes a credible mayfly emerger as well, especially for smaller flies.

Step 1: Attach the thread and position it at the middle of the shank. Mount a CDC feather at the midpoint of the shank so that the tip extends about ½ a shank-length beyond the hook bend. Clip and bind the excess. Mount a length of white thread at the tailing point.

Step 2: With a *flattened thread* (p. 37), form a smooth abdomen over the rear half of the shank. Spiral the white thread forward to rib the abdomen; tie off and clip at the front of the abdomen.

Step 3: Mount two CDC feathers in front of the abdomen, with the tips extending rearward. Bind and clip the excess. Mount a grizzly hackle in front of the CDC as explained in *mounting collar hackle* (p. 37). Finally, secure 3 or 4 strands of peacock herl in front of the hackle.

Step 4: Using the method shown in *wrapping twisted-herl collars* (p. 49), form a herl thorax. Tie off and clip the excess.

Step 5: Spiral the hackle forward over the herl as shown in *palmering hackle* (p. 38). Tie off in front of the herl and clip.

Step 6: Draw the CDC feather over the top of the thorax, using your left fingers to smooth back any hackle barbs away from the tie-down point. Secure the feather behind the hook eye, as shown. Whip finish the fly, then clip the excess CDC to form a small tuft at the head of the fly.

Bighorn Baetis Wonder Nymph

Originator: Brad Downey
Hook: TMC 2487, or other light-wire scud hook, #16-#18
Thread: Dun 8/0
Tail: Woodduck flank fibers
Abdomen: Olive-dun Hareline dubbing
Wing case: Webby base of grizzly hackle feather
Thorax: Dark dun Hareline dubbing

Wyoming tyer Bruce Salzburg highly recommends this pattern. The use of the fluffy base of a hackle feather for the wing case is an unusual use of a material that most tyers discard. Paste floatants will mat the wingcase fibers and diminish their mobility; powder-type floatants are better, though this pattern can be fished in the film with no floatant at all.

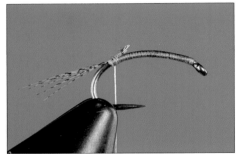

Step 1: Attach the thread and wrap to the tailing point. *Align and strip* (p. 30) 6-8 flank fibers, and mount them atop the shank to make a tail about equal in length to the hook shank.

Step 2: Use the *direct dubbing* method (p. 34) to dub a slightly tapered abdomen over the rear half of the hook shank.

Step 3: Select a hackle feather with fluffy barbs at the base that are about one hook-gap long. With moistened thumb and forefinger, preen back a section of barbs at the base of the feather. This section of barbs should be about a shank-length long.

Step 4: Tie in the feather atop the shank at the front of the abdomen. Mount it just at the base of the moistened barbs, with the concave side of the feather facing upward.

Step 5: Clip the excess hackle and bind down. Dub the thorax. Position the tying thread at the front of the thorax.

Step 6: Fold the wing case over the thorax. With a dubbing needle, stroke forward the hackle barbs that lie ahead of the tying thread, leaving a gap of bare stem directly above the thread. Tie down the wing case by binding down the bare stem, as shown here. Then clip the excess and bind down. Whip finish.

Itty Bitty Emerger

Originator: Hans Weilenmann
Hook: TMC 2487, or other fine-wire scud hook, #18-#26
Thread: Brown 8/0
Abdomen: Hare's ear dubbing
Wing: Brown partridge feather
Legs: Pine squirrel hair
Wing case: Partridge from wing
Thorax: Hare's ear dubbing

This generic emerger can be altered in color to imitate a variety of small insects. The splayed squirrel hair on this pattern acts like a parachute hackle and can be adapted for use on other patterns that have a drawn wing case. Hans Weilenmann prefers squirrel hair, but notes that any straight, smooth hair, or hackle fibers, can be used.

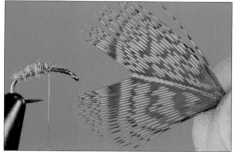

Step 1: Mount the tying thread and position it at the rearmost point of the body. Use the *direct dubbing* method (p. 34) to dub a slender, tapered abdomen to the midpoint of the shank. Select a partridge feather; strip away the fluffy barbs at the base, and snip away the center quill to form a "V" at the tip of the feather.

Step 2: Position the feather atop the shank, directly ahead of the abdomen. Take a soft wrap over the bare stem, then pull the stem toward the hook eye, sliding the feather beneath the thread wrap to form a wing that extends just beyond the hook bend. Secure the feather, and take a turn of thinly dubbed thread over the mounting wraps.

Step 3: Fold the butt of the feather rearward. Cut a small clump of fur from the back of pine squirrel pelt; remove most of the underfur and any excessively long guard hairs. Mount the hair, tips rearward, directly against and slightly on top of the folded feather butt. Clip and bind the excess.

Step 4: Lift the feather butt slightly, and sneak a turn of thinly dubbed thread beneath the folded feather, as close as possible to the abdomen dubbing. Then dub forward, forming a thorax slightly larger in diameter than the front of the abdomen. Finish the thorax 6 or 7 thread-wraps' distance behind the eye.

Step 5: Press your thumbnail against the base of the squirrel hair at the tie-in point to fan the hair in an arc, as shown here from the front.

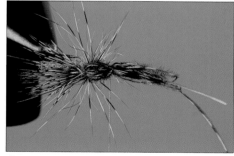

Step 6: Draw the feather butt through the middle of the fanned hair, over the thorax, and down to the hook eye. The drawn feather should force the hair into a horizontal splay of almost 360 degrees, as shown in this top view. Secure the feather, clip the excess, and whip finish.

CDC Emerging Midge

Originator: René Harrop
Hook: TMC 900BL, or equivalent dry-fly hook, #14-#20
Thread: Olive 8/0
Tail: Teal flank fibers
Back: Gray closed-cell foam
Legs: Gray CDC
Body: Olive poly dubbing

CDC and foam make this an excellent flush-floating pattern, while the clean body profile suits it well to flatter waters. This is a relatively simple fly to tie even in small sizes, though softer, less dense foams will tie more easily on small hooks.

Step 1: Attach the thread and wrap to tailing point. Secure a small bundle of teal flank fibers extending rearward from the mounting wraps about one shank-length.

Step 2: Cut a strip of foam equal in width to about one hook-gap. Secure one end of the foam directly atop the tail-mounting wraps. Clip and bind the excess. Position the thread halfway between these mounting wraps and the hook eye.

Step 3: Gather and bundle the barbs from a CDC feather as shown in *stripping CDC barbs* (p. 40). Lay them crosswise atop the shank, directly above the tying thread. Secure them with a series of crisscross wraps, as shown in this top view.

Step 4: Use the *direct dubbing* method (p. 34) to dub a slender body, ending about 5 thread-wraps' distance behind the hook eye. Position the thread at the front of the dubbed body.

Step 5: Fold the foam over the top of the shank, and secure it. Whip finish beneath the foam tag, directly around the hook shank.

Step 6: Clip the foam, leaving a short tag for the head. Clip the legs to one hook-gap in length.

Pop-Top Caddis Emerger

Originator: Andy Burk
Hook: TMC 2487, or other light-wire scud hook, #14-#18
Thread: Tan 8/0
Underbody: Tan dubbing
Body: Tapered strip of tan closed-cell foam, colored on top with brown waterproof marker
Legs: Grouse fibers
Wing: Dun Z-Lon
Antennae: Mallard flank fibers

The foam shellback makes a compact, low-profile, low-floating, highly suggestive pattern. It can be a little difficult to see; fishing it as a dropper behind a larger dry fly can help track the fly on the water.

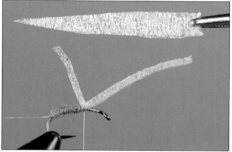

Step 1: Attach the thread at the rear of the hook, leaving a 6" tag of thread. Use the *direct dubbing* method (p. 34) to dub a slender abdomen over the rear half of the shank. Cut a wedge-shaped piece of foam as shown, and secure it atop the shank so that the point of the foam extends about one hook-gap's distance beyond the bend.

Step 2: With the left fingers, draw the tip of the foam over the top of the shank; use the *tag* of tying thread to secure the rear of the foam at the tailing point. Then spiral the thread tag forward to the front of the abdomen, creating 3 body segments. Tie off the thread tag ahead of the foam, and clip the thread tag.

Step 3: Fold the foam rearward, and take a few thread wraps over the base of the fold. Then dub the thorax halfway to the hook eye. Fold the foam forward, and bind down ahead of the dubbing to create another body segment.

Step 4: Mount the legs directly ahead of the foam as shown in *throat hackle* (p. 41). Mount a sparse bundle of Z-Lon on either side of the shank, directly ahead of the foam, to form wings that slant up and rearward. Clip and bind the excess. Draw both wings rearward and clip the tips to reach the midpoint of the abdomen.

Step 5: Mount a mallard flank fiber on either side of the shank, directly ahead of the wing, to form antennae that extend rearward about 1 ½ shank-lengths. Clip the excess and dub the remainder of the thorax to the hook eye.

Step 6: Fold the foam forward again, and bind it down behind the hook eye. Clip and bind the excess foam, and whip finish. If desired, color the top of the foam with a waterproof marker.

Captive Dun

Originator: René Harrop
Hook: TMC 900BL, or equivalent dry-fly hook, #14-#20
Thread: Olive 8/0
Shuck: Gray marabou
Body: Olive-brown dubbing
Legs: Woodduck flank fibers
Wing case: Gray duck or goose wing quill section

This is an older Harrop pattern that uses a quill segment tied shellback style to represent a dun's wings still captured in the shuck. CDC can be substituted for the marabou shuck and woodduck legs.

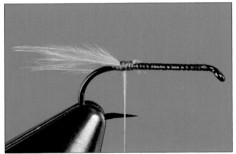

Step 1: Attach the thread and wrap to tailing point. Secure a bundle of marabou fibers extending rearward about the distance of one hook-gap. Clip and bind the butts. Position the thread atop the rearmost thread wraps.

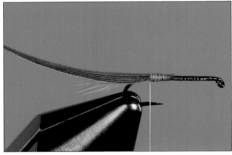

Step 2: Cut a section of duck or goose quill about ⅔ the width of the hook gap. Mount it by the tip atop the tailing wraps, taking care to keep the quill as flat as possible on top of the shank.

Step 3: Use the *direct dubbing* method (p. 34) to dub the rear half of the body.

Step 4: Using the method shown in *side-mounted legs* (p. 39), mount a bundle of woodduck fibers on either side of the shank, extending outward about the distance of one hook-gap, as shown in this top view.

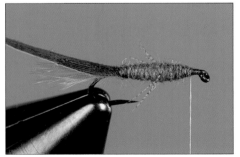

Step 5: Clip and bind the excess fiber butts. Dub the front half of the body, stopping about 6 thread-wraps behind the eye.

Step 6: Fold the quill section over the top of the body, and secure it at the front of the dubbing. Clip and bind the excess. Form the head of the fly and whip finish.

Stillborn Emerger

Originator: Shane Stalcup
Hook: TMC 101, or equivalent dry-fly hook, #14-#22
Thread: Brown 8/0
Shuck: Rust Z-Lon
Rear gills: Rusty brown marabou
Abdomen: Light brown Micro Tubing
Thorax: Pale-yellow fine poly dubbing
Hackle: Dun
Wings: Two Type 1 or Type 2 natural gray CDC feathers

The CDC shellback on this pattern represents wings stuck in the shuck of a stillborn mayfly. Colors and sizes can be changed for a variety of mayfly hatches; the version shown here is a PMD.

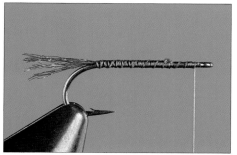

Step 1: Attach the tying thread and position it about ⅓ of a shank-length behind the eye. Secure a sparse bundle of Antron fibers, and wrap rearward, binding the Antron atop the shank and forming a smooth underbody. At the tailing point, reverse direction and wrap back to the hook eye. Clip the Antron to one hook-gap in length.

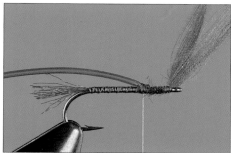

Step 2: Align the tips of the CDC feathers, and secure them atop the shank behind the eye. Position the thread ⅓ of a shank-length behind the eye, and tie in the body tubing.

Step 3: *Prepare a hackle feather* (p. 39) and mount it directly behind the CDC feathers as shown in *mounting collar hackle* (p. 37). Use the *direct dubbing* method (p. 34) to dub a thorax rearward to the tie-in point of the Antron. Position the thread at the rear of the thorax.

Step 4: Spiral the hackle rearward over the thorax as shown in *palmering hackle* (p. 38). Tie off and clip the hackle at the back of the thorax. Wrap the tying thread to the tailing point. Wrap the body tubing rearward; tie off the tubing at the tailing point, and clip the excess.

Step 5: Draw the CDC feathers rearward so that the barbs form a flat "panel" over the body and force the hackle barbs to the sides of the shank. Secure the CDC feather at the tailing point, and clip the excess feather to the length of the shuck. Mount 3-6 strands of marabou, by the tips, atop the CDC tie-off wraps.

Step 6: Using the method shown in *wrapping twisted-herl collars* (p. 49), wrap the marabou forward over the rear ⅓ of the shank. Tie off, clip the excess, and whip finish over these wraps. Trim away the hackle barbs beneath the shank, so that only the fibers projecting to the sides remain.

Tied Down Caddis

Hook: TMC 3761, Mustad 3906B, or equivalent 1XL
    nymph hook, #8-#14
Thread: Orange 6/0
Tail: Deer hair
Shellback: Deer hair
Body: Orange yarn
Hackle: Brown

This is an old standard. We're not sure of its origin, but the design suggests a Pacific Northwest pattern. It is most often fished on lakes as a stillborn/emerger pattern, though it can be fished in moving water where larger species of caddis are found.

Step 1: Attach the thread and wrap to the tailing point. *Clip, clean, and stack* (p. 32) a bundle of deer hair, and mount it to make a tail one hook-gap in length. Secure hair butts along the length of the shank for a uniform underbody over the rear ⅖ of the shank.

Step 2: *Clip, clean, and stack* (p. 32) a second bundle of hair. Clip the butts even, and mount the bundle directly atop the tailing wraps.

Step 3: *Prepare a hackle feather* (p. 39), and mount it atop the tailing wraps as explained in *mounting collar hackle* (p. 37). Mount a length of yarn atop the hackle stem, and bind it along the rear ⅖ of the shank to make a level underbody.

Step 4: Wrap the yarn forward, and tie off at the front of the underbody. Clip and bind the excess.

Step 5: Wrap the hackle forward as explained in *palmering hackle* (p. 38), and tie off at the front of the underbody.

Step 6: Fold the deer hair forward over the top of the body. Secure it atop the shank in front of the hackle. Clip and bind the excess hair. Form the head of the fly and whip finish.

Lady McConnell

Originator: Brian Chan
Hook: TMC 5212, or other 2XL dry-fly hook, #10-#16
Thread: Black 6/0
Shuck: Grizzly hackle tip
Body: Gray poly dubbing
Shellback: Deer hair
Hackle: Grizzly

Brian Chan designed this pattern for McConnell Lake near Kamloops. It represents a fully hatched midge that is still trailing the shuck. A higher-floating pattern, it's easy to see on flat or slightly ruffled lake surfaces.

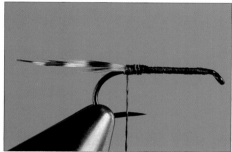

Step 1: Attach the tying thread and wrap to tailing point. Secure a grizzly hackle tip to make a shuck about one shank-length long. Position the thread atop the rearmost tail-mounting wrap.

Step 2: *Clip, clean, and stack* (p. 32) a bundle of deer hair. Use a sparse bundle—just enough to make shellback that will cover the top of the body. Secure the hair by the tips atop the shank, and bind down the tips to make a smooth underbody.

Step 3: Use the *direct dubbing* method (p. 34) to dub a body over the rear ⅓ of the hook shank.

Step 4: Fold the deer hair forward over the top of the shank, and secure it at the front of the body. Cover the butts with thread to make a foundation for the hackle, and position the thread at the rearmost tie-down wrap.

Step 5: *Prepare a hackle feather* (p. 39), and mount it as explained in *mounting collar hackle* (p. 37).

Step 6: Wrap and tie off the hackle as shown in *wrapping dry-fly hackle* (p. 44). Clip and bind down the excess feather. Form the head of the fly and whip finish.

Raccoon

Originator: Paul Lasha
Hook: TMC 100 or 101, or equivalent dry-fly hook, #12-#18
Thread: Black 6/0
Shuck: Teal flank feathers or grizzly hackle tip
Butt: White ostrich herl
Shellback: Deer or elk hair
Body: Black Super Fine dubbing

Philip Rowley introduced us to this pattern. To make the shuck, he substitutes teal flank for the grizzly hackle on the original pattern. It can be tied in a variety of colors by altering thread and dubbing colors.

Step 1: Attach the thread and position it at the tailing point. Secure a bundle of teal flank to make a shuck about ⅔ of a shank-length long. Bind the butts along the top of the shank for a smooth underbody. Mount one ostrich herl above the rearmost thread wraps.

Step 2: Take 5 or 6 wraps of the herl to form a collar as explained in *wrapping single-herl collars* (p. 48).

Step 3: *Clip, clean, and stack* (p. 32) a bundle of deer hair. Mount the hair ahead of the collar, and bind the excess atop the shank for a smooth underbody.

Step 4: Use the *direct dubbing* method (p. 34) to dub a slender body, ending just behind the hook eye.

Step 5: Draw the fibers over the top of the hook shank, and secure them behind the hook eye. Then lift the excess hair, and take a few wraps around the shank only, and whip finish behind the eye.

Step 6: Trim the hair butts to make a short, tuft-like head.

Cooper's Bug

Hook: TMC 101, or equivalent 1X fine dry-fly, #16-#26
Thread: Yellow 6/0
Tail: Elk hair
Body: Yellow tying thread
Shellback: Elk hair
Hackle: Grizzly

We first saw this pattern years ago tied with peacock herl as a beetle imitation. But it is highly adaptable and can be used to imitate both emerging mayflies and midge, depending on size and color. It is an easy pattern to dress in very small sizes.

Step 1: Attach the thread and position at the tailing point. *Clip, clean, and stack* (p. 32) a bundle of elk hair. Mount the hair atop the shank to make a tail about ½ the length of the shank. Bind the hair in with 4-5 smooth, even wraps, since these will be visible on the finished fly.

Step 2: Smooth the hair butts rearward. With a *flattened thread* (p. 37), wrap forward to the hook eye, then back to the tail-mounting wraps, forming a smooth underbody.

Step 3: With a *twisted thread* (p. 42), wrap forward again over the rear ⅔ of the shank to make a segmented body.

Step 4: *Prepare a hackle feather* (p. 39), and mount it as explained in *mounting collar hackle* (p. 37). With a twisted thread, continue forming a segmented body from the hackle-mounting point forward about 5 thread wraps.

Step 5: Wrap the hackle forward 3-5 turns as explained in *wrapping dry-fly hackle* (p. 44). Place the hackle wraps in the "grooves" between the thread wraps. Tie off and clip the feather tip.

Step 6: Fold the elk hair forward over the top of the shank, and secure behind the hook eye. Whip finish beneath the hair butts, around the shank only. Then clip the butts to form a small head.

Shellback Midge Pupa

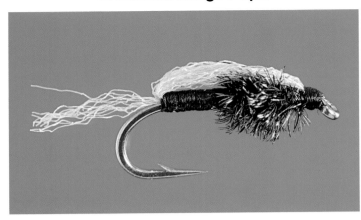

Hook: TMC 100, or equivalent dry-fly hook, #18-#22
Thread: Black 14/0
Shuck: Gray poly yarn
Abdomen: Black tying thread
Shellback: Gray poly yarn
Thorax: Peacock herl

This simple, low-floating pattern can be tied in colors to match any midge hatch. The ease of tying makes this design suitable for small hook sizes.

Step 1: Attach the thread and position it at the tailing point. Mount a few fibers of poly yarn to make a trailing shuck about one shank-length long.

Step 2: Mount the shellback yarn directly over the tail-mounting wraps. Secure the yarn to the top of the shank with smooth, uniform thread wraps to form the abdomen of the fly over the rear ⅔ of the shank.

Step 3: Mount 1-2 strands of peacock atop the abdomen at the midpoint of the shank.

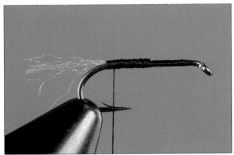

Step 4: Form the thorax as explained in *wrapping twisted-herl collars* (p. 49), stopping about 5 thread-wraps' distance behind the hook eye.

Step 5: Fold the shellback yarn over a dubbing needle placed crosswise atop the shank.

Step 6: Secure the yarn in front of the thorax. Clip and bind the excess. Form the head of the fly and whip finish.

Nymerger

Originator: Darrel Martin
Hook: TMC 900BL, or equivalent dry-fly hook, #18-#24
Thread: Tan 8/0
Tail: Tan CDC
Body: Tying thread
Overbody: Tan CDC fibers
Thorax: Tan CDC dubbing
Wing: Tan CDC

Martin Westbeek of the Netherlands showed us this method of tying Darrel Martin's "nymph/emerger" pattern, the Nymerger. Westbeek says, "If trout are sipping small stuff from the water, the Nymerger is my first choice." This all-CDC pattern sits low in the film. It's an easy pattern to tie even on very small hooks. Westbeek likes olive, natural gray, and black, in addition to the tan variety shown here. Different colors of thread and CDC can combined in one fly to match specific hatches.

Step 1: Attach the thread and position it at the tailing point. Mount 8-10 CDC barbs for the tail. Use a *flattened thread* (p. 37) to wrap forward to the midpoint of the shank, securing the tail fibers atop the shank. Clip the excess CDC and trim the tails to one hook-gap in length.

Step 2: Gather a bundle of long CDC fibers as shown in *stripping CDC barbs* (p. 40) and secure them atop the hook at the midpoint of the shank. Use a flattened thread to wrap rearward, securing the barbs atop the shank right up to the tailing point. Wrap a flattened thread forward again to the midpoint of the shank.

Step 3: Fold the bundle of CDC forward over the top of the shank, Humpy-style. Don't pull the barbs tight; they should form a bubble-like overbody. Continue wrapping forward, binding the bundle to the hook eye.

Step 4: Use the *direct dubbing* method (p. 34) to dub the thorax. Don't twist the CDC dubbing too tightly; the thorax should be shaggy, as shown. Dub from the hook eye rearward, so that the tying thread is positioned at the rear of the thorax after dubbing

Step 5: Draw the CDC fibers rearward over the thorax, again not too tightly; you want the fibers to trap some air beneath the wing case. Secure the CDC at the rear of the thorax. Whip finish the fly at the rear of the thorax.

Step 6: Trim the wing so that it extends to the hook bend, as shown. Use a dubbing teaser or needle to pick out fibers from the sides of the thorax for legs. Clip away any stray or out-of-place fibers.

Whitlock Emerging Pupa

Originator: Dave Whitlock
Hook: TMC 101, or other ring-eye dry-fly hook, #14-#18
Thread: Black 8/0
Shuck: Gray ostrich herl tips
Body: Natural dark deer hair
Rib: Black tying thread
Thorax: Gray ostrich herl

Since deer hair gives this pattern good buoyancy, we fish it without floatant, since paste types can mat the ostrich collar. The key to tying this pattern in smaller sizes is to use finely textured deer hair, which gives a sleek body that still provides floatation.

Step 1: Attach the thread and wrap to the tailing point, leaving a 6" tag of thread. Mount 1 or 2 ostrich herl tips to form a tail about one hook-gap long. Clip and bind the excess. Position the thread ⅓ of a shank-length behind the hook eye.

Step 2: *Clip, clean, and stack* (p. 32) a bundle of deer hair. Clip the tips back ⅛". Position the hair tips as shown, so that they encircle the hook shank. Take a loose wrap of thread completely around the hair, then tighten so that the hair is distributed around the shank.

Step 3: Bind the butts of the hair tightly to the shank, stopping at the tail-mounting point.

Step 4: Position the thread a few thread-wraps' distance behind the eye. Smooth the hair forward so that it encircles the shank in a tight capsule, and bind down.

Step 5: Spiral the thread tag forward to rib the body. Tie off and clip. Mount a strand of ostrich herl atop the ribbing tie-off wraps.

Step 6: Wrap the ostrich forward as shown in *wrapping single-herl collars* (p. 48). Clip and bind down the excess. Whip finish.

BWO Floating Nymph

Originator: A.K. Best
Hook: TMC 100, or equivalent dry-fly hook, #14-#20
Thread: Dark brown 6/0
Tail: Elk hair
Underbody: Elk hair
Rib: Tying thread
Abdomen: Olive-brown fur or synthetic dubbing
Wing case: Goose quill section
Thorax: Brown fur or synthetic dubbing

This inventive design uses the technique for a drawn wing case to form a buoyant underbody on this floating nymph pattern.

Step 1: Attach the thread, leaving a 6" tag for ribbing. Position the thread and tag at the tailing point. *Clip, clean, and stack* (p. 32) about 10-20 elk hairs, depending on fly size. Mount the hair to form a tail one shank-length long. Bind the hair butts atop the shank, as shown, stopping a short distance behind the hook eye.

Step 2: Position the tying thread at the midpoint of the shank. Fold the hair butts back over the top of the shank, and secure as shown. Then return thread to the front of the underbody.

Step 3: Fold the hair forward again over the thorax portion of the fly. Secure the hair in front of the under-body. Clip and bind the excess. Spiral the thread back to the tail-mounting wraps.

Step 4: Use the *direct dubbing* method (p. 34) to dub the abdomen of the fly, and rib with the tag of thread left in Step 1. Tie off and clip the ribbing thread directly ahead of the abdomen.

Step 5: Mount a section of goose wing quill at the front of the abdomen. Dub a thorax, completely covering the elk hair underbody, and position the thread a short distance behind the hook eye.

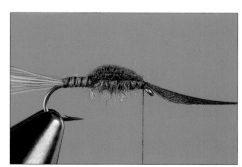

Step 6: Fold the quill section forward to form a wing case. Secure the quill behind the hook eye. Bind and clip the excess. Form the head of the fly and whip finish.

Chapter 7: Tuft Emergers

The defining element of this fly style is a tuft of material—hair, synthetic fibers, feathers or feather barbs—that projects outward over the hook eye. Certainly there are exceptions, but broadly speaking a large number of tuft emerger patterns are really descendents of two design ancestors—the Quigley Cripple, with its distinctive deer-hair tuft; and the European Shuttlecock style, with its conspicuous plume of CDC feathers. On flush-floating patterns, the tuft suggests the emerging wings of the insect. On descending-body designs, where part or all of the fly abdomen hangs beneath the surface, the tuft may suggest the wings and/or the body of the insect climbing out onto the surface film.

In a great many tuft-style emergers the tuft is the component most responsible for floating the fly and positioning it properly on the water. One benefit of the tuft is its visibility to the angler, particularly on low-floating or descending-body designs; many tyers in fact choose light or brightly colored tuft materials to maximize this attribute. Some tuft emergers permit a choice in the type of profile they present in the water. If only the tuft (and sometimes thorax) is dressed with floatant, the fly will sit more vertically; if the entire fly is dressed, the body will lie flush in the film. All in all, its one of the most versatile of emerger styles.

Halo Emerger

Originator: Gary LaFontaine
Hook: Dai Riki 300, or other standard dry-fly hook, #8-#24
Thread: Brown 8/0
Tag: Clear Antron
Tail: Brown marabou fibers
Body: Olive-brown fine poly dubbing
Wing: Thin Ethafoam
Tuft: Dyed orange elk or deer hair

Gary LaFontaine based this unusual design on his underwater observations of hatching mayflies. One of the keys to its effectiveness, he notes, is the orange tuft, and this component should be preserved if tail and body colors are changed to match other hatches.

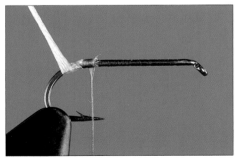

Step 1: Attach the thread and wrap to a point just above the hook barb. Mount a sparse strand of clear Antron. Wrap the Antron down around the hook bend, as shown.

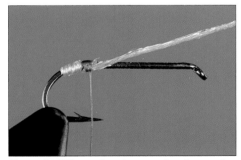

Step 2: Wrap the Antron back up the hook bend to the mounting wraps. Tie off and clip the excess.

Step 3: Tie in a sparse bundle of stripped marabou fibers directly atop the rearmost thread wraps. The tail should be about one shank-length long. Clip and bind down the excess.

Step 4: Advance the tying thread to the hook eye, laying a thread foundation. Return the thread to a point about ⅓ of a shank-length behind the eye. Cut a strip of thin foam about ½ the hook gap in width and 2" long. Position the foam crosswise over the shank, and secure it with crisscross wraps, as shown in this top view.

Step 5: Hold a dubbing needle parallel to the hook shank, and fold the foam strip on the far side of the shank over the top of the needle, making a double thickness of foam about ¼ to ⅓ the length of the hook shank, as shown in this top view.

Step 6: Using 2 or 3 crisscross wraps, secure the folded tag of foam directly atop the original mounting wraps, as shown here from the top.

Step 7: Pull the tag of foam toward you, and clip it close to the thread wraps, as shown in this top view.

Step 8: Repeat Steps 5-7 with the strip of foam on the near side of the shank to form a matching wing, as shown here from the top.

Step 9: Return the tying thread to the tailing position, and use the *direct dubbing* method (p. 34) to dub a slender abdomen.

Step 10: Form the thorax by taking crisscross wraps over the wing-mounting thread. Position the thread ahead of the thorax.

Step 11: *Clip, clean, and stack* (p. 32) a small bundle of deer or elk hair. Mount the hair atop the shank, with the tips extending over the hook eye about ¾ of a shank-length.

Step 12: Trim the hair butts as shown, but do not bind them down with thread. Whip finish behind the eye, under the tuft.

EZ-Sight Cripple

Originator: Richard W. Murphy, Sr.
Hook: TMC 2487 or 206BL, or other light-wire scud hook,
    #14-#20
Thread: Olive-brown 8/0
Shuck: White SAPP Body Fur (6-8 strands) or white
    Micro-Zelon
Abdomen: Olive-brown 6/0 thread
Thorax: Peacock herl
Wing: ¹⁄₃₂" Evasote foam
Hackle: Dun
Tuft: Dyed orange calf or goat body hair

This design combines elements of the Halo Emerger and the Quigley Cripple. Guide Richard W. Murphy favors it in size 20 for spring and fall BWO hatches, and in size 16 for hatches of PMDs. It is easy to see and is effective. He recommends treating only the front half of the fly with floatant so that the tail and abdomen sink beneath the film.

Step 1: Attach the thread and wrap to the tailing point. Mount the shuck fibers to form a shuck one shank-length long. Wrap the tying thread back and forth over the rear half of the hook shank to produce a slim, slightly tapered abdomen. Use a *twisted thread* (p. 42) to give the abdomen a segmented appearance.

Step 2: Cut a pair of foam wings to the shape shown—an hourglass with rounded tips. Overall wing length should be about one shank-length, and the width about ⅓ the hook gap. Use crisscross wraps to mount the wings atop the shank about ⅓ the distance from the front of the abdomen to the hook eye, as shown here from the top.

Step 3: Mount 2-3 strands of peacock herl at the front of the abdomen, and using the technique shown in *wrapping twisted-herl collars* (p. 49), form a thorax. Take the last wrap of herl ahead of the wings.

Step 4: *Clip, clean, and stack* (p. 32) a small bundle of calf or goat body hair. Secure the hair directly atop the shank with the tips extending over the hook eye a distance of about one hook-gap.

Step 5: *Prepare a hackle feather* (p. 39), and use the steps shown in *mounting collar hackle* (p. 37) to secure the feather stem over the thread wraps securing the hair.

Step 6: Using the method shown in *wrapping dry-fly hackle* (p. 44), take one or two wraps of hackle behind the thread wraps used to mount the hair tuft. Secure the hackle tip and clip the excess feather. Whip finish over the tuft-mounting wraps.

Candy Cane

Hook: TMC 900BL, or equivalent dry-fly hook, #12-#20
Thread: White 8/0
Tail: Cream Antron yarn
Abdomen: White tying thread
Rib: Red Flex-Floss
Thorax: Tan Antron dubbing
Tuft: Cream poly yarn

Virtually everything about this standard midge pupa design can be altered to match other hatches—size, colors, body and ribbing materials. Many tyers substitute Antron yarn or a CDC puff for the poly tuft.

Step 1: Attach the thread and position it behind the hook eye. Mount a piece of poly yarn atop the shank, extending over the hook eye. Secure with 5 or 6 tight wraps toward the hook bend. Clip and bind the excess.

Step 2: Mount a sparse length of Antron yarn for the tail just behind the tie-off wraps securing the poly yarn. Bind the Antron atop the shank with smooth, uniform wraps, moving toward the hook bend.

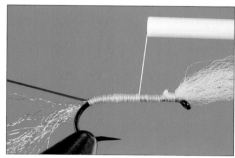

Step 3: Mount the ribbing material directly atop the rearmost wraps securing the Antron. Secure it with 5 or 6 tight thread wraps, then stretch the tag tightly, and clip it. With a *flattened thread* (p. 37) and form a slender, smooth abdomen of tying thread over the rear ¾ of the hook shank.

Step 4: When the abdomen is complete, spiral the ribbing material forward. The rib can be made wide or narrow, depending on how tightly the Flex-Floss is stretched; either way, maintain consistent tension on the material to produce a uniform rib.

Step 5: Tie off the ribbing at the front of the abdomen, and use the *direct dubbing* method (p. 34) to dub a short thorax.

Step 6: Whip finish the fly beneath the poly tuft, around the shank only. Clip the tail to about ½ the hook gap in length; clip the front tuft to about ½ the body length.

Palomino Midge

Originator: Brett Smith
Hook: TMC 2487, or other light-wire scud hook, #18-#22
Thread: Brown 8/0
Abdomen: Olive-brown New Dub
Wing case: White Z-Lon
Thorax: Brown rabbit dubbing

This Brett Smith fly was introduced to tyers about ten years ago and quickly became popular. It is lifelike, simple to tie even in small sizes, and effective, particularly on lakes. Dressing just the tuft will cause the fly to ride vertically.

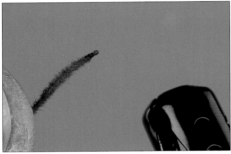

Step 1: Clip a short length of New Dub. Very briefly touch the end of the material to a flame to singe it to a point, as shown.

Step 2: Attach the thread and position it at the tailing point. Secure the New Dub with the pointed end extending rearward from the mounting wraps about one shank-length. Clip and bind down the excess.

Step 3: Mount a length of Z-Lon directly atop the wraps, securing the New Dub abdomen. Clip the excess.

Step 4: Use the *direct dubbing* method (p. 34) to dub a short, ball-like thorax.

Step 5: Fold the Z-Lon over the top of the thorax, and secure behind the hook eye.

Step 6: Fold the Z-Lon tag rearward, and whip finish the fly around the hook shank only. Then clip the Z-Lon to the same length as the thorax.

CDC Tuft Emerger—Trico

Hook: TMC 2488, or other fine-wire scud hook, #14-#20
Thread: Brown 14/0
Shuck: Cream Antron
Abdomen: Olive fine poly dubbing
Thorax: Dark brown fine poly dubbing
Tuft: Dun Type 3 CDC feather (puff)

This simple, but very productive, design seems to have popped up in various places simultaneously. Colors and sizes can be altered to match a variety of mayfly species.

Step 1: Attach the tying thread and position it about ⅓ the shank-length behind the hook eye. Mount a CDC puff at the very base with 2 light thread wraps. Pull the feather butt, sliding the feather beneath the wraps, to produce a wing tuft about one shank-length long.

Step 2: When the wing is properly sized, secure the feather butt and clip the excess. Wrap the thread to a point just around the hook bend, and mount a sparse piece of Antron yarn to make a shuck about ⅔ of a shank-length long.

Step 3: Use the olive dubbing to dub an abdomen over the rear half of the shank.

Step 4: Use the brown dubbing to dub a thorax that reaches to the base of the wing tuft.

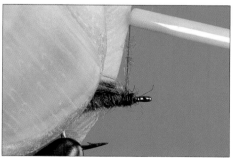

Step 5: When the wing tuft is reached, smooth the CDC fibers rearward, and continue building the abdomen to a point just behind the hook eye. Form the head of the fly and whip finish.

CDC Pop Emerger—BWO

Originators: Tony Gehman and Dave Eshenower
Hook: TMC 900BL, or equivalent dry-fly hook, #14-#20
Thread: Olive 8/0
Shuck: Olive Antron or Z-Lon
Body: Olive fine poly dubbing
Tuft: One or two gray Type 4 CDC feathers

This variation of the preceding pattern is a good way of utilizing Type 4 CDC feathers which would otherwise have limited use. Intact feather tips are shown here, but stripped CDC barbs can also be used. This emerger design seems to have originated simultaneously in many parts of the country. This is our version of a pattern first shown to us by Tony Gehman and Dave Eshenower, who used the name Pop Emerger.

Step 1: Attach the thread and position it about 2-3 thread-wraps behind the hook eye. Stack the CDC feathers so that the tips are aligned and the curvatures match. Mount them using two firm, but not tight, wraps.

Step 2: With the right hand, put a slight tension on the bobbin. With the left fingers, pull the feather butts rearward, sliding the feather beneath the wraps to produce a tuft one shank-length long. Secure the feather with additional tight wraps. Clip and bind the excess.

Step 3: Wrap the thread to the tailing point, and mount the Antron yarn to form a shuck about ¾ the length of the hook shank.

Step 4: Use the *direct dubbing* method (p. 34) to dub a tapered body to the base of the wing tuft.

Step 5: Draw the tuft fibers rearward, fanning them over the top half of the body. Take a few thread wraps against the base of the CDC to secure them. Whip finish the fly.

Step 6: The finished wing should be slightly arced, as shown in this front view, and angled about 45 degrees over the hook eye.

Once and Away

Originator: Hans van Klinken
Hook: TMC 200R, or other curved long-shank hook, #12-#18
Thread: Black 8/0
Abdomen: Blue dun hackle quill
Thorax: Peacock herl
Wing case and tuft: Four natural gray Type 2 CDC feathers

The use of stripped hackle quill for the abdomen gives this fly a slender, elegant, and realistic appearance. But other materials can be used as well—tying thread, moose mane, peccary, horse hair, peacock or ostrich quill.

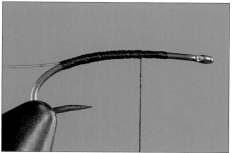

Step 1: Attach the thread and wrap to the tailing point. Secure the hackle quill by the tip with a *flattened thread* (p. 37). Wrap forward, securing the fiber and laying a smooth thread foundation along the rear ⅔ of the shank.

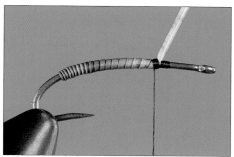

Step 2: Wrap the quill forward in touching, but not overlapping, turns. When the front of the thread foundation is reached, bind and clip the excess quill.

Step 3: Stack the CDC feathers so that the tips are aligned and the curvatures match. Mount them near the butts, directly ahead of the abdomen. Then mount 3 strands of peacock herl directly ahead of the CDC feathers.

Step 4: Using the method explained in *wrapping twisted-herl collars* (p. 49), form the thorax; tie off and clip the herls a short distance behind the hook eye.

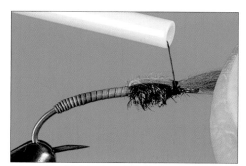

Step 5: Fold the CDC feathers over the herl, keeping all the barbs atop the thorax. Secure the CDC feathers behind the hook eye.

Step 6: Elevate the CDC feather tips by pulling them rearward with the left fingers and building a thread bump ahead of them until the feather tips are held nearly vertical. Whip finish behind the hook eye, around the shank only. Clip the feather tips to about the length of the abdomen.

Lace Midge Emerger

Originator: Bruce Salzburg
Hook: TMC 2487, or other fine-wire scud hook, #16-#22
Thread: Red 8/0
Abdomen: Clear vinyl tubing
Thorax: Golden brown rabbit dubbing
Wing case and tuft: One white Type 1 or Type 2 CDC feather

This pattern takes advantage of both the lifelike effects and the durability that are achieved by wrapping clear vinyl tubing over a colored thread underbody.

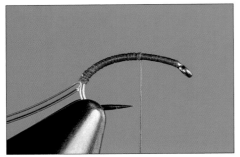

Step 1: Attach the thread behind the hook eye. Wrap a *flattened thread* (p. 37) to the rearmost point of the body, laying a smooth thread foundation. Trim the tip of the tubing at an angle, and mount the tubing by the point. Secure it firmly and wrap a flattened thread forward ⅔ of the distance to the hook eye.

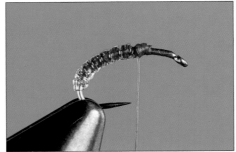

Step 2: Wrap the tubing forward, stretching it with enough tension to produce body segments proportional to the hook size. When the tying thread is reached, secure the tubing firmly. Lift the tubing and take two wraps around the shank only, against the base of the tubing. Stretch the tubing tag, clip, and firmly bind the end.

Step 3: Mount one CDC feather, tip to the rear, directly ahead of the tubing.

Step 4: Use the *direct dubbing* method (p. 34) to dub a ball-like thorax, ending a short distance behind the hook eye.

Step 5: Draw the CDC feather forward over the top of the thorax, and secure behind the hook eye.

Step 6: Whip finish beneath the feather tip, around the shank only, to elevate the tip slightly. Trim the feather tip to about the length of the wing case.

Mighty Midge

Originator: Hans van Klinken
Hook: Partridge K14ST, or other light-wire scud hook, #16-#18
Thread: Black 8/0
Abdomen: Two very fine dun hackle tips
Thorax: Peacock herl
Wing case and tuft: Four small natural gray CDC feather

This pattern is essentially a Once and Away (p. 129) tied with hackle points, instead of quill, for the abdomen. Except for the tuft, the whole fly slims down when wet and takes on a very lifelike appearance.

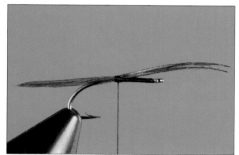

Step 1: Attach the thread and position it at the tailing point. Mount the hackle feathers to extend beyond the hook bend a distance equal to the hook gap; clip the excess. Position the thread atop the rearmost mounting wrap.

Step 2: Stack the CDC feathers so that the tips are aligned and the curvatures match. Mount the feathers with two light thread wraps. Take the thread wraps near the butt, with the tips of the feathers extending rearward.

Step 3: With the left fingers, put a bit of tension on the bobbin. With the right fingers, pull the butts of the feathers toward the hook eye, sliding the feathers beneath the thread wraps. Stop when the tips of the feathers are about half again as long as the hackle feathers forming the abdomen.

Step 4: Secure the CDC feathers and clip the excess. Mount two strands of peacock herl directly ahead of the CDC feathers. Position the thread 6-7 thread-wraps' distance behind the hook eye.

Step 5: Form the thorax as shown in *wrapping twisted-herl collars* (p. 49). Bind and clip the excess herl, and position the thread at the front of the thorax.

Step 6: Draw the CDC feathers over the top of the thorax, taking care to keep all the barbs atop the herl. Secure the CDC behind the hook eye to form a tuft that extends horizontally. Build a bump of thread ahead of the tuft to elevate it slightly. Whip finish, and trim the tuft to the length of the thorax.

CDC Bubble Emerger

Originator: A. Piller
Hook: TMC 900BL, or equivalent dry-fly hook, #14-#20
Thread: Black 12/0 or 14/0
Shuck: CDC feather tip from body
Abdomen: Natural Type 1 or Type 2 CDC feather
Thorax/tuft: Natural Type 1 or Type 2 CDC feather

This unusual use of CDC was shown to us by Italian tyer Giuseppe Nova, who notes that it is an excellent slow-water emerger pattern. Feather length is important—the longer, the better; a long feather minimizes wraps taken with the thick end of the feather stem. CDC feathers vary significantly in their conformation, and each fly tied may be slightly different than the next. They all fish, however.

Step 1: Mount the tying thread and position it at the tailing point. Select a CDC feather and preen the lower barbs downward, leaving a tip section 2-3 times the hook-shank length.

Step 2: Mount the feather by taking two moderately tight turns over the bare stem just ahead of the preened-back lower barbs. Draw the butt of the feather forward, sliding the tip beneath the thread wraps to form a shuck about one hook-gap in length.

Step 3: When the tail is sized, bind it securely over the original mounting wraps. Lift the butt of the feather, and advance the tying thread to the mid-point of the shank.

Step 4: Clip the butt of the feather in hackle pliers, and begin wrapping. The first turn should cover the mounting wraps; then wrap forward to form the abdomen. Tie off the feather at the midpoint of the shank.

Step 5: Clip the excess CDC feather. Mount a second CDC feather directly ahead of the abdomen as shown in *tip-mounted hackle* (p. 41).

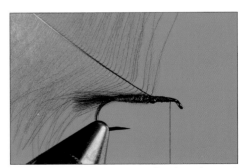

Step 6: Clip the excess feather tip and position the thread about 4 thread-wraps' distance behind the hook eye.

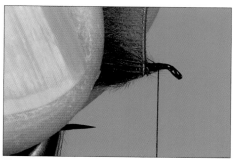

Step 7: Take 2-4 turns of the feather as explained in *wrapping wet-fly hackle* (p. 50). On each wrap, use the left fingers to preen the flared barbs of the previous wrap rearward to avoid trapping them beneath the stem.

Step 8: Wrap the thread rearward to the last hackle wrap; tie off the feather and clip the excess. Position the thread 3-4 wraps' distance behind the eye. Use a dubbing needle to free any trapped barbs, and to straighten any tangled barbs so that the CDC fibers all extend outward from the shank.

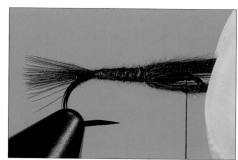

Step 9: With the right fingers, draw all the barbs smoothly and evenly forward past the tying thread to form a uniform capsule around the thorax. Pinch the bundle with the fingertips just beyond the hook eye.

Step 10: Push your fingertips back toward the hook so that they pinch the hook eye as well. This will bulge the CDC fibers to form a capsule. With the left fingers, take a soft wrap of thread behind the hook eye, capturing all the fibers. Then tighten down the wrap. Take additional firm wraps with the right hand.

Step 11: With the right fingers, draw all the CDC barbs up to the top of the shank, and take a few wraps toward the hook eye to secure them. Then lift the bundle and take a few wraps against the base of the barbs to elevate them to about 45 degrees. Whip finish the fly beneath the fibers, around the hook shank only.

Step 12: Clip the CDC tuft to about one shank-length.

CDC Suspender Buzzer Pupa

Originator: Henk Verhaar
Hook: TMC 2487, or other fine-wire scud hook, #12-#22
Thread: Bright red 6/0
Abdomen: Clear 5X tippet material
Thorax: Bright red angora goat dubbing
Tuft: Two Type 2 white CDC feathers

The tuft on this pattern from Henk Verhaar of the Netherlands is actually tied like a loop wing over the hook eye. The loop incorporates a generous amount of material and captures air in the interior, making this a good-floating pattern. Color can be varied to match other naturals.

Step 1: Attach the thread behind the hook eye, and wrap to the rear of the body in smooth wraps. Take a length of tippet material and crimp the end flat with pliers, as shown.

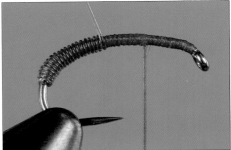

Step 2: Mount the flattened end of the mono, and wrap a *flattened thread* (p. 37) forward to form a smooth, uniform underbody over the rear ⅔ of the shank. Wrap the mono over the thread.

Step 3: Advance the thread to just behind the hook eye. Stack the two CDC feathers so that the tips are aligned and the curvatures match. Tie in the tips of the feathers behind the hook eye, as shown.

Step 4: Fold the butts of the feathers rearward, forming a loop over the hook eye that is about ¾ the overall hook length. On smaller patterns, folding the CDC feathers over a dubbing needle, as shown here, may help in forming a properly sized loop.

Step 5: Secure the feather butts directly atop the thread wraps used to mount the feather tips. Clip and bind the excess.

Step 6: Use the *direct dubbing* method (p. 34) to dub a shaggy thorax. Whip finish in front of the loop tuft.

Holographic Midge Suspender

Originator: Henk Verhaar
Hook: TMC 2487, or other fine-wire scud hook, #14-#18
Thread: Gray 8/0
Abdomen: Silver holographic tinsel
Thorax: Hare's ear dubbing
Wing: White CDC feather barbs

By varying the quantity of CDC used on the pattern, you can make a fly that sits either very high or very low in the water. Dutch tyer Henk Verhaar uses other body materials on this basic design—floss, tying thread, almost any material that makes a light, slender abdomen that sinks readily.

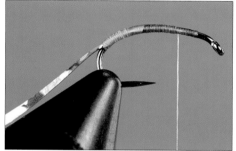

Step 1: Attach the thread and position it about ⅓ of the way around the hook bend. Secure a strand of tinsel. Wrap forward, binding the tag of tinsel to the shank and forming a smooth underbody. Wrap the thread ⅔ of the distance to the hook eye.

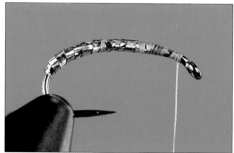

Step 2: Wrap the tinsel forward to form the abdomen. Tie off and clip the excess. Position the thread 2-3 thread-wraps' distance behind the eye.

Step 3: Gather a bundle of CDC barbs as explained in *stripping CDC barbs* (p. 40). Mount them atop the shank so that the tips extend over the hook eye a distance of about two shank-lengths. Clip the butts and bind the excess. Position the thread midway between the CDC and the abdomen.

Step 4: Fold the CDC barbs rearward, forming a loop wing about ½ the hook gap in height. Secure the fibers atop the shank.

Step 5: Fold the CDC barbs forward so that they lean against the loop wing. Wrap the thread forward to the base of the loop wing, securing the CDC fibers in position. You can use thread pressure to force the barbs around the shank to encircle the loop wing, almost like a parachute hackle, or just slant them over the top of the tuft.

Step 6: Use the *direct dubbing* method (p. 34) to dub a thorax from the front of the abdomen to the base of the wing. Whip finish around the shank only, beneath the loop wing.

Shuttlecock Buzzer

Originator: Clive Perkins
Hook: TMC 2487, or other fine-wire scud hook, #10-#18
Thread: Brown 8/0
Body: Brown Larva Lace
Wing case and tuft: Two to six Type 1, Type 2, or Type 4 CDC feathers

The Shuttlecock, more a style than a specific pattern, is a popular midge emerger design in the U.K. Body material can be varied, but the pattern should sit vertically in the water, so non-buoyant body materials are advisable. The tuft here is, obviously, designed to be highly visible to the angler.

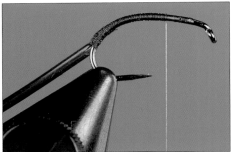

Step 1: Attach the thread and position it about halfway down the hook bend. Clip the Larva Lace to a point, and mount it by the point at the thread position. Position the thread ⅓ of a shank-length behind the hook eye.

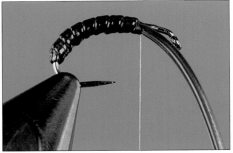

Step 2: Wrap the tubing forward to form the abdomen. Tie off the tubing ⅓ of a shank length behind the eye. Clip and bind the excess.

Step 3: Align the tips of the CDC feathers, and mount them directly ahead of the abdomen so that the feather tips extend rearward about two shank-lengths. Bind and clip the excess.

Step 4: Mount 2-4 strands of peacock herl directly ahead of the CDC.

Step 5: Form the thorax as shown in *wrapping twisted-herl collars* (p. 49), ending about 5 thread-wraps' distance behind the hook eye. Clip and bind the excess. Position the thread at the front edge of the thorax.

Step 6: Fold the CDC feathers over the thorax, forming a smooth wing case. Bind the feathers atop the shank directly ahead of the thorax. Lift the CDC tips and whip finish around the hook shank only.

Perky

Originator: Paul Canning
Hook: TMC 900BL, or equivalent dry-fly hook, #10-#12
Thread: Black 6/0
Body: Stripped grizzly hackle stem
Tuft: One Type 2 or 4 white or gray CDC feather

Designed primarily for stillwater fishing, this simple pattern can be tied with a variety of body materials and colors. Flies fished in rougher water can be dressed with two or more CDC feathers for the tuft.

Step 1: Attach the thread and position it behind the hook eye. Mount the CDC feather atop the shank, extending over the hook eye a distance of about two shank-lengths. Clip and bind the feather butt. Wrap the thread to the rearmost point of the body.

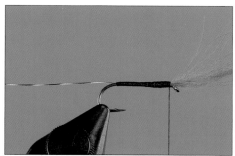

Step 2: Mount the hackle stem by the tip. Advance a *flattened thread* (p. 37) to the base of the CDC feather, creating a smooth underbody as you wrap forward.

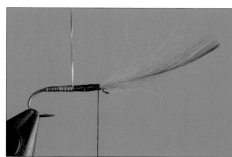

Step 3: Wrap the hackle stem forward to the base of the CDC.

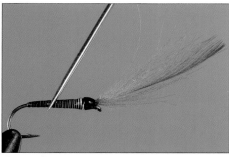

Step 4: Tie off the hackle stem to form a neat head, and whip finish. Coat the quill with head cement to improve durability.

CDC Crippled Emerger

Originator: Vladimir Markov
Hook: Mustad 94840, or other standard dry-fly hook, #10-#16; or light-wire scud hook #8-#14
Thread: Olive 8/0
Shuck: One Type 1 or 2 gray CDC feather
Body: Olive-brown poly dubbing
Hackle: Dun
Wings: Two Type 4 gray CDC feathers

This pattern emphasizes two of the most important triggers on an emerger pattern—the shuck and the wings. With CDC fore and aft, and hackle in the middle, this pattern floats high and well even in rougher water. It can be modified for many mayfly hatches.

Step 1: Attach the thread and position it behind the hook eye. Stack the CDC wing feathers front-to-front, so that they curve away from one another. Mount the feathers to form wings that extend beyond the eye about one hook-length. Clip and bind the butts.

Step 2: Wrap the thread to the tailing point. Form the shuck as explained in *reverse CDC shuck* (p. 53).

Step 3: Use the *direct dubbing* method (p. 34) to dub the abdomen to the midpoint of the shank.

Step 4: *Prepare a hackle feather* (p. 39), and secure it to the shank as explained in *mounting collar hackle* (p. 37).

Step 5: Dub the remainder of the body to the base of the CDC feathers.

Step 6: Spiral the hackle over the dubbed thorax as shown in *palmering hackle* (p. 38). Tie off and clip behind the hook eye. Form the head of the fly and whip finish.

Left-Handed Shortstop

Originator: Thomas C. Duncan, Sr.
Hook: TMC 200R, or other long-shank curved hook, #14-#20
Thread: Black 8/0
Shuck: White CDC barbs
Body: Mink fur with guard hairs
Hackle: White hen
Wing: One Type 1 or Type 2 white CDC feather

This is one of those patterns that looks like nothing in particular and everything in general. The pattern sits low in the film and is best suited to flatter water; in rougher currents, tyer Thomas Duncan tops the CDC tuft with some elk hair. He also ties the pattern in gray, using muskrat dubbing with the guard hairs left in.

Step 1: Attach the thread and position it behind the hook eye. Mount the CDC feather atop the shank so that it extends over the eye a distance of one shank-length. Clip and bind the excess. Position the thread at the tailing point.

Step 2: Mount a sparse bundle of CDC barbs atop the hook to make a shuck about ½ a shank-length long.

Step 3: Use the *direct dubbing* method (p. 34) to dub a slender, but slightly shaggy body, stopping 6-7 thread-wraps' distance behind the CDC tuft.

Step 4: *Prepare a hackle feather* (p. 39) and mount it directly ahead of the body as shown in *mounting collar hackle* (p. 37). Clip and bind the excess, and position the thread at the base of the CDC tuft.

Step 5: Take 2-4 wraps of the feather as explained in *wrapping wet-fly hackle* (p. 50). Tie off and clip the excess. Preen the hackle barbs rearward, and take a few thread wraps over the base of the barbs to slant them rearward. Then form a tapered head on the fly.

Step 6: Lift the CDC tuft, and take a few thread wraps against the front base to post the tuft slightly upward. Whip finish beneath the tuft, around the shank only.

Snowshoe-Hare Emerger

Originator: Jim Cannon
Hook: Orvis 1639, or other fine-wire scud hook, #18-#22
Thread: Olive 8/0
Abdomen: Olive goose biot
Thorax: Olive beaver underfur
Wing: Dun snowshoe hare fur

This midge emerger can be tied in a variety of colors, and we suspect the olive version pictured here would make a credible *Baetis* emerger as well. Jim Cannon's technique for preparing snowshoe hare fur for winging makes this effective material more practical and efficient for use on small patterns.

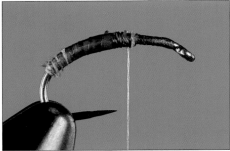

Step 1: Mount the thread and position it at the tailing point. Use the method shown in *biot body—smooth* (p. 31) to form an abdomen over the rear half of the hook shank. Clip and bind the excess biot.

Step 2: Trim a pinch of fur from a snowshoe hare's foot, preferably taking the fur anywhere from the midpoint of the foot to the heel. Cut once through the center of the fur bundle. Mix the hair as you would blend dubbing, by pulling the clump in two, stacking the halves, and repeating until the different textures of hair are well mixed.

Step 3: Take a small pinch of fur. Pull the hairs from one edge of the dubbing. Carefully stack the remaining dubbing atop these hairs, and pull out the hairs on the edge of the clump once again. The goal here is to produce a small bundle of aligned fibers pulled from the randomized dubbing.

Step 4: Take the small bundle of aligned hairs and mount them atop the shank about halfway between the front of the abdomen and the hook eye.

Step 5: Use the *direct dubbing* method (p. 34) to dub a thorax. Use wraps of dubbing to elevate the rear half of fur bundle to the vertical. Trim the rear portion of the hair parallel with the hook shank, leaving a tuft of hair over the hook eye.

Step 6: Take a turn or two of dubbing in front of the hair to elevate the forward bundle about 45 degrees upward. Whip finish beneath the tuft, around the shank only.

ILR PMD

Originator: Howard Cole
Hook: TMC 2487, or other fine-wire scud hook, #10-#20
Thread: Rust-brown 8/0
Undertail: Amber Z-Lon
Tail: Pheasant-tail barbs
Rib: Fine copper wire
Abdomen: Pheasant-tail barbs
Wing case: Gray snowshoe hare's foot
Thorax: Amber dubbing

This pattern makes good use of the floatation and sheen of snowshoe rabbit's foot by incorporating it into a slightly looped wing case and wing tuft. It can be modified for almost any mayfly hatch. The "ILR," says Howard Cole, stands for "I love rabbit."

Step 1: Attach the thread and position it at the tailing point. Mount a sparse bundle of Z-Lon atop the shank to make an undertail about one hook-gap in length. Clip and bind the excess. Mount three pheasant-tail barbs atop the Antron with two tight wraps to make a tail slightly longer than the Antron. Do not clip the excess.

Step 2: Mount the ribbing wire atop the wraps securing the pheasant barbs. Lift the barbs and bind the wire tag to the shank, stopping at the midpoint. Clip and bind the wire tag. Form an abdomen over the rear half of the hook shank as explained in *wrapping feather-barb bodies* (p. 45).

Step 3: *Counter-rib* (p. 33) the wire; clip and bind at the front of the abdomen. Clip a pinch of hair from near the heel of the rabbit foot. It should of relatively uniform length, moderately fine in texture, and crinkly. Mount it atop the shank ahead of the abdomen, so that the tips extend rearward about 1 ½ shank-lengths.

Step 4: Use the *direct dubbing* method (p. 34) to dub a thorax slightly thicker than the abdomen. Position the thread at the front of the thorax.

Step 5: Fold the hair over the thorax. Don't pull the hair tight; it should balloon out to the sides, forming a roughly hemispherical wing case. Secure the hair atop the shank, ahead of the thorax. Lift the hair, take a few wraps against the front base to post up the wing to 45 degrees, and whip finish around the shank.

Step 6: Here is a view of the underside. There should be enough space between shuck and thorax to trap a little air when the fly is resting on the surface film.

Pop Top Midge Emerger

Originator: Andy Burk
Hook: TMC 101, or other ring-eye dry-fly hook, #16-#24
Thread: Brown 8/0
Tuft: 2mm white closed-cell foam
Hackle: Grizzly hen neck
Thorax: Dark brown Superfine dubbing
Rib: One strand pearl Krystal Flash (#16-#20); fine gold wire (#22-#24)
Abdomen: Light brown Superfine dubbing

This unusual midge emerger is tied in reverse; it is simple to dress, highly durable, and places the most buoyant material directly above the heaviest part of the hook.

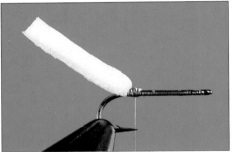

Step 1: Attach the thread and position it at the rear of the shank. Mount a length of 2mm foam that is roughly square in cross section. Bind and clip the butt.

Step 2: *Prepare a hackle feather* (p. 39), and mount it directly ahead of the foam strip as explained in *mounting collar hackle* (p. 37).

Step 3: Take two turns of the hackle feather as show in *wrapping dry-fly hackle* (p. 44). Bind and clip the feather tip.

Step 4: Use the *direct dubbing* method (p. 34) to dub a thorax extending about ⅓ the distance to the hook eye. Mount one strand of Krystal Flash (or fine gold wire on smaller hooks) just ahead of the thorax.

Step 5: Dub a slender abdomen, stopping a few thread-wraps behind the hook eye.

Step 6: Rib the body. Tie off the ribbing behind the hook eye and clip. Whip finish. Trim the foam tuft to about ¼ the shank length.

Quigley Cripple—Green Drake

Originator: Bob Quigley
Hook: TMC 900BL, or equivalent standard dry-fly hook, #8-#12
Thread: Olive 6/0
Tail: Olive grizzly marabou
Abdomen: Olive dubbing
Rib: Yellow floss
Thorax: Dark brown dubbing
Wing case and tuft: Deer hair
Hackle: Olive grizzly

Tied in the appropriate sizes and colors, the Quigley Cripple is one of the most widely used and effective emerger designs for almost any mayfly hatch. It is the precursor of many tuft-style emerging-mayfly patterns.

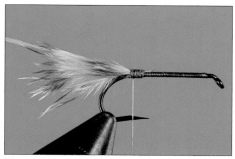

Step 1: Attach the thread and position it at the tailing point. Mount the marabou to form a tail about one shank-length long. Mount the ribbing material directly atop the rearmost tailing wraps.

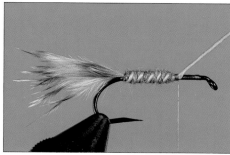

Step 2: Use the *direct dubbing* method (p. 34) to dub the abdomen over the rear half of the hook shank. Spiral the ribbing forward, and tie it off in front of the abdomen.

Step 3: Dub a thorax that extends from the front of the abdomen halfway to the hook eye. Position the thread at the front of the thorax.

Step 4: *Clip, clean, and stack* (p. 32) a bundle of deer hair. Mount the hair atop the shank directly in front of the thorax so that the tips extend forward about one shank-length. Bind the hair with 3 or 4 thread wraps toward the hook eye to lay a short foundation for the hackle.

Step 5: Clip the hair butts even with the back of the thorax. *Prepare a hackle feather* (p. 39) and mount it directly in front of the thorax as explained in *mounting collar hackle* (p. 37).

Step 6: Wrap the hackle forward as shown in *wrapping dry-fly hackle* (p. 44). Take 2 or 3 wraps of the feather behind the wing tuft. Elevate the tuft, and take one wrap of hackle ahead of the deer hair. Tie off the feather against the shank and clip. Form the head of the fly and whip finish.

PMD Cripple

Originator: Version of Bob Quigley design
Hook: TMC 900BL, or equivalent dry-fly hook, #14-#16
Thread: Yellow 8/0
Shuck: Amber Antron
Abdomen: Fine pale-yellow dubbing
Thorax: Arizona Synthetic Peacock dubbing, bronze
Wing case and tuft: Deer hair
Hackle: Dun

This pattern is hackled around the tuft only, making it a kind of parachute Quigley Cripple. Applying floatant to the entire fly will position it flush in the film. Dressing just the tuft, hackle, and wing case with floatant allows the abdomen to sink for a descending-body emerger.

Step 1: Attach the thread and position it at the tailing point. Mount a sparse bundle of Antron yarn to make a shuck one shank-length long. Use the *direct dubbing* method (p. 34) to dub a slender, slightly tapered abdomen over the rear half of the shank.

Step 2: Dub a thorax from the front of the abdomen halfway to the hook eye.

Step 3: *Clip, clean, and stack* (p. 32) a bundle of deer hair. Mount the hair atop the shank directly in front of the thorax so that the tips extend forward about one shank-length. Bind the hair tightly with 3 or 4 closely spaced thread wraps. Clip the hair butts even with the back of the thorax.

Step 4: *Prepare a hackle feather* (p. 39) and mount it at the rear base of the tuft, as explained in *horizontal-mount parachute hackle* (p. 37). Secure the feather with a couple of wraps behind the tuft; then fold the stem toward the hook eye and secure with additional wraps. Clip the excess. Take one thread wrap around the base of the post and hackle.

Step 5: The hackle is wrapped as explained in *wrapping parachute hackle* (p. 46). Spiral the bare feather stem a short distance up the tuft, and take each wrap of hackle *beneath* the preceding one. Raise the tuft with your left fingers each time the feather passes in front of the post.

Step 6: Take 3 or 4 wraps of hackle around the tuft, and tie off the feather tip in front of the tuft. Clip the excess and whip finish the fly. Put a drop of head cement at the base of the uppermost hackle wrap, and let it bleed downward into the base of the tuft.

Crippled CDC & Elk

Originator: Bruce Salzburg
Hook: TMC 2487, or other light-wire scud hook, #12-#16
Thread: Gray 6/0
Body: Type 1 or Type 4 natural dark dun CDC feather
Wing: Fine-tipped deer hair

This design combines the CDC & Elk with the Quigley Cripple. It can be fished in the film or submerged. It's easy to tie, floats well, and we've found it to be quite effective.

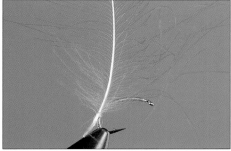

Step 1: Attach the thread and position it at the rearmost point of the body. Select a feather with the longest barbs equal to twice the shank length. Mount the feather at the butt with two light thread wraps.

Step 2: Pull the feather rearward, sliding it beneath the thread wraps to preen the barbs toward the feather tip. Leave a short tag of feather. Pull the thread to tighten the wraps, and take one more very tight wrap over the feather tip. Slip a turn of thread beneath the tag of feather to elevate it, then bind the tag down tightly.

Step 3: Wrap the thread forward, stopping 3-4 wraps behind the hook eye. Clip the feather butt in a hackle pliers, and wrap it forward in touching turns. When feather barbs begin to stand out from the shank, like a palmered hackle, stroke them rearward as each feather wrap is made.

Step 4: Tie off the feather where the thread is positioned. Bind and clip the excess.

Step 5: *Clip, clean, and stack* (p. 32) a bundle of deer hair. Mount it atop the shank, tips forward, to make a tuft about one shank-length long.

Step 6: Clip the butts to about ¼ the shank length. Whip finish around the shank, beneath the tuft.

Poxyback Green Drake Emerger

Originator: Mike Mercer
Hook: TMC 200R, or other curved long-shank hook, #12
Thread: Olive 6/0
Tail: 3 gray ostrich herl tips; brown Z-Lon; gray marabou, pearl Angel Hair
Abdomen: Olive turkey biot, pearl Flashabou
Gills: Natural gray marabou
Wing case: Dark mottled brown turkey tail coated with 5-minute epoxy
Thorax: Olive dubbing
Hackle: Grizzly saddle feather dyed olive
Wing: Deer hair
Head: ⅛" green closed-cell foam

This is one example of Mike Mercer's popular Poxyback Nymph series and a good illustration of his detailed and meticulous tying style. This pattern can be tied to represent a variety of mayflies, though Mercer omits the foam head on smaller patterns.

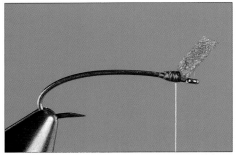

Step 1: Attach the thread and position it behind the hook eye. Cut a piece of foam one hook-gap in width, and secure it atop the shank so that it projects over the hook eye about ⅓ of a shank-length. Clip and bind the excess. Position the thread at the base of the foam.

Step 2: *Clip, clean, and stack* (p. 32) a bundle of deer hair. Mount it atop the shank, directly behind the foam to form a tuft about ¾ of a shank-length long. Clip and bind the excess. Advance the thread to the tailing point. Mount three ostrich herl tips atop the shank to form tails one shank-length long. Do not clip the excess.

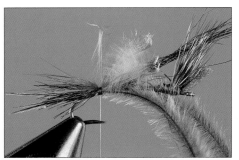

Step 3: Mount a sparse bundle of Z-Lon directly atop the herl-mounting wraps to form a tail about one hook-gap in length. Do not clip the excess. Mount a sparse bundle of marabou atop the Z-Lon to form a tail equal in length to the Z-Lon. Do not clip the excess.

Step 4: Mount a sparse bundle of Angel Hair over the marabou to make a tail equal in length to the marabou and Z-Lon. Do not clip the excess. Mount the turkey biot as explained in *biot bodies—fringed* (p. 30). With a flattened thread, bind the tags of all materials atop the hook, forming a smooth underbody to the midpoint of the shank.

Step 5: Wrap the biot forward to form the abdomen. Tie off and clip the excess at the midpoint of the shank. Tie in one strand of pearl Flashabou atop the shank, directly ahead of the abdomen. Clip the excess. Trim the Flashabou to the length of the Z-Lon tail.

Step 6: Using the technique shown in *side-mounted legs* (p. 39), mount a sparse clump of marabou on each side of the hook shank directly ahead of the abdomen, as shown in this top view. The marabou should extend rearward to the end of the abdomen. Clip and bind the excess.

Step 7: Cut a strip of turkey tail one hook-gap in width. Mount it with the dull, or back, side of the feather facing upward. Clip and bind the excess.

Step 8: Use the *direct dubbing* method (p. 34) to dub a thorax halfway to the hook eye. Position the thread at the front of the thorax.

Step 9: Fold the turkey tail over the thorax, and bind it down directly in front of the thorax.

Step 10: *Prepare a hackle feather* (p. 39) and mount it directly atop the thread wraps securing the front of the wing case as shown in *mounting collar hackle* (p. 37). With a flattened thread, wrap forward, forming a smooth underbody up to the base of the deer hair tuft.

Step 11: Wrap the hackle forward as shown in *wrapping dry-fly hackle* (p. 44). Place the hackle wraps very close together to produce a dense collar. Tie off the hackle atop the thread wraps at the base of the deer-hair tuft. Clip the excess. Whip finish around the shank, beneath the foam.

Step 12: Trim the hackle underneath the shank even with the hook point, as shown in this front view.

Step 13: Place a drop of 5-minute epoxy atop the turkey wing case to form a smooth, glossy "bubble."

Eastern Green Drake Emerger

Originator: Stephen Lopatic
Hook: Mustad 37160, or other scud hook, #10-#14
Thread: Black 8/0
Shuck: Grizzly olive marabou
Abdomen: Grizzly olive marabou
Tails: 3 moose mane hairs
Collar: Olive Antron dubbing
Hackle: Dark dun
Wings: Hen grizzly hackle tips
Thorax/head: ⅛" black closed-cell foam

Using hackle-tip wings on this Quigley Cripple allows for a closer match of the natural mayfly. Stephen Lopatic's original design uses mono eyes; we've omitted them here for slightly simpler tying. This pattern is particularly well suited to larger mayfly species, such as the green drake shown here, or *Hexagenia*.

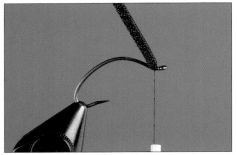

Step 1: Mount the tying thread and position it behind the hook eye. Cut a foam strip about ⅔ the hook gap in width. Secure it behind the hook eye. Stretch the tag of foam beyond the hook eye, and clip it close to the thread wraps. Bind down the excess.

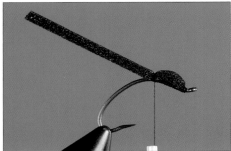

Step 2: Raise the foam and wrap the thread rearward to the front bend of the hook, or about ⅓ the shank length behind the eye. Fold the foam rearward, forming a humped thorax. Bind and clip the excess.

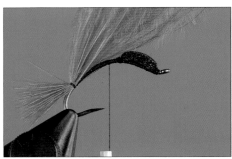

Step 3: Wrap the thread to the tailing point shown. Mount a marabou blood feather atop the shank to form a shuck equal in length to the hook gap. Secure it tightly. Lift the feather butt and wrap the thread forward to the midpoint of the shank.

Step 4: Grasp the feather butt, and wrap forward to form the abdomen. Tie off and clip the excess marabou at the midpoint of the shank.

Step 5: Align the tips of three moose mane fibers. Mount them atop the shank, directly ahead of the thorax, so that the tips extend rearward as far as the end of the marabou shuck and the fibers are slightly splayed. Bind and clip the excess.

Step 6: Position the thread at the rear of the foam thorax. Prepare two grizzly hen hackles by stripping away the lower barbs to leave feather tips as long as the overall hook length.

Step 7: Place one feather, with the front side facing outward, against the near side of the shank. Secure it directly behind the foam thorax. The feather should be butted against the foam, which splays the feather tip outward. Bind and clip the excess.

Step 8: Mount the second feather on the far side of the shank. Bind and clip the excess. The wings should splay apart, as shown in this top view.

Step 9: Wrap back to the front of the abdomen. Use the *direct dubbing* method (p. 34) to wrap a narrow collar of dubbing directly in front of the abdomen. *Prepare a hackle feather* (p. 39), and mount it directly ahead of the dubbed collar as explained in *mounting collar hackle* (p. 37)

Step 10: Wrap the hackle to the base of the feather-tip wings, about 4-5 wraps, as explained in *wrapping dry-fly hackle* (p. 44). Then tie off the feather behind the wings. Whip finish the fly behind the feather-tip wings.

Fancy PMD Emerger

Originator: Stephen Lopatic
Hook: Mustad 80260BR, or other light-wire scud hook, #12-#16
Thread: Black 8/0
Tail: Olive marabou
Rib: Green copper wire
Abdomen: Yellow Antron dubbing
Wing: Dyed-yellow mallard flank fibers
Hackle: Dark dun

The use of a feather-barb wing on this version of the Quigley Cripple gives wider latitude in matching the wing color or markings of specific hatches. And on small hooks, the feather barbs tie more easily, with less bulk, than the standard deer hair, making this version well suited to imitating smaller mayfly species.

Step 1: Mount the thread behind the hook eye, and wrap to the tailing point. *Align and strip* (p. 30) a sparse bundle of marabou fibers. Secure them atop the shank to make a tail one shank-length long. Mount the ribbing wire atop the rearmost thread wraps.

Step 2: Use the *direct dubbing* method (p. 34) to dub a slender abdomen over the rear ⅔ of the shank. Spiral the ribbing forward to rib the abdomen. Clip and bind the excess.

Step 3: Position the thread about four thread-wraps behind the hook eye. *Align and strip* (p. 30) a bundle of mallard flank fibers. Mount the bundle to form a wing one hook-length long. Hold the fibers butts atop the shank, and bind them down to the front of the abdomen. Clip the butts even with the middle of the abdomen.

Step 4: Wrap the thread forward to the wing. As you wrap, pinch the wing fibers flat to make a panel-like wing. Take a few thread wraps ahead of the wing to elevate it as shown. Then position the thread at the front of the abdomen.

Step 5: *Prepare a hackle feather* (p. 39), and mount it directly ahead of the abdomen as explained in *mounting collar hackle* (p. 37). Wrap the hackle to the base of the wing, about 4-5 wraps, as explained in *wrapping dry-fly hackle* (p. 44).

Step 6: Tie off the feather behind the wing. Whip finish the fly behind the wing. Then clip off the barbs on the underside of the shank, as shown in this front view.

Bug Lite Callibaetis

Originator: Herb Burton
Hook: TMC 200BR, or other curved long-shank hook, #12-#18
Thread: Olive 6/0
Tail: Golden pheasant tippet dyed olive
Rib: Fine copper wire
Abdomen: Olive-brown rabbit fur
Wing case: Coastal deer hair
Thorax: Olive-brown rabbit fur
Wing: Clipped butts from wing case

This emerger design by Herb Burton resembles the Warren Emerger (p. 152), but it is a bit simpler to tie and incorporates the more buoyant deer-hair butts into the wing. Burton notes that the key to fishing this fly is to soak the body with water and dress only the top of the wing with floatant in order to position the fly properly.

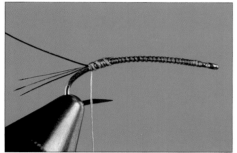

Step 1: Mount the tying thread and position it at the tailing point. Mount three golden pheasant fibers atop the shank to make a tail about ½ a shank-length long. Mount the ribbing wire directly atop the tailing wraps.

Step 2: Use the *direct dubbing* method (p. 34) to dub a slender abdomen over the rear half of the hook shank. Spiral the ribbing forward to the front of the abdomen; then tie off and clip the wire.

Step 3: *Clip, clean, and stack* (p. 32) a bundle of deer hair. Clip off about ⅛" of an inch from the tip of the bundle. Mount the hair by the tips atop the shank directly ahead of the abdomen. Clip and bind the excess.

Step 4: Dub a slender thorax to a point about 4-5 thread-wraps behind the hook eye.

Step 5: Form the wing case and elevate the wing as explained in Warren Emerger—March Brown, Steps 9-11, (p. 152).

Step 6: Whip finish beneath the tuft, around the hook shank only. Draw the hair butts upward, and clip them to a length equal to the length of the wing case.

Warren Emerger—March Brown

Originator: Gary Warren
Hook: TMC 900BL, or other standard dry-fly hook, #10-#14
Thread: Brown 6/0
Shuck: Mottled brown hen hackle fibers
Abdomen: Olive-brown dubbing
Wing case: Deer hair
Thorax: Olive-brown dubbing
Wing: Deer-hair tips from wing case

Oregon tyer Gary Warren showed us this design some years back, and it's become our "go-to" pattern, particularly in tough hatches. Colors and sizes can be varied to match almost any mayfly hatch, though for smaller hooks, the CDC version of this design (see Loop-Tuft BWO, p. 300) is easier to tie. The technique shown for forming the wing case in that tying sequence can also be used here with deer hair for a pronounced hump above the thorax. You can treat the whole fly with floatant, but we often treat only the wing case and wing to let the abdomen hang below the surface film.

Step 1: Mount the hook and wrap the thread to the tailing position. *Align and strip* (p. 30) a small bundle of mottled hen fibers. Secure them atop the shank to make a tail about ¾ the length of the shank.

Step 2: Use the *direct dubbing* method (p. 34) to form a tapered abdomen over the rear half of the hook shank.

Step 3: *Clip, clean, and stack* (p. 32) a bundle of deer hair. With your right fingers, size the hair against the shank, as shown, until the fingertips are positioned at the hook eye and hair tips aligned with the bend of the hook.

Step 4: Maintaining your pinch on the hair, slide the right fingers back so that the fingertips are aligned with the front of the abdomen.

Step 5: Without moving the hair, grip the bundle with your left fingers, freeing the right hand for wrapping.

Step 6: Take 3 or 4 tight thread wraps around the hair, directly ahead of the abdomen. Maintain a firm grip with your lefts fingers to keep all the hair atop the shank.

Step 7: Clip and bind down the excess hair.

Step 8: Dub the thorax, stopping 5-6 thread-wraps' distance behind the hook eye.

Step 9: Draw all the deer-hair fibers evenly forward, keeping them atop the shank to form a smooth wing case.

Step 10: While holding the deer hair in position, use your left hand to take 3 or 4 tight wraps to secure the hair to the shank.

Step 11: Preen the hair rearward and use the thread to form a tapered head against the base of the hair. These wraps will keep the wing in an upright position. Whip finish the fly behind the eye.

Step 12: If necessary, preen the hair over the top of the shank to fan the wing into an arc of about 180 degrees, as shown in this front view.

Tom Thumb

Hook: TMC 100, or equivalent dry-fly hook, #8-#14
Thread: Black 6/0
Tail: Deer or elk hair
Body: Olive dubbing
Shellback and tuft: Deer or elk hair

The Tom Thumb has been a popular stillwater pattern in the Pacific Northwest, and particularly in Canada, for half a century. The profile suggests a hatching caddis; it can be fished motionless on the film or stripped to imitate a hatching natural struggling on the surface.

Step 1: Attach the tying thread near the eye, and wrap a thread foundation to the tailing point. *Clip, clean, and stack* (p. 32) a bunch of deer or elk hair. Mount it at the tailing point atop the shank to make a tail about ½ a shank-length long. Clip and bind the excess.

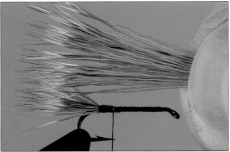

Step 2: Position the thread about ¼ of a shank length ahead of the tail. Clip, clean, and stack a second bunch of hair. Align the tips of the hair with the tips of the tail.

Step 3: Secure the hair atop the shank, wrapping rearward until the thread reaches the rearmost tailing wrap. Clip and bind the excess hair. Use the *direct dubbing* method (p. 34) to dub a body over the rear ¾ of the hook shank.

Step 4: Fold the hair over the top of the shank, and tie it down directly in front of the dubbing. Pinch the hair tightly when you secure it to keep the fibers from migrating around the hook shank.

Step 5: Preen back the hair tips, and take a few tight thread wraps against the base of the hair to elevate it to about 45 degrees and to spread the hair in an arc. Whip finish beneath the hair, around the shank only.

Step 6: Here's a front view of the fanned wing.

Hatchmaster

Originator: Dave Lambroughton
Hook: TMC 9300, or other 1X heavy nymph hook, #12-#20
Thread: Olive 6/0
Tail: Deer hair
Body: Olive tying thread
Shellback: Deer hair
Wing: Deer hair
Hackle: Grizzly

This design combines the shellback and wing tuft of a Tom Thumb with the hackle of a Quigley Cripple. Hatch-specific variations can be tied by altering body and hackle colors. This is fine general-purpose emerger.

Step 1: Attach the thread and wrap to the tailing point. *Clip, clean, and stack* (p. 32) a bundle of deer hair. Mount the hair to make a tail equal in length to the hook shank. Bind the hair butts to the top of the shank to make a level underbody over the rear ⅔ of the shank. Return the thread to the tailing point.

Step 2: Clip, clean, and stack a second bundle of hair. Pinch the bundle of hair, as shown, so that it reaches from the hook eye to the tip of the tail fibers.

Step 3: Slide your fingers down the shank, and secure the hair to the top of the shank directly atop the tail-mounting wraps. With a *flattened thread* (p. 37), bind the hair butts to the top of the shank, forming a smooth underbody, stopping ⅓ of a shank-length behind the eye.

Step 4: Fold the deer hair forward over the top of the shank, and secure at the front of the thread body. Keep the hair atop the shank. Continue binding the hair forward to the hook eye, forming a smooth foundation for the hackle.

Step 5: *Prepare a hackle feather* (p. 39) and mount it as explained in *mounting collar hackle* (p. 37) at the front edge of the shellback.

Step 6: As shown in *wrapping dry-fly hackle* (p. 44), wrap the hackle over the thread foundation. Secure the feather at the base of the wing tuft, and clip the excess. Lift the wing tuft and take several turns of thread against the base of the hair to elevate the tuft to about 45 degrees. Whip finish around the shank.

Parachute Midge Emerger

Originator: Scott Sanchez and Gary Willmott
Hook: Dai-Riki 310, or other ring-eye dry-fly hook, #16-#22
Thread: Black 8/0
Body: Arizona Synthetic Peacock dubbing, natural
Rib: Rainbow Krystal Flash
Tuft: White poly or Antron yarn
Hackle: Grizzly

Though not technically a parachute pattern, this fly sits with the abdomen under water and the hackle spread horizontally on the film. Dress only the hackle and post with floatant; tying the fly to the leader with a loop knot helps properly position the fly on the water.

Step 1: Attach the thread and position it behind the hook eye. Mount a length of yarn atop the shank to make a tuft as long as the hook shank. Clip and bind the yarn butt. Mount a strand of Krystal Flash atop the shank, and secure it by wrapping the thread rearward to the end of the hook shank.

Step 2: Use the *direct dubbing* method (p. 34) to dub a slightly tapered body, stopping 4-5 thread-wraps behind the rear of the yarn tuft.

Step 3: Rib the body. Tie off and clip the rib in front of the dubbing.

Step 4: *Prepare a hackle feather* (p. 39) and mount it directly ahead of the body as explained in *mounting collar hackle* (p. 37).

Step 5: Take 2-5 wraps of the hackle behind the tuft as shown in *wrapping dry-fly hackle* (p. 44). Tie off the hackle feather just behind the tuft.

Step 6: The tuft should be slightly elevated. If the yarn lies too horizontally, lift the tuft and take a few wraps at the front of the base to elevate it. Whip finish beneath the tuft.

Gray Midge Emerger

Hook: TMC 100, or equivalent dry-fly hook, #16-#22
Thread: Gray 8/0
Shuck: Cream Antron yarn
Rib: Fine silver wire
Body: Gray 8/0 tying thread
Hackle: Dun
Tuft: Gray poly yarn

This is a version of the previous pattern, the Parachute Midge Emerger, tied with a shuck. Depending on how floatant is applied, the body of this fly can sit horizontally on the film or suspended vertically beneath it.

Step 1: Attach the tying thread and position it behind the hook eye. Mount a length of poly yarn atop the shank. Secure it by wrapping rearward another 5 or 6 thread wraps, forming a smooth foundation for the hackle. Clip the excess and bind down. Clip the poly tuft to about ¾ the shank length.

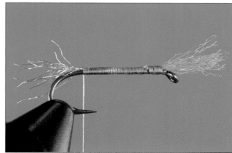

Step 2: Mount a sparse bundle of Antron behind the yarn. Bind it atop the shank with smooth wraps to the tailing point. Trim the yarn to form a shuck about ½ the shank length.

Step 3: Mount the ribbing wire over the rearmost thread wraps. Secure the tag of wire along the hook shank over the entire length of the fly body. These thread wraps form the body, so keep them smooth and uniform.

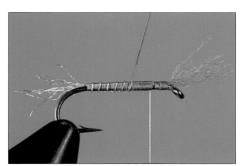

Step 4: Form the thread body right up to the base of the yarn tag that was clipped and bound down in Step 1. When the body is complete, spiral the ribbing wire forward.

Step 5: Tie off and clip the rib at the front of the body. *Prepare a hackle feather* (p. 39), and mount it directly ahead of the body as explained in *mounting collar hackle* (p. 37).

Step 6: Take 3-5 wraps of hackle and secure the feather tip as shown in *wrapping dry-fly hackle* (p. 44). Tie off the feather and whip finish the fly around the hook shank only, beneath the yarn tuft.

Suspender Midge

Originator: John Mundinger
Hook: Mustad 94840, or other standard dry-fly hook, #18-#20
Thread: Black 8/0
Tuft: White closed-cell foam strip, square in cross-section
Shuck: Beige Z-Lon
Abdomen: Black tying thread
Rib: Peacock Krystal Flash
Thorax: Peacock herl
Hackle: Grizzly

We've seen a number of versions of this basic design. Tyer John Mundinger showed us this one. He also ties this pattern in a PMD emerger version, using a #16 hook, a dun shuck, yellow thread body, chartreuse Krystal Flash rib, yellow dubbing thorax, and yellow foam tufts. Dress only the hackle with floatant. The fly should sit vertically in the water.

Step 1: Attach the thread, lay a short foundation behind the eye, and position the thread behind the hook eye. Mount the foam atop the shank with a couple of firm wraps, then make a few crisscross wraps over the butt end of the foam. If necessary, take a few wraps beneath the post to elevate it as shown.

Step 2: Clip and bind the excess foam, and trim the tuft to about one hook-gap in length. Mount the shuck material behind the foam butt and bind it atop the shank to the tailing point. Trim to make a shuck slightly longer than the hook gap.

Step 3: Mount the ribbing material atop the rearmost wrap, and form a thread abdomen over the rear ⅔ of the shank. Rib the body, tie-off the Krystal Flash, and clip it. Mount a strand of peacock herl directly ahead of the abdomen.

Step 4: Form a short thorax as shown in *wrapping single-herl collars* (p. 48). Tie off and clip the herl.

Step 5: *Prepare a hackle feather* (p. 39) and mount it as explained in *mounting collar hackle* (p. 37).

Step 6: Take 3-4 turns of hackle as explained in *wrapping dry-fly hackle* (p. 44). Tie off and clip the feather tip. Whip finish around the hook shank beneath the foam post.

Vertimerger

Originator: Paul Dieter
Hook: TMC 206BL, or other fine-wire scud hook, #12-#20
Thread: Gray 8/0
Abdomen: Olive McLean's Quill Body
Hackle: Dun
Wing: Tulle

This pattern sits vertically in the surface film. Tulle is a mesh-like material available in fabric stores, though tyer Paul Dieter also uses CDC and turkey flats for the wing. The version shown here is a BWO emerger, but component colors can be altered to match other mayfly species. It also makes a credible midge emerger in smaller sizes.

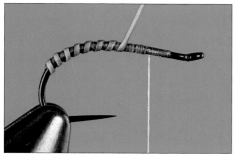

Step 1: Attach the thread and position it at the tailing point. Mount a McLean's quill by the tip, and wrap a *flattened thread* (p. 37) over the rear ⅔ of the shank, forming a smooth underbody. Wrap the quill in an open spiral over the thread to segment the abdomen. Tie off and clip the quill ⅓ a shank-length behind the eye.

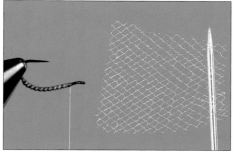

Step 2: Position the hook in the vise as shown. Position the thread 5 or 6 thread-wraps' distance behind the hook eye. Cut a piece of tulle about 1" square, and "weave" the point of a dubbing needle through the mesh along one edge, as shown here.

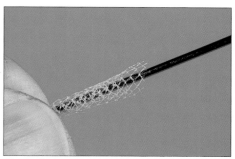

Step 3: Pinch the corner of the tulle near the point of the needle, and twirl it between the left thumb and forefinger to roll the tulle around the needle into a cone-shaped tube. Twist the point of the cone tightly.

Step 4: Maintain the pinch on the tulle, and remove the needle. Use a *pinch wrap* (p. 38) to mount the wing at the thread position. Bind the butt to the front of the abdomen and clip the excess.

Step 5: Trim the wing at an angle, as shown, to about one shank-length in height. *Prepare a hackle feather* (p. 39) and mount it directly ahead of the abdomen as shown in *mounting collar hackle* (p. 37). Wrap the thread forward forming a smooth foundation to the base of the wing.

Step 6: Take 5 or 6 turns of hackle as described in *wrapping dry-fly hackle* (p. 44). Secure the feather tip behind the wing with one wrap of thread. Take additional wraps over the feather tip in front of the wing, using thread wraps to force the rear of the wing against the wrapped hackle. Clip the excess and whip finish. Coat the body with head cement.

CHAPTER 8: Parachute Emergers

The parachute design is a natural for emergers, since it places the fly body flush against, or even underneath, the surface film, offering much the same profile as the natural insect. Parachute patterns can be tied in both flush-floating and descending-body designs, and the hackle fibers pressing against the surface may, as some have suggested, dimple the film and scatter light in much the same way as the disorganized, rumpled shuck and body of a hatching nymph or pupa. At the same time, parachute flies generally float well and are quite visible to the angler—a combination that makes the style useful in rougher or broken currents as well as on smooth water.

It is one of the most versatile approaches to representing emergers, and given the variety in different types and characteristics of post materials—hair, synthetic fibers, foam, and feather barbs among them—and colors of hackle, there is little wonder that parachute-hackle flies are among the most popular of emerger styles.

One of the more interesting recent developments in parachute patterns is the use of CDC as a hackling material. In addition to the usual benefits of a parachute design, the very mobile CDC barbs give the fly a lifelike movement. Three such patterns using two different hackling techniques are shown in this chapter.

Vertical Emerger—Parachute Hendrickson

Originator: Harold McMillan
Hook: TMC 400T, or other swimming nymph hook, #12-#14
Thread: Wine 14/0
Shuck: Brown Darlon
Abdomen: Brown dubbing, blend of synthetic, rabbit, and squirrel
Ribbing: Gold wire
Thorax: Hendrickson blend to match natural
Wing post: White calf body hair
Hackle: Light dun

This unusual emerger style takes advantage of the swimming-nymph hook to give a lifelike shape to the pattern. Harold McMillan also dresses this pattern with a CDC loopwing or snowshoe hare's foot downwing and omits the hackle.

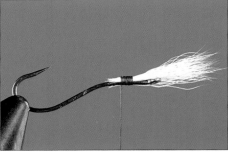

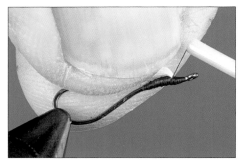

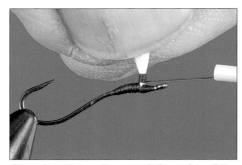

Step 1: Mount the hook upside down as shown. Lay a thread foundation over the bent portion of the hook shank. Position the thread at the middle of the foundation. *Clip, clean, and stack* (p. 32) a bundle of calf body hair. Secure the hair atop the shank to form a post 1 ½ hook-gaps in height. Clip the butts at an angle.

Step 2: Bind down the exposed hair butts. Post the bundle upright by drawing the hair rearward with the left fingers. At the front base of the bundle, build a bump of thread to keep the wing post elevated. The bump should be cone-shaped, with the base of the cone abutting the hair and tip tapered toward the hook eye.

Step 3: With a *flattened thread* (p. 37), take 2 or 3 tight wraps horizontally at the base of the wing post. Take 4 or 5 firm wraps vertically up the wing post, then 4 or 5 more wraps back down to the base of the post. Maintain a flattened thread throughout to make a smooth base for winding the parachute hackle.

Step 4: Position the tying thread behind the wing post. *Prepare a hackle feather* (p. 39) Using the steps shown in *vertical-mount parachute hackle* (p. 42), secure the feather to the parachute post.

Step 5: Mount the hook in the normal position. Wrap the tying thread to the tailing point. Mount the shuck material at the tailing point, and clip it to the length of one hook gap. Mount the ribbing wire directly atop the thread wraps securing the shuck.

Step 6: Use the *direct dubbing* method (p. 34) to dub a tapered abdomen along the rear half of the shank.

Step 7: Spiral the wire forward to rib the abdomen. Tie off the ribbing in front of the abdomen and bind down the excess.

Step 8: Mount the hook upside down. Use the direct dubbing method to dub the thorax of the fly. When you come to the wing post, use a crisscross wrap of dubbing formed beneath the hook shank to dub the area directly under the post. Then continue dubbing to point just behind the hook eye.

Step 9: Form the parachute hackle as explained in *wrapping parachute hackle* (p. 46).

Step 10: Secure the feather tip and clip the excess. Form the head of the fly and whip finish.

Klinkhamer Special

Originator: Hans van Klinken
Hook: Partridge GRS15ST, or other fine-wire scud hook, #8-#18
Body thread: Tan 8/0
Hackling thread: Danville Spiderweb, or other very fine, strong thread
Abdomen: Light-tan Fly-Rite poly dubbing
Wing post: White poly yarn
Thorax: 3 strands peacock herl
Hackle: Dun, one size larger than normally used for the hook size

There are dozens of variations of this popular pattern tied in different sizes and colors to match midge, mayfly, and caddis hatches. The following sequence shows van Klinken's original pattern and the unusual hackling technique he employs, but a conventional parachute hackling method can also be used.

Step 1: Lay a foundation of the body thread over the front ⅓ of the shank, and position the thread at the winging point. Take a 2" length of poly yarn half the thickness of the finished wing, and fold it around the thread as shown.

Step 2: With left fingers, put tension on the yarn. With right fingers put tension on the bobbin. Slide the yarn down the thread and position directly atop the hook shank.

Step 3: Release the yarn and take 2 or 3 additional tight thread wraps over the first wrap to secure the yarn. Then draw the yarn upward with the left fingers and take several tight thread wraps horizontally around the base of the yarn.

Step 4: *Prepare a hackle feather* (p. 39) and secure it as explained in *vertical-mount parachute hackle* (p. 42).

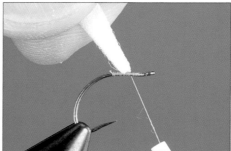

Step 5: Wrap the thread to the rear of the shank, forming a smooth, slightly tapered underbody. Apply dubbing to the thread sparsely to maintain a slim body profile, and dub a tapered body to a point just behind the wing post.

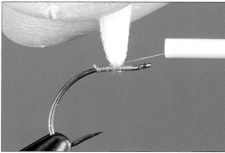

Step 6: Mount three peacock herls and a 4" length of tying thread directly in front of the body. As you bind down the tips of the herl, keep the underbody smooth. Position the thread directly behind the hook eye.

Step 7: Using the technique shown in *wrapping twisted-herl collars* (p. 49), take two or three wraps behind the wing post. Wrap the twisted herl directly beneath the wing post, and continue wrapping to a point just behind the hook eye. Tie off the herl and clip the excess. Whip finish the head of the fly, and clip the thread.

Step 8: Position the hook as shown, with the eye downward. Attach the Spiderweb thread at the base of the wing post, just as you would attach the thread to a hook shank. Take a few wraps toward the tip of the post, then position the thread at the base of the post, against the herl thorax.

Step 9: Wrap the hackle as explained in *wrapping dry-fly hackle* (p. 44), except here you're wrapping from right to left. Take 5 wraps on smaller hooks, 6 or 7 on larger ones. After the last wrap, hold the hackle pliers in your left hand, and hold the feather horizontally, pointing to the left. With the right hand, secure the feather tip against the base of the wing post with 3 or 4 thread wraps.

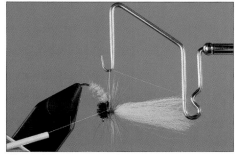

Step 10: Clip the feather tip and whip finish the fly with 3 or 4 wraps at the base of the wing post beneath the low-ermost wrap of hackle. Clip the wing post to a length of about one hook-gap.

Parachute Emerger Sparkle Pupa

Originator: Vladimir Markov
Hook: Mustad 94840, or other standard dry-fly hook, #12-#18
Thread: Olive 6/0
Shuck: Gray Antron dubbing fibers
Abdomen: Gold or pearl Lite-Brite (hank form)
Bubble shuck: Gray, gold, or green Antron yarn
Thorax: Peacock herl
Wing post: White poly yarn
Hackle: Brown or cream

This variation of Gary LaFontaine's Sparkle Pupa produces a fly that floats better and is more visible than the original, suiting it to rougher water.

Step 1: With pliers, bend the front ⅕ of the hook to produce the hook shape shown on the right. Wrap a thread foundation on the bent portion of the shank. Using the technique shown in the Klinkhamer Special (p. 162), Steps 1-3, secure the yarn post at the winging point. *Prepare a hackle feather* (p. 39) and using the method shown in *horizontal-mount parachute hackle* (p. 37), secure the feather to the hook shank.

Step 2: Wrap the thread to the tailing point. Pull out a sparse pinch of fibers from a skein of Antron dubbing, and mount them to form a tail equal in length to the hook shank. Using the method shown in *Antron bubble*, Steps 1-3, (p. 69), attach a piece yarn to the far side of the hook, and a second piece to the near side.

Step 3: Pull a sparse pinch of fibers from a hank of Lite-Brite and mount them over the rearmost thread wraps securing the Antron yarn. Twist the strands to make a cord, and wrap an abdomen that extends ¾ the distance to the angle you bent in the shank.

Step 4: Using the technique shown in *Antron bubble*, Steps 5-6, pull the yarn strands forward and secure them to make the bubble.

Step 5: Clip the yarn tags from the bubble and secure the butts with thread. Mount three strands of peacock herl and a 4" piece of tying thread directly atop the thread wraps securing the bubble. Form the thorax as explained in *wrapping twisted-herl collars* (p. 49). Tie off and clip the excess.

Step 6: Use the method shown in *wrapping parachute hackle* (p. 46) to take 4-6 wraps of hackle around the post. Secure the hackle and clip the excess. Form the head of the fly and whip finish. Trim the wing to a height of one hook gap.

Parachute Adams Emerger

Hook: TMC 100, or equivalent dry-fly hook, #14-#20
Thread: Gray 8/0
Shuck: Cream Antron
Body: Gray Superfine dubbing
Wing post: Light gray poly yarn
Hackle: Grizzly

This generic emerger, a simplified version of one of fly-fishing's most popular dry flies, has accounted for more than its share of trout. It produces during midge, mayfly, or caddis emergences, and is especially useful in smaller sizes. Anglers who resist carrying a lot specialty patterns for hatches can cover a pretty fair range of situations with this fly.

Step 1: Attach the thread and position it ⅓ of a shank-length behind the eye. Form a wing post as shown in Klinkhamer Special, Steps 1-3, (p. 162).

Step 2: Wrap to the tailing point, and secure a sparse bundle of Antron to make a shuck one shank-length long.

Step 3: Use the *direct dubbing* method (p. 34) to dub a tapered abdomen to the rear of the wing post.

Step 4: *Prepare a hackle feather* (p. 39), and secure it using the technique shown in *horizontal-mount parachute hackle* (p. 37).

Step 5: Dub the remainder of the body.

Step 6: Using the method shown in *wrapping parachute hackle* (p. 46), take 4-6 turns of the feather down the post; tie off the hackle and clip the excess. Whip finish. Clip the wing post to one hook-gap in height.

Reverse Midge Emerger

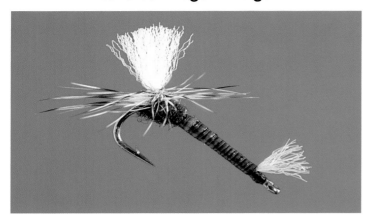

Hook: TMC 101, or other ring-eye, dry-fly hook, #12-#16
Thread: Black 8/0
Wing: White poly yarn
Hackle: Grizzly
Thorax: Brown Superfine dubbing
Abdomen: Stripped peacock quill
Shuck: White Antron

This reverse style can be used for a variety of emerger types. It presents a clear and uncluttered profile of the body and shuck of the insect by placing the hook bend and spear at the head of the fly. Leave your tippet ungreased so that the hook shank will sink.

Step 1: Mount the hook in the vise as shown. Attach the thread and position it about ⅓ the way around the hook bend. Cut a 3" length of poly yarn, half the thickness of the finished wing. Secure the center of the strand. Lift both ends vertically, and take 4 or 5 thread wraps up the base, and then 4 or 5 wraps down to the hook.

Step 2: When the wing strands are posted vertically and consolidated with wraps around the base, *prepare a hackle feather* (p. 39) and mount it as explained in *horizontal-mount parachute hackle* (p. 37). Bind and clip the excess. Use the *direct dubbing* method (p. 34) to dub a thorax ⅓ the distance to the hook eye.

Step 3: Take 4 or 5 turns of hackle as explained in *wrapping parachute hackle* (p. 46). When the last wrap is taken, tie off the hackle at the rear of the thorax, as shown here. Clip and bind the excess.

Step 4: Re-mount the hook in the vise in the conventional way. Position the thread 6-8 thread-wraps' distance behind the eye. Mount a sparse length of Antron yarn. Bind the yarn to the top of shank, wrapping rearward to the thorax, forming a smooth under-body, as shown. Clip, and bind the excess right up to the thorax.

Step 5: Mount a stripped peacock herl by the butt end, directly behind the thorax. Bind down the excess with a *flattened thread* (p. 37) to form a smooth underbody. Continue wrapping the thread beyond the Antron to the hook eye.

Step 6: Wrap the quill in adjacent turns toward the hook eye. Bind and clip the quill just beyond the shuck. Whip finish. Use a dubbing needle to apply a drop of head cement to the body for durability. Clip the wing post and shuck to ½ the hook gap in length.

E/C Caddis

Originator: Ralph Cutter
Hook: TMC 9300, or other 1XH hook, #12-#20; TMC 100, or equivalent dry-fly hook, #22-#24
Thread: Olive
Shuck: Amber Antron or fine amber Z-Lon
Body: Rear half—brownish dubbing; front half—green, yellow, or tan dubbing
Wing: Elk or deer hair
Hackle: Grizzly

This pattern evolved over several seasons as Ralph Cutter donned scuba gear and watched trout react to various versions of this fly. In small sizes, it makes a good midge emerger pattern. During a mayfly hatch, tug the wing upward to elevate almost vertically for a mayfly emerger. One of the keys to the pattern, says Cutter, is the two-toned body, which significantly outfishes one with a single-color body.

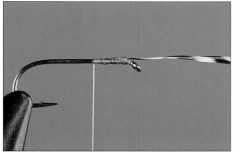

Step 1: Attach the thread and lay a thread foundation over the front ⅓ of the hook shank. Position the thread a short distance behind the hook eye. *Prepare a hackle feather* (p. 39), and secure it to the shank, shiny side up, with feather extending horizontally over the hook eye, as shown.

Step 2: Wrap the thread to the tailing point. Take a few fibers of Antron or Z-Lon, and fold them in half to form a loop. Mount the loop at the tailing point; the length of the loop should be about one hook-gap.

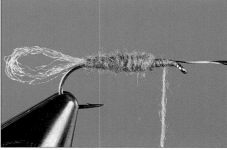

Step 3: Dub the rear half of the body with a slight taper. Dub the front half of the body, stopping at a point about ¼ of shank-length behind the hook eye. Then, with a very thinly dubbed thread, take a few wraps toward the hook eye. This foundation will help grip the winging fibers as they are being secured.

Step 4: *Clip, clean, and stack* (p. 32) a bundle of elk or deer hair. Position it atop the hook, just above the thinly dubbed portion of the shank. Secure the bundle with tight wraps of thread. When the hair is secure, advance the thread to a point just behind the hook eye.

Step 5: Clip the butt ends of the wing hair as shown. Using the method explained in *wrapping parachute hackle* (p. 46), take 3-5 wraps of hackle. As you wrap, the hackle passes beneath the rear wing and ahead of the clipped butts. Wrap snugly, but not so tightly that you elevate the wing to a vertical position.

Step 6: Secure and clip the hackle tip. Whip finish the fly.

Parachute Puff Emerger

Originator: Bruce Salzburg
Hook: TMC 2487, or other light-wire scud hook, #14-#18
Thread: Brown 8/0
Abdomen: Olive vinyl lace
Wing: Type 3 CDC feather (puff)
Thorax: Dark brown fine poly dubbing
Hackle: Dun

The use of a CDC puff as a parachute post makes for a very light fly that lands gently on the water and is quite visible to the angler. This design is adaptable to many mayfly and midge species, and the wing height can be altered to suit the tyer's taste.

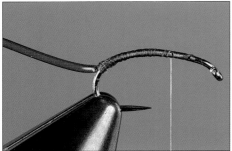

Step 1: Attach the thread and position it at the rearmost point of the body. Cut a length of vinyl lace, and clip the end at an angle. Mount the strand by the point, binding it with a *flattened thread* (p. 37) to make a smooth underbody. Position the thread ⅓ of a shank length behind the eye.

Step 2: Wrap the strand forward in touching turns, and tie off ⅓ of a shank length behind the eye. Bind the excess. Position the thread halfway between the front of the abdomen and the hook eye.

Step 3: Mount a CDC puff with the butt of the feather toward the hook bend so that the feather tip extends one shank length beyond the mounting wraps. Build a thread bump ahead of the feather to post it vertically, and take 4 or 5 thread wraps up the base of the post, then 4 or 5 more back down the post.

Step 4: *Prepare a hackle feather* (p. 39) and mount it as explained in *horizontal-mount parachute hackle* (p. 37).

Step 5: Use the *direct dubbing* method (p. 34) to dub the thorax. Take a criss-cross wrap of dubbing beneath the wing to cover the shank. Position the thread behind the hook eye.

Step 6: Take 3 or 4 turns of the feather as shown in *wrapping parachute hackle* (p. 46), and tie off behind the hook eye. Whip finish.

PMD Foam Emerger

Originator: Ross Purnell
Hook: TMC 2487, or other light-wire scud hook, #14-#18
Thread: Brown 6/0
Shuck: Brown Z-Lon
Abdomen: Brown stretch-floss
Thorax: Pale yellow Superfine dubbing
Post: White Rainey's Float Foam, ⅛" diameter
Hackle: Light dun

Foam-post parachute patterns have grown increasingly popular in recent times, and with good reason. The foam can give added buoyancy on sparsely hackled patterns, and it's quite visible to the angler. Colors and sizes of this design can be modified for virtually any mayfly hatch.

Step 1: Attach the tying thread and wrap to the tailing point. Mount the Z-Lon to form a shuck about one hook-gap in length; do not trim the excess. Mount the body material atop the tailing wraps, leaving a 1" tag. Draw the excess shuck and body materials along the top of the shank, and bind them down with a *flattened thread* (p. 37) to make a smooth underbody.

Step 2: Tie off the tags about ⅓ of a shank-length behind the eye. Wrap the floss forward to form the abdomen. Use a consistent tension on the material in order to create uniform segments.

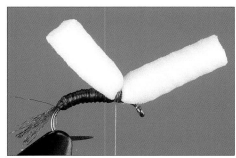

Step 3: Form the abdomen over the rear ⅔ of the shank; tie off and clip the floss. Position the thread about halfway between the abdomen and hook eye. Tie in the foam post, with the tag end pointing rearward.

Step 4: Clip and bind the tag of the foam. Build a bump of thread in front of the foam post to position it upright. *Prepare a hackle feather* (p. 39) and mount it as explained in *horizontal-mount parachute hackle* (p. 37).

Step 5: Use the *direct dubbing* method (p. 34) to dub the thorax, taking a crisscross wrap of dubbing beneath the foam post to cover the exposed thread wraps. Position the thread behind the hook eye.

Step 6: Take 4 or 5 turns of hackle as explained in *wrapping parachute hackle* (p. 46). Secure the feather and clip the excess. Form the head of the fly and whip finish. Trim the foam post to ½ the hook gap in height.

Hi-Vis Caddis Pupa Emerger

Hook: TMC 2487, or other fine-wire scud hook, #12-#16
Thread: Brown 8/0
Shuck: Tan Antron
Rib: Brown 6/0
Abdomen: Olive dubbing
Wing: Brown Antron
Post: ⅛" yellow closed-cell foam
Thorax: Brown dubbing
Hackle: Dun

An Antron shuck and wings give this emerger lots of sparkle, and the yellow post makes this low-floating fly easy to spot even in riffly water. Other high-visibility colors can of course be used. This generic pattern can be altered in size and color to match other caddis.

Step 1: Mount the thread behind the hook eye and wrap to the tailing point. Form a *burned teardrop shuck* (p. 58), and secure it atop the shank so that it extends one shank-length beyond the mounting wraps. Mount a length of thread for the ribbing atop the shuck-mounting wraps.

Step 2: Use the *direct dubbing* method (p. 34) to dub an abdomen over the rear ⅔ of the shank. *Counter-rib* (p. 33) the abdomen. Tie off and clip the excess ribbing. Position the thread about 5 thread-wraps ahead of the abdomen.

Step 3: Mount the brown Antron atop the shank with 2 or 3 very tight wraps. Split the yarn in half, and hold one strand on each side of the body. Wrap the thread back to the front of the abdomen, forming a wing on either side of the body, as shown in this top view. Clip the wings even with the rear of the abdomen.

Step 4: Cut a strip of foam half the hook gap in width. Mount it as shown in PMD Foam Emerger, Steps 3-4, (p. 169). *Prepare a hackle feather* (p. 39) and mount it as explained in *horizontal-mount parachute hackle* (p. 37).

Step 5: Dub the thorax, taking a crisscross wrap of the dubbing beneath the foam post to cover the exposed thread wraps.

Step 6: Take 4 or 5 turns of hackle as explained in *wrapping parachute hackle* (p. 46). Secure the feather and clip the excess. Form the head of the fly and whip finish. Trim the foam post to ½ the hook gap in height.

Low Rider Emerger—Sulfur

Originator: Ryan Meulemans
Hook: TMC 100, or equivalent dry-fly hook, #14-#20
Thread: Pale yellow 8/0
Shuck: Brown Z-Lon
Abdomen: Pheasant-tail fibers
Ribbing: Fine copper wire
Thorax: Pale yellow dubbing
Wing case: White closed-cell foam
Hackle: Ginger

This pattern offers the virtues of parachute hackling without the high wing post that is more characteristic of an adult insect. The foam wing case builds in some extra floatation, so the hackle can be kept very sparse if desired. The version shown here is tied to represent a mayfly, but this is a good general-purpose emerger design.

Step 1: Attach the thread, wrap to the tailing point, and secure the Z-Lon to make a shuck one shank-length long. Mount the ribbing and 3-5 pheasant-tail fibers atop the rearmost thread wraps. Advance the thread to the mid-point of the shank.

Step 2: Using the method shown in *wrapping feather-barb bodies* (p. 45), form the abdomen over the rear half of the shank. Then *counter-rib* (p. 33) the abdomen with the wire.

Step 3: Mount a strip of foam, about ⅔ the hook gap in width, ahead of the abdomen; clip and bind the excess. Take a few thread wraps behind the foam to stand the strip vertically. Mount the hackle feather as explained in *horizontal-mount parachute hackle* (p. 37).

Step 4: Use the *direct dubbing* method (p. 34) to dub a thorax slightly larger in diameter than the abdomen. The thorax should end about 5 thread-wraps behind the hook eye.

Step 5: Wrap the hackle as shown in *wrapping parachute hackle* (p. 46), taking 2 or 3 wraps around the foam post. Tie off the hackle directly in front of the thorax, and clip the excess feather.

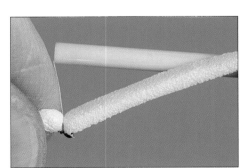

Step 6: Fold the foam post forward, using the left fingers to preen the hackle barbs in front of the post rearward, to avoid binding them down. Bind down the foam in front of the thorax, as shown. Clip the foam and secure the tag, forming the head of the fly. Whip finish.

CDC Parachute Emerger

Originator: Cliff Sullivan
Hook: TMC 206BL, or other fine-wire scud hook, #14-#22
Thread: Black 8/0
Shuck: Turkey tail
Rib: Fine copper wire
Abdomen: Turkey tail
Thorax: Brown Superfine dubbing
Wing: White Float-Vis or Para Post Wing
Hackle: Two white Type 1, Type 2, or Type 4 CDC feathers

This light, very visible pattern uses a CDC dubbing loop to form the parachute hackle. This unusual hackling approach can be adapted to a wide variety of parachute patterns and is particularly useful on small hooks.

Step 1: Attach the thread and position it ⅓ of a shank-length behind the hook eye. Cut a 2" length of wing material that is half the desired thickness of the finished wing. Secure the center of the strand. Lift both ends vertically, and take 4 or 5 thread wraps up the base, then 4 or 5 back down to the hook.

Step 2: When the wing strands are posted vertically and consolidated with wraps around the base, position the thread at the tailing point. Cut a strip of 3 or 4 interlocking barbs from a turkey tail. Use a *pinch wrap* (p. 38) to mount the strip on its edge, broadside to the tyer, to form a tail one hook length long. Clip and bind the excess.

Step 3: Mount the ribbing atop the rearmost tailing wraps. Clip 3-4 more turkey-tail barbs, and mount them as a strip atop the rearmost tailing wrap. Position the thread at midshank. Wrap the barbs forward as a strip to form an abdomen over the rear half of the shank.

Step 4: *Counter-rib* (p. 33) the wire over the abdomen. Tie off and clip ahead of the abdomen. Position the thread at the base of the wing. Form a *dubbing loop*, Steps 1-2, (p. 35). When the loop is formed, raise it vertically and take a horizontal thread wrap to bind the loop to the wing post. Use the *direct dubbing* method (p. 34) to dub the thorax.

Step 5: Position the thread behind the hook eye. Clip the two CDC feathers in a paper clamp and transfer them to the loop as shown in *CDC dubbing loop* (p. 31). Twist tightly. Take 3 or 4 wraps around the post as described in *wrapping parachute hackle* (p. 46). On each wrap, lift the CDC barbs on the post upward to avoid trapping them with the next wrap.

Step 6: Tie off the dubbing loop behind the hook eye, and clip. Whip finish the fly and clip the thread. Preen the CDC barbs and wingpost upward, applying a uniform tension to all the fibers. Clip them as a bundle to the length of the hook shank.

Para-Emerger

Originator: Gerhard Laible
Hook: TMC 900BL, or equivalent dry-fly hook, #12-#18
Thread: Black 8/0
Tail: Brown hackle barbs
Body: Brown mink dubbing
Wing case: Yellow closed-cell foam
Hackle: Two tan Type 1, Type 2, or Type 4 CDC feathers

Using CDC as parachute hackle around a folded foam post gives a well-defined hackle and the suggestion of emerging wings. Using a brightly colored foam will make smaller patterns easier to see on the water. This basic design can be modified in size and color to match mayflies, caddis, and midges.

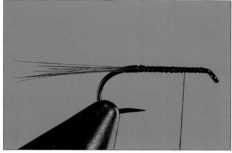

Step 1: Attach the tying thread and position it at the tailing point. *Align and strip* (p. 30) 6-8 hackle barbs, and mount them atop the shank to form a tail one shank-length long. Clip and bind the excess. Position the thread ⅓ of a shank-length behind the hook eye.

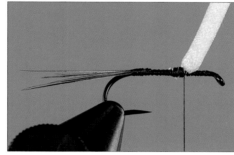

Step 2: Cut a strip of foam about one hook-gap in width. Secure it atop the shank, wrapping rearward. Clip and bind the excess, and then position the thread at the frontmost thread wrap used to secure the foam.

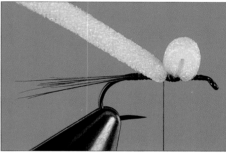

Step 3: Fold the foam strip rearward to form a ball about one hook gap in height. Bind down the foam over the frontmost thread wrap used to mount the foam; this will give it a ball-like shape. Wrap rearward to secure the foam; then bind and clip the excess.

Step 4: Use the *direct dubbing* method (p. 34) to dub a tapered thorax to the rear of the foam ball. At the rear base of the foam, form a *dubbing loop*, Step 1-2, (p. 35).

Step 5: Dub the thorax and position the thread behind the hook eye. Clip two CDC feathers in a paper clamp and transfer them to the dubbing loop as shown in *CDC dubbing loop* (p. 31). Twist tightly.

Step 6: Take 3-4 turns of the dubbing loop around the foam as explained in *wrapping parachute hackle* (p. 46). On each wrap, lift the CDC barbs on the post upward to avoid trapping them beneath the next wrap. Tie off behind the hook eye and clip. Whip finish. Preen the barbs upward, and clip to the length of the hook shank.

CDC Midge Emerger

Originator: Shane Stalcup
Hook: TMC 2487, or other light-wire scud hook, #16-#22
Thread: Black 14/0
Body: Gray, black, brown-olive, tan, or red goose biot
Wing post: White poly yarn
Hackle: 2 Gray CDC feathers

Because CDC barbs are sparsely distributed on the stem, conventional parachute hackling techniques give poor results with CDC feathers. Colorado tyer Shane Stalcup devised this unusual method for combining the virtues of CDC with the effectiveness of a parachute design. The fly style can also be used to imitate smaller mayfly emergers, especially blue-winged olives or pale morning duns.

Step 1: Mount the tying thread near the hook eye, and wrap it rearward to the bend of the hook, using a flattened thread to form a smooth foundation. Secure a goose biot by the tip as shown in *biot body—smooth* (p. 31). Bind down the biot tip, forming a smooth underbody to a point just forward of the midpoint of the shank.

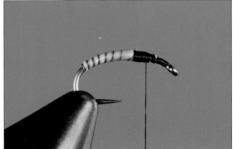

Step 2: Using the method explained in *biot body—smooth* (p. 31), wrap the biot forward in overlapping turns. Tie off and clip the excess.

Step 3: Using the method shown in *stripping CDC barbs* (p. 40), remove the barbs from 2 CDC feathers; keep the barbs aligned as much as possible. Pinch the barbs between the right thumb and forefinger. Cut a 3" piece of poly yarn that is half the thickness desired in the finished wing. Slip the yarn between your thumb and forefinger so that it is positioned atop the CDC fibers.

Step 4: Transfer the bundle of fibers to your left fingers; the CDC fibers should now be closest the fingertips. Use a *pinch wrap* (p. 38) to mount the bundle with one thread wrap to the top of the shank. If all goes well, the yarn should be on top, with the CDC fibers bundled beneath it. Take an additional wrap atop the first.

Step 5: Carefully rotate the whole bundle of fibers crosswise on the shank, as shown in this top view. Secure the bundle with a series of tight crisscross wraps.

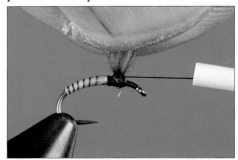

Step 6: With the left fingers, draw all the fibers upward so that the yarn halves are folded together and sandwiched between the bundles of CDC. Take 3 or 4 tight turns of thread around the base of the elevated fibers.

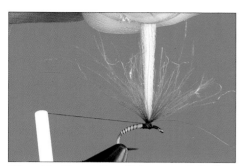  

Step 7: Carefully slide your left fingertips upward until the CDC barbs are released, but you still have hold of the tip of the yarn post. Take a couple of additional wraps around the post beneath (not through) the CDC fibers. These wraps will further distribute the CDC barbs in a radial pattern.

Step 8: Release the wing post. The CDC barbs should be drawn around the wing post in a fairly uniform distribution, as shown in this top view. When the CDC barbs are satisfactorily distributed around the post, whip finish the fly and clip the thread.

Step 9: With the right fingers, draw the yarn post upward by the tip. With the left fingers, preen all the CDC fibers downward below the shank. Try to pull the fibers downward with a uniform tension. Then clip the CDC fibers parallel to the hook shank. The cut length should be about one hook-gap, as shown here.

Step 10: Draw the yarn post upward and clip it to a height of about one shank-length. Here the finished fly, pictured from above, shows the distribution of CDC into a parachute-hackle configuration.

Ma's Hatching Dun—March Brown

Originator: Vladimir Markov
Hook: TMC 2487, Mustad 80250, or TMC 200R, #10-#18
Thread: Brown 6/0
Tail: 3-6 woodduck, partridge, or hackle fibers
Nymphal skin: Brown Antron dubbing fibers or Z-Lon
Nymphal thorax: Olive-brown Antron and poly dubbing, blended
Nymphal legs: 6 partridge or hen hackle fibers
Rib: Fine silver wire
Body of dun: Same as nymphal thorax
Thorax of dun: Same as body of dun
Wing post: 5X mono tippet material
Hackle and wing: Grizzly rooster hackle

This is certainly one of the more difficult patterns presented in this book, but the results are undeniably impressive. In this transitional pattern, the front half of the fly imitates a mayfly as it is emerging from the nymphal skin, which is represented on the rear half of the hook. The postless parachute technique used here allows the tyer to fashion hackle and wings from the same feathers. Markov notes that if a specific representation demands hackle and wings of different colors, the excess hackle feathers can be trimmed, and feather tips of a different color mounted, as noted below in Step 10.

Step 1: Lay a thread foundation over the rear half of the hook. Using the method shown in *tailed shuck* (p. 63), dress the trailing shuck and tails. Use the *direct dubbing* method (p. 34) to dub a short, thick nymphal thorax over the rear ⅓ of the shank.

Step 2: Use the technique shown in *side-mounted legs* (p. 39) to mount three partridge fibers on each side of the nymphal thorax as shown in this top view. Then mount the ribbing wire directly in front of the legs.

Step 3: Dub the slim, tapered body of the dun, stopping at a point about ¼ of a shank-length behind the hook eye.

Step 4: Spiral the wire forward to rib the dun body. Tie off the rib directly ahead of the dubbing, and advance the tying thread about two wraps forward.

Step 5: Cut a 4" length of 5X tippet material. Cross the ends to form a loop about 1" tall. Use crisscross wraps of tying thread, under light tension, to secure the loop to the near side of the shank. The thread wraps should secure the mono at the point where two ends of material cross to form the loop.

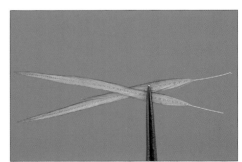

Step 6: Take two hackle feathers and place them together front to back, so their curvatures match. Strip off the lower barbs to leave a feather tip long enough to take 5 or 6 wraps of hackle and then produce wings that are proportional to the hook size. This takes a bit of experimentation.

Step 7: Mount the stacked hackles using the method shown in *horizontal-mount parachute hackle* (p. 37), except that they should be mounted in front of the mono loop, with the stems bound toward the hook eye. After the feathers are mounted, bend them outward, directly away from you to keep them out of the tying field, as shown here from the top.

Step 8: Return the tying thread to the front of the dubbed body. Dub a thorax slightly larger in diameter than the abdomen. Use light, but still firm, wraps. Finish dubbing the thorax a few thread-wraps' distance behind the hook eye.

Step 9: Grasp both feather tips and wind the hackles together (as though they were one feather) as explained in *wrapping parachute hackle* (p. 46). As you wrap, pass the feather tips from hand to hand, using one hand to wrap and the other to support the mono loop.

Step 10: When the last wrap of hackle is taken, pull the feather tips over the hook eye, and secure them behind the eye with 2 tight turns of thread. (Note: if wings of a different color are required, clip the hackle tips and mount two hackle tips of the desired color.)

Step 11: With the right fingers, take the mono loop and bend it forward so that the hook eye passes through the loop. With your left fingers, raise the two feather tips upward, through the loop, and angle them back toward the hook bend.

Step 12: Raise the mono loop vertically. Release the loop and with the right fingers, pull downward on the two mono tags below the hook shank, closing the loop. With your left fingers, maintain a slight upward and rearward tension on the feather tips.

Step 13: Snug the loop down firmly. Pull the two tags ends of mono forward on the underside of the shank. Secure them behind the hook eye. Clip the tags and whip finish.

Step 14: Clip away any stray hackle barbs that project upward and obscure the wing silhouette. If necessary or desired, gently spread the wings to divide them slightly. Put a drop of head cement at the hub of the parachute hackle.

Parachute Caddis Emerger

Originator: Shane Stalcup
Hook: Daiichi 1130, or other fine-wire scud hook, #10-#16
Thread: Brown 8/0
Bubble shuck: Golden brown Ice Dubbing
Body: Amber D-Rib
Wing post: White poly yarn
Wing: Dark dun Medallion sheeting
Hackle: Dun
Thorax: Golden brown Ice Dubbing

Perhaps more than any other tyer, Shane Stalcup has explored the uses of synthetic-film wings. The parachute style here places wings and body close to the water for a clean silhouette; at the same time, the pattern is suited to fishing in broken or turbulent water.

Step 1: Mount the thread and position it at the middle of the hook. Secure a pinch of Ice Dubbing, and wrap rearward. As you wrap, pull the dubbing fibers slightly downward to distribute them around the hook shank. Secure the dubbing fibers at the rear of the shank with 2 or 3 tight thread wraps.

Step 2: Cut a piece of D-Rib and trim the end at an angle. Secure the trimmed end atop the rearmost thread wrap. Advance the thread ⅔ the distance to the hook eye.

Step 3: Wrap the D-Rib forward in firm, touching wraps. When you reach the tying thread, tie off and clip the excess.

Step 4: Draw the dubbing fibers forward to surround the body material in a loose sheath. With the bobbin in the left hand, secure the fibers ahead of the body with a few tight wraps. Clip off the excess and bind down. Then trim away any stray dubbing fibers to neaten up the bubble sheath.

Step 5: Cut a length of poly yarn. Bind the center of the yarn atop the shank directly ahead of the body. Raise both ends, and take several thread wraps horizontally around the base to consolidate the two ends into a bundle. Wrap a short thread foundation up the post, and then back down, as shown.

Step 6: Cut a strip of wing material about 2" long and ⅔ the width of the hook gap. Mount the strip crosswise atop the shank, ahead of the wingpost, using a series of crisscross wraps.

Step 7: Fold the wings rearward, one down each side of the body. Wrap the thread rearward over the wing butts, securing the wings in position, until you reach the front of the abdomen.

Step 8: Trim the wings at angle, as shown, so they extend rearward to the end of the body. *Prepare a hackle feather* (p. 39) and mount it as shown in *horizontal-mount parachute hackle* (p. 37). Clip the excess feather stem and position the thread at the rear base of the wings.

Step 9: Use the *direct dubbing* method (p. 34) to dub the thorax. Position the thread behind the hook eye.

Step 10: Take 4-6 wraps of the hackle as explained in *wrapping parachute hackle* (p. 46). Tie off and clip the excess feather. Form the head of the fly and whip finish.

Step 11: Clip the wing post to a height about equal to the hook gap.

Chapter 9: Parasol and Umbrella Emergers

The purpose of these two designs is to imitate a nymph or pupa hanging just beneath the surface film prior to emergence. In the parasol style, the fly is suspended beneath a "puff" formed from a buoyant material that is joined to the fly by a stem or post. Post and puff materials, and their placement on the fly, vary and form the primary differences among the parasol patterns in this chapter. Fran Betters uses deer hair and thread; we use poly yarn and monofilament; and number of European tyers use CDC to form both the parasol puff and the post. Umbrella emergers are identical in their function to parasol emergers but use hackle wrapped atop a tall post to float the fly. The hackle and post are perhaps less conspicuous to the fish, but they are more complicated to tie.

The use of an umbrella or parasol accomplishes a couple of functions. It positions the fly just beneath the film, in much the same way that is achieved by fishing an ordinary nymph pattern on tippet that is greased to within a few inches of the fly. But unlike the greased-tippet approach, the parasol gives a visible component to a sunken fly that helps in detecting strikes. And it allows the angler to track the behavior of the fly on the water and determine if it is drifting freely or dragging. Though specific imitations are illustrated in the tying sequences, almost any mayfly nymph, caddis pupa, or midge pupa can be tied with the parasols shown in this chapter.

Piggy-Back Nymph

Originator: Fran Betters
Hook: TMC 3761BL, or other 1XL nymph hook, #14-#18
Thread: Tan 6/0
Tail: Australian possum guard hairs
Rib: Copper wire
Abdomen: Australian possum
Parasol: Clipped deer hair with tying thread post
Wing case: Mottled turkey tail
Thorax: Same as abdomen

As far as we know, this is the original incarnation of the parasol idea. Though deer hair is a bit more involved to tie than some of the other parasol materials, Betters favors this approach because it allows a very flexible post material.

Step 1: *Clip and clean* (p. 32) a bundle of deer hair, but do not stack it. Pinch the hair in your left fingers with the hair tips exposed.

Step 2: Clip the tips so that ¼" or so projects beyond your fingertips.

Step 3: Pinch a 3" tag of tying thread beneath your thumb.

Step 4: With the bobbin, take 10-12 wraps next to your fingertips, tightening the wraps as you wind to flare the hair.

Step 5: Pull 3" of tying thread from the bobbin, and clip. Now use both hands to tie 2 or 3 overhand knots in the center of the bundle. When the hair is secured, clip it to a ball shape of the desired diameter, usually about ¼"-⅜".

Step 6: Mount the tying thread and wrap to the tailing point. Secure a sparse bundle of guard hairs to form a tail about one hook-gap in length. Mount the ribbing material atop the rearmost tailing wrap.

Step 7: Use the *direct dubbing* method (p. 34) to dub a slightly tapered abdomen over the rear ⅔ of the shank. *Counter-rib* (p. 33) the wire to the front of the abdomen; tie off and clip.

Step 8: Mount the parasol directly ahead of the abdomen with the deer-hair ball extending rearward. The thread post between the shank and the deer hair can be adjusted to the tyer's preference, but Fran Betters leaves about 1" of thread.

Step 9: Cut a strip of turkey tail about ⅔ the width of the hook gap, and mount it directly in front of the abdomen. Then dub a thorax slightly thicker than the abdomen.

Step 10: Fold the wing case over the thorax, and secure it behind the hook eye. Clip and bind the excess. Form the head of the fly and whip finish.

Parasol March Brown

Originator: Jim Schollmeyer and Ted Leeson
Hook: TMC 3761BL, or other 1XL nymph hook, #12-#14
Thread: Brown 6/0
Parasol puff: Two 1" pieces of light gray carded poly yarn (for hooks #18 and smaller, use one piece)
Parasol post: 8-inch length of 4X tippet (for hooks #18 and smaller, use 5X)
Tail: Mottled brown hen fibers
Rib: Fine copper wire
Abdomen: Light brown Antron dubbing
Thorax: Brown Haretron dubbing
Legs: Mottled brown hen fibers

We came up with this parasol design in attempt to devise a suspended-nymph pattern that rode deeper beneath the film than we could get with a float pod. It takes little poly yarn to float the fly, so the puff can be made smaller than is shown here, though the visibility decreases.

Step 1: To form the puff: align the two pieces of yarn (left); stack them (middle); and tie a clinch knot around the center of the bundle with the tippet material (right).

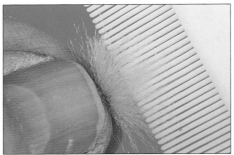

Step 2: Clip the tag of the tippet material. Run a dubbing needle or comb through the yarn to fluff and separate the fibers.

Step 3: Lay a thread foundation over the middle ⅓ of the shank. Position the thread ⅓ of a shank-length behind the eye. Bind the parasol atop the shank. The length of the mono post can be varied; here, we're using a parasol height of about ¼". When the height is correct, bind the mono tag tightly and clip the excess.

Step 4: Position the thread at the tailing point. Mount the tail material to form a tail about one hook-gap in length. Mount the ribbing material atop the rearmost tailing wrap.

Step 5: Use the *direct dubbing* method (p. 34) to dub a tapered abdomen over the rear half of the shank. *Counter-rib* (p. 33) the wire to the front of the abdomen. Clip and bind the excess.

Step 6: Position the tying thread directly ahead of the mono post. Lift the post and take several wraps of thread in front of it, building a thread bump that holds the post in a vertical position.

Step 7: Dub the thorax, leaving enough room behind the hook eye to mount the legs.

Step 8: *Align and strip* (p. 30) a small bundle of mottled hen fibers, and use the method explained in *side-mounted legs* (p. 39) to mount them on the near side of the shank. Repeat to mount the legs on the far side, as shown in this view from underneath. Clip and bind the excess.

Step 9: Whip finish the fly. Draw the yarn fibers evenly upward.

Step 10: Clip them to a height of about ³⁄₁₆". (On hooks #18 and smaller, clip to a height of about ⅛".)

Parasol Caddis

Originator: Jim Schollmeyer and Ted Leeson
Hook: Mustad 37160, or other scud hook, #14-#20
Thread: Brown 6/0
Parasol puff: Two 1" pieces of light gray carded poly yarn (for hooks #18 and smaller, use one piece)
Parasol post: 8-inch length of 4X tippet (for hooks #18 and smaller, use 5X)
Shuck: Amber Antron dubbing fibers
Abdomen: Arizona Synthetic Peacock dubbing, bronze
Thorax: Arizona Synthetic Peacock dubbing, natural
Legs: CDC fibers

The parasol approach has proven effective on caddis patterns as well. Post height can be varied, but posts longer than an inch can make the fly spin or catch on the leader.

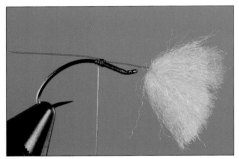

Step 1: Form and mount the parasol as explained in Parasol March Brown, Steps 1-3, (p. 182).

Step 2: Wrap the thread to the tailing point, and secure a bundle of Antron dubbing fibers to form a shuck about one hook-gap in length.

Step 3: Use the *direct dubbing* method (p. 34) to dub an abdomen over the rear ⅔ of the shank.

Step 4: Elevate the parasol and build a thread bump in front of the mono post to stand it up vertically, as explained in Parasol March Brown, Step 6. (p. 182).

Step 5: Dub the thorax, leaving enough room behind the hook eye to mount the legs.

Step 6: Use the method shown in *stripping CDC barbs* (p. 40) to gather a bundle of fibers. Mount them underneath the shank as explained in *throat hackle* (p. 41) to form legs that extend to the hook point. Whip finish the fly and trim the parasol as explained in Parasol March Brown, Steps 9-10, (p. 182).

Parasol Midge Emerger

Originator: Jim Schollmeyer and Ted Leeson
Hook: TMC 2487, or other fine-wire scud hook, #14-#20
Parasol puff: Two 1" pieces of light gray carded poly yarn (for hooks #18 and smaller, use one piece)
Parasol post: 8-inch length of 4X tippet (for hooks #18 and smaller, use 5X)
Thread: Black 8/0
Shuck: Sparse bundle (about 15 strands) white Z-Lon
Rib: Fine copper wire
Abdomen: 2-3 strands green Krystal Flash
Thorax: Dark brown rabbit fur

In this version of the design, the parasol is angled out over the hook to orient the fly almost vertically beneath the film, which is a more natural position for a midge pupa.

Step 1: Form and mount the parasol as explained in Parasol March Brown, Steps 1-3, (p. 182). Bind the mono tag to the midpoint of the shank and clip. Position the thread at the tailing point.

Step 2: Mount the Antron to form a shuck about ½ the hook gap in length. Mount the Krystal Flash atop the rear-most tailing wrap. Mount the rib wire atop the Krystal Flash. Leave all the tags long, and bind them as a group atop the shank until you reach the clipped end of the mono.

Step 3: Trim the tags even with end of the mono. Wrap the thread forward, forming a smooth underbody. Wrap the strands of Krystal Flash forward as a group, and tie off at a point ¼ the shank-length behind the eye.

Step 4: *Counter-rib* (p. 33) the wire over the abdomen. Bind and clip the excess at the front of the abdomen.

Step 5: Build a bump of tying thread in front of the mono post to elevate the parasol to an angle of about 45 degrees above the hook shank.

Step 6: Use the *direct dubbing* method (p. 34) to form a ball-like thorax. Whip finish the fly and trim the parasol as explained in Parasol March Brown, Steps 9-10, (p. 182).

Parasol PMD Pop-Up

Originator: Jim Schollmeyer and Ted Leeson
Hook: TMC 3761BL, or other 1XL nymph hook, #14-#18
Thread: Brown 8/0
Tail: Mottled brown hen hackle fibers
Rib: Fine copper wire
Abdomen: Olive-brown dubbing
Parasol puff: Two 1" pieces of light gray carded poly yarn (for hooks #18 and smaller, use one piece)
Parasol post: 8-inch length of 4X tippet (for hooks #18 and smaller, use 5X)
Thorax: Brown dubbing
Legs: Mottled brown hen hackle fibers

Pop-ups and puff emergers are among our favorite styles for imitating hatching mayflies. Flies of this style tied with poly yarn are quite durable, but best restricted to hooks larger than #20. For smaller hooks, we think CDC, tied as shown on the PMD Puff Emerger (p. 269) or the Puff Emerger—BWO (p. 270), is a more practical material.

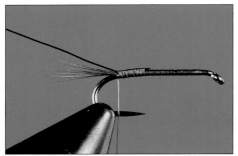

Step 1: Mount the thread and position it at the tailing point. *Align and strip* (p. 30) a sparse bundle of hen fibers. Mount them atop the shank to form a tail about one hook-gap in length. Mount the ribbing wire atop the rearmost tailing wraps.

Step 2: Use the *direct dubbing* method (p. 34) to dub a tapered abdomen over the rear half of the shank. Then *counter-rib* (p. 33) the wire to the front of the abdomen. Bind and clip the wire.

Step 3: Dub a thorax about ⅓ the distance to the hook eye.

Step 4: Form the parasol as explained in Parasol March Brown, Steps 1-2, (p. 182). Mount the parasol atop the shank with the puff to the rear, directly in front of the thorax. Use 3-4 moderately light thread wraps; don't wrap tightly, since you need to slide the mono beneath these wraps later.

Step 5: Dub the rest of the thorax, stopping about one hook-eye's distance behind the eye. Grasp the mono tag, and pull to draw the puff down so that it touches, or nearly touches the thorax.

Step 6: Bind the mono tag tightly, and clip. Trim the parasol as explained in Parasol March Brown, Steps 9-10, (p. 182). *Align and strip* a bundle of hen hackle fibers, and use the technique shown in *throat hackle* (p. 41) to mount them beneath the shank for legs. Bind the butts, clip, and whip finish the fly.

Quill Parasol

Hook: TMC 2487, or other fine-wire scud hook, #12-#18
Thread: Dark brown 6/0
Parasol: Two to four Type 2 CDC feathers wrapped with stripped peacock quill
Body: Tying thread
Rib: Yellow 6/0 thread
Thorax: Dark brown fur dubbing

We've seen a couple of versions of this European midge emerger, designed primarily for lake fishing. The quill-wrapped post on the parasol suggests the emerging adult body, while the dressing on the hook suggests the abandoned shuck.

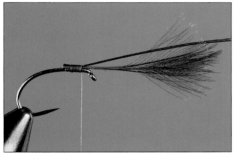

Step 1: Mount the thread, prepare the CDC feathers, and mount the feathers as explained in Parasol Buzzer, Steps 1-2, (p. 188). Mount a stripped peacock quill by the tip directly atop the frontmost thread wrap behind the hook eye.

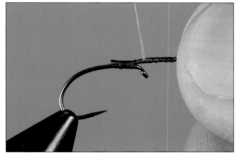

Step 2: Using the technique shown in Parasol Buzzer, Steps 3-5, (p. 188), wrap the feather stems and the quill together with a flattened thread. Then wrap back down the stems, forming a smooth underbody, again with a flattened thread. When you reach the hook, take a couple of thread wraps rearward.

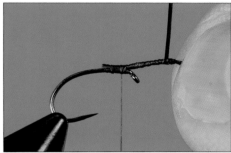

Step 3: Clip the butt of the quill in a hackle pliers, and wrap it in smooth turns down the thread-wrapped post. Support the feather tips with the right fingers, and wrap with the left hand. It may help to hold the bobbin out of the tying field by propping it on the vise head or clipping the thread in a material clip.

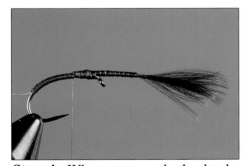

Step 4: When you reach the hook, take a wrap of quill around the shank. Then bind the quill and clip the excess. Wrap the thread to a point just around the hook bend, and mount the ribbing material. Wrap the thread forward over the rear ¾ of the shank to form the abdomen.

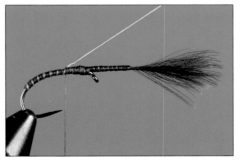

Step 5: Spiral the ribbing thread forward. Tie off the wire in front of the abdomen, and clip the excess.

Step 6: Use the *direct dubbing* method (p. 34) to form a ball-like thorax. Whip finish the fly behind the hook eye, around the shank only. Use a dubbing needle to coat the quill-wrapped post with head cement to improve durability.

Parasol Buzzer

Originator: Graydon Bell
Hook: TMC 2487, or other fine-wire scud hook, #10-#16
Thread: Black 6/0
Body: Black tying thread
Rib: Fine holographic tinsel
Thorax: Arizona Synthetic Peacock dubbing, natural
Wing buds: Orange floss
Parasol: Three natural CDC feathers, preferably Type 2

Graydon Bell showed us this pattern a few years ago, and we were much impressed with the ingenuity of the style, designed for midge fishing in the U.K. Though not especially difficult to tie, it is a bit more time consuming than other designs.

Step 1: Mount the thread, lay a short foundation behind the hook eye, and position the thread behind the eye. Measure one hook-length down the tip on the CDC feathers, and strip away the barbs below that point.

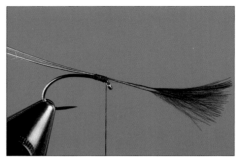

Step 2: Align the tips of the CDC feathers. Mount them as a bundle directly behind the hook eye so that the length of the stripped stem between the mounting wraps and the lowermost barbs is about equal to one hook-length. Clip and bind the CDC butts.

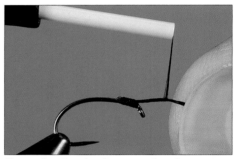

Step 3: Beginning at the frontmost mounting wrap, use a *flattened thread* (p. 37) to wrap around the CDC stems, moving toward the tip. Use the right fingers to put tension on the feather tips. Use left hand to wrap. You will have to release the bobbin after each full wrap, and reposition your hand for the next wrap.

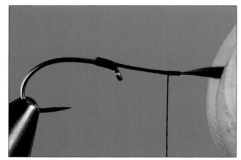

Step 4: Continue wrapping up to the lowermost CDC barbs, periodically stopping to spin the bobbin for a flattened thread. When you reach the CDC barbs, reverse direction and begin wrapping downward to the hook.

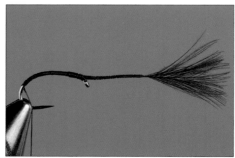

Step 5: When you reach the shank, continue wrapping the thread rearward to a point just around the hook bend.

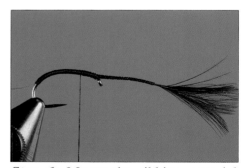

Step 6: Mount the ribbing material with a few thread wraps. Then continue wrapping forward to form the abdomen over the rear ¾ of the shank.

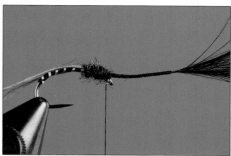

Step 7: Spiral the ribbing forward and tie it off at the front of the abdomen. Clip and bind the excess.

Step 8: Attach one strand of floss on the near side of the shank, directly ahead of the abdomen. Attach a second strand on the far side, as shown in this top view.

Step 9: Use the *direct dubbing* method (p. 34) to form the thorax.

Step 10: Draw one wing case strand forward along each side of the dubbing, and secure them in front of the thorax. Clip and bind the excess. Whip finish the fly behind the eye, around the hook shank only.

Step 11: When the fly is complete, use a dubbing needle to apply a thin coat of head cement to the thread-wrapped CDC stems to improve durability.

Umbrella Parachute Emerger—*Callibaetis*

Originator: Version of Tatsuhiro Saido design
Hook: TMC 900BL or equivalent dry-fly hook, #12-#18
Thread: Gray 8/0
Shuck: Gray Z-Lon or Antron
Body: Gray-brown dubbing, preferably natural fur
Wing post: Light dun poly yarn
Hackle: Grizzly

This unusual style suspends the fly body just below the surface film, while the tip of the wing post remains visible to the angler. The use of natural fur rather than poly dubbing helps the body sink. This basic design can be modified to imitate a variety of mayfly species.

Step 1: Lay a thread foundation over the front half of the shank, and position the thread about ¼ of a shank-length behind the eye. Cut a 4" length of poly yarn half the thickness desired in the finished wing. Double the yarn to form a loop, and mount the cut ends. Build a bump of thread at the front base of the post to stand the loop upright.

Step 2: Prepare a hackle feather as shown by removing the barbs from the tip and butt of the feather. The stripped portions of the stem should be at least 1 ½ times the shank length. The intact section of barbs should also be about 1 ½ times the shank length.

Step 3: Using the method explained in *horizontal-mount parachute hackle* (p. 37), secure the hackle to the hook shank. Note that the length of bare feather stem between the mounting wraps and the base of the hackle barbs is about one shank-length.

Step 4: After the hackle is secure, raise it vertically and prop it against the front of the poly loop to keep the feather out the way when dressing the rest of the fly. Position the thread at the tailing point, and secure a sparse bundle of Antron to make a shuck about one hook-gap in length.

Step 5: Dub a slightly tapered abdomen over the rear ⅔ of the shank.

Step 6: Dub a thorax with a slight bulge, and position the thread behind the hook eye.

Step 7: Clip the feather tip in a pair of hackle pliers. Insert your left index finger into the yarn loop and apply tension upward. With the right hand, spiral the bare hackle stem up the wing post. Wrap as far toward the rear of the hook as you can. Then capture the pliers in your left fingers, as shown.

Step 8: Reposition your right hand in front of the wing post. Take the hackle pliers in your right hand again, and continue spiraling the bare stem up the shank. When you reach the section of feather with barbs on it, wrap the hackle as explained in *wrapping parachute hackle* (p. 46), placing each wrap of the feather directly beneath the previous one.

Step 9: When the barbed portion is fully wrapped, spiral the remaining section of bare stem back down the wing post. Secure the feather stem just as you would tie off a parachute hackle.

Step 10: Clip the excess hackle stem, and whip finish the head. Clip the wing post to about one hook-gap in height.

Dandelion Emerger

Hook: TMC 2487, or other fine-wire scud hook, #16-#20
Thread: Light gray 8/0
Abdomen: Green wire
Wing: Gray Antron
Thorax: Peacock herl
Wing post: White Antron
Hackle: Grizzly

We've seen a number of versions of (and names for) this design which, as far as we've been able to determine, originated in Colorado. The umbrella-style hackle here can be used on virtually any nymph or sunken emerger pattern. The version shown here is also effective tied with red or black wire.

Step 1: Attach the thread and position it behind the hook eye. Cut a 4" length of Antron, half the thickness of the finished wing post. Double it over, forming a loop, and secure the two ends atop the shank, behind the hook eye. Raise the loop vertically, and hold it in a gallows tool.

Step 2: Prepare a hackle feather. Wrap the thread up the Antron post about ½". At the top of the post, pinch the hackle feather against the yarn post, and secure the butt of the feather by wrapping the thread downward, laying a smooth foundation. Wrap ⅓ of the way down to the hook.

Step 3: Wrap the hackle downward as shown in *wrapping parachute hackle* (p. 46). Take 5 or 6 turns of hackle. Unwrap the tying thread from the post until it abuts the last wrap of hackle. Tie off the hackle against the post. Trim off the hackle tip and the excess stem, and wrap the thread smoothly down to the hook.

Step 4: Remove the yarn from the gallows tool, and cut the wing post to about one hook-gap in height. Add a drop of Super Glue to the wing post and thread wraps.

Step 5: Wrap to the tailing point. Mount a length of wire, and bind the excess to the top of the shank so that it abuts the base of the wing post, forming a smooth underbody.

Step 6: Wrap the wire forward to form an abdomen over the rear ⅔ of the shank. Bind and clip the excess.

Step 7: Mount a piece of Antron yarn directly ahead of the abdomen to form a wing about ½ the hook gap in length. Clip and bind the excess Antron.

Step 8: Mount 2-3 strands of peacock herl directly atop the wing-mounting wraps. Position the tying thread at the base of the wing post.

Step 9: Form a thorax as shown in *wrapping twisted-herl collars* (p. 49). Tie off and clip the excess. If necessary, take a few thread wraps at the base of the post to lean it at a shallow angle over the hook eye.

Step 10: Build a small thread bump ahead of the post to help hold it at the desired angle. Whip finish beneath the post, around the shank only.

Chapter 10: Paraloop Emergers

This unusual hackling technique appears to have evolved independently in at least two places—among a group of West Coast tyers in the U.S., most notably Ned Long, Bob Quigley, and Jim Cramer; and in U.K. by tyer Ian Moutter. It's been given different names—"hackle stacker," "twisted hackle," "pullover hackle," and finally, "paraloop," the name used by Ian Moutter and the one we've chosen since Moutter literally wrote the book on the subject—*Tying Flies the Paraloop Way*.

The paraloop design is well suited to emergers. The effect of this hackle style is somewhere between a parachute hackle and a Comparadun-type arc wing, and it produces a fly that rides low in the water with an unobstructed body silhouette, but floats well and is reasonably visible to the angler. Though forming the paraloop is a bit more involved than other tying techniques, it is not difficult. The paraloop assembly can be dressed in a drawn wing case fashion, as a loopwing, or even a shellback style on both flush-floating and descending-body emergers. Tyers interested in this very recent design should most certainly consult Moutter's book, where the versatility of this hackling style is shown in great detail.

Paraloop BWO Emerger

Originator: Adaptation of Ian Moutter design
Hook: TMC 206BL, or other fine-wire scud hook, #14-#18
Thread: Dun 8/0
Shuck: Amber Antron
Abdomen: Olive floss
Paraloop post: Olive or gray size A or 3/0 polyester tying thread
Hackle: Dun rooster saddle
Thorax: Olive fine poly dubbing

This is a simple adaptation of Ian Moutter's paraloop dun design. It can be modified to match almost any mayfly hatch. The following illustrates the construction of the "hackle brush" that is the central component of the paraloop method.

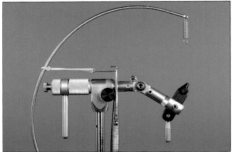

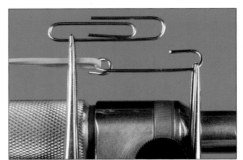

Step 1: The hackle brush can be fashioned without a gallows tool, but is much easier if one is used, as shown here. Shown on the stem of the gallows tool is a simple homemade tool Moutter calls a "neckbreaker." It holds the hackle brush out of the way when dubbing the thorax and is shown in detail in the next step.

Step 2: To make the neckbreaker, bend a paper clip to the shape shown. Fold a rubber band around the stem of the gallows tool, and insert one end through the loop of the other end, making a slip knot that holds the rubber band in place. Slip the rubber band into the "eye" bent in the paper clip.

Step 3: Mount the tying thread behind the hook eye, and wrap a thread foundation to the midpoint of the shank. Cut a 5" length of post material and fold it in half. Mount this loop at the midpoint of the shank, cut ends toward the hook eye. Take 2-3 wraps behind the loop to elevate it vertically.

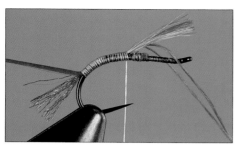

Step 4: Fold the loop forward over the hook eye. Mount a sparse bundle of Antron behind the loop, and bind it to the top of the shank, stopping about ⅓ the distance around the hook bend. Clip it to form a shuck about one shank-length long. Mount a strand of floss. Bind the tag atop the shank to the rear of the loop.

Step 5: Clip the floss tag. Wrap the floss forward to form a tapered abdomen that extends to the rear of the loop threads. Tie off and clip the excess.

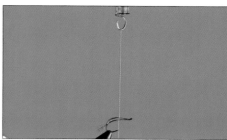

Step 6: Hook the looped thread post in a gallows tool, as shown. Adjust the tension on the gallows tool to put a very firm tension on the loop threads. A tight post will greatly facilitate the hackle wrapping.

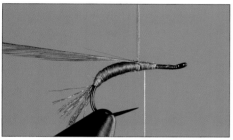

Step 7: *Prepare a hackle feather* (p. 39). Mount the feather as explained in *horizontal-mount parachute hackle* (p. 37), except no bare feather stem is left between the lowermost barbs and the post.

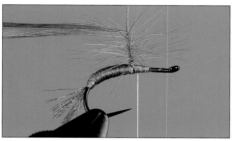

Step 8: Wrap the hackle up the post threads in close, but not touching turns. Wrap up the threads to a height that equals the distance from the base of the post to the back of the hook eye.

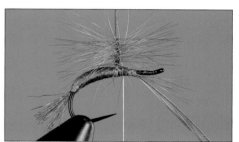

Step 9: When the proper height is reached, wrap the hackle back down to the base of the post. Tie off the hackle at the front base of the post, and the hackle brush is complete.

Step 10: Remove the thread post from the gallows tool, and hook the thread loop on the paper-clip hook. This holds the hackle brush out of the tying field so that the remainder of the fly can be dressed.

Step 11: Use the *direct dubbing* method (p. 34) to dub the thorax of the fly. Position the thread at the front of the thorax.

Step 12: Remove the hackle brush from the neckbreaker. Fold the hackle brush forward over the top of the thorax. Tie it off directly in front of the thorax. Clip the excess and bind down, forming the head of the fly. Whip finish.

Step 13: Here is a front view of the completed fly.

Brown Sedge Emerger

Originator: Ian Moutter
Hook: TMC 2487, or other fine-wire scud hook, #10-#12
Thread: Brown 8/0
Paraloop post: Gray size A or 3/0 polyester tying thread
Shuck: Cream and brown Antron fibers, furled
Abdomen: Cream and brown Antron dubbing
Hackle: Brown
Thorax: Rusty-olive fine poly dubbing

This caddis pattern illustrates the way in which the paraloop design can be used to create an open loop atop the thorax to suggest the humped profile of an emerging insect.

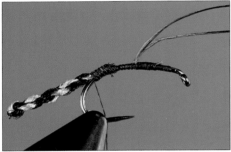

Step 1: Mount the thread post as shown in Paraloop BWO Emerger, Step 3, (p. 194). Wrap the thread to the hook bend. Bundle together strands of brown and cream Antron yarn to make a single strand. Use the method shown in *furled shuck* (p. 61) to furl the strand, and mount it to form a shuck one shank-length long. Clip and bind the excess.

Step 2: With scissors, clip the excess shuck yarns into ⅛" pieces and mix to make dubbing. Use the *direct dubbing* method (p. 34) to dub the abdomen up to the base of the thread post.

Step 3: Use the procedure shown in Paraloop BWO Emerger, Steps 6-9, (p. 195), to form a hackle brush that is as tall as 1 ½ times the distance from the thread post to the hook eye. Remove the post from the gallows tool, and gently pull the two threads apart. Moutter calls this "compacting" the hackle.

Step 4: Use the left thumb and forefinger to gently stroke the hackle fibers rearward. Repeat a few times. This "doubling" as Moutter calls it creates a gap in the front of the hackle brush that produces a neater finished fly.

Step 5: Hook the loop in the neckbreaker as shown in Paraloop BWO Emerger, Step 10, (p. 195). Use the poly dubbing to dub a thorax from the front of the post to just behind the hook eye.

Step 6: Fold the hackle brush over the thorax, creating a loop as shown. Secure the hackle brush behind the hook eye. Clip the excess and whip finish the fly. Reverse the fly in the vise. Use a lighter to melt the very end of the shuck. As the fibers begin to melt, pinch them with moistened thumb and forefinger to make a slight point.

Reverse Paraloop Emerger

Originator: Version of Roy Christie design
Hook: TMC 101, or other ring-eye dry-fly hook, #12-#18
Thread: Brown 8/0
Trailing shuck: Brown Antron
Dubbed shuck: Brown dubbing
Adult abdomen: Tan dubbing
Adult thorax: Brown dubbing
Paraloop post: Brown Super Floss
Hackle: Grizzly

British tyer Roy Christie specializes in this reverse-style dressing, which puts the greatest floatation atop the heaviest part of the hook and takes advantage of the straight shank in imitating the abdomen of the emerger. The version show here represents a March brown, but the design can be modified for almost any hatch.

Step 1: Position the hook in the vise as shown. Attach the thread and wrap it ⅓ the way around the hook bend. Mount the Super Floss post as shown in Paraloop BWO Emerger, Step 3, (p. 194).

Step 2: Use the *direct dubbing* method (p. 34) to dub a thorax ¼ the distance to the hook eye. Position the thread at the rear of the thorax. Use the procedure shown in Paraloop BWO Emerger, Steps 6-9, (p. 195), to form a hackle brush just tall enough to reach the rear of the thorax.

Step 3: Reposition the hook in the vise. Fold the hackle brush over the thorax. Tie off the hackle-brush loop directly in front of the thorax and clip the excess. Advance the thread to the hook eye. Mount a sparse bundle of Antron fibers atop the shank.

Step 4: Return the thread to the rear of the thorax. Dub a tapered abdomen ⅔ the distance to the hook eye.

Step 5: Use the shuck dubbing to dub a shuck that begins slightly wider than the abdomen, then tapers to the hook eye and covers the thread wraps securing the Antron.

Step 6: Lift the shuck fibers and build a small thread bump; elevating the fibers gives easier access to the hook eye when tying fly to tippet. Clip the Antron to ¼ of a shank length. Whip finish beneath the Antron, around the hook shank only.

PMD Paraloop

Originator: Version of Ian Moutter design
Hook: TMC 206BL, or other fine-wire scud hook, #14-#16
Thread: Gray 8/0
Paraloop post: Gray size A or 3/0 polyester tying thread
Shuck: Olive Z-Lon
Body: Yellow fine poly dubbing
Hackle: Dun
Wing: Dun hackle tips

Ian Moutter ties some mayfly and midge emergers with feather-tip wings to suggest more precisely the silhouette of the emerging fly. Colors and sizes can be varied to match almost any hatch.

Step 1: Mount the thread behind the hook eye. Wrap to the midpoint of the shank, and return the thread to a point about five thread-wraps behind the eye. Prepare two dun hackle tips by clipping away the lower barbs to leave tips that are about one shank-length long.

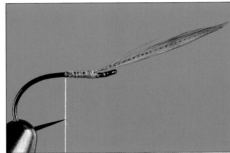

Step 2: Place the hackle tips front-to-front, so they flare away from one another. Mount them atop the shank about five thread-wraps behind the eye. Note that a small section of bare stem is left between the mounting wraps and lowermost barbs. Clip the excess. Wrap the thread rearward and position it just above the hook point.

Step 3: Form and mount the thread post as shown in Paraloop BWO Emerger, Step 3, (p.194). Wrap the thread rearward to a point just above the hook barb. Take a sparse length of olive Z-Lon and prepare it as shown in *furled shuck* (p. 61). Mount it atop the hook to form a shuck as long as the hook shank. Clip and bind the excess.

Step 4: With scissors, clip the excess shuck yarn to ⅛" lengths, and mix to randomize the fibers into dubbing. Use the *direct dubbing* method (p. 34) to dub the shank from the front of the shuck to the rear of the thread post.

Step 5: Use the procedure shown in Paraloop BWO Emerger, Steps 6-10, (p. 195), to form hackle brush that is as tall as twice the distance from the thread post to the hook eye. Clip the hackle brush in the neckbreaker.

Step 6: Dub the yellow poly from the front of the thread post to the front-most mounting wrap securing the hackle tips. Remove the post from the neckbreaker, and gently pull the two threads apart, forcing the hackle wraps downward to make a hackle brush that is 1 ½ times the length from the post to the hook eye.

Step 7: Fold the hackle brush over the dubbed body, forming an open loop. Tie off the brush directly in front of the dubbing, behind the hackle tips. Clip and bind the excess.

Step 8: Lift the feather tips and take a wrap of thread directly in front of the stems to elevate the wings slightly. Use your fingertips to separate the wings in a narrow "V".

Step 9: Draw the wings rearward with your left fingers, and take a few thread wraps to hold them in position. Whip finish the fly. The finished wings should angle back over the body. Melt the end of the abdomen as shown in Brown Sedge Emerger, Step 6, (p. 196).

Brown Midge Emerger

Originator: Variation of Ian Moutter pattern
Hook: TMC 206BL, or other fine-wire scud hook, #14-#18
Thread: Brown 8/0
Shuck: Cream Antron
Abdomen: Brown tying thread
Wings: Dun hackle tips
Paraloop post: Brown size A or 3/0 polyester tying thread
Hackle: Brown
Thorax: Dark brown fine poly dubbing

Ian Moutter calls this looped hackle-wing design a "locked wing" and uses it on some of his emerging midge patterns; it could be used in mayfly emergers as well. This interesting wing design seems to us as though it might have applications in more conventional patterns as well.

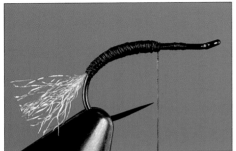

Step 1: Mount the thread behind the eye and wrap rearward ⅓ of a shank length. Mount a sparse strand of Antron and wrap rearward, binding it atop the shank. Stop at the rearmost point of the body, and clip to make a shuck ½ a shank-length long. Wrap the thread forward to form a slender abdomen. Clip the excess Antron.

Step 2: Take two dun hackles with barbs about one hook-gap in length. Mount one feather by the tip on the near side of the shank. The front of the feather should face the tyer. Mount the second feather on the far side of the shank, with the front facing away from the tying. Clip and bind the excess.

Step 3: Form and mount the thread post as shown in Paraloop BWO Emerger, Step 3, (p. 194). Use the procedure shown in Paraloop BWO Emerger, Steps 6-10, (p. 195), to form hackle brush that is as tall as the distance from the thread post to the hook eye. Clip the hackle brush in the neckbreaker.

Step 4: Use the *direct dubbing* method (p. 34) to dub a thorax ⅔ the distance from the front of the abdomen to the hook eye. Fold the hackle brush over the thorax, and tie it off directly in front of the thorax. Clip and bind the excess.

Step 5: Fold the hackle on the near side toward the hook eye, forming a loop about ⅔ the hook gap in height. Secure the feather against the side of the shank in front of the thorax.

Step 6: Repeat Step 5 with the feather on the far side, forming a matching wing. Clip the excess feather butts and bind down, forming the head of the fly. Whip finish. Here's a view of the finished fly from the front.

Ned's Emerger

Originator: Ned Long
Hook: TMC 2487, or other fine-wire scud hook, #12-#16
Thread: Brown 8/0
Shuck: Tan Z-Lon
Abdomen: Red Superfloss
Paraloop post: Red Superfloss
Hackle: Brown
Thorax: Reddish brown fine poly dubbing

Ned Long's use of a stretch floss body material for the paraloop post on this midge emerger is an interesting innovation. When tension on the floss is relaxed after wrapping the hackle, the hackle wraps compress closely together, and the expansion of the floss inside the wraps helps secure them.

Step 1: Mount the thread behind the eye and wrap rearward ⅓ of a shank length. Mount a strand of Antron and wrap rearward, binding it atop the shank. Stop at the rearmost point of the body, and clip to make a shuck ½ a shank-length long. Melt the end of the shuck with a lighter to hold the yarns strands together.

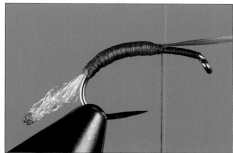

Step 2: Mount a strand of Superfloss tightly atop the rearmost shuck wrap. Wrap the thread forward, forming a tapered underbody over the rear ⅔ of the shank. Wrap the Superfloss forward to form the abdomen. Tie off the floss on top of the shank, but do not clip the excess.

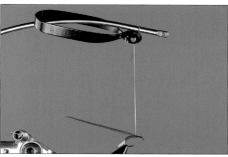

Step 3: Clip the Superfloss tag in hackle pliers, and hang the pliers from the gallows tool, as shown. The Superfloss should be taut. *Prepare a hackle feather* (p. 39). Mount the feather as explained in *horizontal-mount parachute hackle* (p. 37), except no bare feather stem is left between the lowermost barbs and the post.

Step 4: Advance the thread to the hook eye. Use the *direct dubbing* method (p. 34) to dub a thorax. Wrap rearward to the base of the paraloop post.

Step 5: Use the procedure shown in Paraloop BWO Emerger, Steps 6-9, (p. 195), to form the hackle brush. Ned Long takes 8 wraps up the post and 4 wraps back down. When the hackle is tied off at the base of the post, spiral the thread forward over the thorax to a point a few thread-wraps behind the hook eye.

Step 6: Release the floss from the hackle pliers, and let it relax until there's no tension. Fold the hackle brush over the thorax, and secure it behind the hook eye. Clip the excess and bind it down, forming the head of the fly. Whip finish.

Chapter 11: Collar Hackle and Herl Collar Emergers

This chapter contains fly designs incorporating materials wrapped collar fashion—most notably hackle, but also aftershaft, ostrich herl, and fibers spun in a dubbing loop. Flies collared with wet-fly hackle, particularly those tied in the "soft hackle" or "North Country spider" style, are certainly one of the oldest designs in fly-fishing. And though we tend to think of these flies as tied for fishing on the swing, they make excellent emerger patterns fished dead-drift on or in the film. The mobility of the hackle is one of the key features of the style, and recently tyers such as Jack Gartside have used soft, fluffy, flexible aftershaft feathers to give lifelike movement to the fly. And many patterns have appeared that incorporate CDC for the hackle, which floats the fly better for dead-drift presentations and gives excellent mobility to flies fished subsurface or on the swing. Collars of dry-fly hackle are used on some designs, though tyers often trim the hackle beneath the shank to bring the fly body closer to the surface of the water, as in Wayne Luallen's Stuck Shuck Midge.

Other patterns are tied with unclipped dry-fly hackle in a design that suspends the hook vertically in the water with most of the shank submerged; the hackle spreads radially on the film, much like a parachute style. Typically, these flies are dressed with a tuft over the eye to represent the emerging wings or body, and we've included two such patterns, the Grey Midge Emerger and the Suspender Midge, in Chapter 7, Tuft Emergers.

Stuck Shuck Midge

Originator: Wayne Luallen
Hook: Daiichi 1130, or other light-wire scud hook, #18-#26
Thread: Gray 10/0
Shuck: Light dun Micro-Zelon
Abdomen: Tying thread
Rib: Dark gray 8/0 or 10/0 tying thread
Wing: Dun or white Type 3 CDC feather
Thorax: Gray mole dubbing
Hackle: Dun

Tyer Wayne Luallen designed this midge emerger for fishing the San Juan River. Fine thread and finely textured materials make it well suited to very small hooks. Colors can be varied to match the many colors of natural midges.

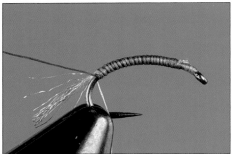

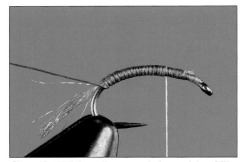

Step 1: Attach the thread and position it behind the hook eye. Mount the shuck fibers atop the shank. Secure them by wrapping rearward, forming a smooth underbody as you go. Trim the shuck to about one hook gap in length. Mount the ribbing thread.

Step 2: With a *flattened thread* (p. 37), form a smooth abdomen over the rear ¾ of the hook shank.

Step 3: With a *twisted thread* (p. 42), spiral the ribbing forward and tie off at the front of the abdomen. Mount the tip of a CDC feather directly in front of the abdomen to form a sparse wing that extends just to the rear of the body. Wrap forward, binding the CDC atop the shank, and clip the butt to form a small tuft over the hook eye.

Step 4: *Prepare a hackle feather* (p. 39) and mount it directly in front of the abdomen as explained in *mounting collar hackle* (p. 37). Use the *direct dubbing* method to dub a thorax that covers the thread wraps used to secure the hackle stem.

Step 5: Wrap the hackle forward in a close spiral over the thorax as explained in *palmering hackle* (p. 38). Tie off and clip the hackle and whip finish around the shank at the base of the CDC to elevate the tuft slightly.

Step 6: Trim away the hackle fibers below the hook shank to form a V-shaped gap, as shown in this front view.

Baetis Soft Hackle

Hook: TMC 900BL, or equivalent dry-fly hook, #16-#20
Thread: Gray 8/0
Tail: Dun hen hackle fibers
Rib: Fine gold wire
Body: Olive Antron dubbing
Hackle: Dun hen hackle

This versatile pattern can be varied in size and color; it can be fished on the swing or greased and fished dead-drift in the surface film. One of the simplest of all emergers to tie, it is still one of the most effective.

Step 1: Attach the thread and position it at the tailing point. Mount 4-6 hen hackle fibers to make a tail equal in length to the hook gap. Mount the ribbing wire atop the rearmost thread wraps.

Step 2: Use the *direct dubbing* method (p. 34) to dub a slender, slightly tapered abdomen over the rear ⅔ of the shank. Spiral the wire forward to rib the abdomen.

Step 3: Tie off the ribbing in front of the abdomen; dub a thorax slightly larger in diameter than the abdomen, stopping 5-6 thread-wraps' distance behind the hook eye.

Step 4: *Prepare a hackle feather* (p. 39), and mount it as explained in *mounting collar hackle* (p. 37). The front side of the feather should face the tyer.

Step 5: Take 2-3 turns of the feather as explained in *wrapping wet-fly hackle* (p. 50). Tie off and clip the feather.

Step 6: Draw the feather fibers rearward, and take a few wraps of thread at the base of the hackle to slant the barbs slightly toward the hook bend. Whip finish.

Partridge & Green

Hook: TMC 3761BL, or equivalent 1XL wet-fly hook, #10-#16
Thread: Green Pearsall Gossamer silk
Abdomen: Tying thread
Thorax: Dark hare's mask dubbing
Hackle: Brown partridge

This pattern from the north country of England is old but good. The hackling technique shown here can be used on any pattern where a very sparse hackle is desired. This same design is often tied with a hot orange or yellow body. While some tyers insist on Pearsall's silk for the abdomen, we've had good luck with synthetic materials as well.

Step 1: Attach the thread directly behind the hook eye with four turns of thread moving toward the bend. Select a partridge feather with barbs about twice the hook-gap in length. Prepare the feather by stripping the barbs from the base and one side, as shown.

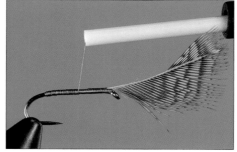

Step 2: Secure the feather atop the shank as shown. Bind the stem to the top of the shank in smooth, touching wraps. When you reach a point ⅓ the shank-length behind the eye, clip the stem. Continue wrapping the thread to the rear of the shank, then reverse direction and wrap forward in smooth wraps.

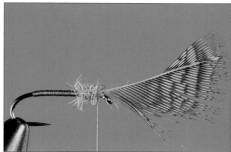

Step 3: Stop wrapping the abdomen at a point ⅓ the shank-length behind the eye. Use the *direct dubbing* method (p. 34) to form a thorax from the front of the abdomen to the tie-in point of the hackle.

Step 4: Clip the tip of the feather in a pair of hackle pliers, and take two turns *rearward*, toward the thorax, laying the bare side of the hackle stem against the hook shank.

Step 5: Take one turn of thread over the hackle tip. Take 2 or 3 turns of thread forward, through the wrapped hackle, ending on the bare shank directly ahead of the first hackle wrap. As you wrap forward, wiggle thread from side to side to avoid trapping any feather barbs.

Step 6: Clip the feather tip and whip finish to form a small, neat head in front of the first hackle wrap.

Hare's Ear Flymph

Originator: Jim Leisenring
Hook: Mustad 3906, or other standard wet-fly hook, #12-#16
Thread: Red Pearsall's Gossamer silk
Tail: Brown hen hackle fibers
Rib: Oval gold tinsel
Body: Hare's mask dubbing
Hackle: Brown hen hackle

This generalized emerger pattern is usually fished on the swing and is productive in both mayfly and caddis hatches.

Step 1: Attach the thread and position it behind the hook eye. *Prepare a hackle feather* (p. 39). Mount it directly behind the hook eye with a few tight wraps, as shown, with the front of the feather facing you. Clip the excess, and wrap to the tailing point.

Step 2: Mount 6-8 hen hackle fibers to form a tail as long as the hook shank. Strip a bit of the metallic coating from the end of the tinsel to expose the thread core. Mount the tinsel by binding down the core atop the rearmost thread wrap.

Step 3: Form a *dubbing loop* (p. 35) using the hare's mask dubbing, and twist tightly to produce a spikey cord. Wrap the dubbing forward, leaving a few wraps of thread exposed at the tail for a tag. Wrap forward over the rear ⅔ of the shank. Tie off and clip the dubbing loop.

Step 4: Rib the body tightly to press the tinsel into the fur. Tie off and clip the ribbing directly in front of the dubbing. Wrap the thread rearward to a point just forward of the middle of the body. Take two turns of hackle toward the rear of the shank, just behind the eye.

Step 5: Take a third wrap of hackle rearward halfway to where the tying thread is positioned. Take the last wrap of hackle directly in front of the tying thread. Take a wrap of thread to secure the hackle tip.

Step 6: Wrap the thread forward, "weaving" it through the hackle barbs to avoid trapping them, ending directly in front of the first wrap of hackle. Clip the hackle tip. Draw the hackle barbs back, and form a small, neat head at the base to slant the fibers slightly rearward. Whip finish.

Denny's All Purpose Emerger

Originator: Denny Rickards
Hook: TMC 5262, or other 2XL hook, #10-#14
Thread: Black 6/0
Tail: Woodduck flank barbs
Rib: Copper wire
Abdomen: Hare's ear dubbing
Thorax: Peacock herl
Wing case: Woodduck flank barbs
Hackle: Partridge

Stillwater guru Denny Rickards ranks this among his top four most effective patterns. Soft materials give this generic fly good movement in the water; it can be fished with a strip or twitch to simulate the action of an emerging insect.

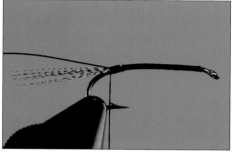

Step 1: Attach the thread and position it at the tailing point. *Align and strip* (p. 30) a bundle of 8-10 woodduck flank barbs, and mount them atop the shank to produce a tail one shank-length long. Clip and bind the excess. Mount the rib material atop the rear-most tailing wrap.

Step 2: Use the *direct dubbing* method (p. 34) to dub a tapered abdomen over the rear half of the shank. Spiral the wire forward to rib the abdomen. Bind and clip at the front of the abdomen.

Step 3: Cut a strip of woodduck flank barbs about ½ the hook gap in width. Mount the strip directly ahead of the abdomen. Clip and bind the excess. Mount 3-5 strands of peacock herl directly ahead of the woodduck.

Step 4: Using the method shown in *wrapping twisted-herl collars* (p. 49), form the thorax of the fly, stopping about 6-7 thread-wraps' distance behind the hook eye. Bind and clip the herl.

Step 5: Fold the woodduck barbs over the thorax, forming the wing case. Tie off and clip directly ahead of the thorax. *Prepare a hackle feather* (p. 39), and mount the partridge feather directly ahead of the thorax. Advance the tying thread 3-4 wraps toward the hook eye.

Step 6: Take 2-4 turns of the feather as explained in *wrapping wet-fly hackle* (p. 50). Tie off the feather and clip the excess. Do not take extra thread wraps over the hackle to slant the barbs rearward. Form the head of the fly, and whip finish.

Foam Midge Emerger

Originator: Craig Mathews and Verlyn Klinkenborg
Hook: TMC 100, or equivalent dry-fly hook, #16-#26
Thread: Gray 8/0
Shuck: Amber Z-Lon
Rib: Fine copper wire
Abdomen: Black closed-cell foam
Hackle: Gray partridge
Thorax: Peacock herl

A foam body makes this pattern ride flush in the film. Ordinary fly-tying foam can be rather stiff for small hooks; try Ethafoam, often used a packing material for home electronics, colored with a black marker. CDC can be substituted for the partridge.

Step 1: Attach the thread and position it at the tailing point. Mount a bundle of Antron fibers to form a shuck about ½ the shank-length. Mount the ribbing wire atop the rearmost thread wraps. Mount a narrow strip of foam atop the thread wraps securing the rib.

Step 2: Bind the Antron and wire tags atop the shank to a point 6-7 thread-wraps' distance behind the hook eye. Clip and bind the excess. Under firm, but not tight, tension, wrap the foam strip forward in close, touching turns. Tie off and clip the excess foam. *Counter-rib* (p. 33) the copper wire.

Step 3: Secure the rib in front of the foam abdomen. Select a partridge feather with barbs that are about 1 ½ times the hook gap. Strip away the fluffy barbs at the base, and mount the feather ahead of the abdomen as explained in *mounting collar hackle* (p. 37).

Step 4: Take one wrap of the feather as shown in *wrapping wet-fly hackle* (p. 50). Tie off the feather, and clip the tip.

Step 5: Mount a strand of peacock herl directly ahead of the hackle.

Step 6: Wrap the herl to the hook eye as shown in *wrapping single-herl collars* (p. 48). Tie off and clip the excess. Form the head of the fly and whip finish.

CDC Spider

Hook: TMC 900BL, or equivalent dry-fly hook, #10-#16
Thread: Gray 8/0
Shuck: Cream Antron
Abdomen: Gray CDC dubbing
Thorax: Gray CDC dubbing
Hackle: Natural gray Type 1 or 4 CDC feather

We first heard of this pattern from English angler and writer Charles Rangeley Wilson. Our version uses CDC dubbing rather than fur for the abdomen. At the end of a dead-drift, the fly can be skated across the surface or pulled under and fished on the swing.

Step 1: Attach the thread and position it about six thread-wraps' distance behind the hook eye. Select a CDC feather with barbs about twice the length of the hook gap. Prepare and secure the CDC feather as explained in *tip-mounted hackle* (p. 41).

Step 2: Wrap the thread to the rearmost point of the body. Mount a sparse bundle of Antron fibers to form a shuck about one hook-gap in length. Use the *direct dubbing* method (p. 34) to dub a slender abdomen over the rear ⅔ of the shank.

Step 3: Dub a thorax slightly larger in diameter than the abdomen. The thorax should be dubbed right up to the frontmost thread wrap securing the CDC feather. Position the thread about three thread-wraps' distance behind the hook eye.

Step 4: Take 4-6 wraps of the feather as explained in *wrapping wet-fly hackle* (p. 50).

Step 5: Tie off the feather and clip the excess. Whip finish to form a small head.

Simple Swimming Caddis Pupa

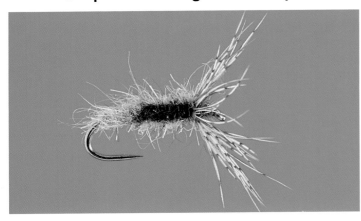

Originator: Doug Swisher and Carl Richards
Hook: TMC 3761, or equivalent 1XL nymph hook,
  #14-#20
Thread: Tan 8/0
Body: Tan fur dubbing
Wings: Black waterproof marker
Hackle: Gray partridge
Head: Dark brown dubbing

The forward-pointing hackle on this pattern gives the feather barbs more water resistance for a swimming action when the fly is twitched.

Step 1: Attach the thread and position it ¼ of a shank-length behind the eye. Select a partridge feather with barbs about twice the hook gap. Prepare it as explained in *preparing hackle feathers* (p. 39). Mount it as shown in *mounting collar hackle* (p. 37), placing the front, or concave side, of the feather toward the hook eye.

Step 2: Take 2-3 wraps of the hackle as shown in *wrapping wet-fly hackle* (p. 50), except wrap toward the hook bend. Tie off and clip the excess.

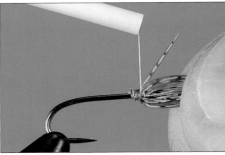

Step 3: Preen the barbs forward with the right fingers; with the left hand take several thread wraps at the base of the hackle to slant the barbs forward.

Step 4: Spiral the thread to the rearmost point of the body, and use the *direct dubbing* method (p. 34) to dub a thick, tapered body that abuts the wrapped hackle. You can use the dubbing to force the hackle barbs further forward if needed.

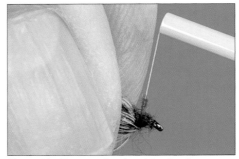

Step 5: Preen the hackle barbs rearward with the left fingers, and dub a head from the base of the hackle to the hook eye. Form the head of the fly and whip finish.

Step 6: With a waterproof marker, color in wing buds on either side of the body.

CDC Soft Hackle

Hook: TMC 900BL, or equivalent dry-fly hook, #16-#20
Thread: Olive 8/0
Abdomen: Olive fine poly dubbing
Thorax: Dyed olive hare's ear dubbing
Hackle: Natural dun CDC

The use of a dubbing loop permits dressing smaller patterns with a CDC hackle. This fly can be fished like the CDC Spider (p. 209).

Step 1: Attach the thread and position it at the rearmost point of the body. Use the *direct dubbing* method (p. 34) to dub a slender abdomen over the rear ¾ of the hook shank.

Step 2: Dub a thorax from the front of the abdomen to a point about 4-5 thread-wraps behind the hook eye.

Step 3: Form a thread loop about 2" long and insert a CDC feather as shown in *CDC dubbing loop* (p. 31). The barb tips should extend beyond the loop threads a distance of twice the hook gap.

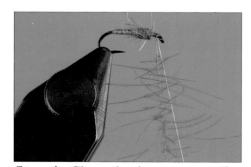

Step 4: Close the loop to trap the feather barbs between the threads. Carefully trim away the stem side of the feather. Insert a dubbing hook into the loop, and twist to capture and flare the barbs.

Step 5: Wrap the spun loop as though you were *wrapping wet-fly hackle* (p. 50), stroking the barbs rearward with each wrap. Take 2-6 wraps, depending on the desired density of hackle in the finished fly.

Step 6: Tie off the loop behind the hook eye, and clip the excess. Stroke the barbs rearward with the left fingers, and take a few turns of thread at the base of the hackle to force any wayward barbs toward the rear of the hook. Clip any stray barbs, and whip finish.

Hair Hackle Caddis

Hook: TMC 2487, or other fine-wire scud hook, #12-#16
Thread: Brown 8/0
Abdomen: Tan Larva Lace
Thorax: Brown SLF dubbing
Hackle: Red fox squirrel hair

Hair spun in a dubbing loop and wrapped can be used to collar-hackle emergers. This fly can be fished on the swing, but it also effective when greased and fished dead-drift in the film. Floatant will not mat the hair hackle in the way it can a traditional soft hackle.

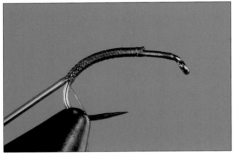

Step 1: Attach the thread and position it ⅓ of a shank-length behind the hook eye. Mount the body tubing, and secure it atop the shank, wrapping back to the rearmost point of the body.

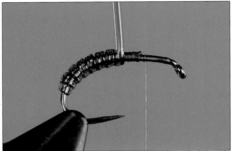

Step 2: Position the thread at the tubing tie-in point. Wrap the tubing forward over the rear ⅔ of the shank; tie off and clip the excess.

Step 3: Use the *direct dubbing* method (p. 34) to dub a thorax from the front of the abdomen to a point about 6-7 thread-wraps' distance behind the eye. Use a dubbing teaser or needle to pick out fibers from the thorax.

Step 4: As shown in *dubbing loop* (p. 35), form a dubbing loop at the front of the thorax and insert the squirrel hair so that the tips of the guard hairs project about one shank-length beyond the loop threads. Twist the loop tightly, as shown.

Step 5: Take 2-3 wraps of the loop, stroking each wrap rearward as a new wrap is taken, as explained in *wrapping wet-fly hackle* (p. 50). Tie off the dubbing loop threads behind the hook eye; clip and whip finish.

Tunkwanamid

Originator: Tom Murray
Hook: Mustad 9671, or other 2XL hook, #4-#16
Thread: Black 6/0
Tag: Fine silver oval tinsel (or silver wire on smaller hooks)
Body: Peacock herl
Rib: Fine silver oval tinsel (or silver wire on smaller hooks)
Collar: White ostrich herl

This pattern was designed for the larger Chironomid hatches on stillwaters. It can be treated with floatant and fished on the surface film, fished just beneath the surface on a greased leader, or deeper on an ungreased one. Treating only the collar with floatant will cause the pattern to sit vertically in the water.

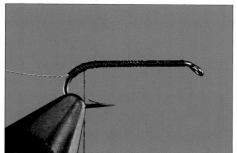

Step 1: Attach the thread and position it ⅓ of the way down the hook bend. Strip ⅛" of the metallic part of the tinsel from one end of the strand, exposing the fiber core. Mount the tinsel by securing the core. Position the thread about 4 wraps forward of the mounting point.

Step 2: Take 3 or 4 turns of the tinsel to form a tag. Tie off the tinsel, but do not clip it. Mount 3-5 strands of peacock herl ahead of the tag.

Step 3: Using the method shown in *wrapping twisted-herl collars* (p. 49), wrap a body to a point about 6 or 7 thread-wraps behind the hook eye. Tie off and clip the herl.

Step 4: Spiral the tinsel forward to rib the body. Tie off in front of the herl and clip.

Step 5: Mount a strand of ostrich herl in front of the peacock.

Step 6: Wrap the herl as explained in *wrapping single-herl collars* (p. 48). Tie off the herl, clip the excess, and whip finish.

TDC (Thompson's Delectable Chironomid)

Originator: Richard Thompson
Hook: TMC 5262, or equivalent 2XL heavy-wire hook, #12-#16
Thread: Black 8/0
Abdomen: Black rabbit fur
Rib: Fine flat silver tinsel
Thorax: Black rabbit fur
Collar: White ostrich herl

Like the Tunkwanamid (p. 213), the TDC is one of the classic patterns for imitating larger Chironomids in lakes, and it can be fished with the same variety of approaches.

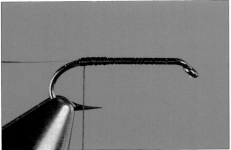

Step 1: Attach the thread and position it at the rear of the shank. Mount a length of flat silver tinsel.

Step 2: Use the *direct dubbing* method (p. 34) to form a tapered abdomen over the rear ⅔ of the shank.

Step 3: Spiral the tinsel forward to rib the abdomen. Tie off and clip the excess directly in front of the abdomen.

Step 4: Dub a thorax 1 ½ times the diameter of the abdomen, stopping about 6 or 7 thread-wraps behind the hook eye.

Step 5: Mount a strand of ostrich herl in front of the thorax.

Step 6: Wrap the herl forward as explained in *wrapping single-herl collars* (p. 48). Tie off the herl behind the hook eye. Clip the excess and whip finish.

CDC October Caddis

Hook: TMC 900BL, or equivalent dry-fly hook, #8-#12
Thread: Brown 6/0
Abdomen: Orange Antron yarn
Wing buds: Mottled brown hen hackle, burned or clipped
Hackle: Dark brown Type 1 or 4 CDC feather
Thorax/head: Dark brown dubbing

The CDC in this pattern is used more to give some movement to the fly than for floatation. It can be fished awash in the film or slightly beneath the surface. Tying it on as a dropper behind a dry fly can help detect strikes.

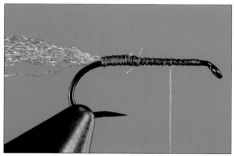

Step 1: Attach the thread and position it ⅔ of a shank-length behind the eye. Mount a strand of Antron yarn atop the shank, binding it rearward to the rearmost point of the body. Clip the excess. Position the thread ⅓ of a shank-length behind the eye.

Step 2: Twist the yarn tightly clockwise to produce a segmented body, and wrap forward over the rear ⅔ of the shank. As you take the last few wraps, relax the twist in the yarn to flatten it and produce a smooth base for mounting the wing buds.

Step 3: Tie off and trim the yarn. Fashion and mount a pair of cut wings as shown in Spotted Sedge Emerger, Steps 3-8, (p. 324).

Step 4: Use the *direct dubbing* method (p. 34) to dub a short thorax from the front of the abdomen about halfway to the hook eye. Prepare and secure the CDC feather as explained in *tip-mounted hackle* (p. 41).

Step 5: Take 2 or 3 wraps of the feather as explained in *wrapping wet-fly hackle* (p. 50). Bind the tip and clip the excess.

Step 6: Dub the head to a point just behind the hook eye, and whip finish.

Aftershaft Mayfly Emerger—March Brown

Originator: Jack Gartside
Hook: TMC 2312, or other fine-wire 2XL hook, #12-#16
Thread: Brown 6/0
Tail: Woodduck flank fibers
Body: Arizona Synthetic Peacock dubbing, bronze
Wings: Pheasant aftershaft feather
Legs: Woodduck flank fibers

Jack Gartside pioneered the use of aftershaft feathers to give a pattern mobility in the water. Aftershaft feathers can be found at the base of many of the body feathers on a pheasant skin. This simple, slender design can be varied to match a variety of mayfly hatches. As with CDC, use no floatant on aftershaft feathers.

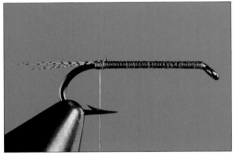

Step 1: Attach the thread and position it at the tailing point. Mount a small bundle of woodduck flank fibers to make a tail about one hook-gap in length.

Step 2: Use the *direct dubbing* method (p. 34) to form a slender tapered body over the rear ⅔ of the hook shank.

Step 3: Strip the fluff from the bottom ¼" of an aftershaft feather. Secure the stem to the shank directly ahead of the body dubbing, as shown.

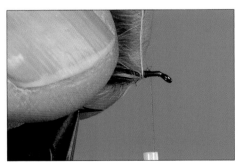

Step 4: Using the technique shown in *wrapping wet-fly hackle* (p. 50), take 5-6 wraps of the aftershaft feather, working very carefully, as the material is quite fragile.

Step 5: Tie off and secure the feather. Trim away all the feather barbs on the underside of the shank, as shown in this front view.

Step 6: Mount a bundle of woodduck flank on the underside of the shank as shown in *throat hackle* (p. 41). These legs should extend rearward to the hook point. Take a few wraps of thinly dubbed thread to cover the leg-mounting wraps, and whip finish.

Aftershaft Caddis Emerger

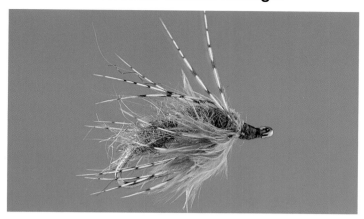

Originator: Jack Gartside
Hook: Mustad 37160, or equivalent scud hook, #8-#18
Thread: Brown 6/0
Body: Blend of olive squirrel, rabbit, and Antron dubbings
Legs: Gray partridge
Wing/thorax: Pheasant aftershaft feather

Jack Gartside recommends fishing this pattern just under the surface, on the swing or with small twitches to imitate the movement of an emerging caddis. It can be tied in a variety of colors. Use no floatant on this pattern; it will mat the aftershaft and destroy its motion in the water.

Step 1: Attach the thread and position it at the rearmost point of the body. Use the *direct dubbing* method (p. 34) to dub a thick body over the rear ⅔ of the hook shank.

Step 2: Select a partridge feather with barbs about 1 ½ to 2 times the shank length. Prepare the feather as explained in *preparing hackle feathers* (p. 39), and mount it directly in front of the body dubbing as explained in *mounting collar hackle* (p. 37)

Step 3: Take one wrap of the feather as shown in *wrapping wet-fly hackle* (p. 50). Secure the feather tip and clip the excess.

Step 4: Strip the fluff from the bottom ¼" of an aftershaft feather. Secure the stem to the shank directly ahead of the wrapped hackle.

Step 5: Using the technique shown in *wrapping wet-fly hackle* (p. 50), take 5-6 wraps of the aftershaft feather, working very carefully, as the material is quite fragile. Tie off and clip the excess aftershaft.

Step 6: Trim away the aftershaft fibers on the top of the hook shank, taking care not to trim away the partridge hackle. Preen the aftershaft fibers rearward, and take a few thread wraps over the base of the wrapped feather to slant the fibers rearward. Then whip finish the fly.

Chapter 12: Downwing Emergers

One might reasonably expect that downwing emergers—tied with wings that slant rearward over the back of the body—would have evolved from traditional winged wet flies, which make credible emergers both in their appearance and in the way they are customarily fished on a down-and-across swing. Yet in the development of modern emerger patterns, this older style appears largely to have been abandoned. Tyers generally seem to approach downwing emerger design from the direction of downwing dry flies. But where downwing dry flies are most often tied to represent the slanting, tentwing profile of caddis, downwing emerger patterns are more varied and are used to imitate hatching mayflies and midges as well as caddis. Emerger downwings tend to be short and may represent a point of emergence at which these three types of insects look more alike than different.

But there's no question that the downwing style can effectively represent the gamut of hatching insects in a trout stream. And many downwing patterns are productive during more than one type of hatch—Rim Chung's popular RS2, for instance, is equally useful as an emerging midge or small mayfly—making downwing emergers among the most versatile of all styles.

The downwings on patterns in this chapter range from wings that lie flat across the back of the fly to those that stand virtually upright; their distinguishing feature from the tying standpoint is that they are mounted with the wing butts toward the hook eye. Upright wings, as we use the term, are mounted in the opposite orientation.

Hex Foam Emerger

Originator: Jim Schollmeyer
Hook: TMC 206BL, or other fine-wire scud hook, #10
Thread: Brown 6/0
Body: ¹⁄₁₆" yellow foam, cut ⅛" wide and 3" long
Tails: Tan Antron fibers
Wing: Deer hair
Thorax: Yellow dubbing

The foam body and deer-hair wing make this pattern float well. The extended-body style can be used to imitate other mayfly species, though it is most practical for larger patterns.

Step 1: Mount a needle in the vise as shown. Push the very center of the foam into the needle, and slide the foam down the needle shank. Mount the tying thread on the needle. Slide the foam forward so it abuts the mounting wraps, as shown in this top view.

Step 2: Mount a very sparse bundle of Antron fibers directly atop the thread-mounting wraps.

Step 3: Fold the two halves of the foam forward around the sides of the needle. Hold them in position with the right hand. With the left hand, take a thread wrap around the foam very close to the fold, as shown. Take 2 or 3 more moderately tight wraps over the first one.

Step 4: Place three half-hitches over the thread wraps, using a dubbing needle to guide the half-hitches into place.

Step 5: Fold the foam rearward. Advance the thread, under very little tension, about three wraps forward on the needle, binding down the Antron fibers as you wrap.

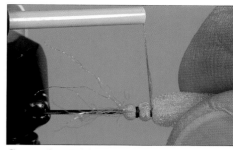

Step 6: Fold the foam forward as shown in Step 2, and form the next body segment, slightly larger than the first.

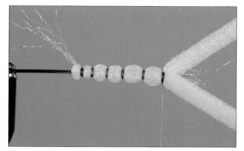

Step 7: Repeat Steps 3, 5, and 6, four more times, making each segment slightly larger than the previous one to give this extended abdomen a taper. Secure the thread with three half-hitches directly atop the thread wraps used to form the last body segment.

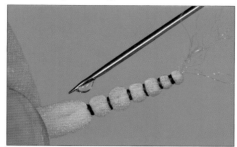

Step 8: Clip the thread. Pinch the needle directly behind the tail, and carefully pull the foam body from the needle. Trim the excess Antron fibers and place a drop of flexible head cement on the frontmost and rearmost thread wraps.

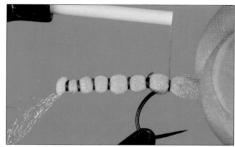

Step 9: Mount the thread on the hook and wrap rearward to the end of the straight portion of the shank. Fold the foam around the sides of the shank, and form another body segment.

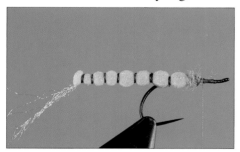

Step 10: Advance the thread and form one more body segment. Then clip the foam tags and secure the butts tightly.

Step 11: *Clip, clean, and stack* (p. 32) a bundle of deer hair. Position the hair atop the shank so that the tips extend just beyond the hook bend.

Step 12: Secure the hair to the top of the shank, letting it flare to the sides, or with your fingers preen the hair to distribute it down the sides of the shank. The wing should form an arc of about 180 degrees when viewed from the front.

Step 13: Clip the hair butts and cover the exposed butts with thread. Whip finish the fly. Here is a front view of the fly showing the spread of the wing fibers.

Emergent Sparkle Pupa—Green

Originator: Gary LaFontaine
Hook: TMC 900BL, or equivalent dry-fly hook, #14-#16
Thread: Olive 8/0
Bubble shuck: Cream or tan Antron yarn
Body: Green Antron dubbing
Wing: Deer hair
Head: Brown marabou

This floating version of LaFontaine's Deep Sparkle Pupa (p. 76) is a widely used and very effective caddis emerger pattern. Sizes and colors can be varied to meet most caddis hatches. The fly can be treated with floatant to ride higher in the water, or left untreated to sit flush in the film.

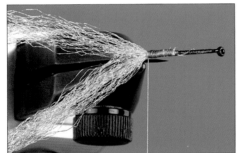

Step 1: Attach the thread and position it at the rear of the shank. Use the technique shown in *Antron bubble* (p. 69), Steps 1-3, to prepare and mount two yarn strands to form the bubble.

Step 2: Use the *direct dubbing* method (p. 34) to dub the body, stopping about ¼ of a shank-length behind the hook eye.

Step 3: Use the method shown in Antron bubble shuck, Steps 3-6, to form the bubble sheath. Lay a short thread foundation ahead of the bubble, and return the thread to the rearmost wrap of the thread base.

Step 4: *Clip, clean, and stack* (p. 32) a bundle of deer hair. Use a *pinch wrap* (p. 38) to secure the hair atop the shank, forming a wing that extends to the rear of the bubble shuck.

Step 5: Clip the butt ends of the hair and secure with thread. Mount 3-6 marabou herls at the base of the wing.

Step 6: Use the technique shown in *wrapping twisted-herl collars* (p. 49) to form the head of the fly. Tie off the herl, and clip the excess. Whip finish the fly.

Callibaetis Emerger

Hook: TMC 900BL, or equivalent dry-fly hook, #14-#16
Thread: Olive 8/0
Shuck: Amber Z-Lon
Rib: Fine copper wire
Abdomen: Pale olive Ligas Ultra Translucent Dubbing
Wing: Deer hair
Thorax: Same as abdomen
Legs: Mallard flank fibers

The wing on this pattern incorporates the most buoyant part of the deer hair and produces a compact emerging wing impression. The pattern is easy to tie and can be modified to represent almost any mayfly species.

Step 1: Mount the thread and advance to the tailing point. Secure a sparse bundle of Antron to make a shuck equal in length to the hook shank. Secure the ribbing wire atop the rearmost shuck-mounting wrap.

Step 2: Use the *direct dubbing* method (p. 34) to dub a slightly tapered abdomen over the rear ⅔ of the shank. *Counter-rib* (p. 33) the abdomen; secure and clip the wire directly in front of the abdomen.

Step 3: *Clip and clean* (p. 32) a bundle of deer hair. Secure the hair at the middle of bundle, tips forward, directly ahead of the abdomen.

Step 4: Trim off the hair tips and secure tightly with thread. Dub the thorax.

Step 5: Using the *throat hackle* method (p. 41), secure 6-8 mallard flank fibers to the underside of the shank to make legs equal in length to about ½ a shank-length.

Step 6: Form the head of the fly and whip finish. Clip the deer hair tips to make a wing that extends rearward about ½ the length of the abdomen.

Bead-Shuck Caddis Emerger

Originator: Jim Schollmeyer and Ted Leeson
Hook: TMC 206BL, or other light-wire scud hook, #12-#16
Thread: Brown 8/0
Shuck: Amber beads and cream Antron
Abdomen: Orange Krystal Flash
Wing: Deer hair
Thorax: Dark brown fine poly dubbing
Legs: Tips from deer-hair wing

This is one of our own designs that we've found quite effective, though we're the first to admit that tying the bead shuck can be tedious. Other shuck styles can be substituted, but dress only the wing and cross-hackle legs with floatant; the shuck should sink below the surface film.

Step 1: Mount the hook with eye angled downward as shown. Attach the thread and wrap to a point about halfway around the hook bend. Assemble and mount the shuck as shown in *bead shuck* (p. 65). Take three strands of Krystal Flash, fold them in half, clip the tips even, and mount them directly in front of the first bead.

Step 2: Advance the thread ½ the distance to the hook eye. Adjust the hook in the vise to the normal position. Insert the dubbing twister into the loop, twist the strands, and wrap halfway to the hook eye. Tie off and clip the Krystal Flash.

Step 3: *Clip, clean, and stack* (p. 32) a bundle of deer hair. Mount the hair atop the shank so that the tips extend beyond the mounting wraps a distance equal to the length of the abdomen.

Step 4: Use crisscross wraps to separate the hair tips into two bundles. Use additional wraps to post the bundles in a horizontal plane, perpendicular to the hook shank, as shown in this top view. When the legs are positioned, apply a drop of head cement to the thread wraps.

Step 5: With a very thinly dubbed thread, dub over the crisscross wraps to cover the thread.

Step 6: Whip finish the fly. Clip the wing hair at an angle so that it extends rearward just to the front edge of the shuck.

Snowshoe Emerger—Flav

Hook: TMC 206BL, or other fine-wire scud hook, #12-#14
Thread: Olive 6/0
Shuck: Amber Z-Lon
Rib: Yellow size "A" thread
Abdomen: Olive dubbing
Wing: Snowshoe hare's foot, light dun
Thorax: Peacock herl

This is one of those straightforward, adaptable, easy-to-tie patterns that can be varied to match many mayfly and caddis emergences. It's a basic snowshoe-hare design that is becoming more and more popular.

Step 1: Attach the thread and position it halfway around the hook bend. Mount a sparse bundle of Z-Lon to form a shuck about ½ the hook gap in length. Clip and bind the excess. Mount the ribbing material directly atop the rearmost thread wraps.

Step 2: Use the *direct dubbing* method (p. 34) to dub a tapered abdomen over the rear ⅔ of the shank.

Step 3: Spiral the ribbing forward and tie off directly ahead of the abdomen.

Step 4: Clip a bundle of fur from the rear half of a hare's foot (see Snowshoe Hare's Foot, p. 27). Hold it by the tips and pull out any short hairs. Secure the hair atop the shank to form a wing that extends to the rear of the abdomen. Clip the butts at an angle and bind down with a *flattened thread* (p. 37) to form a smooth foundation.

Step 5: Mount 3-5 strands of peacock herl directly ahead of the wing.

Step 6: Form the thorax as explained in *wrapping twisted-herl collars* (p. 49). Tie off and clip the excess. Whip finish.

Snowshoe Hendrickson Emerger

Hook: TMC 900BL, or equivalent standard dry-fly hook, #12-#14
Thread: Bright orange 6/0
Shuck: Snowshoe hare's foot
Abdomen: Snowshoe hare's foot dubbing
Wing: Snowshoe hare's foot
Thorax: Snowshoe hare's foot dubbing

This is a more substantial and more heavily dressed version of the preceding pattern that uses all snowshoe hare—a kind of emerger version of The Usual (p. 268). This simple design can be adapted to a variety of hatches. The thread underbody gives a hint of color to the fly when wet, so choose a thread color to match the natural.

Step 1: Attach the thread behind the hook eye and wrap to the rear of the shank, laying a uniform foundation. Clip a small bundle of hair from the rear half of a snowshoe hare's foot (see "Snowshoe Hare's Foot," p. 27). Mount the hair at the tailing point to make a shuck that extends rearward about one shank-length.

Step 2: Use a sparsely dubbed thread and the *direct dubbing* method (p. 34) to form a tapered abdomen along ⅔ of the hook shank.

Step 3: Clip a bundle of hair from the center of the foot. If necessary, align the fibers by drawing out the longer hairs and stacking them with the remaining hair so that the tips are even. Repeat a couple of times to roughly align the hair. It need not be exact.

Step 4: Mount the hair atop the shank in front of the abdomen so that the tips extend rearward to the end of the body. Secure the hair tightly.

Step 5: Clip the hair butts and cover with thread. Dub the thorax, and whip finish the fly.

Wotton's Hatching Caddis

Originator: Davy Wotton
Hook: Mustad 3906B, or other 1XL wet-fly hook, #8-#18
Thread: Rust 6/0
Rib: Gold oval tinsel
Abdomen: Rusty brown dubbing
Wing case: Brown Swiss straw
Wing: Natural rabbit fur
Thorax: Rusty brown dubbing
Hackle: Brown partridge

This pattern employs fine, soft rabbit underfur for the wings and a soft hackle for lots of movement in the water. Body and hackle colors can be varied to suit local caddis hatches.

Step 1: Attach the tying thread and wrap to the rear of the shank. Strip ¼" of tinsel from the core, and mount the ribbing by the core material. Use the *direct dubbing* method (p. 34) to dub the abdomen over the rear ⅔ of the shank. Spiral the tinsel forward to rib the abdomen.

Step 2: Cut a strip of Swiss straw about ½ the hook gap in width. Mount it flat directly ahead of the abdomen.

Step 3: Cut a pinch of rabbit fur from the skin. Pull out the guard hairs, then hold the hair by the tip and pull out any short fibers or fluff from the cut base. Mount the hair atop the shank, tips rearward, to make a wing equal in length to the hook shank.

Step 4: Trim away the hair butts and secure with thread. Dub the thorax.

Step 5: Prepare the hackle and mount it as explained in *tip-mounted hackle* (p. 41). Take 2 turns of the feather as described in *wrapping wet-fly hackle* (p. 50). Tie off and clip the excess.

Step 6: Divide the hair to form two wings, and draw the wing case forward between the halves. Divide the hackle fibers, and bring the wing case forward through the gap. Pull the wing case forward to splay the wings outward, as shown in this top view. Tie down and clip the wing case. Whip finish the fly.

RS2

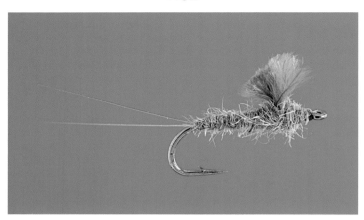

Originator: Rim Chung
Hook: TMC 101, or other ring-eye dry-fly hook, #12-#24
Thread: Brown 8/0
Tail: Dark dun Micro Fibetts
Body: Muskrat fur
Wing: Dark dun fluff from base of saddle hackle

The RS2 (Rim's Semblance #2) is one of the most popular emergers in the Rocky Mountain states. It can be fished near the surface like a traditional emerger, and many tyers substitute CDC for the wing. But the fly is often fished deep using split shot or lead putty or as a dropper off a larger nymph. Sizes and colors can be varied for local waters.

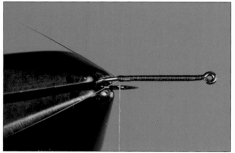

Step 1: Attach the thread, and position it at the tailing point. Mount a Micro Fibett on each side of the shank to make tails one shank-length long. Pull the fibers outward to make a split tail with a 60-70-degree spread, as shown in this top view. Take a few crisscross wraps of thread between the fibers to hold them in position.

Step 2: Use the *direct dubbing* method (p. 34) to dub a sparse abdomen over the rear ⅔ of the shank. Take the first wrap of dubbing behind the tails, and keep the dubbing tightly twisted to produce a segmented body.

Step 3: Strip a bundle of fluffy fibers from the base of a saddle hackle. Mount them atop the shank directly in front of the abdomen, as shown.

Step 4: Trim away the excess wing material, and secure the butts with thread.

Step 5: Dub the thorax, taking wraps both ahead of and behind the wing.

Step 6: Whip finish and clip the thread. Trim the wing by holding it under tension with the left fingers and making an angle cut from above.

Surface Emerger

Hook: TMC 100, or equivalent dry-fly hook, #14-#20
Thread: Olive 8/0
Tail: Mallard flank fibers dyed wood duck
Rib: Fine copper wire
Abdomen: Olive-brown Superfine dubbing
Wing case: Turkey tail
Legs: Brown partridge
Head: Same as abdomen

This simple, easily tied design is quite versatile. It can be fished deep or in the film and tied in any color or size to match prevailing mayfly hatches.

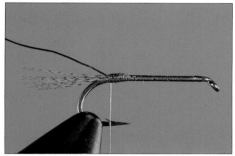

Step 1: Attach the thread and wrap to the rear of the shank. Clip a small bundle of mallard flank, and mount it to make a tail about ½ the length of the shank. Mount the ribbing material directly atop the rearmost thread wrap securing the tail.

Step 2: Use the *direct dubbing* method (p. 34) to form a tapered body over the rear ⅔ of the hook shank. Spiral the ribbing forward. Tie off the ribbing in front of the abdomen and clip the excess.

Step 3: Wrap the tying thread a few turns rearward, back over the front of the abdomen. Mounting the wing case and legs over this thicker portion of the body, rather than the bare hook shank, will prevent excess flare of the materials.

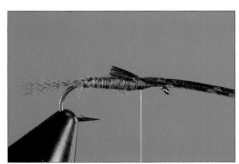

Step 4: Clip a section of turkey tail about ½ the hook gap in width. Mount the wing case flat on the front of the abdomen, securing tightly. Clip the wing case to about ½ the length of the abdomen. Clip and bind the excess turkey quill.

Step 5: Using the method shown in *side-mounted legs* (p. 39), mount a sparse bundle of partridge fibers on either side of the shank, directly over the rearmost wraps securing the wing case.

Step 6: Dub the head of the fly, taking the rearmost wraps of dubbing over the thread wraps securing the legs and wing case. Whip finish.

Stillborn Midge

Hook: TMC 2487, or other fine-wire scud hook, #10-#20
Thread: Black 14/0
Shuck: Gray Antron yarn
Abdomen: Stripped peacock quill
Wings: Grizzly hackle tips
Thorax: Peacock herl

This basic design can be modified for mayfly emergers by using dyed hackle stems for the body and dun hackle tips for the wings. The thorax here can also be fashioned by forming a dubbing loop with CDC fibers.

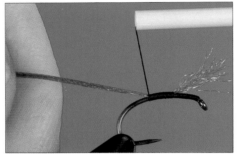

Step 1: Attach the tying thread behind the hook eye, and wrap rearward ⅓ a shank length. Mount a sparse length of Antron yarn, and bind it to the shank with smooth wraps of *flattened thread* (p. 37). Binding the material along the length of the shank will give a smooth underbody for the quill.

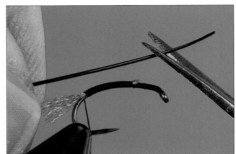

Step 2: Bind the Antron to a point about ⅓ of the way down the hook bend. Clip the front tag. Clip the shuck to about one hook-gap in length. Draw your thumbnail down a piece of peacock herl, from tip to butt, until all the fibers are removed. Clip about ¼" from the thin tip of the quill.

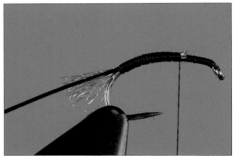

Step 3: Using a flattened thread, mount the quill atop the rearmost thread wrap. Continue wrapping forward with a flattened thread, forming a smooth, uniform underbody. Wrap forward to the point where the shuck material was first tied in.

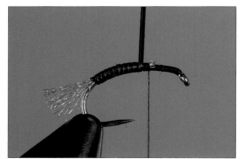

Step 4: As shown in *wrapping quill bodies* (p. 47), wrap the quill forward in precisely adjacent wraps; don't overlap the quill or the effect of segmentation will be lost. Use firm, but not tight, wrapping pressure.

Step 5: Wrap forward to the tying thread. Tie off and clip the excess quill. Mount a strand of peacock herl at the front of the abdomen.

Step 6: Take 2-3 wraps of the herl as explained in *wrapping single-herl collars* (p. 48). Tie off the herl on the underside of the shank, but do not clip the excess. This rear portion of the thorax will help elevate and position the wings.

Step 7: Position a grizzly hackle tip crosswise atop the shank, pointing rearward at a 45-degree angle to the shank. Hold it in position with two firm, but not tight, thread wraps, as shown in this top view.

Step 8: With the right fingers, carefully pull the butt end of the feather, sliding it beneath the thread wraps, until the tip forms a wing slightly shorter than the abdomen. If the feather starts to slip out of position, hold the feather tip with the left fingers as you draw the wing to length.

Step 9: Secure the wing with 2 tight wraps. Repeat Steps 7-8 to mount the wing on the near side of the shank. Secure the near wing with tight thread wraps. Clip the feather butts, cover with thread, and position the tying thread behind the hook eye.

Step 10: Resume wrapping the front portion of the herl thorax, taking the first wraps of herl over the thread wraps securing the wings. Wrap to a point just behind the hook eye. Secure the herl and clip the excess.

Step 11: Whip finish the fly. Carefully apply a drop of head cement to the quill abdomen to improve durability.

Wonder Wing Emerger—March Brown

Hook: TMC 900BL, or equivalent dry-fly hook, #12-#14
Thread: Brown 8/0
Shuck: Amber Antron
Rib: Fine gold wire
Abdomen: Brown-olive dubbing
Wing: Two matched webby dun saddle feathers
Hackle: Dun dry fly

The wonder-wing design produces a delicate, realistic, and reasonably durable wing. It can be used on a variety of mayfly emergers but is most practical on hook sizes #16 and larger. Colors can be altered to match other mayflies.

Step 1: Attach the thread and wrap to the rear of the shank. Mount a sparse bundle of Antron to form a shuck equal in length to the hook shank. Mount the ribbing material atop the rearmost wrap securing the shuck.

Step 2: Use the *direct dubbing* method (p. 34) to dub a tapered abdomen over the rear ⅔ of the shank. *Counter-rib* (p. 33) the abdomen. Bind and clip the ribbing directly in front of the abdomen.

Step 3: Select a pair of dun saddle feathers. Place them front-to-front, so that they flare away from one another, with the tips aligned. Clip the butts so that all the fluffy barbs are removed.

Step 4: Hold the feathers in your left hand. With the right fingers, preen a section of barbs (from both feathers) back and beyond the clipped feather butt. The section of quill enclosed by the barbs should be about ⅓ of a shank-length long.

Step 5: With the right fingers, position the wings atop the shank directly ahead of the abdomen. The wings should slant rearward about ½ the shank length.

Step 6: With the left fingers, take a wrap of thread over the top of the hook shank, and let the bobbin hang. With the left fingers, gently pull the feather tip to straighten out any twisted barbs and to make the wing shape symmetrical.

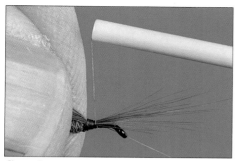

Step 7: With the left fingers, pinch the wings against the shank at the mounting point. With the right hand, draw the bobbin tight and take additional tight thread wraps toward the hook eye.

Step 8: Pull the feather tips apart to separate the wings. Clip off the excess feather tips above the uppermost barbs forming the wing. Clip away the excess barbs pointing forward and secure with thread.

Step 9: *Prepare a hackle feather* (p. 39), and using the method shown in *mounting collar hackle* (p. 37), mount the hackle directly ahead of the wings.

Step 10: Wrap the hackle forward to a point just behind the hook eye using the technique shown in *wrapping dry-fly hackle* (p. 44). Tie off and clip the feather. Whip finish the fly.

Step 11: Clip away the hackle barbs above and below the shank, leaving only the barbs extending from each side of the hook shank, as shown in this front view.

Scary Harey

Originator: Howard Cole
Hook: TMC 2487, or other fine-wire scud hook, #14-#20
Thread: Tan 8/0
Abdomen: Gray and ginger Antron dubbing mixed in fine silver wire dubbing loop
Thorax: Silver glass bead
Wing: Gray snowshoe hare's foot
Hackle: Medium dun CDC

This pattern gets a wonderfully "buggy" look from the rough-dubbed abdomen and the CDC hackle, and a bit of flash from the bead thorax. Howard Cole notes that tan and olive versions are also effective. The hackle in the following sequence is applied with a dubbing loop, but a very fine-stemmed CDC feather can also be used. It should be tip-mounted and wrapped like wet-fly hackle.

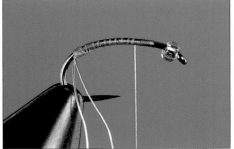

Step 1: Slide the thorax bead on the shank up to the hook eye. Attach the thread and position it at the tailing point. Cut a 4" length of silver wire, fold it in half to make a loop, and secure the ends at the rearmost point of the body. Position the tying thread at the midpoint of the shank.

Step 2: Wax one of the wire strands, and insert the dubbing as shown in *dubbing loop* (p. 35). The dubbing should be roughly chopped to produce a shaggy body. Twist the wire tightly, and wrap the dubbing loop forward to the midpoint of the shank. Tie off and clip the excess.

Step 3: Clip a bundle of fur from the rear half of a hare's foot (see Snowshoe Hare's Foot, p. 27), choosing hair that is crinkly and moderately fine in texture. Secure the hair atop the shank to form a wing that extends to the rearmost point of the abdomen. Do not clip the excess.

Step 4: Slide the bead rearward so that it abuts the wing-mounting wraps, and wrap the thread to the front of the bead. Form a dubbing loop from the tying thread, and advance the tying thread 3 or 4 wraps toward the hook eye. Place CDC fibers in the loop as shown in *CDC dubbing loop* (p. 31) and twist tightly.

Step 5: Take 2 or 3 wraps of the dubbing loop directly ahead of the bead. Tie off and clip the loop.

Step 6: Fold the butts of the wing hair over a dubbing needle held crosswise atop the bead, forming a loop-style wing case over the bead and hackle. Secure the hair directly in front of the hackle, behind the hook eye. Clip the butts to form a tuft-like head, and whip finish the fly.

Rose's Sulphur Emerger

Originator: Gary Rose
Hook: Daiichi 1251, or equivalent scud hook, #14-#18
Thread: Yellow 8/0
Tail: Medium blue dun ostrich herl tip
Abdomen: Sulphur yellow rabbit fur
Ribbing: One strand yellow Krystal Flash
Wing: One to three slate-gray Type 3 CDC feathers (puffs)
Thorax: Sulphur yellow rabbit fur mixed with small amount of chartreuse rabbit fur

The basic CDC downwing fly is an essential emerger pattern. This simple dressing can be altered in size, color, and shuck style to match virtually any mayfly.

Step 1: Attach the thread and wrap rearward halfway down the hook bend. Mount the tip of an ostrich herl atop the shank to form a tail about one hook-gap long. Secure the strand of Krystal Flash atop the rearmost tail-mounting wraps.

Step 2: Use the *direct dubbing* method (p. 34) to form a tapered thorax over the rear ⅔ of the hook shank.

Step 3: Spiral the Krystal Flash forward to rib the abdomen. Tie off the ribbing directly in front of the abdomen. Position the thread against the front of the abdomen.

Step 4: Hold the CDC puff (or puffs if using more than one) by the stem, and preen the barbs to the tip to align them. With the right fingers, position the feather atop the shank, directly ahead of the thorax, so that the barbs extend rearward about ⅔ the length of the abdomen.

Step 5: When the feather is properly positioned, pinch it with the left fingers and secure it to the top of the shank with 4-5 tight wraps. Clip the excess feather butt and secure with thread.

Step 6: Hold the wing in position with the left fingers, and with a thinly dubbed thread, take a few wraps against the base of the wing to cover the wing-mounting wraps and force the CDC against the front of the abdomen. Then dub the remainder of the thorax. Form the head of the fly and whip finish.

CDC BWO Emerger

Originator: Bruce Salzburg
Hook: TMC 2487, or other light-wire scud hook, #18-#22
Thread: Olive 8/0
Tail: Woodduck flank fibers
Rib: Fine copper wire
Abdomen: Olive-brown dubbing
Wing: Two Type 4 CDC feathers (or one CDC puff)
Legs: Woodduck flank fibers
Head: Dark dun dubbing

Tied in shades to match local BWOs, this is an essential emerger pattern for anglers across the country. It can, of course, be modified to match other mayfly hatches as well.

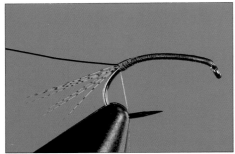

Step 1: Attach the thread and wrap to the tailing point. Secure 4-6 woodduck fibers to form a tail slightly shorter than the shank length. Mount the ribbing material atop the rearmost tailing wraps.

Step 2: Use the *direct dubbing* method (p. 34) to form a slightly tapered abdomen over the rear ⅔ of the hook shank. *Counter-rib* (p. 33) with the copper wire. Secure the rib in front of the abdomen and clip the excess.

Step 3: Align the tips of the two CDC feathers. With the right fingers, position the tips atop the shank in front of the abdomen to form a wing that extends rearward just shy of the end of the abdomen.

Step 4: When the wings are properly sized, pinch them in position with the left fingers and secure with 4-5 thread wraps moving toward the hook eye. Clip the feather butts and secure with thread.

Step 5: Using the method shown in *side-mounted legs* (p. 39), secure a small bundle of woodduck flank fibers to each side of the shank.

Step 6: Hold the wing in position with the left fingers, and with a thinly dubbed thread, take a few wraps against the base of the wing to cover the wing-mounting wraps and force the CDC against the front of the abdomen. Then dub the remainder of the head. Whip finish the fly.

Balloon Emerger

Originator: Roman Moser
Hook: TMC 900BL, or equivalent dry-fly hook, #12-#18
Thread: Brown 8/0
Abdomen: Brown tying thread
Wing: One Type 2 CDC feather (or Type 3 on smaller hooks)
Thorax: Dirty olive dubbing
Legs: Partridge hackle

Though designed as an emerger caddis pattern, this fly is effective during mayfly hatches as well. Dyed CDC can be substituted to match caddis of other colors, particularly ginger, cream, and brown.

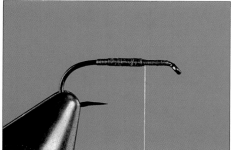

Step 1: Attach the thread behind the hook eye, and wrap back to a point just short of the hook bend. Then wrap forward again, forming a slightly tapered abdomen that ends ⅔ of a shank-length behind the eye.

Step 2: Use a *pinch wrap* (p. 38) to mount the CDC feather so that the broad side of the feather faces the tyer, as shown. The wing should extend just beyond the hook bend.

Step 3: Clip the excess CDC feather, and secure the end with thread. Use the *direct dubbing* method (p. 34) to dub a small, round thorax, covering the thread wraps used to mount the wing.

Step 4: Prepare a partridge feather by snipping away the tip at a point on the stem where the barbs are slightly shorter than the length of the hook shank. Preen the lower barbs downward, to leave a "V" of 4 or 5 fibers on either side of the stem, as shown.

Step 5: Hold the feather flat over the hook, with the dubbed thorax in the notch of the "V", and the fibers slanting rearward along each side of the shank.

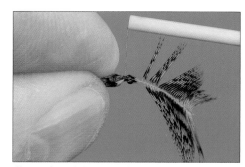

Step 6: With the left fingers, pinch the barbs against the sides of the thorax. Take 4 or 5 tight wraps to secure the fibers. Clip the feather butt and secure with thread, forming the head of the fly at the same time. Whip finish.

CDC BWO

Originator: Martin Westbeek
Hook: TMC 100, or equivalent dry-fly hook, #18
Thread: Olive 8/0
Tail: Dun Micro Fibetts
Abdomen: Olive Superfine dubbing
Wing: Dark gray Type 1 or Type 2 CDC feather
Wing case: Olive foam
Thorax: Olive squirrel

This trim, clean design rides low in the water but gets good floatation from both the wing and the wing case. It is a relatively simple fly to tie, even in small hook sizes, and it can be varied to match a variety of smaller mayflies.

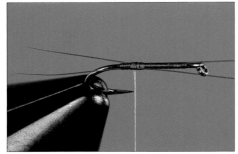

Step 1: Attach the thread and position it at the tailing point. Take 2 or 3 wraps forward with a flattened thread to form a slim tag at the rear of the shank. Mount a Micro Fibett on each side of the shank ahead of the tag to form split tails about one shank-length long, as shown in this top view.

Step 2: Clip and bind the tail tags. Use the *direct dubbing* method (p. 34) to dub a slender, tapered abdomen to the midpoint of the shank.

Step 3: Mount the CDC feather atop the shank, directly ahead of the abdomen, to form a wing that extends to the rearmost point of the body. Clip and bind the excess.

Step 4: Cut a strip of thin foam about half the hook gap in width, and mount it directly ahead of the CDC wing. Clip and bind the excess.

Step 5: Dub the thorax, stopping 3-4 thread-wraps' distance behind the eye.

Step 6: Fold the foam over the thorax and secure behind the hook eye. Bind and clip the excess, and whip finish the fly. Use a dubbing needle to tease out some of the dubbing fibers on the bottom and sides of the thorax.

CDC Transitional Caddis—Tan

Originator: René Harrop
Hook: TMC 900BL, or equivalent standard dry-fly hook, #12-#16
Thread: Tan 6/0
Shuck: Golden-tan dubbing
Rib: Fine gold wire
Abdomen: Golden-tan dubbing
Legs: Speckled turkey or mottled hen feather fibers
Antennae: Two speckled turkey feather fibers
Wing: Two Type 4 gray CDC feathers
Head: Brown dubbing

Like many of René Harrop's designs, this pattern combines realistic elements with a general impression of bugginess. Though the pattern sits low on the water, the CDC still gives it good visibility.

Step 1: Attach the thread and wrap to the tailing point. Mount a small tuft of dubbing to form a shuck about ½ a shank-length long. Mount the ribbing wire. Form a *dubbing loop* (p. 35), insert the dubbing, twist tightly, and wrap forward to produce a well-segmented abdomen over the rear ⅔ of the shank.

Step 2: *Counter-rib* (p. 33) the abdomen. Clip and bind the excess wire directly ahead of the abdomen.

Step 3: Align 6-10 turkey or mottled hen fibers, and mount them as shown in *throat hackle* (p. 41) to form legs that extend rearward to the end of the abdomen.

Step 4: Take two turkey fibers and mount them atop the shank to form antennae that extend rearward to the end of the shuck. Select two matched CDC feathers, and place them front-to-front, so that they flare away from one another, with the tips aligned.

Step 5: Position the wings atop the shank so that the tips extend to rear of the abdomen. Use a *pinch wrap* (p. 38) to secure the wings atop the shank. The finished wings should be symmetrical and maintain the flare shown in Step 4.

Step 6: Use the *direct dubbing* method (p. 34) and a thinly dubbed thread to cover the wing-mounting wraps; then dub the remainder of the head. Whip finish.

E-Merger

Originator: Joe Evans
Hook: TMC 101, or other ring-eye dry-fly hook, #16-#24
Thread: Dark brown 8/0
Shuck: Light amber Z-Lon
Abdomen: Natural gray muskrat fur
Wing: Light dun or white crinkled Z-Lon
Thorax: Dark brown mink fur with guard hairs

This simple pattern was designed for caddis emergences on the upper Yellowstone River. Joe Evans attributes its effectiveness to the use of muskrat and mink furs, two materials that float extremely well. Evans recommends against using head cement on the whip finish; it can bleed into the thorax fur, marring the appearance and reducing buoyancy.

Step 1: Attach the thread and position it at the tailing point. Mount 12-15 Z-Lon fibers (for a #16 hook; smaller hooks require fewer fibers) atop the shank. Trim to make a shuck ¾ the shank length.

Step 2: Use the *direct dubbing* method (p. 34) to dub a tapered abdomen over the rear ⅔ of the shank.

Step 3: Mount a bundle of Z-Lon fibers directly ahead of the abdomen, and secure it tightly. Place enough thread wraps behind the Z-Lon to elevate the wing to about 60 degrees above the shank.

Step 4: When the wing fibers are positioned, clip and bind the excess Z-Lon. Trim the wing so that it extends rearward just to the end of the abdomen.

Step 5: Dub a thorax about twice the thickness of the abdomen. Whip finish the fly.

Step 6: Use a dubbing needle or teaser to pick out the thorax fur and guard hairs for legs. Evans considers this a crucial step in tying the fly. He then treats the fly with Scotch Guard or other waterproofing treatment.

Rivergod Emerger—Hendrickson

Originator: Dennis M. Potter
Hook: TMC 100, or equivalent dry-fly hook, #12-#14
Thread: Brown 6/0
Tail: Woodduck flank fibers
Shuck: Rust Hi-Vis wing material
Abdomen: Light brown poly dubbing
Wing: Dark dun Z-Lon
Head: Same as abdomen

The synthetic wing material makes this pattern a snap to tie and very durable; colors and sizes can be altered to match other mayfly species.

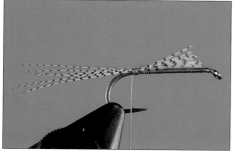

Step 1: Attach the thread and wrap to the tailing point. Mount 6-8 woodduck fibers to make a tail one hook-length long. Clip and bind the excess.

Step 2: Mount a bundle of shuck fibers directly atop the tailing wraps to form a shuck half the length of the tail. Clip and bind the excess.

Step 3: Use the *direct dubbing* method (p. 34) to form a slightly tapered abdomen over the rear ¾ of the hook shank.

Step 4: Use tight thread wraps to mount a piece of Z-Lon directly ahead of the abdomen. The wing should slant rearward just to the end of the abdomen.

Step 5: Preen the sides of the wing outward so that the fibers are spread through a 90-degree arc over the top of the shank, as shown in this front view.

Step 6: When the wing fibers are positioned, secure the wing butts tightly, and clip the excess. Dub the head of the fly, and whip finish.

KF Midge Emerger—Brown

Hook: TMC 2487, or other fine-wire scud hook, #16-#24
Thread: Dark brown 8/0
Rib: Fine gold wire
Abdomen: Dark brown tying thread
Wing: 3-5 strands pearl Krystal Flash
Thorax: Dark brown dubbing

This design is ideal for dressing on smaller hooks since it's easy to tie and requires no complicated material handling. Abdomen color can be varied to represent locally prevailing midge species.

Step 1: Attach the thread and wrap to the rear of the shank. With a *flattened thread* (p. 37), mount the rib material. Bind the tag to the shank with adjacent, touching thread wraps moving toward the hook eye to form a smooth abdomen over the rear ⅔ of the shank.

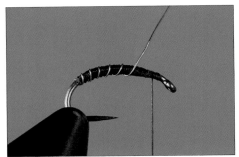

Step 2: Spiral the wire forward to rib the abdomen. Tie off the ribbing directly in front of the abdomen.

Step 3: Take the strands of Krystal Flash and clip the tips even. Mount them atop the shank directly ahead of the abdomen to form a wing that extends to the rearmost point of the body.

Step 4: Clip and bind down the excess Krystal Flash. Use the *direct dubbing* method (p. 34) to dub the thorax. Form the head of the fly and whip finish.

CDC Emerger

Originator: Shane Stalcup
Hook: TMC 2487, or other light-wire scud hook, #10-#16
Thread: Tan 8/0
Tail: Partridge fibers
Abdomen: Olive turkey biot
Wings: Medallion sheeting
Thorax: Natural dun CDC barbs

This fly offers a clean, precise silhouette. Since it sits low in the film and all floatation is provided by the CDC thorax, the pattern is best suited to flatter water. Sizes and colors can be varied, though the film wings here are most practical on hooks larger than #18.

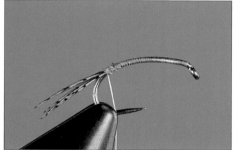

Step 1: Mount the thread and position it at the tailing point. *Align and strip* (p. 30) a small bundle of partridge fibers. Secure them at the tailing point to make a tail about one hook-gap long.

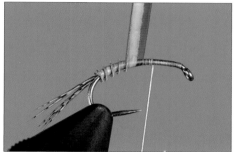

Step 2: Mount and wrap a turkey biot as explained in *biot body—fringed* (p. 30) to form an abdomen over the rear ⅔ of the shank. Bind and clip the excess. Position the thread midway between the front of the abdomen and the hook eye.

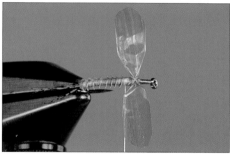

Step 3: Cut a strip of Medallion sheeting about ⅔ the hook gap in width and 1 ½ shank-lengths long. Fold the strip crosswise, and trim the ends to rounded tips. Unfold the strip and lay it crosswise atop the shank. Secure it with crisscross wraps. Position the thread at the front of the abdomen.

Step 4: Form a *CDC dubbing loop* (p. 31), and position the working thread behind the hook eye.

Step 5: Twist the loop tightly to flare the CDC fibers. Take a couple of wraps behind the wings.

Step 6: With the left fingers, draw the wings rearward and slightly upward. Continue wrapping the CDC forward over the wing butts to secure the wings in position. Wrap the CDC to the hook eye; secure and clip the excess. Whip finish. Trim the CDC fibers to make a bushy thorax, leaving long barbs beneath the shank for legs.

X-Caddis

Originator: Craig Mathews
Hook: TMC 900BL, or equivalent dry-fly hook, #12-#16
Thread: Brown 8/0
Shuck: Amber Z-Lon
Body: Olive Antron dubbing
Wing: Natural deer hair

Lacking a palmer hackle over the body, this version of an Elk Hair Caddis floats lower and is a proven producer during caddis hatches. Sizes and colors can be varied; on smaller hooks, a CDC puff can be substituted for the deer-hair wing for easier tying and better floatation.

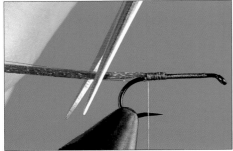

Step 1: Mount the thread and wrap to the tailing point. Mount a length of Z-Lon atop the shank; wrap forward to secure it and return the thread to the rearmost wrap. Clip the shuck, as shown, to about one hook-gap in length.

Step 2: Using the *direct dubbing* (p. 34) method, apply dubbing loosely to the thread and wrap it forward to form a slightly tapered body over the rear ⅔ of the shank. Position the thread at the front of the body.

Step 3: *Clip, clean, and stack* (p. 32) a bundle of deer hair. Position it atop the shank so that the tips extend rearward to the end of the hook bend.

Step 4: Secure the hair with tight thread wraps. Lift the hair butts, and whip finish around the shank behind the hook eye.

Step 5: Gather the hair butts, elevate them slightly, and clip at an angle to form the head.

Deer-Hair Compara-Emerger

Originator: Al Caucci and Bob Nastasi
Hook: TMC 900BL, or equivalent dry-fly hook, #8-#18
Thread: Brown 6/0
Tail: Dun rooster hackle fibers
Body: Blended gray dubbing
Wing: Natural deer hair

The Compara-emerger has been the starting point for many similar patterns. The fly is usually tied to imitate emerging mayflies, and the colors can be altered to match the desired hatch. The dressing shown here—with split, hackle-fiber tails—is the original, but it's often tied these days with a straight, undivided Antron or Z-Lon shuck.

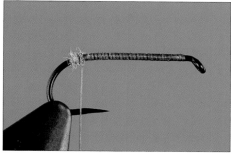

Step 1: Mount the tying thread and position it at the tailing point. Using the *direct dubbing* method (p. 34), twist a very small amount of dubbing tightly on the thread. Wrap rearward to form a small ball of dubbing just where the shank begins to bend.

Step 2: *Align and strip* (p. 30) 4-6 hackle barbs. Mount them on the far side of the shank with two tight thread wraps, as shown in this top view, so that the barbs extend about one shank-length beyond the dubbing ball.

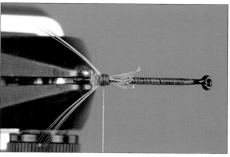

Step 3: Repeat Step 2, mounting an equal number of barbs on the near side of the shank. If necessary, take a thread wrap against the base of the dubbing to flare the tails at roughly a 90-degree angle, as shown in this top view.

Step 4: Secure the tail butts with a few tight wraps and clip the excess. Dub a slender, tapered thorax over the rear ⅔ of the hook shank.

Step 5: *Clip, clean, and stack* (p. 32) a small bundle of deer hair. Mount the hair ahead of the body to form a wing that extends about halfway to the rear of the shank. Lift the hair butts, and take several tight turns around the shank directly against the base of the butts to elevate them.

Step 6: Clip the butts at an angle, as shown, and add a small amount of dubbing to cover the thread wraps between the wing and the trimmed hair. Whip finish behind the eye, around the shank only.

Everything Emerger

Originator: Scott Sanchez
Hook: Dai Riki 310, or other ring-eye dry-fly hook, #14-#18
Thread: Rust-brown 8/0
Shuck: Brown Z-Lon
Rib: Tying thread
Abdomen: Tan dubbing
Wing: Elk or deer hair
Thorax: Tan dubbing

Scott Sanchez points out that emergers of different types of insects may well look more alike to the fish than different—"a shuck, a compressed body, and a disarray of legs." He designed this pattern as a multi-purpose emerger and fishes it for mayflies, caddis, and midges. He ties it in dun, black, and olive, and notes that CDC or snowshoe hare's foot can be used for the wing/leg material.

Step 1: Attach the thread and position it at the tailing point. Mount a sparse bundle of Antron to form a shuck one shank-length long. Form a loop of thread at the rearmost thread wrap as described in *dubbing loop*, Steps 1-2, (p. 35). (This loop is only used to rib the fly, not dub the body.)

Step 2: Use the *direct dubbing* method (p. 34) to dub a tapered body ⅔ the distance to the hook eye. Twist the loop threads together, and spiral them forward to rib the abdomen. Tie off and clip at the front of the abdomen.

Step 3: *Clip, clean, and stack* (p. 32) a bundle of elk hair. Mount the bundle atop the shank, directly ahead of the abdomen, so that the hair tips extend to the hook bend. Secure the hair tightly, then clip out the center portion of the hair butts, leaving about 5 fibers on either side for legs, as shown here.

Step 4: Pull the leg fibers outward, perpendicular to the shank. Cut the hair butts to one hook-gap in length. Wrap a thinly dubbed thread up to the base of the legs, as shown in this top view.

Step 5: Use crisscross wraps of dubbed thread to hold the legs perpendicular to the shank, as shown here from the top.

Step 6: Dub the remainder of the head up to the hook eye. Whip finish. Using your thumb and forefinger, pinch the legs inward to crumple them into a more lifelike shape, as shown in this top view.

CDC & Elk

Originator: Hans Weilenmann
Hook: TMC 102Y, or equivalent dry-fly hook, #11-#17
Thread: Brown 6/0
Body/hackle: One Type 1 CDC feather
Wing: Fine-tipped natural deer hair

This easy-to-tie pattern is highly effective during both caddis and mayfly hatches. It can be fished high-and-dry by applying a bit of floatant to the wing only (not the CDC); it can be fished in the film by applying no floatant; and it can be fished as a wet as well.

Step 1: Select a Type 1 CDC feather on which the longest barbs are twice the shank length. Stroke the barbs to the tip of the feather, and bunch them. Mount the feather by the tip with two tight wraps. Lift the tips, and take one more wrap. Follow with a fourth wrap, just ahead of the third, that binds the tips down.

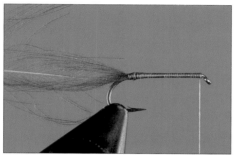

Step 2: Spiral the thread forward in touching wraps to the hook eye. Then take one wrap rearward.

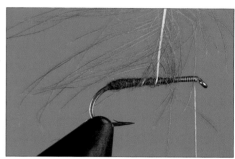

Step 3: Clip the feather butt in a pair of hackle pliers, and wrap forward in touching turns.

Step 4: Continue wrapping forward. As you approach the eye, loose barbs will splay out to form the hackle. When you reach the tying thread, bind down the stem with 2 or 3 tight wraps. Clip the excess feather stem.

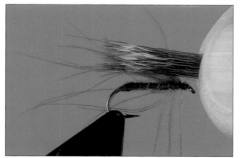

Step 5: *Clip, clean, and stack* (p. 32) a bundle of deer hair. Measure the hair against the shank, with the tips aligned with the hook bend. Clip the butts even with the hook eye.

Step 6: Mount the hair atop the shank with two tight wraps. Make a third wrap at 45 degrees to the shank through the clipped butts, as shown here. Take a fourth wrap under the hair butts, and whip finish around the shank.

U-Con 2 Caddis Emerger

Originator: Howard Cole
Hook: TMC 900BL, or equivalent dry-fly hook, #14-#20
Thread: Dun 8/0
Tail: Amber Z-Lon
Body: Dark olive dubbing
Overbody: Dark olive Z-Lon
Thorax: Silver glass bead
Wing: Natural deer hair

The simplified version of the bubble shuck on this Howard Cole design places the fly body on the surface film and is easy to tie.

Step 1: De-barb the hook if it's not barbless, and slide the glass bead over the shank to the hook eye. Mount the thread and position it at the tailing point. Secure a sparse bundle of Z-Lon atop the shank to make a trailing shuck about the length of the hook shank. Position the thread at the midpoint of the shank.

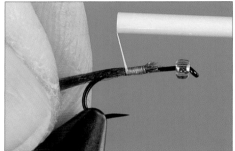

Step 2: Mount a strand of Z-Lon at the midpoint of the shank with a few tight wraps. Wrap the thread toward the tail, and as you do, draw the strand slightly downward with the left fingers, so that the Z-Lon fibers are secured to the top and sides, but not bottom, of the shank. Stop at the rearmost tailing wrap.

Step 3: Use the *direct dubbing* method (p. 34) to dub body over the rear ⅔ of the shank. Make sure that the front edge of the body is thick enough to prevent the glass bead from sliding rearward. Secure the thread behind the bead with a few half-hitches, and remount the thread ahead of the bead.

Step 4: Pull the overbody Z-Lon forward to form a loose bubble around the top and sides of the shank. Secure the Z-Lon atop the shank with two thread wraps. If necessary, use a dubbing needle to distribute the fibers uniformly around the top half of the shank. Then secure the Z-Lon with tight wraps and clip the excess.

Step 5: The finished overbody bubble should surround the top and sides of the shank but be open on the bottom, as shown in this view of the fly from underneath.

Step 6: *Clip, clean, and stack* (p. 32) a bundle of deer hair. Mount it atop the shank, behind the hook eye, to form a wing that extends to the rear of the overbody bubble. Lift the hair butts and whip finish around the shank. Clip the hair butts at an angle to form the head.

Traveling Sedge Emerger (Chan)

Originator: Brian Chan
Hook: TMC 5212, or other fine-wire 2XL hook, #6-#10
Thread: Olive 6/0
Rib: Bright green Super Floss
Body: Brown seal substitute dubbing
Wing: Deer hair
Hackle: Dark brown

This pattern, from stillwater expert Brian Chan, can also be tied with an olive or green body and a ginger hackle. The fly sits low in the water, like an emerging natural, but is quite visible to the angler.

Step 1: Attach the thread, position it at the rearmost point of the body, and tie in the ribbing material. Use the *direct dubbing* method (p. 34) to dub a body over the rear ¾ of the hook shank.

Step 2: *Counter-rib* (p. 33) the Super Floss; tie off and clip at the front of the body.

Step 3: *Clip, clean, and stack* (p. 32) a bundle of deer hair. Mount the hair atop the shank to form a wing that extends slightly beyond the hook bend.

Step 4: *Prepare a hackle feather* (p. 39) and mount it as shown in *mounting collar hackle* (p. 37).

Step 5: Take two wraps of hackle toward the hook eye as explained in *wrapping dry-fly hackle* (p. 44), then reverse direction and wrap rearward, over the first hackle wraps, back to the tying thread. Tie off and clip the excess hackle. Lift the deer-hair tips, and wrap the tying thread back to the midpoint of the shank.

Step 6: Draw the deer hair rearward over the top of the shank, and secure it at the midpoint of the shank to make a humped wing case. Whip finish over these thread wraps. Trim the deer hair to form a tuft-like head, and trim the hackle atop and underneath the shank, leaving only the barbs projecting from the sides.

Mayfly Emerger

Originator: Doug Swisher and Carl Richards
Hook: TMC 5212, or other fine-wire 2XL hook, #14-#18
Thread: Dun 8/0
Tail: Grizzly hen hackle fibers
Body: Dun dubbing
Wings: 2 dun hen hackle tips
Legs: Grizzly hen hackle fibers

This pattern can be fished in the film or as a wet fly. The colors can be varied to match specific mayfly species, and the fly is also productive during caddis hatches.

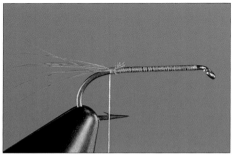

Step 1: Mount the thread and wrap to the tailing point. *Align and strip* (p. 30) 6-8 barbs from a grizzly hen feather. Secure them atop the shank at the tailing point to form a tail about one hook-gap long.

Step 2: Use the *direct dubbing* method (p. 34) to dub a slightly rough body over ⅔ of the hook shank.

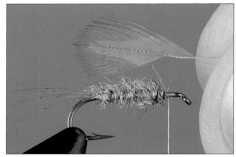

Step 3: Prepare the wings by stacking two hen hackles back-to-back, with the concave sides together. Strip away the lower barbs so that the tip section is as long as the fly body. Then strip additional fibers from one side of the feather stems, as shown.

Step 4: Place the feathers atop the body, with the stems lying side-by-side. Secure them in this position by taking the first wrap or two just over the dubbing at the front edge of the body. Check the wing position—the feathers should be vertical. If not, adjust them to vertical.

Step 5: When the wings are properly positioned, bind the stems toward the hook eye, and clip the excess. Align and strip a small bundle of grizzly barbs, and mount them to the underside of the shank using the technique shown in *throat hackle* (p. 41). Clip the excess. Form the head of the fly and whip finish.

Winger

Originator: Shane Stalcup
Hook: TMC 2487, or other fine-wire scud hook, #12-#22
Thread: Tan 8/0
Shuck: Dun hen hackle fibers
Body: Olive Micro Tubing
Wings: Dun hen hackle feathers
Thorax: Light olive fine poly dubbing

The use of hen hackle-tip wings for emerger patterns was popularized by Swisher and Richards in their Mayfly Emerger (p. 248). The wrapped hackle is used for greater lateral stability in the pattern; and the scud hook gives a descending-body profile.

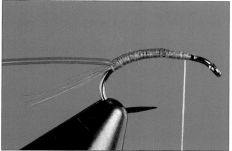

Step 1: Attach the thread and position it at the tailing point. *Align and strip* (p. 30) a sparse bundle of hen hackle fibers, and mount them to form a tail one shank-length long. Trim a length of vinyl tubing to a point. Mount the tubing by the point over the rearmost thread wraps securing the tail.

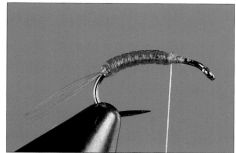

Step 2: Wrap the tubing forward to form an abdomen over the rear ⅔ of the hook shank. Tie off; clip and bind the excess. Position the thread at the front of the abdomen.

Step 3: *Prepare a hackle feather* (p. 39) and secure it in front of the abdomen as shown in *mounting collar hackle* (p. 37). Use the *direct dubbing* method (p. 34) to dub a tapered thorax, stopping about 6 or 7 thread-wraps' distance behind the hook eye.

Step 4: Spiral the hackle over the thorax as explained in *palmering hackle* (p. 38). Tie off the feather in front of the abdomen, and clip the excess. Prepare two hen hackles by stripping away the lower barbs, leaving feather tips equal in length to the fly body, as shown.

Step 5: Place the feathers front-to-front, so they flare away from one another. Position them in front of the thorax so that the stems straddle the hook shank and the tips are angled upward. Secure them with a firm, but not tight, wrap; adjust the position if necessary; then secure with tight thread wraps.

Step 6: Clip the excess wing butts. Dub a head that covers the wing-mounting wraps, and whip finish the fly.

Timberline Emerger

Originator: Randall Kaufmann
Hook: TMC 3761BL, or equivalent 2XL heavy nymph
hook, #12-#16
Thread: Gray 8/0
Tail: Gray fluff from base of pheasant body feather
Rib: Fine copper wire
Body: Gray Angora goat mixed with gray Haretron dubbing
Wings: Grizzly hen hackle tips
Hackle: Brown wet-fly

Randall Kaufmann originally designed this classic emerger pattern for high-elevation lakes as a midge and mayfly emerger. It can be fished damp, in the film, or just under the film with a slow, hand-twist retrieve. Tan and olive versions are also effective.

Step 1: Mount the thread and position it at the tailing point. Strip a generous clump of fluff from the base of a pheasant body feather, and secure it to make a tail about one hook-gap in length. Bind the butts toward the hook eye, and return the thread to the rearmost wrap. Mount the ribbing wire.

Step 2: Use the *direct dubbing* method (p. 34) to dub a slightly rough, tapered body over ¾ of the hook shank.

Step 3: Spiral the ribbing wire forward. Tie it off directly in front of the body, and clip the excess.

Step 4: Select and *prepare a hackle feather* (p. 39) with barbs about ¾ the length of the body. Mount the feather at the front edge of the body as shown in *mounting collar hackle* (p. 37).

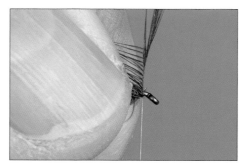

Step 5: Take 3-5 turns of the feather as shown in *wrapping wet-fly hackle* (p. 50).

Step 6: Secure the feather tip, and clip the excess feather.

Step 7: Draw the hackle fibers rearward around the body, and take 3 or 4 wraps over the base of the barbs to slant them rearward and lay a thread foundation for the wings.

Step 8: Select a matched pair of grizzly hen hackles, and place them front-to-front, with the convex sides together and the tips aligned. Strip away the lower fibers until the remaining tips are about one hook-length long.

Step 9: Place the feathers atop the shank so that the tips extend rearward ¾ the length of the body.

Step 10: Transfer the tips to the left fingers, and use a *pinch wrap* (p. 38) to secure them to the top of the shank. Take another pinch wrap atop the first.

Step 11: Check to make sure the wings are vertical, and flare away from one another slightly, as shown in this top view. If the wings are out of position, adjust them.

Step 12: When the wings are in position, secure with additional wraps toward the hook eye. Then clip the feather stems, form the head of the fly, and whip finish.

CDC Pheasant-Tail Emerger

Hook: TMC 900BL, or equivalent dry-fly hook, #12-#20
Thread: Brown 8/0
Tail: Pheasant-tail fibers
Abdomen: Pheasant-tail fibers
Ribbing: Fine copper wire
Wing case: Pheasant-tail fibers
Thorax: Arizona Synthetic Peacock dubbing, natural
Wing: Gray CDC fibers or Type 3 "puff"

We've seen a number of versions of this pattern; this one is typical. It's a good example of how the addition of a simple CDC wing can make almost any standard nymph into a floating nymph or emerger. Absorbent materials allow the body to ride in or just under the film, while the wing is visible to the angler.

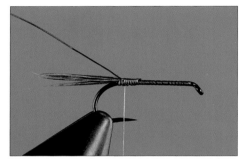

Step 1: Attach the thread and position it at the tailing point. *Align and strip* (p. 30) 3-6 pheasant-tail fibers, and mount them to make a tail about one hook-gap in length. Bind and clip the excess. Mount the ribbing wire atop the rearmost tailing wrap.

Step 2: Mount 3-6 pheasant-tail fibers by the tips at the tailing point. Advance the thread to the midpoint of the shank. Wrap the pheasant fibers forward, as shown in *wrapping feather-barb bodies* (p. 45) to form an abdomen over the rear half of the shank. Bind down the fibers and clip the excess.

Step 3: *Counter-rib* (p. 33) the wire to the front of the abdomen. Tie off and clip.

Step 4: Align and strip 6-10 more pheasant fibers, and clip off the bottom ⅓ of the bundle. Secure the fiber butts directly ahead of the abdomen. Use the *direct dubbing* method (p. 34) to dub a thorax slightly wider than the abdomen.

Step 5: Fold the pheasant fibers over the thorax, and secure with a few tight wraps.

Step 6: Clip the excess fibers and bind down. Gather a bundle of CDC barbs as explained in *stripping CDC barbs* (p. 40), or select a CDC puff. Mount the CDC directly ahead of the thorax so that it extends rearward to the midpoint of the abdomen. Clip the excess CDC and secure the butts tightly. Whip finish the fly.

Fratnick Caddis Emerger

Originator: Version of Marjan Fratnick design
Hook: TMC 900BL, or equivalent dry-fly hook, #14-#22
Thread: Black 8/0
Shuck: One strand pearl Krystal Flash
Body: One Type I or Type 2 CDC feather
Wing: CDC barbs or Type 3 CDC "puff"

The original Fratnick is an adult caddis pattern. This version has a simple shuck and a shorter wing to imitate emerging caddis. It is simple to tie and particularly effective in smaller sizes. Colors can be varied to match other naturals.

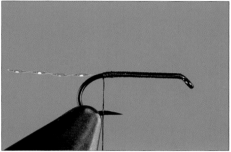

Step 1: Mount the thread and position it at the tailing point. Secure a strand of Krystal Flash atop the shank. Clip the strand to form a shuck about ⅔ the shank length. Return the thread to the tailing point.

Step 2: Select a CDC feather for the body. Take two wraps under light tension over the bare stem of the feather, just below the lowermost barbs.

Step 3: Apply light tension to the bobbin with the right hand. With the left fingers, draw the feather rearward, sliding it beneath the thread wrap to consolidate the barbs. When you are within ⅛" or so of the feather tip, stop pulling the feather, and tightly bind the tip to the shank.

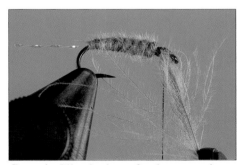

Step 4: Clip the bare feather stem in a pair of hackle pliers, and wrap the feather forward, stopping about ¼ of a shank length behind the hook eye. Tie off the feather and clip the excess.

Step 5: Gather a bundle of CDC barbs as shown in *stripping CDC barbs* (p. 40), or for larger flies, select a CDC puff. Mount the CDC atop the shank, directly ahead of the body to make a wing about ⅔ of a shank-length long. If using stripped barbs, you can clip or break the barbs to length. Then clip and bind the excess. Whip finish.

Harrop Brown Drake Biot Emerger

Originator: René Harrop
Hook: TMC 5212, or other fine-wire 2XL hook, #8-#12
Thread: Brown 8/0
Tail: Three woodduck flank fibers
Abdomen: Tan-yellow turkey biot
Thorax: Tan-yellow dubbing
Hackle: Brown partridge fibers
Wings: Two Type 2 dark brown or dark dun CDC feathers

Designed for fishing the brown drake hatch on Henrys Fork, this pattern is an excellent example of René Harrop's trim, precise fly styles.

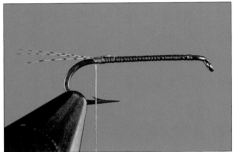

Step 1: Mount the tying thread and position it at the tailing point. *Align and strip* (p. 30) three woodduck flank fibers. Mount them atop the shank to form a tail slightly longer than one hook-gap. Use a *flattened thread* (p. 37) to bind the butts and lay a smooth foundation for the biot body.

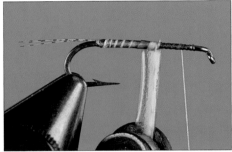

Step 2: Mount a turkey biot atop the rearmost tailing wrap as shown in *biot body—smooth* (p. 31), and wrap the biot forward over the rear ⅔ of the shank. Bind and clip the excess.

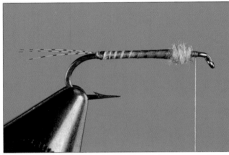

Step 3: Use the *direct dubbing* method (p. 34) to form a tight ball of dubbing for a thorax about twice as thick as the body.

Step 4: Align and strip a small bundle of partridge fibers. Mount them beneath the shank, directly ahead of the thorax, as explained in *throat hackle* (p. 41), to make legs slightly longer than one hook-gap.

Step 5: Select two CDC feathers and stack them front-to-front, with the convex sides together. Mount them directly ahead of the thorax to form wings that extend to the rearmost point of the body. Bind and clip the excess.

Step 6: The finished wings should sit vertically atop the shank and flare away from one another, as shown in this top view.

PMD Shiny Tail Emerger

Originator: Joseph Burket
Hook: TMC 2487G, or other fine-wire scud hook, #18
Thread: Light yellow 8/0
Tail: Amber Z-Lon or Darlon
Abdomen: Fine yellow tubing such as Larva Lace
Thorax: Rusty brown Ice Dub
Wings: Two Type 2 natural CDC feathers
Legs: Brown micro rubber

This unusual extended-body emerger uses tubing to suggest translucence and build a bit flotation into the rear of the fly. We haven't tried this pattern for other hatches but see no reason why the fly style couldn't be adapted to other mayflies.

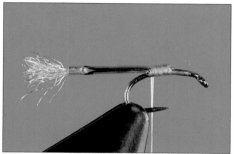

Step 1: Fold a length of fine copper wire around a length of tailing material and insert the ends of the wire through the tubing, as shown on the left. Then pull the ends of the wire to draw the tail material a short distance into the tubing, as shown on the right. Clip the tail to one hook-gap in length.

Step 2: Mount the tying thread and position it at the rear of the shank. Secure the tail/abdomen assembly with tight thread wraps moving toward the hook eye. Bind and clip the excess. Return the thread to the rear-most wrap.

Step 3: Use the *direct dubbing* method (p. 34) to dub a thorax about ⅔ the distance to the hook eye.

Step 4: Place two CDC feather front-to-front, with convex sides together. Mount them directly in front of the thorax so that the wings extend halfway to the end of the tail. Bind and clip the excess

Step 5: Take a length of rubber leg material and fold it around the tying thread. Mount the leg material on the far side of the shank, as shown in this top view.

Step 6: Repeat Step 5 to mount another pair of legs on the near side of the shank. Clip the legs to the overall length of the body. Whip finish behind the hook eye, ahead of the front legs.

QD Mayfly Emerger/Stillborn

Originator: Bob Braendle
Hook: TMC 200R, or curved long-shank hook, #16
Thread: Gray 8/0
Tail: Mallard flank fibers
Bubble shuck: Rust Antron or Z-Lon
Body: Light brown Superfine dubbing
Hackle: Grizzly dyed olive
Wing: Gray poly yarn

This simple pattern can be modified in size and color to match various mayflies. Bob Braendle also notes that the wing can be tied from deer hair or snowshoe hare's foot.

Step 1: Mount the thread and position it at the tailing point. *Align and strip* (p. 30) 4-6 mallard flank fibers. Secure them atop the shank to make a tail about ¾ the shank length. Bind and clip the excess fibers; then position the thread at the midpoint of the shank.

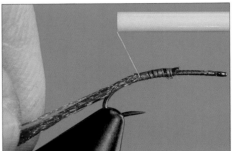

Step 2: Secure a strand of shuck material at the middle of the shank. Bind it down moving toward the hook bend. As you wrap, draw the strand slightly downward with your left fingers to distribute the shuck fibers around the shank. Secure the strand tightly around the rearmost tailing wraps.

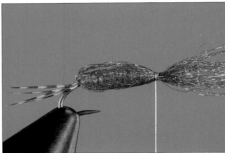

Step 3: Using *direct dubbing* method (p. 34) to dub a body ¾ the distance to the hook eye. Draw the shuck material forward evenly to form a slender bubble-like capsule around the dubbed body. Secure the shuck material tightly at the front of the body.

Step 4: Trim the excess shuck material. Mount the hackle feather directly ahead of the body as shown in *mounting collar hackle* (p. 37). Take 3-4 wraps of the feather as explained in *wrapping dry-fly hackle* (p. 44). Tie off and clip the feather.

Step 5: Trim the top and bottom of the hackle so only the fibers projecting to the sides remain. Cut a short length of poly yarn; trim the end to even the fibers. Mount the yarn ahead of the hackle to form a wing that extends to the midpoint of the body.

Step 6: Whip finish the fly behind the eye, underneath the tag of yarn. Clip the tag of yarn to form a tuft-like head. This front view shows the hackle fibers extending to the sides and the spread of the poly wing.

Pop Top PMD Emerger

Originator: Andy Burk
Hook: TMC 101, or other ring-eye dry-fly hook, #14-#18
Thread: Light olive 6/0
Tail: Mallard flank fibers dyed wood duck
Abdomen: Rusty brown stripped hackle quill
Thorax: Pale yellow-olive Superfine dubbing
Legs: Mallard flank fibers dyed wood duck
Float pod: Gray 2mm foam

Here's one for minimalist tyers. The slender silhouette and sparse dressing make this a good choice for flat water. It is an easy pattern to tie, even in small sizes.

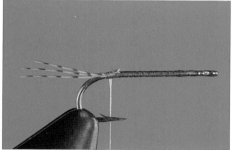

Step 1: Mount the thread and position it at the tailing point. *Align and strip* (p. 30) 3-5 mallard flank fibers, and secure them atop the shank to make a tail about one hook-gap in length. Use a *flattened thread* (p. 37) to bind down the fiber butts and create a smooth underbody.

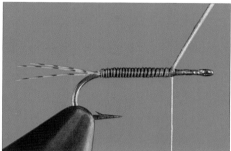

Step 2: Mount the tip of the hackle quill atop the rearmost tailing wraps, as shown in *wrapping quill bodies* (p. 47), and wrap the quill forward over the rear ⅔ of the hook shank. Tie off and clip the excess.

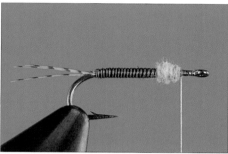

Step 3: Use the *direct dubbing* method (p. 34) to form a thorax slightly wider than the body and tapering toward the hook eye. The taper helps position the foam float pod.

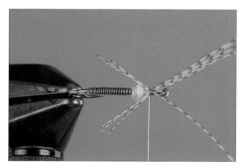

Step 4: Use the technique shown in *side-mounted legs* (p. 39) to mount 3-5 mallard fibers on either side of the shank, directly ahead of the thorax. Take a wrap or two of thread abutting the thorax to flare the legs slightly. When the legs are positioned, clip and bind down the excess fibers.

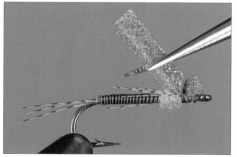

Step 5: Cut a strip of foam about ½ the hook gap in width. Secure it atop the shank directly ahead of the legs. Whip finish. Trim the front tag to make a stubby head. Trim the rear tag to make a wing that extends just past the thorax.

Tan Caddis Emerger

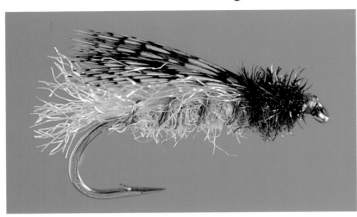

Originator: Mike Lawson
Hook: TMC 100, or equivalent dry-fly hook, #14-#20
Thread: Tan 8/0
Shuck: Tan Z-Lon
Rib: Fine copper wire
Abdomen: Tan Antron
Underwing: Tan Z-Lon
Wing: Two mottled brown partridge hackle tips
Thorax: Peacock herl

The liberal use of Z-Lon gives this pattern a lot of sparkle, both above and below the water. The partridge feathers make it especially well suited to imitating caddis with mottled wings.

Step 1: Mount the thread and position it at the tailing point. Mount the ribbing wire. Use the *direct dubbing* method (p. 34) to dub a tapered abdomen ⅔ the distance to the hook eye.

Step 2: Cut a length of Z-Lon about four times the shank length. Secure the middle of the strand atop the shank with tight wraps directly ahead of the abdomen. Draw the rear tag of the yarn along the top of the abdomen, and secure it by spiraling the ribbing wire forward. Tie off the ribbing ahead of the front yarn tag.

Step 3: Fold the front tag of yarn over the abdomen. Take several thread wraps over the base of the folded yarn so that it angles to the rear. Clip this wing even with the hook bend. Clip the shuck to about ½ the length of the abdomen.

Step 4: Strip the barbs from two partridge feathers until the remaining tips are as long as the abdomen. Stack them front-to-back so the curvatures match, and mount them atop the shank with the concave side facing down, lying against the Z-Lon underwing.

Step 5: Mount 2-3 strands of peacock herl, and wrap a thorax as explained in *wrapping twisted-herl collars* (p. 49). Clip the excess and bind it down, forming the head of the fly. Whip finish.

Brass Assed Emerger

Originator: Paul Dieter
Hook: TMC 205BL, or other light-wire scud hook, #14-#18
Thread: Black 8/0
Abdomen: Green copper wire
Thorax: Hare's ear dubbing
Wing: Stripped CDC barbs
Legs: Partridge fibers
Wing case: Strip of turkey tail coated with flexible cement

Washington tyer Paul Dieter designed this interesting split wing case with emerging wing, and it could be used on other emerger patterns as well. His original fly uses standard copper wire for the body; we use green wire for a general-purpose emerger.

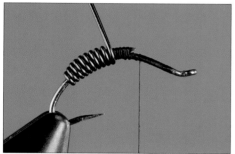

Step 1: Mount the thread and position it at the tailing point. Mount a length of wire atop the shank. Bind the tag on top of the shank ⅔ the distance to the hook eye to make a uniform underbody. Wrap the wire evenly forward to form an abdomen over the rear ⅔ of the shank. Tie off and clip.

Step 2: Use the *direct dubbing* method (p. 34) to dub a thorax half the distance to the hook eye.

Step 3: Gather a bundle of CDC barbs as shown in *stripping CDC barbs* (p. 40). Mount them directly ahead of the thorax to form a wing that extends rearward to the midpoint of the body.

Step 4: *Align and strip* (p. 30) a sparse bundle of partridge hackle fibers. Use the method shown in *throat hackle* (p. 41) to mount them to the underside of the shank to form legs that extend to the hook point.

Step 5: Cut a strip of turkey tail feather about ½ the hook gap in width. Coat with flexible cement and let dry. Fold the strip crosswise, and trim the tips even. Cut a "V" notch in the trimmed ends.

Step 6: Mount the folded wing case atop the shank. It should extend rearward to the end of the thorax, and the CDC fibers should be centered in the "V" notch, as shown in this front view. Clip and bind the excess. Whip finish the fly.

PMD PT Emerger

Originator: Mike Lawson
Hook: TMC 100, or equivalent dry-fly hook, #10-#20
Thread: Brown 8/0
Tail: Dun Z-Lon
Shellback: Dun Z-Lon
Abdomen: Pheasant-tail fibers
Rib: Fine red wire
Thorax: Pale yellow fine poly dubbing
Underwing: Dun Z-Lon
Overwing: Two Type 1 or Type 2 gray CDC feathers
Legs: Partridge body feather fibers

Like many of Mike Lawson's emerger patterns, this one incorporates a Z-Lon underwing. The basic design here can be modified to match a number of mayfly species. This is a good flat-water pattern.

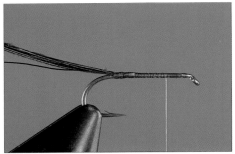

Step 1: Mount the tying thread and position it at the tailing point. Mount 4-6 pheasant-tail fibers by the tips. Mount the ribbing wire directly atop the thread wraps securing the pheasant tail. Advance the thread ⅔ the distance to the hook eye.

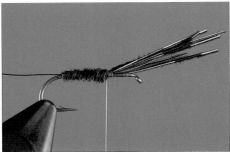

Step 2: Wrap the pheasant-tail fibers forward as shown in *wrapping feather-barb bodies* (p. 45) to form an abdomen over the rear ⅔ of the shank. Tie off and clip the excess.

Step 3: Mount a sparse Z-Lon yarn directly ahead of the abdomen. Clip and bind the front tag.

Step 4: Draw the Z-Lon rearward over the top of the abdomen. Secure it in this position by spiraling the ribbing wire forward. Bind and clip the wire at the front of the abdomen.

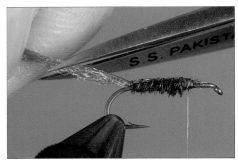

Step 5: Clip the Z-Lon to make a tail as long as the abdomen.

Step 6: Use the *direct dubbing* method (p. 34) to dub a thorax from the front of the abdomen halfway to the hook eye.

Step 7: Mount another sparse bundle of Z-Lon directly ahead of the thorax to form a wing about as long as the abdomen.

Step 8: Clip and bind the front tag of the Z-Lon. Align the tips of the CDC feathers, and mount them atop the wraps securing the Z-Lon. This CDC overwing should extend rearward the same distance as the Z-Lon underwing.

Step 9: Using the method shown in *side-mounted legs* (p. 39), mount a bundle of partridge fibers on either side of the shank to form legs as the long as the body. Clip the excess.

Step 10: Put a drop of head cement on the wrappings to help secure all the materials.

Step 11: Dub a tapered head, covering the thread wraps securing the wing materials. Whip finish the fly.

CDC Green Drake Emerger

Originator: Shane Stalcup
Hook: TMC 2302, or equivalent 2XL dry-fly hook, #10-#12
Thread: Olive 6/0
Tail: Brown partridge fibers
Rib: Fine copper wire
Abdomen: Olive turkey biot
Thorax: Chartreuse Superfine dubbing
Underwing: Natural gray Type 2 CDC feather
Legs: Brown partridge fibers
Overwing: Dun Z-Lon

The Z-Lon overwing makes this low-floating pattern more visible to the angler. It can be tied to represent other mayfly species, and a smooth biot body can be used in place of the fringed one shown here.

Step 1: Mount the thread and position at the tailing point. *Align and strip* (p. 30) a sparse bundle of partridge fibers, and mount them at the tailing position to form a tail about ½ the shank-length long. Secure the ribbing material atop the tail fibers. Mount the biot atop the rib as explained in *biot body—fringed* (p. 30).

Step 2: Wrap the biot forward over the rear ⅗ of the shank. Tie off and clip. Wrap the ribbing forward, placing each wrap just behind the fringe on the biot abdomen. Tie off and clip the ribbing in front of the abdomen.

Step 3: Use the *direct dubbing* method to dub a thorax halfway to the hook eye. Mount the CDC feather directly in front of the thorax to make an underwing that extends to the midpoint of the abdomen. When the wing is secure, clip and bind the excess.

Step 4: Use the method shown in *side-mounted legs* (p. 39) to affix a small bundle of partridge fibers on either side of the shank, directly alongside the CDC wing. The legs should be about ⅔ the hook gap in length, as shown in this top view. When the legs are positioned and secure, clip and bind the excess.

Step 5: Dub the remainder of the thorax, stopping about 5 thread-wraps short of the hook eye.

Step 6: Mount a strand of Z-Lon at the front of the thorax to make an overwing about ¾ of shank-length long. Clip and bind the excess. Whip finish the fly.

CDC Floating Callibaetis Nymph/Emerger

Hook: TMC 5212, or other fine-wire 2XL hook, #14-#16
Thread: Tan 8/0
Tail: Mallard flank dyed wood duck
Rib: Fine copper wire
Abdomen: Tan Antron
Wing: Brown partridge flanking medium-dun Type 2 CDC feather over brown Z-Lon
Thorax: Tan Antron

This generic emerger design can be altered to match most mayfly hatches. It is a basic, workmanlike, but effective pattern.

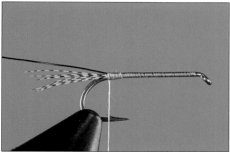

Step 1: Mount the thread and position it at the tailing point. *Align and strip* (p. 30) 6-8 mallard flank fibers and secure them atop the shank at the tailing point. Bind and clip the excess. Mount the ribbing wire atop the rearmost tailing wrap and bind down the excess.

Step 2: Use the *direct dubbing* method (p. 34) to dub a slender tapered abdomen over the rear ⅔ of the shank. Spiral the ribbing forward, and tie off in front of the abdomen.

Step 3: Mount a strand of Z-Lon directly in front of the abdomen to make an underwing that extends to the tail-mounting point. Clip and bind the excess Z-Lon.

Step 4: Mount a CDC feather atop the Z-Lon that extends to the tail-mounting point. Clip and bind down the excess feather.

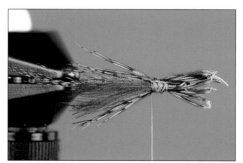

Step 5: Use the technique shown in *side-mounted legs* (p. 39) to secure a small bundle of partridge fibers on each side of the wing. The fibers should extend to the tail-mounting point, as shown in this top view.

Step 6: Clip and bind the excess partridge fibers. Dub a thorax to just behind the hook eye. Form the head of the fly and whip finish.

Chapter 13: Upwing Emergers

Upwing emergers, unsurprisingly, tend to be modified versions of upright-wing mayfly patterns and often represent mayflies in a very late phase of emergence, with wings almost fully extended. Thus the fly body is frequently dressed in the color of the adult insect rather than the nymphal or pupal form. Some flies in fact, such as the popular Sparkle Dun, are almost indistinguishable from standard mayfly duns, with the presence of a trailing shuck the only real difference. We've even included one fly in this category, Fran Betters' Usual, which is not, strictly speaking, an emerger pattern at all; but so many anglers have found it effective on emerger-feeding trout that we'd be remiss not to present it.

Some upwing patterns strongly resemble downwing designs, the chief difference being in the mounting orientation of the wing material; upright wings are usually mounted with the material butts toward the hook bend, which facilitates posting the wing vertically. The upwing design places the fly body flush against or just under the surface film, and the elevated wings make these flies among the more visible emerger patterns. On virtually all the patterns here, the wing length can be altered to suit the tyer's taste. We've found the Puff Emerger patterns shown here to be especially effective during hatches of smaller mayflies, and Howard Cole's CDC Split Wing Cripple suggests, among other things, the interesting possibility of using dark-colored wing materials on an emerger, which are more visible in low-light conditions.

Sparkle Dun—Flav

Originator: Craig Mathews
Hook: TMC 100, or equivalent dry-fly hook, #14-#16
Thread: Olive 8/0
Shuck: Brown Z-Lon
Body: Olive dubbing
Wing: Natural deer hair

The lineage of this design extends back through the Compara-dun to Fran Betters' Usual (p. 268). It is simple to tie, fishes well as both an emerger and dun pattern, and can be altered to match a variety of mayfly species.

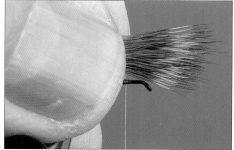

Step 1: Attach the thread and lay a thread foundation over the middle ⅓ of the shank. Position thread about ⅓ of a shank-length behind the eye. *Clip, clean, and stack* (p. 32) a bundle of deer hair. Position it atop the shank so that the tips extend beyond the tying thread a distance of one shank-length.

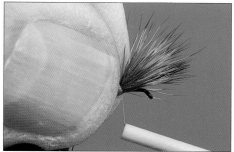

Step 2: Take two snug, but not tight, wraps over the hair. Then pull downward on the thread to cinch the hair to the shank. Pinch the bundle tightly in your left fingers to prevent the hair from slipping around the shank.

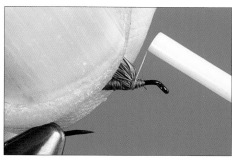

Step 3: Take additional tight wraps toward the hook bend to secure the hair. Clip the hair butts at an angle, and cover with thread. Wrap the thread forward to the front base of the hair. With the left fingers, preen the hair toward the bend. Build a bump of thread, tightly abutting the front base of the hair, to post it vertically.

Step 4: Use your fingers to fan the hair evenly from side to side, forming an arc of 180 degrees, as shown in this front view.

Step 5: Spiral the thread to the tailing point, and mount a sparse bundle of Z-Lon to form a shuck one hook-gap in length.

Step 6: Use the *direct dubbing* method (p. 34) to dub a slender, tapered abdomen. Take a few crisscross wraps of dubbing beneath the wing to cover the exposed thread wraps. Then dub ahead of the wings to form the head. Whip finish.

CDC Sparkle Dun

Originator: Version of Craig Mathews pattern
Hook: TMC 100, or equivalent dry-fly hook, #16-#20
Thread: Gray 8/0
Shuck: Amber Z-Lon
Body: Gray fine poly dubbing
Wing: One to three Type 1, Type 2, or Type 3 natural CDC feathers

Sizes and colors can be varied to match many mayfly hatches, but the CDC wing is particularly well-suited to smaller patterns, where deer hair can be bulky to mount and produces a sparse wing.

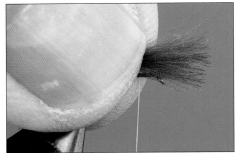

Step 1: Attach the thread and lay a foundation over the middle ⅓ of the shank. Position thread about ⅓ of a shank-length behind the eye. If more than one feather is used, align the tips. Position the CDC feather(s) atop the shank so that the tips extend beyond the tying thread a distance of one shank-length.

Step 2: Secure the butt end of the feather(s) to the top of the shank. Clip and bind the excess.

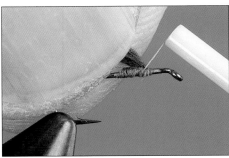

Step 3: With the left fingers, preen the feather toward the bend. Build a cone-shaped bump of thread, tapered toward the hook eye, tightly abutting the front base of the feather to post it vertically.

Step 4: Spiral the thread to the tailing point, and mount a sparse bundle of Z-Lon to form a shuck one hook-gap in length.

Step 5: With a sparsely dubbing thread, use the *direct dubbing* method (p. 34) to dub a tapered abdomen. Take a few crisscross wraps beneath the wing to cover the shank, and then dub the head of the fly. Whip finish.

Step 6: Here's a front view of the finished fly, showing the wing.

Wyatt's Deer Hair Emerger

Originator: Bob Wyatt
Hook: TMC 2487, or other light-wire scud hook, #10-#16
Thread: Gray 8/0
Abdomen: Hare's mask underfur and olive SLF dubbing
Rib: Tag end of tying thread
Thorax: Spiky hare's mask dubbing
Wing: Deer hair

Sizes and colors of this pattern can be varied, but Bob Wyatt advises treating only wing and thorax with floatant so that the abdomen hangs beneath the surface film. Alternate body materials include stripped quill, peacock herl, and seal-fur dubbing.

Step 1: Attach the tying thread, leaving a tag of thread 6" long. Lay a thread foundation over the middle ⅓ of the shank, and position the thread ⅓ of a shank-length behind the eye. *Clip, clean, and stack* (p. 32) a bundle of deer hair, and position it atop the shank so that tips extend one hook-length beyond the thread.

Step 2: Hold the hair tightly atop the shank, and secure with several thread wraps, moving toward the hook bend. Clip the butts at an angle, and bind down.

Step 3: Wrap the thread to the middle of the hook bend, securing the tag end of the thread as you go. Use the *direct dubbing* method (p. 34) to dub a slightly tapered abdomen along the shank that covers the thread wraps securing the wing.

Step 4: *Counter-rib* (p. 33) the tag end of the thread to rib the abdomen. Tie off the ribbing behind the wing. Position the tying thread behind the hook eye.

Step 5: Dub the thorax from the eye rearward, using the dubbing to force the deer-hair wing upright. The wing fibers will fan slightly, but not in a full arc, as shown in this front view.

Step 6: Spiral the thread through the thorax back to the eye, and whip finish. With a dubbing needle or teaser, pick out the thorax fibers.

The Usual

Originator: Fran Betters
Hook: TMC 900BL, Mustad 94840, or equivalent dry-fly
   hook, #12-#16
Thread: Burnt-orange 6/0
Tail: Snowshoe hare's foot
Body: Snowshoe hare's foot dubbing
Wing: Snowshoe hare's foot

An all-purpose pattern, the Usual (or Phillips Usual, as it was originally called) fishes well as both an emerger and dun. Thread color shows through slightly when the body is wet, and it can be varied to give the desired shade to the fly. Snowshoe hare gives this pattern good floatation and sheen.

Step 1: Attach the thread and position it ⅓ of a shank-length behind the hook eye. Clip a bundle of hair from the rear half of a snowshoe hare's foot (see Snowshoe Hare's Foot, p. 27). Hold it by the tips and pull out any very short hairs. Reserve this material, if there is any, for dubbing.

Step 2: Position the hair atop the shank, extending one shank-length beyond the tying thread. Secure the hair to the top of the shank. Clip the butts at an angle and bind down.

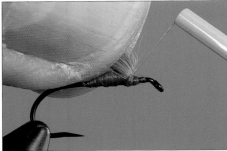

Step 3: With the left fingers, preen the hair rearward. Build a cone-shaped bump of tying thread, tapering toward the hook eye, and tightly abutting the front base of the hair to post it vertically.

Step 4: Spiral the thread to the tailing point. Clip a bundle of hair from the same area of the hare's foot where you clipped the wing material. Mount it to make a tail one shank-length long. Clip and bind the excess.

Step 5: Using the *direct dubbing* method (p. 34), form a slightly tapered abdomen. Apply dubbing sparsely so that the thread shows through. When you reach the wings, use crisscross wraps of dubbing to cover the underside of the shank. Then dub a tapered head. Whip finish the fly.

Step 6: Here's a view of the fly from the front.

PMD Puff Emerger

Icon: Mayfly
Hook: TMC 900BL, or equivalent dry-fly hook, #16-#18
Thread: Olive 8/0
Shuck: Stalcup's Trailing Shuck, tan
Abdomen: Light olive turkey biot
Wing: One natural gray Type 3 CDC feather (puff)
Thorax: Pale-olive fine poly dubbing

This style is one of our all-time favorites for fishing mayfly hatches. It's very easy to tie, floats well, and takes fish. We frequently dress it with a simple Antron shuck, particularly when imitating smaller mayflies.

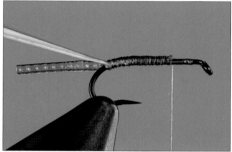

Step 1: Mount the thread and position it at the tailing point. Secure the trailing shuck so that it extends one shank-length beyond the mounting wraps. Secure a turkey biot by the tip atop the rearmost thread wrap as explained in *biot body—smooth* (p. 31). Position the thread ⅓ of a shank-length behind the hook eye.

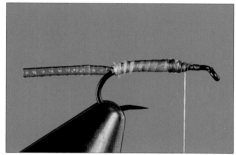

Step 2: Wrap the biot forward, and tie it off ⅓ of a shank-length behind the hook eye. Bind and clip the excess.

Step 3: Mount a CDC puff directly ahead of the abdomen. Take tight mounting wraps over the center of the puff. Do not clip the excess.

Step 4: Raise both the feather tips and butt end of the feather, and take 3 or 4 thread wraps horizontally around the base of the wing fibers to consolidate them.

Step 5: Use the *direct dubbing* method (p. 34) to dub the thorax, taking a crisscross wrap or two of dubbing beneath the wings to cover the thread wraps. Whip finish behind the hook eye.

Step 6: Raise the wing fibers and trim them to a height of one shank-length.

Puff Emerger—BWO

Hook: TMC 206BL, or other fine-wire scud hook, #16-#22
Thread: Olive 8/0
Shuck: Natural gray CDC feather barbs
Body: Olive fine poly dubbing
Wing: Stripped CDC barbs

This simple design is very effective for a variety of mayflies. Using stripped CDC barbs is a good way to utilize Type 4 CDC feathers that may be unsuitable for other applications. In small sizes, this makes a good midge emerger as well.

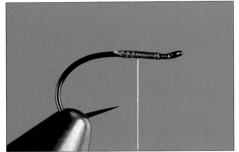

Step 1: Attach the thread and position it ⅔ of a shank-length behind the eye.

Step 2: Strip the fibers from 2-6 CDC feathers as shown in *stripping CDC barbs* (p. 40). Mount them with 4 tight thread wraps over the middle of the bundle. (Note: if a dense wing is desired, strip and mount 2 or 3 smaller bundles of barbs rather than a single large one.)

Step 3: Pull the fibers upward and take 3-5 thread wraps around the base to consolidate the barbs and post them vertically.

Step 4: Wrap the thread to the rear, and mount a sparse bundle of CDC barbs to make a shuck about one hook-gap in length.

Step 5: Use the *direct dubbing* method (p. 34) to dub a slender abdomen. Take a few crisscross wraps of dubbing beneath the wing to cover the shank. Then dub a tapered head. Whip finish behind the eye.

Step 6: Draw the wing fibers upward and trim them to the desired length, usually about one hook-gap.

CDC Split Wing Cripple

Originator: Howard Cole
Hook: TMC 100, or equivalent dry-fly hook, #14–#20
Thread: Olive-dun 8/0
Undertail: Amber Z-Lon
Tail: Woodduck flank barbs
Abdomen: Dark-olive hackle quill
Thorax: Olive dubbing
Wing case: One dark-olive Type 1, Type 2, or Type 4 CDC feather
Wings: Black poly yarn

The black wing on this pattern stands out on the water, particularly on overcast days. The version shown here is a BWO, but colors can be altered for other mayfly hatches.

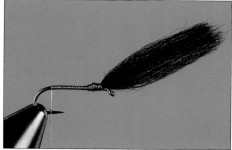

Step 1: Attach the thread and position it 4-5 thread-wraps' distance behind the hook eye. Mount a 1" length of poly yarn atop the shank; bind the tag rearward. Clip the excess, bind down, and wrap the thread to the tailing point.

Step 2: Mount a sparse bundle of Z-Lon atop the shank to form an undertail about one hook-gap in length. Do not clip the excess. Mount 3-4 woodduck flank fibers atop the Z-Lon to form tails one shank-length long. Do not clip the excess.

Step 3: Mount a hackle quill atop the rearmost tailing wraps. Bind all tags atop the hook to the midpoint of the shank, forming a smooth underbody, and clip. Form the abdomen as explained in *wrapping quill bodies* (p. 47). Tie off and clip at the midpoint of the shank.

Step 4: Mount a CDC feather by the tip atop the shank, directly ahead of the abdomen. Use the *direct dubbing* method (p. 34) to dub the thorax up to the base of the poly yarn. Position the tying thread ahead of the poly yarn.

Step 5: With a dubbing needle, divide the poly yarn into two equal wings. Pull the wing tips outward to create a gap. Fold the CDC through the gap in the wings and pinch it against the hook eye. Do not pull the CDC tight; the wing case should form a loop.

Step 6: With the left fingers, preen the wing fibers rearward and pinch the CDC in position. Secure the CDC behind the hook eye, wrapping rearward to elevate the wings to about 45 degrees, slanting forward. Clip the CDC and whip finish the fly. Lift both wings simultaneously, and clip to one shank-length in height.

Funnelwing Caddis

Originator: Variation of Henning von Monteton design
Hook: TMC 206BL, or other light-wire scud hook, #12-#18
Thread: Brown 8/0
Abdomen: Tan dubbing
Wing: Two natural gray Type 4 CDC feathers
Thorax: Dark brown natural fur dubbing

This unusual winging style from Henning von Monteton of Frankfurt, Germany, makes use of CDC feathers that otherwise have limited application. The abdomen material should absorb water so that it sinks below the surface film. Body colors can be varied to match other naturals.

Step 1: Attach the tying thread and wrap to the midpoint of the hook bend. Use the *direct dubbing* method (p. 34) to dub an abdomen to a point ⅓ of a shank-length behind the hook eye.

Step 2: Form a 3"-4" *dubbing loop*, Steps 1-2, (p. 35), at a point halfway between the front of the abdomen and the hook eye. Do not wax the loop. Advance the tying thread to the hook eye. Take two CDC feathers and stack them, tip to butt, and with the curvatures matching.

Step 3: Preen the barbs so that they stand out perpendicular to the stems. As explained in *CDC dubbing loop*, (p. 31), capture the barbs on one side in a paper clamp, leaving about ¼" between the edge of the clamp and the feather stems. Trim the barbs from the stems.

Step 4: Carefully position the butts of the barbs inside the dubbing loop. The butts should project beyond the loop threads about ⅛".

Step 5: Pull the loop threads firmly to trap the barbs. With the right fingers, slide the barbs up toward the hook shank to consolidate them. Don't push them tight against the shank. Leave about 1/32" or so of bare thread between the barbs and the shank.

Step 6: Spin the dubbing hook or twister about 10 times to lock in the fibers. Maintain tension on the loop and push the barbs upward again to form an even tighter stack.

Step 7: Spin the dubbing loop very tightly. With the right hand, raise the dubbing loop vertically atop the shank.

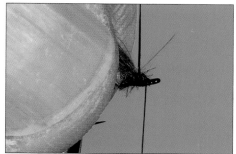

Step 8: With the left fingers, preen all the barbs to the rear of the hook. With the dubbing-loop threads (not the tying thread), take 3 tight wraps at the front base of the CDC bundle.

Step 9: Raise the CDC bundle, and use the dubbing-loop thread to take one wrap under light tension around the base of the CDC.

Step 10: Draw the CDC bundle toward the hook eye, and use the dubbing-loop thread to take 3 very tight wraps against the rear base of the bundle.

Step 11: Wrap the dubbing-loop threads to the hook eye. Secure them with the tying thread, and clip the excess.

Step 12: Dub the thorax, taking criss-cross wraps beneath the wing to cover the exposed shank. Whip finish behind the hook eye. Trim the wing fibers to a height of about one shank-length.

Chapter 14: Loopwing Emergers

Loopwings have been used from time to time on dry flies, but with the increasing popularity of emerger patterns, this wing style is seen far more often now. It's a logical choice for emergers since the style nicely blends a representational function with a structural one. The loop of material suggests the rounded form of emerging wings or thorax, and at the same time, it is often the primary component contributing to the floatation of the fly. The loop form efficiently incorporates material into the pattern without producing a wing that is disproportionately dense or heavy, and on many patterns, the open interior of the loop traps air that aids floatation and may give a bit of sparkle to the fly when viewed from beneath.

Loopwings can be tied in a variety of fashions: the loop can be placed behind, in the middle of, or in front of the thorax, or it may be dressed to span over the thorax or even the entire body. All of these approaches are represented in this chapter. A wide range of materials are suitable, though tyers tend to choose buoyant or water-resistant materials—hollow hair, poly yarn, foam, and increasingly, CDC and snowshoe hare's foot—to improve floatation.

Loopwing PMD Emerger

Hook: TMC 206BL, or other fine-wire scud hook, #16-#18
Thread: Gray 14/0
Tail: Three pheasant-tail barbs
Rib: Fine gold wire
Abdomen: Pheasant-tail barbs
Wing: One or two Type 1 or Type 2 CDC feathers
Legs: CDC barbs from wing
Thorax: Golden-olive Superfine dubbing

There are dozens of variations on this basic, but highly versatile, CDC loopwing style. This is one we tie. We've incorporated legs into the pattern to show it can be done. The same technique can be used to add legs to a loopwing pattern made of stripped CDC barbs, such as the TWE (p. 276). Legs can be omitted, particularly on smaller hooks where they are troublesome to tie. Sizes and colors can be varied for other hatches, and an un-tailed version can be used to imitate caddis.

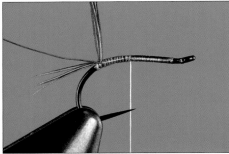

Step 1: Mount the thread and position it at the tailing point shown. Mount three pheasant-tail fibers atop the shank to form a tail about 1 hook-gap in length. Fold the fiber butts rearward, and take one wrap of thread over the wraps used to mount the tail. Then mount the ribbing wire atop this last wrap.

Step 2: Position the thread ⅗ the distance to the hook eye. Wrap the pheasant fibers as shown in *wrapping feather-barb bodies* (p. 45). When you reach the tying thread, tie off and clip the excess. *Counter-rib* (p. 33) the wire over the abdomen. Bind and clip the excess.

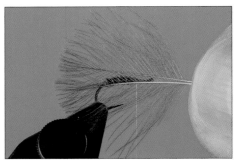

Step 3: Prepare the CDC feathers by stacking them so that the tips are aligned and the curvatures match. Strip away the lower barbs until the remaining feather tip is about twice the hook length.

Step 4: Mount the feathers flat atop the shank, with the concave side up, directly ahead of the abdomen. Take two snug, but not tight, wraps over the bare stem below the lowermost barbs.

Step 5: With the left fingers, put light downward tension on the bobbin. With the right fingers, pull the feather stems toward the hook eye, sliding the feather beneath the thread wraps until the exposed feather tips are about one hook-length long.

Step 6: Secure the feather butts with additional wraps; bind and clip the excess. Position the thread directly in front of the abdomen. With your left hand on the far side of the hook, position a dubbing needle crosswise atop the shank. With the right fingers, fold the feather tips firmly over the top of the needle.

Step 7: If a more pronounced wing is desired, maintain your grasp on the feather tips and pull upward on the dubbing needle to enlarge the loop. Tastes seem to vary in wing size; we use a loop about ½ to ⅔ the hook gap in height.

Step 8: When the wing is properly sized, use the left hand to take a light wrap over the feather tips, directly atop the mounting wraps used to secure the base of the feather. Then pull the bobbin to tighten the thread, keeping the CDC loop atop the shank. Secure the CDC with additional tight wraps.

Step 9: Don't worry if a few stray barbs project from the back of the loop or from the sides. We prefer it that way, and you can even snip a few barbs from the front of the loop and preen them rearward to enhance the effect.

Step 10: To form legs, clip away the excess CDC barbs, but leave a few on each side the shank. Pull them rearward, one bundle on either side of the shank, and wrap back over the base of the barbs to secure them in this position.

Step 11: Use the *direct dubbing* method (p. 34) to dub a thorax tapering toward the hook eye. Form the head of the fly and whip finish. If desired, break or clip the legs to the desired length.

TWE (Tom's Working Emerger)

Originator: Tomaz Modic
Hook: TMC 900BL, or equivalent dry-fly hook, #16-#20
Thread: Dark brown 8/0
Rib: Black 3/0 thread
Tail: Black rooster hackle fibers
Abdomen: Dark brown tying thread
Wing: Dark dun CDC barbs
Thorax: Dark brown rabbit dubbing

This design, by Slovenian tyer Tomaz Modic, is representative of a large number of patterns that use a CDC loopwing tied in at the rear of the thorax. The simplicity of tying it makes this design well suited to smaller hook sizes, and the clean, low silhouette fishes well in flat water. Modic uses full CDC feathers for the loopwing. On small hooks, we prefer bundled, stripped barbs, as shown in the following sequence. Stripped barbs give better control over the quantity of material on a small hook; they tie with less bulk than a full feather; and they are a way of making use of damaged, imperfect, or thick-stemmed CDC feathers.

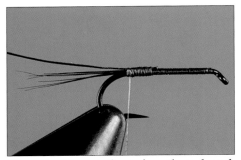

Step 1: Mount the tying thread and position it at the rear of the shank. *Align and strip* (p. 30) a sparse bundle of rooster hackle barbs. Secure them atop the shank to form a tail equal in length to the hook shank. Mount the ribbing thread atop the rearmost tail-mounting wrap.

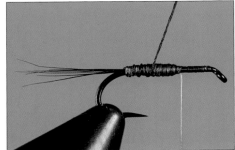

Step 2: Use the working thread to build a tapered abdomen over the rear ⅔ of the shank. Wrap forward and back several times, gradually building the taper. Spiral the ribbing thread forward over the abdomen. Tie off the ribbing at the front of the abdomen, and clip.

Step 3: Gather a bundle of CDC barbs as shown in *stripping CDC barbs* (p. 40). Mount them directly in front of the abdomen. If necessary, mount additional bundles until the wing density is satisfactory; remember, though, that the wing is looped and will appear twice as dense as the bundle of single fibers. Bind and clip the excess.

Step 4: With the right fingers, draw all the CDC fibers evenly toward the rear of the hook, then fold them forward to form a loopwing of the desired height, here about ¾ the hook gap.

Step 5: Hold the CDC in position, and with the left hand take a soft wrap over the bundle, directly ahead of the abdomen, keeping all the fibers atop the shank. Pull the thread to tighten the wrap. Add additional tight wraps to secure the CDC barbs.

Step 6: Clip the excess CDC. Use the *direct dubbing* method (p. 34) to form a thinly dubbed thorax, placing one wrap behind the wing. Form the head of the fly and whip finish.

Callibaetis Emerging Dun

Originator: Wayne Luallen
Hook: Daiichi 1260, or other curved long-shank hook, #16
Thread: Tan 8/0
Tail/shuck: Mallard flank fibers and gray-brown Z-Lon
Rib: Dark brown thread
Rear abdomen: Gray-brown dubbing blend
Front abdomen/thorax: Olive-tan dubbing blend
Wing: Mallard flank and one Type 1 or Type 2 gray CDC
   feather

Wayne Luallen's design shows how loopwing materials can be combined to imitate more closely the patterned or veined mayfly wings—in this case, a *Callibaetis*. The dubbing color for the front of the abdomen and thorax should be chosen to match the underside of the natural insect.

Step 1: Attach the thread and position it at the tailing point. Mount three mallard flank fibers atop the shank to make tails one hook-gap long. Press the mounting wraps with the thumbnail to splay the fibers; then secure them. Mount a sparse bundle of Antron fibers, one-half the hook gap in length, over the mallard. Clip and bind.

Step 2: Mount a short length of thread for the rib. Use the *direct dubbing* method (p. 34) to form a slender, tapered abdomen over the rear half of the shank. Spiral the thread forward to rib the abdomen, then tie off and clip. Use the second dubbing color to dub a thorax about half the distance to the hook eye.

Step 3: Preen back the lowermost fibers from a mallard flank feather, leaving a tip section containing about 10-15 barbs, as shown at the right. Mount the feather by the tip, concave side up, directly ahead of the thorax. Mount the CDC feather by the tip, directly atop the mallard.

Step 4: Continue dubbing the thorax half the distance to the hook eye.

Step 5: Fold the wing feathers over a dubbing needle to form a loopwing that extends rearward, even with the hook point. Keep the mallard positioned over the CDC.

Step 6: Secure the wing feathers; clip and bind the excess. Dub half the distance to the hook eye. Thinly dub a short length of thread, then form a whip finish using the dubbed thread to conceal the finish wraps.

Iris Caddis

Originator: Craig Mathews and John Juracek
Hook: TMC 100, or equivalent dry-fly hook, #14-#16
Thread: Camel 8/0
Shuck: Gold Z-Lon
Body: Olive-brown rabbit dubbing
Wing: Gray Antron yarn
Head: Tan Haretron dubbing

This loopwing style is unusual in that it is formed laterally rather than vertically. It gives the fly a broad, caddis-like silhouette when viewed from any angle.

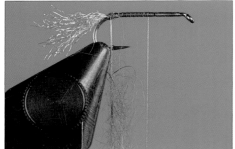

Step 1: Attach the thread and position it at the tailing point. Secure a length of Antron yarn for the shuck, and clip to the length of the hook gap. Position the thread at the tailing point. Form a *dubbing loop* (p. 35) over the rearmost thread wraps, and insert the body dubbing in the loop.

Step 2: Twist the loop to form a shaggy yarn, and wrap the body slightly beyond the halfway point on the shank. Tie down and clip off the dubbing loop.

Step 3: Take a length of Antron yarn and secure it to the far side of the shank directly ahead of the body, as shown in this top view.

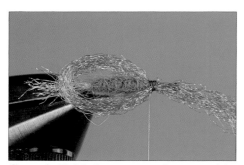

Step 4: Fold the yarn to form a wide loop at the rear of the fly, and secure the end of the yarn on the near side of the shank with one snug, but not tight, wrap of thread.

Step 5: Pull the tag of yarn to shorten the loop, forming a wing that extends rearward just to the hook bend.

Step 6: When the wing is properly sized, bind the yarn tag tightly, clip and bind the excess. Dub the head of the fly; it should be shaggy, as shown. Then whip finish the fly.

CDC Emerging Caddis

Originator: Wayne Luallen
Hook: Daiichi 1310, or other short-shank fine-wire dry-fly
hook, #12-#20
Thread: Brown 8/0
Shuck: Gold Z-Lon
Body: Green (#10) SLF dubbing
Wing: Type 1, Type 2, or Type 4 dun CDC feather

This is Wayne Luallen's CDC version of the popular Iris Caddis. It can be varied to match a variety of naturals, and the simplicity of tying suits the pattern well to small hooks.

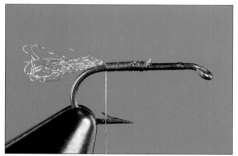

Step 1: Attach the thread and position it at midshank. Use the technique shown in *twisted furled shuck* (p. 62) to form a shuck one hook-gap in length. Position the thread at the rearmost wrap securing the shuck.

Step 2: Use the *direct dubbing* method (p. 34) to dub an abdomen over the rear ¾ of the hook shank.

Step 3: Secure the CDC feather by the tip directly ahead of the abdomen.

Step 4: Fold the feather over a dubbing needle held crosswise atop the shank to form a wing that extends just to the rear of the abdomen. Secure the feather directly ahead of the abdomen, atop the thread wraps used to mount the feather.

Step 5: Dub a head that tapers to the hook eye. Whip finish.

Midge 1

Originator: Chip Drozenski
Hook: TMC 2487, or other light-wire scud hook, #20-#24
Thread: Black 8/0
Shuck: Narrow grizzly dun hackle tip
Wing: One Type 1 or Type 2 natural dun CDC feather
Thorax: Peacock herl

This light, spare pattern is a fine flat-water design. The CDC feather should be chosen to give the proper density in the wing and tuft; larger feathers can be stripped of the lowermost barbs to give the feather the proper proportions.

Step 1: Attach the thread and position it ⅓ of a shank-length behind the eye. Tie in a hackle tip to form a shuck about twice the length of the hook shank. Clip and bind the excess. Position the thread at the rearmost shuck-mounting wrap.

Step 2: Tie in the CDC feather—with the dull side facing up—so that the tip extends rearward of the mounting wraps a distance of about three shank-lengths. Tie in a strand of peacock herl directly atop the wraps used to mount the CDC. Position the thread at the rearmost wrap used to mount the herl.

Step 3: Fold the CDC feather forward to form a loopwing that extends rearward to the hook bend.

Step 4: Preen a few CDC barbs rearward to form part of the trailing shuck.

Step 5: Secure the CDC feather atop the wraps used to mount the herl. Use a *flattened thread* (p. 37) to bind the feather atop the shank, stopping 4-5 thread-wraps' distance behind the hook eye.

Step 6: Wrap the herl forward as explained in *wrapping single-herl collars* (p. 48). Tie off atop the frontmost wrap securing the CDC. Clip and bind the excess. Lift the CDC tip, take a few thread wraps beneath the feather to elevate the tuft slightly, and whip finish around the shank only, behind the hook eye.

CDC Loopwing Midge Emerger

Hook: TMC 206BL, or other fine-wire scud hook, #10-#18
Thread: Black 8/0
Shuck: One to three strands pearl Krystal Flash
Rib: One strand pearl Krystal Flash
Abdomen: Fine-textured brown dubbing
Thorax: Dark brown Haretron dubbing
Wing: One or two Type 1 or Type 2 gray CDC feathers

Though CDC loopwings are most commonly tied on flush-floating emergers, they can make effective descending-body designs particularly if they are tied in, as shown in the midge pattern, ahead of the thorax. This position allows the entire fly body to sink beneath the film with only the wing projecting above the surface.

Step 1: Mount the tying thread behind the hook eye, and lay a thread foundation to the tailing point. Secure the strands of Krystal Flash atop the shank to make a shuck about one hook-gap in length. Clip the excess, leaving one strand of Krystal Flash long. Fold the strand rearward, and bind it back to the tailing point.

Step 2: Use the *direct dubbing* method (p. 34) to form an abdomen over the rear ⅔ of the shank. Spiral the strand of Krystal Flash forward to rib the abdomen. Tie off and clip directly ahead of the dubbing.

Step 3: Dub a thorax from the front of the abdomen halfway to the hook eye.

Step 4: Align the tips of the CDC feathers. Mount them directly ahead of the thorax with two firm, but not tight, thread wraps.

Step 5: Put light tension of the bobbin with the left hand. With the right fingers, pull the feather stems, sliding the feathers beneath the thread wraps until the tips extend just to the rear edge of the thorax. Then secure the feathers in this position with a few tight thread wraps.

Step 6: With the right fingers, form a loop in the feathers about one hook-gap in height. With the left hand, take one soft wrap around the feathers directly ahead of the thorax. Pull the thread to tighten the wrap, keeping the feather stems atop the shank. Then secure with additional tight wraps; clip and bind the excess. Whip finish.

Drake Mackerel Emerger

Originator: Craig Mathews and John Juracek
Hook: TMC 5212, or fine-wire 2XL hook, #12
Thread: Camel 8/0
Shuck: Amber Z-Lon
Body: Tan rabbit dubbing
Rib: Brown Pearsall's silk thread
Wing case: Gray Fly Foam
Hackle: Duck shoulder

This fly was designed for the tan-colored autumn green drakes (*Timpanoga hecuba*), but can be altered to match hatches of PMD and Flav (*Drunella Flavilinea*) emergers.

Step 1: Attach the thread and position it at the tailing point. Mount a length of Antron yarn for the shuck, and clip to ½ a shank-length. Mount the ribbing thread atop the tailing wraps.

Step 2: Use the *direct dubbing* method (p. 34) to dub a slender abdomen over the rear ⅔ of the hook shank, and *counter-rib* (p. 33) the thread over the abdomen. Tie off the ribbing and clip in front of the abdomen.

Step 3: Secure a strip of foam about ⅔ the width of the hook-gap at the front of the abdomen. Clip the excess, and take a few turns of dubbed thread over the mounting wraps to conceal them.

Step 4: Fold the foam strip over a dubbing needle to make doubled section about the height of the hook gap.

Step 5: Secure the foam directly in front of the end already mounted. Clip and bind the excess. Prepare and mount the hackle directly ahead of the foam as explained in *tip-mounted hackle* (p. 41).

Step 6: Take two wraps of the feather, as shown in *wrapping wet-fly hackle* (p. 50). Then tie off the feather; clip and bind the excess. Whip finish the fly.

Pearl Midge Emerger

Originator: Jim Schollmeyer and Ted Leeson
Hook: TMC 2487, or other fine-wire scud hook, #14-#20
Thread: Black 12/0
Shuck: Pearlescent Krystal Flash
Rib: Black tying thread
Abdomen: Pearlescent Krystal Flash
Thorax: Arizona Synthetic Peacock dubbing, natural
Wing: Gray closed-cell foam

Ease of tying makes this pattern particularly well suited to small hooks. The position of the foam loopwing causes the fly body to sit vertically beneath the film. The fly floats well and is durable.

Step 1: Attach the thread, leaving a 6-inch tag, and wrap to the tailing point. Furl one strand of Krystal Flash as shown in *furled shuck* (p. 61). Mount the furled portion with two tight wraps to form a shuck about ⅔ the shank length. With a *flattened thread* (p. 37), form a smooth underbody about ⅔ the distance to the hook eye.

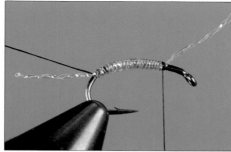

Step 2: Wrap the tags of Krystal Flash forward as you would tinsel, forming a smooth abdomen over the rear ⅔ of the shank. Tie off and clip the excess.

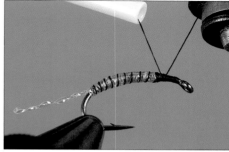

Step 3: Twist the tag of tying thread (grip it with a pair of hackle pliers if necessary), and spiral the thread forward to rib the abdomen. Tie off and clip the ribbing at the front of the abdomen. Position the thread behind the hook eye.

Step 4: Cut a strip of foam about ½ the hook gap in width, and ¼ the hook gap thick. Mount it directly behind the hook eye, as shown. Bind and the clip the tag.

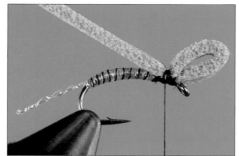

Step 5: Fold the foam rearward to form a loop about one hook-gap in length. Secure the foam behind the hook eye.

Step 6: Bind and clip the excess foam. Position the thread at the front of the abdomen, and use the *direct dubbing* method (p. 34) to dub the thorax. Whip finish the fly beneath the foam loop, around the hook shank only.

CDC Loop-Wing Emerger

Originator: Hans Weilenmann
Hook: TMC 5212, or other fine-wire 2XL hook, #12-#20
Thread: Olive 6/0
Shuck: Light gray poly yarn
Abdomen: Medium olive hare's ear dubbing
Thorax: Dark olive hare's ear dubbing
Wing: One or two Type 2 gray CDC feathers

The use of a long-shank hook combined with a loopwing that spans the thorax incorporates a generous amount of CDC in this pattern for good floatation. Type 2 CDC feathers can produce a very neat, uniform wing, but we often dress this style with Type 4 feathers to produce some stray barbs at the sides of the wings.

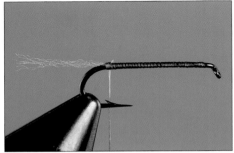

Step 1: Attach the thread and position it at the tailing point. Tie in a few strands of poly yarn fibers to make a sparse shuck about one shank-length long.

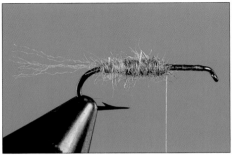

Step 2: Use the *direct dubbing* method (p. 34) to dub a slender, slightly tapered abdomen on the rear half of the hook shank.

Step 3: Mount the CDC feathers directly ahead of the abdomen. The tip of the feather should extend rearward far enough to form the loopwing—at least one shank-length or so.

Step 4: Dub the thorax.

Step 5: Hold a dubbing needle crosswise over the midpoint of the abdomen. Fold the CDC around the needle, toward the hook eye, to make a loop about one hook-gap in height.

Step 6: Withdraw the needle. With the left fingers, pinch the feather tip against the hook shank just behind the eye. Bind the tip down, clip the excess, and form the head. Whip finish the fly.

Skopje Emerger

Hook: TMC 900BL, or equivalent dry-fly hook, #12-#16
Thread: Brown 6/0
Tail: Brown partridge or rooster hackle fibers
Rib: Gold wire
Abdomen: Olive Antron mixed with hare's ear dubbing
Thorax: Darker shade of mixture used for abdomen
Wing case: Brown closed-cell foam
Wing: Two Type 2 gray CDC feathers

This pattern comes from Macedonia where, some authorities speculate, fly-fishing originated. It was shown to us by Andrija Urban.

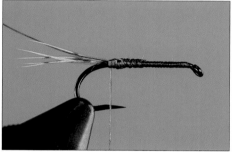

Step 1: Attach the thread and position it at the tailing point. Mount six tailing fibers that extend rearward about one shank-length. Mount the ribbing material atop the tail-mounting wraps.

Step 2: Use the *direct dubbing* method (p. 34) to dub a slender tapered abdomen over the rear half of the hook shank. Rib the abdomen; tie off and clip the excess ribbing.

Step 3: Stack two CDC feathers so the tips are aligned and curvatures match. Tie them in together at the front of the abdomen so that the tips extend rearward.

Step 4: Clip and bind the CDC butts. Mount a strip of foam, about ½ the hook gap in width, ahead of the CDC. Clip and bind the excess foam. Dub the thorax, stopping 6 or 7 thread-wraps behind the hook eye.

Step 5: Fold the foam forward over the thorax, and secure it atop the shank. Clip and bind the excess.

Step 6: Hold a dubbing needle crosswise over the midpoint of the thorax. Fold the CDC around the needle, toward the hook eye, to make a loop about one hook-gap in height. Tie down the feather tips, clip and bind the excess. Whip finish the fly.

CDC Cream Pupa

Originator: Andrija Urban
Hook: TMC 2487, or other light-wire scud hook, #8-#18
Thread: Dark brown 6/0
Abdomen: Chopped aftershaft fibers mixed with cream Antron dubbing
Wing: One Type 2 gray CDC feather, at least twice the hook-shank length
Thorax: Dark brown Antron dubbing mixed with hare's mask
Legs: Partridge hackle

Serbian tyer Andrija Urban, well-known throughout Europe for his CDC patterns, designed this unusual method for handling CDC when forming loopwings.

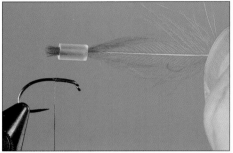

Step 1: Attach the thread and position it at a point ⅓ of a shank-length behind the hook eye. Insert the CDC feather into a short length of plastic tubing until just the tips are exposed. The tubing can be made from anything—a piece of insulation stripped from wire, the hollow plastic barrel of a cotton swab.

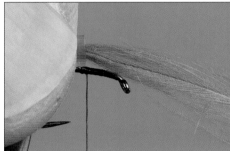

Step 2: Holding the tube, position the feather as shown, directly above the tying thread.

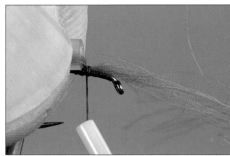

Step 3: Take two thread wraps under light tension around the feather just where it enters the tube. Keep the feather fibers positioned atop the shank. Do not use too much thread pressure or the feather barbs will migrate around the shank.

Step 4: Slide the tube off the tip of the feather, and take additional, tighter thread wraps toward the hook bend to secure the feather.

Step 5: Use the *direct dubbing* method (p. 34) to dub a tapered abdomen up to the base of the CDC feather.

Step 6: Pull the butt of the feather rearward, and take additional thread wraps over the fold of the feather, toward the hook bend. Again, take care to keep the entire feather positioned on top of the shank.

Step 7: Dub the thorax, stopping at a point 6 or 7 wraps behind the hook eye.

Step 8: Fold the CDC feather forward—you can use a dubbing needle as shown here—and secure it ahead of the thorax. The looped wing should extend nearly to the end of the abdomen and be about one hook-gap in height.

Step 9: Clip and bind the excess CDC. Mount a partridge hackle as shown in *tip-mounted hackle* (p. 41).

Step 10: Take one or two wraps of the feather as explained in *wrapping wet-fly hackle* (p. 50). Tie off and clip the feather tip. Form the head, and whip finish.

Bubble CDC Hatching Grey-Olive Dun

Originator: Andrija Urban
Hook: Mustad 94840, or equivalent dry-fly hook, #14-#18
Thread: Black 8/0
Shuck: One gray Type 2 CDC feather
Abdomen: Gray-olive dubbing
Wing: One gray Type 2 CDC feather
Thorax: Gray-olive dubbing
Wing case: Gray closed-cell foam

Andrija Urban notes that this pattern can be given extra floatation by using an extra CDC feather for the loopwing and dressing the wings using the double-tube method shown in Bubble CDC Emerger—March Brown (p. 296).

Step 1: Attach the thread and position it at the tailing point. Form the shuck as explained in *pulled CDC shuck* (p. 54).

Step 2: Position the thread ⅓ of a shank-length behind the hook eye. Mount the wing feather as shown in CDC Cream Pupa, Steps 1-4, (p. 286). Then fold the feather rearward, and wrap the thread back over the fold to the midpoint of the shank.

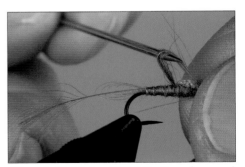

Step 3: Dub the abdomen to the base of the wing feather. Mount a strip of gray foam, ½ the hook-gap in width, directly ahead of the wing feather. Clip and bind the excess.

Step 4: Dub the thorax, stopping about 6-7 thread-wraps behind the hook eye.

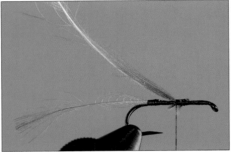

Step 5: Fold the foam forward over the thorax, and secure it directly ahead of the dubbing. Clip and bind the excess foam.

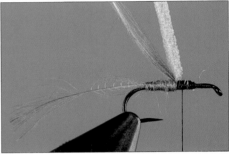

Step 6: Fold the CDC feather forward around a dubbing needle to form a loopwing that extends back to the rear of the abdomen. The wing should be about one hook-gap in height. Secure the CDC behind the hook eye. Clip and bind the excess. Whip finish the fly.

H & L Emerger

Originator: Brett Clark
Hook: TMC 2487, or other light-wire scud hook, #12-#20
Thread: Black 8/0
Tail: White poly yarn
Abdomen: Stripped peacock quill
Thorax: Peacock herl
Wing: White poly yarn

This midge pattern is an emerger version of the famous H & L Variant.

Step 1: Attach the thread and position it at the tailing point. Mount a length of poly yarn to form a tail about ½ a shank-length long. Secure the excess yarn atop the shank, forming a smooth underbody to a point just beyond mid-shank. Return the thread to the tailing point.

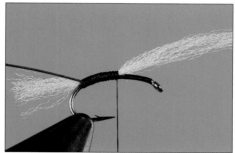

Step 2: Mount a stripped peacock herl atop the tailing wraps. Wrap a *flattened thread* (p. 37) forward, binding in the quill tip and forming a smooth underbody up to the frontmost wraps securing the yarn.

Step 3: Form the abdomen as shown in *wrapping quill bodies* (p. 47).

Step 4: Fold the yarn rearward and take a couple of wraps over the fold, so that the yarn now angles back over the tail. Secure 3-4 peacock herls directly ahead of the yarn.

Step 5: Form the thorax as explained in *wrapping twisted-herl collars* (p. 49). Tie off and clip the herl about 6 thread wraps behind the hook eye, and bind the excess.

Step 6: Fold the yarn forward around a dubbing needle, and secure it behind the hook eye to the form the loopwing. Secure the yarn, and trim it to leave tuft extending over the eye. Whip finish beneath the tuft.

Hatching Midge

Originator: Randall Kaufmann
Hook: TMC 900BL, or equivalent dry-fly hook, #12–#20
Thread: Black 6/0
Tail: Dark dun Type 1 or 2 CDC feather
Rib: White thread
Abdomen: Black 6/0 thread
Wing case: Dark dun Type 2 CDC feather
Thorax: Peacock herl
Hackle: Grizzly

This fly is a loopwing version of Randall Kaufmann's CDC Hatching Midge (p. 107), that gives a more distinct emerging-wing profile. It floats a bit better and is easier to see.

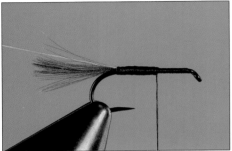

Step 1: Attach the thread and position it at the tailing point. Mount a CDC feather so that the tip forms a tail about equal in length to the hook shank. Clip and bind the excess. Mount the ribbing thread atop the tailing wraps. Advance the tying thread forward, forming a smooth abdomen to the midpoint of the shank.

Step 2: Spiral the ribbing thread forward over the abdomen. Bind down and clip the rib material. Mount a second CDC feather directly in front of the abdomen, so that the feather tip extends rearward beyond the end of the tail.

Step 3: *Prepare a hackle feather* (p. 39) and mount it atop the thread wraps securing the CDC as shown in *mounting collar hackle* (p. 37). Clip and bind the excess. Mount 2-4 peacock herls atop the thread wraps securing the hackle.

Step 4: Form the thorax as shown in *wrapping twisted-herl collars* (p. 49). Clip and bind the excess.

Step 5: Spiral the hackle through the thorax as shown in *palmering hackle* (p. 38). Clip and bind the excess.

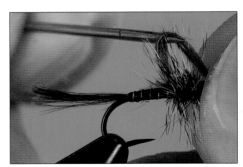

Step 6: Fold the CDC feather forward over a dubbing needle to produce a loopwing about one hook-gap in height. Secure the feather in front of the thorax, and clip to produce a short tuft. Whip finish beneath the tuft.

Loopwing P.T.

Hook: TMC 900BL, or equivalent dry-fly hook, #16-#18
Thread: Yellow 8/0
Tail: Pheasant-tail fibers
Rib: Fine gold wire
Abdomen: Pheasant-tail fibers
Wing tuft: Natural gray Type 1 or 2 CDC feather
Thorax: Yellow fine poly dubbing
Wing: CDC from wing tuft
Legs: CDC

We've seen a number of emerger patterns that combine a rear CDC tuft with a loopwing. This PMD imitation is representative of the approach, though it can be modified to match other hatches.

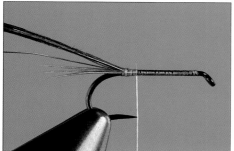

Step 1: Attach the thread and position it at the tailing point. Mount 3-4 pheasant-tail fibers atop the shank for a tail. Secure them with two tight wraps toward the hook eye. Fold the butts rearward and take a couple turns of thread back toward the hook bend, atop the original wraps. Mount the ribbing wire.

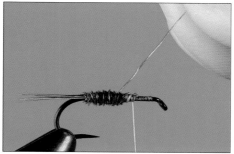

Step 2: Wrap the thread forward the midpoint of the shank. Form the abdomen over the rear half of the shank as explained in *wrapping feather-barb bodies* (p. 45). *Counter-rib* (p. 33) the abdomen; then bind and clip the ribbing wire.

Step 3: Mount a CDC feather directly ahead of the abdomen so that the tip extends to the rearmost point of the body. Use 3 or 4 tight wraps moving toward the hook eye.

Step 4: Fold the butt of the feather rearward, then wrap back over the folded base of the feather until the front of the abdomen is reached, and the feather butt slants back toward the rear of the fly.

Step 5: Use the *direct dubbing* method (p. 34) to dub the thorax, stopping 5 or 6 wraps behind the hook eye. Strip a bundle of CDC barbs, and mount them as explained in *throat hackle* (p. 41), directly ahead of the thorax.

Step 6: Fold the feather butt forward over a dubbing needle to form a loopwing about half the height of the hook gap. Secure behind the hook eye. Clip and bind the excess. Whip finish the fly.

Hatching Mayfly

Originator: Andrija Urban
Hook: Mustad 94840, or equivalent dry-fly hook, #12-#16
Thread: Brown 8/0
Tail: Dun hackle barbs
Abdomen: Pheasant-tail fibers
Rib: Yellow 3/0 thread
Wing: Two or three Type 2 natural gray CDC feathers
Thorax: Olive-brown Superfine dubbing
Hackle: Dun

This Andrija Urban style is highly versatile and can be altered to match a variety of mayfly hatches. The collar hackle and well-formed wings suggest a mayfly dun almost fully emerged.

Step 1: Attach the thread and position it ¼ of a shank-length behind the eye. Stack the CDC feathers so that the tips are aligned and the curvatures match. Mount the CDC feathers as shown in CDC Cream Pupa, Steps 1-4, (p. 286).

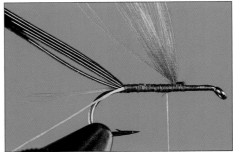

Step 2: Wrap the thread to the tailing point. *Align and strip* (p. 30) a bundle of hackle barbs. Mount them to form a tail about one shank-length long. Mount 4-6 pheasant-tail fibers over the tailing wraps. Mount the ribbing material atop the wraps securing the pheasant tail. Wrap the thread forward to the base of the CDC.

Step 3: Wrap the abdomen as explained in *wrapping feather-barb bodies* (p. 45), and *counter-rib* (p. 33) it with the thread. Tie off the rib in front of the abdomen, and clip.

Step 4: *Prepare a hackle feather* (p. 39) and mount it as explained in *mounting collar hackle* (p. 37). Use the *direct dubbing* method (p. 34) to dub a thorax of the same thickness as the front of the abdomen, stopping about 6 or 7 thread wraps behind the eye.

Step 5: Wind the hackle as shown in *palmering hackle* (p. 38); tie off and clip the excess.

Step 6: Fold the CDC forward over a dubbing needle to form a loopwing about one hook-gap in height and extending rearward to the midpoint of the abdomen. Secure the CDC feathers, and clip the excess. Form the head of the fly and whip finish.

Snowshoe Floating Nymph—Hendrickson

Originator: Steven Williams
Hook: TMC 100, or equivalent dry-fly hook, #12
Thread: Olive 6/0
Tail: Bronze mallard fibers over dun snowshoe hare's foot
Body: Grayish mahogany blend of imitation seal fur and Australian opossum dubbing
Wing: Dun snowshoe hare's foot
Hackle: Mottled brown partridge fibers

This basic design is highly adaptable in imitating other mayfly hatches. If dun snowshoe hare's foot is unavailable, you can use natural cream fur and color it with a gray Pantone marker.

Step 1: Attach the thread and position at the tailing point. Clip a sparse bundle of snowshoe hare fur from the rear half of the foot (see Snowshoe Hare's Foot, p. 27). Mount it to form a tail slightly shorter than the hook-shank length. Mount 10-12 strands of slightly longer bronze mallard fibers atop the hair.

Step 2: Use the *direct dubbing* method (p. 34) to dub a slightly tapered abdomen over the rear ⅔ of the shank.

Step 3: Clip a second bundle of fur, and pull out any short hairs. Mount the bundle by the tip directly in front of the abdomen.

Step 4: Dub the thorax, stopping 7 or 8 thread-wraps' distance behind the hook eye.

Step 5: Fold the hair forward to form a loopwing about one hook-gap in height. Secure the hair at the front of the thorax, and clip the excess. Snip the tip from a partridge feather, and preen the lower barbs downward to make a "V" with 6-8 barbs on each side of the stem.

Step 6: Use two light thread wraps to mount the partridge feather beneath the shank so that the barbs flank the body on either side. Pull the feather stem beneath the mounting wraps until the barbs just reach the hook point. Then secure the feather with tight wraps; bind and clip the excess. Whip finish.

RV Teardrop Emerger

Originator: Howard Cole
Hook: TMC 2487, or other fine-wire scud hook, #14-#18
Thread: Tan 8/0
Abdomen: Olive Antron dubbing
Shuck: Olive Z-Lon
Thorax: Silver glass bead
Wing case: Two natural gray Type 2 CDC feathers
Wing: Tips of wingcase feathers
Hackle: Medium dun

Z-Lon, Antron, and a glass bead give this caddis emerger some sparkle. Though the tying is a bit more involved than on other patterns in this chapter, the fly has good bugginess and shape. The shuck here, formed of a loop tied laterally, can be used on other caddis emerger patterns.

Step 1: De-barb the hook; slide the bead over the point and position it behind the hook eye. Attach the thread at the rear of the hook, and use the *direct dubbing* method (p. 34) to dub the abdomen over the rear ⅓ of the hook shank.

Step 2: Tie in a length of Z-Lon directly ahead of the abdomen on the far side of the shank.

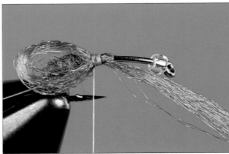

Step 3: Form a loop in the Z-Lon that extends just beyond the hook bend. Secure the free end of the Z-Lon to the near side of the shank, directly ahead of the abdomen.

Step 4: Use a dubbing needle to distribute the Z-Lon fibers around the shank to form a teardrop-shaped bubble. Take a few turns of dubbing to cover the thread wraps securing the Z-Lon.

Step 5: Stack the two CDC feathers so that the tips are aligned and the curvatures match. Hold them above the shank so that the tips extend rearward beyond the hook bend a distance of about one hook-length.

Step 6: Mount the CDC feathers atop the shank. Use very tight, non-overlapping thread wraps to form a compact tie-in, since the bead must fit over these mounting wraps. Clip the excess feathers. Tie off the thread with a few half hitches, and clip it.

Step 7: Slide the bead over the CDC mounting wraps. If the fit is loose, slide the bead forward, reattach the thread, and build up the thread foundation so that the beads fit very snugly. Then tie off the thread and clip it.

Step 8: Re-attach the tying thread in front of the bead. Fold the CDC forward over a dubbing needle to form a loop-style wing case.

Step 9: Secure the CDC directly in front of the bead.

Step 10: Pull the feather tips rearward, and build up a bump of thread, tapering toward the hook eye, to hold the feathers vertically. Make a smooth, gradual taper of thread, since the hackle must be wrapped over it.

Step 11: *Prepare a hackle feather* (p. 39), *and secure it directly in front of CDC wing as shown in* mounting collar hackle (p. 37).

Step 12: Wrap the hackle as explained in *wrapping dry-fly hackle* (p. 44). Tie off and clip the excess. Form the head of the fly and whip finish.

Bubble CDC Emerger—March Brown

Originator: Andrija Urban
Hook: TMC 900BL, or equivalent dry-fly hook, #10-#16
Thread: Brown 8/0
Tail: Partridge hackle fibers
Abdomen: Hareline March Brown dubbing
Rib: Stripped peacock herl
Wing: Two gray Type 4 CDC feathers
Wing case: Gray closed-cell foam
Thorax: Hare's ear dubbing

We've adapted this Andrija Urban mayfly-emerger design to imitate the western March brown, though many other versions are possible. This pattern also illustrates another of Urban's inventive ways of handling CDC feathers.

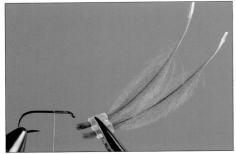

Step 1: Attach the thread and position it ⅓ of a shank-length behind the eye. Urban uses a homemade tool fashioned from two short lengths of plastic tubing glued together, or wrapped together with tying thread and varnished. Insert a feather in each tube, so that they are flat, side-by-side, curving in the same direction.

Step 2: Position the tubing atop the shank, as shown, so that the point where the feathers enter the tube lies directly above the tying thread. If the feathers curve, they should curve upward.

Step 3: Secure the two feathers by taking two light thread wraps, then pulling the thread to tighten. This prevents the CDC fibers from migrating around the shank.

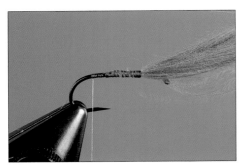

Step 4: Secure the feathers with additional tight thread wraps, and remove the tubing. Clip the feather tips at an angle, and bind down with thread. Position the thread at the tailing point.

Step 5: Mount the partridge fibers to form a tail about ¾ of a shank-length long. Mount the ribbing material directly atop the tail-mounting wraps.

Step 6: Use the *direct dubbing* method (p. 34) to dub a slightly tapered abdomen to the midpoint of the shank. Rib the abdomen, clip, and bind the excess. Position the thread at the front of the abdomen.

Step 7: Fold both CDC feathers rearward, and secure them directly in front of the abdomen, keeping the feathers side-by-side atop the shank.

Step 8: Mount a strip of foam, ½ the hook-gap in width, directly in front of the CDC feathers. Clip and bind the excess.

Step 9: Dub the thorax, stopping 5-6 thread-wraps behind the hook eye.

Step 10: Fold the foam forward over the top of the thorax, and bind down. Clip the excess.

Step 11: Fold both CDC feathers forward over a dubbing needle to form wings one hook-gap in height, and pinch them against the shank behind the hook eye.

Step 12: Secure the feathers, clip and bind the excess. Whip finish the fly. Here are the loopwings shown in a front view.

Bead-Shuck Tan Emerger

Originator: Jim Schollmeyer and Ted Leeson
Hook: TMC 206BL, or other light-wire scud hook, #12-#18
Thread: Brown 8/0
Shuck: Tan Antron over brown beads
Abdomen: Tan fine poly dubbing
Wing case: Deer hair
Thorax: Tan fine poly dubbing
Wing: Tips of wingcase hair

This generic mayfly emerger can be tied in any color. It can be dressed to float flush in the film by extending the shuck straight from the shank and treating it with floatant. Or it can be tied as a descending-body emerger by angling the shuck downward, in which case only the front half of the fly is dressed with floatant.

Step 1: Form and mount the bead-shuck assembly, dub the rear of the abdomen, and form the Antron bubble, all as explained in *bead shuck* (p. 65).

Step 2: Dub the rest of abdomen to cover the rear ½ of the shank, building a slight taper as you dub forward. *Clip, clean, and stack* (p. 32) a bundle of deer hair. Position the hair atop the shank so that the tips extend just to the end of the shuck.

Step 3: Mount the hair atop the shank directly in front of the abdomen. Clip and bind the excess.

Step 4: Dub the thorax, stopping about 4 or 5 thread-wraps behind the eye. Position the thread at the front of the thorax.

Step 5: Position a toothpick (as shown here), or thick monofilament, or any short rod with a diameter about equal to the finished loopwing height. Position it crosswise atop the thorax. Fold the hair over the toothpick, and pinch it atop the shank behind the eye.

Step 6: Secure the hair atop the shank, and remove the toothpick. Pull the hair tips rearward and take a few thread wraps against the base of the hair to fan out and slightly elevate the fibers. Whip finish beneath the hair tips, around the shank only.

CDC Hatching Dun

Originator: Andrija Urban
Hook: TMC 400T, or other swimming-nymph hook, #14
Thread: Brown 8/0
Tail: Light-brown mottled hen
Nymphal body: Light-olive dubbing
Adult abdomen: Yellow Antron dubbing
Adult thorax: Brown dubbing
Wing: One Type 2 CDC feather, natural gray

In this unusual pattern, the rear half of the body represents the nymphal body, while the front portion represents the abdomen and thorax of the emerging adult dun. Colors and sizes can be varied to match a variety of mayflies, though you may need to bend your own swimming-nymph hooks for smaller patterns, since commercially available sizes are limited.

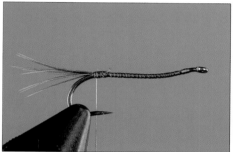

Step 1: Mount the thread and position it at the tailing point. Mount the tail material to form a tail about ½ the hook shank in length.

Step 2: Use the *direct dubbing* method (p. 34) to dub the nymphal body over the rear half of the shank. Position the thread directly in front of the body.

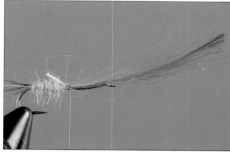

Step 3: Strip the barbs from the base of a CDC feather to leave ¼" of bare stem. Position the feather flat atop the shank; if the feather is curved, place the concave side upward. Take two soft thread wraps over the bare stem, directly in front of the abdomen.

Step 4: Put a slight tension on the bobbin with the right hand. With the left hand, pull the butt of the feather rearward, sliding the feather beneath the two thread wraps. When all but the last ¼" of feather tip has been drawn beneath the wraps, secure the tip with several tight turns of thread.

Step 5: Dub the abdomen of the adult fly half the distance to the hook eye. Then dub the thorax of the adult fly, stopping about 6 thread wraps behind the eye. Position the thread behind the hook eye.

Step 6: Fold the CDC feather forward (you can fold it around a dubbing needle if it is easier). The loopwing should extend almost to the rear of the abdomen. When the wing is properly sized, secure the butt of the feather behind the hook eye. Bind and clip the excess. Whip finish.

Loop-Tuft BWO

Hook: TMC 2487, or other fine-wire scud hook, #14-#18
Thread: Brown 8/0
Shuck: Dun hen hackle fibers
Abdomen: Medium olive Antron dubbing
Wing case: One to three (depending on hook size) Type 1 or Type 2 natural CDC feathers
Thorax: Arizona Synthetic Peacock dubbing, bronze
Wing: Tips from CDC feathers

We've seen perhaps a dozen patterns of this same basic design. It can be varied in size and color to match other mayfly hatches, and in small sizes, it makes a credible midge emerger as well. The "spacer" method for forming the wing case is especially useful on very small hooks, since the short wing fibers can be pulled tight and still produce a hump over the thorax. A spacer can be made from a toothpick, as in the following sequence, thick monofilament line, or almost any rod-like object with a diameter that will give the desired height on the wing case. Whatever the material, it should be a short length, about ½", to keep out of the tying field.

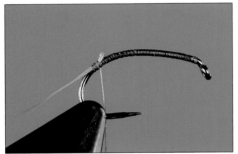

Step 1: Mount the hook and wrap the thread to the tailing position. *Align and strip* (p. 30) a small bundle of dun hen fibers. Secure them atop the shank to make a tail about ¾ the length of the shank.

Step 2: Use the *direct dubbing* method (p. 34) to form a tapered abdomen over the rear half of the hook shank.

Step 3: Align the tips of the CDC feathers; we're using 3 feathers for a #14 hook. Size the feathers by holding them above the hook shank, as shown. Your fingertips should be aligned with the front of the abdomen; the feather tips should reach the end of the shuck, or slightly beyond.

Step 4: Mount the feathers as a group directly in front of the thorax with 4 or 5 tight wraps.

Step 5: Clip and bind down the feather butts. Dub the thorax, stopping 5 to 6 thread-wraps behind the hook eye.

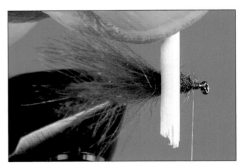

Step 6: Position a short length of a round toothpick (or other round spacer) crosswise atop the thorax, as shown in this top view.

Step 7: With your right fingers, draw the CDC tips vertically. Then fold them forward tightly over the toothpick, and hold them atop the shank directly behind the hook eye. Hold them firmly, and then release your grip on the toothpick. It should stay in position.

Step 8: With your left hand, take 2 or 3 tight wraps to secure the CDC atop the shank.

Step 9: Remove the toothpick. Preen the feather tips rearward and use the thread to form a tapered head against the base of the hair. These wraps will keep the feather tips in an upright position.

Step 10: Whip finish and clip the thread. If necessary, preen the feather tips apart to spread them over the top of the shank to fan-shaped arc, as shown in this front view.

MP 43

Originator: Marc Petitjean
Hook: TMC 100, or equivalent dry-fly hook, #12-#16
Thread: Black 8/0
Tag: Fine silver wire
Tail: Coq de leon feathers and brown UNI Stretch Floss
Rib: Fine silver wire
Abdomen and thorax: Olive Type 1 or Type 2 CDC feather
Wing case: Olive CDC fibers

This low-riding pattern floats quite well and can be adapted to match a variety of mayfly hatches by changing the CDC color or using separate colors for the body and wing case. This is our slight variation of a pattern by Swiss tyer Marc Petitjean.

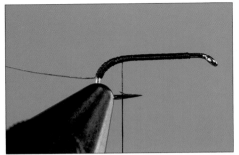

Step 1: Attach the thread and position it halfway around the hook bend. Tie in a length of silver wire, and position the thread at the rearmost point on the straight part of the shank.

Step 2: Wrap the wire in touching turns up to the tying thread. Tie off, but do not clip the excess. Cut a length of Stretch Floss, double it, and tie in the ends atop the shank over the rearmost wraps securing the wire.

Step 3: *Align and strip* (p. 30) 8-10 coq de leon fibers, and mount them atop the shank, directly atop the wraps securing the Stretch Floss, to make a tail as long as the hook shank.

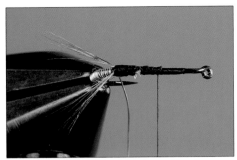

Step 4: With a dubbing needle, form a gap in the center of the tail fibers. Draw the floss up through the gap, dividing the tail fibers into two equal bunches that flare away from the shank symmetrically, as shown in this top view. When the fibers are properly positioned, bind the floss atop the shank and clip the excess.

Step 5: Position the thread directly ahead of the tail. Mount the CDC feather by the tip atop the shank. Position the tying thread ⅓ of a shank-length behind the eye. Twist the butt of the feather to form the barbs into a cord.

Step 6: Wrap the twisted feather forward over the rear ⅔ of the shank. Tie off, but do not clip the excess.

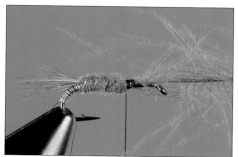

Step 7: Spiral the silver wire over the abdomen to rib it. Tie off and clip the excess at the front of the abdomen.

Step 8: Gather a generous bunch of CDC fibers as shown in *stripping CDC barbs* (p. 40). Mount them atop the shank, directly ahead of the thorax. The fibers will be uneven in length, but mount the bundle so that most of the fibers extend rearward about 1 to 1 ½ shank-lengths. Bind and clip the excess.

Step 9: Retwist the CDC feather, and continue wrapping forward, forming the thorax. (If the feather is too short to form the thorax, clip it off and mount a second feather.) Stop about 6 or 7 thread-wraps distance behind the hook eye. Tie off and clip the feather. Position the thread at the front of the thorax.

Step 10: Fold the CDC barbs over a dubbing needle held crosswise atop the shank, forming a looped wing case about ½ the hook gap in height. Secure the barbs in front of the thorax, with a few tight thread wraps, but do not clip the excess.

Step 11: Draw the CDC barb tips back over the wing case. Wrap the thread over the base of the CDC to slant the barbs rearward over the wing case. Whip finish the fly. Marc Petitjean trims away the stray barbs, leaving only wing and wing case. We leave the stray fibers to give the fly some motion in the water.

Kimball's Diptera Emerger

Originator: Mike Kimball
Hook: Mustad 94833, or other 3X fine dry-fly hook,
   #20-#28
Thread: Dark gray 14/0
Shuck: Teal flank fibers
Thorax: Black fine poly dubbing
Wing case: White poly yarn

This trim, minimalist pattern is superbly simple to tie, which makes it ideal for emerging-midge imitations on very small hooks. The thorax can be tied in any color, and some tyers substitute CDC for the yarn to form the wing case.

Step 1: Attach the thread and position it midshank. Tie in the teal flank fibers to form a tail about 1 ½ times the shank length.

Step 2: Mount a length of poly yarn directly atop the tail-mounting wraps. Clip and bind the excess.

Step 3: Use the *direct dubbing* method (p. 34) to dub the thorax, ending about 5 thread-wraps behind the hook eye.

Step 4: Fold the yarn over a dubbing needle to form a loopwing.

Step 5: Secure the yarn with four tight thread wraps.

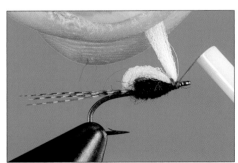

Step 6: Fold the tag of yarn rearward, and place a few thread wraps at the base of the yarn to elevate the tag. Whip finish the fly beneath the yarn, around the hook shank only. Clip the yarn to leave a small tag in front.

Step 7: Use crisscross wraps to mount the wing atop the shank directly ahead of the body, as shown in this top view.

Step 8: Fold the wings rearward, flat down the sides of the body, and wrap rearward to secure the wings in this position.

Step 9: Gather a bundle of CDC fibers as shown in *stripping CDC barbs* (p. 40), and use the technique shown in *throat hackle* (p. 41) to mount them underneath the shank, forming legs that extend just beyond the hook point.

Step 10: Clip and bind down the excess CDC fibers. Use the *direct dubbing* method (p. 34) to form the head of the fly. Whip finish.

Cut-Wing Green Drake Emerger

Hook: TMC 900BL, or equivalent dry-fly hook, #10
Thread: Brown 8/0
Shuck: Green Antron
Body: Olive Antron
Rib: Yellow size A thread
Wings: Dun hen hackle
Legs: Mottled brown hen hackle fibers

Cut-Wing Emergers take advantage of the lifelike markings of hen necks and saddles. This wing style is somewhat more time consuming to tie than other types, but the wings are quite durable.

Step 1: Attach the thread behind the hook eye and spiral to the tailing point. Mount a sparse bundle of Antron atop the shank to form a shuck about one shank-length long. Mount the ribbing thread atop the rearmost thread wrap.

Step 2: Use the *direct dubbing* method (p. 34) to dub a tapered abdomen over the rear ⅔ of the hook shank. *Counter-rib* (p. 33) the abdomen with the yellow thread. Tie off and clip directly in front of the abdomen.

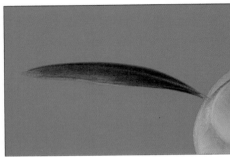

Step 3: Select a pair of dun hen hackles. Place them back-to-front, so that the curvatures match. Strip away the fluffy barbs at the base.

Step 4: With nail clippers or scissors, trim the feather tips, well down into the webby portion of the feathers.

Step 5: Trim the edges to produce a wing-like shape, as shown.

Step 6: Strip away the lower fibers on the stem so that the remaining feather is as long as the fly body.

Step 7: Mount one of the feathers on the near side of the shank, directly ahead of the abdomen. The concave side of the feather should face the tyer; that is, the feather should flare away from the abdomen.

Step 8: Mount the other feather on the far side of the shank, as shown in this top view. Make any adjustments needed to produce symmetrical wings, then bind down the feather stems tightly and clip the excess.

Step 9: Using the method shown in *throat hackle* (p. 41), mount a bundle of mottled hen barbs directly ahead of the wings, beneath the shank, to make legs that extend to the hook point.

Step 10: Clip and bind down the excess leg fibers. Dub the head of the fly, and whip finish.

Spotted Sedge Emerger

Hook: TMC 900BL, or equivalent dry-fly hook, #12-#16
Thread: Brown 8/0
Shuck: Tan Antron
Body: Tan Antron dubbing
Wings: Mottled brown hen hackle
Legs: Olive-brown CDC fibers
Head: Brown dubbing

Like cut wings, burned wings are durable and have a lifelike quality that synthetic materials cannot rival. Wing burners are commercially available and produce more uniform and symmetrical wings than cutting, and the process is a bit faster as well.

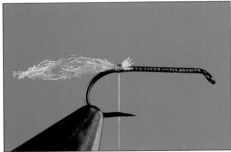

Step 1: Mount the thread behind the hook eye, and lay a foundation to the tailing point. Form and mount a *burned teardrop shuck* (p. 58) that is as long as the hook shank. Position the thread at the rearmost wrap securing the shuck.

Step 2: Use the *direct dubbing* method (p. 34) to form a tapered body about ¾ the distance to the hook eye. Use thread wraps to form a tapered foundation from the front of the abdomen to the hook eye. These will form a foundation for mounting the wings and prevent them from flaring excessively.

Step 3: Select a matched pair of mottled hen hackles, and strip away the fluffy barbs from the base.

Step 4: Place one of the feathers, convex side facing you, in a wing burner. We're using a Renzetti caddis-wing burner here.

Step 5: Pinch the feather in the burner. Note that the feather stem is centered inside the burner halves.

Step 6: Pinch the feather firmly, and use a lighter or candle to burn away the barbs protruding beyond the edges of the burner.

Step 7: Repeat Steps 4-6 for the second feather, but in this case, place the feather in the burner with the concave side facing you. Reversing the feather will ensure that the finished wings have opposing curvatures.

Step 8: Mount the first feather on the thread foundation directly at the front edge of the abdomen to form a wing that extends about halfway to the end of the abdomen. Note that the front of the feather, the most distinctly marked side, faces the tyer, and the lobe-shaped tip points downward.

Step 9: Mount the second feather on the far side of the shank to produce symmetrical wings, as shown in this top view. When the wings are properly positioned, secure the feather stems tightly and clip the excess.

Step 10: Gather a bundle of CDC fibers as explained in *stripping CDC barbs* (p. 40). Mount them beneath the shank as shown in *throat hackle* (p. 41) to produce legs that extend just beyond the hook point.

Step 11: Clip and bind down the excess feather butts. Dub the head of the fly, and whip finish.

Chapter 16: Bullethead Emergers

Bullethead emergers are characterized by a material mounted at the hook eye that is drawn rearward and secured at the front of the abdomen to make a large, almost bubble-like head and thorax. Because the excess bullethead material slants rearward, this style is almost always tied in conjunction with some form of downwing. The bullethead design is more common in dry flies than emerger patterns, but it has some advantages in imitating hatching flies. It gives density and bulk to the front of the fly, which roughly reproduces the visual impression of a hatching natural.

Because bullethead materials are typically buoyant—deer hair and foam are the most common—the combination of head and wing make a fly that floats well, even on patterns with slender, non-buoyant bodies. And since the floatation is concentrated near the front of the fly, this style is an excellent choice for descending-body emergers.

But judging by our research into emerger patterns, tyers have not extensively explored the possibilities of this style, which is perhaps unfortunate, since bullethead patterns make effective, easy-to-tie, durable emergers.

Vulnerable Caddis

Originator: Vladimir Markov
Hook: Mustad 94840, or other standard dry-fly hook, #10-#18
Thread: Brown 6/0
Shuck: Light gray Antron and one strand pearlescent Flashabou
Abdomen: Olive-brown Antron dubbing
Hackle: Dun
Wing: Natural deer hair

Components on this pattern can be varied in color to match hatches as needed. Dress only the wing with floatant so that the body hangs below the surface film.

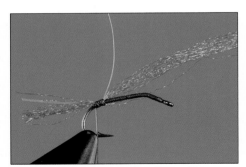

Step 1: Using a pair of needle-nose pliers, bend the front ⅓ of the shank downward, as shown. Secure the hook in the vise. Mount the thread and position it at the bend. Mount a small bundle of Antron fibers and a strand of Krystal Flash to form a shuck about ⅔ the length of the shank. Clip and bind the excess materials.

Step 2: Use the *direct dubbing* method (p. 34) to dub a slightly tapered abdomen. Stop far enough behind the bend you formed in the shank to allow 4-5 wraps of hackle. Position thread behind the hook eye. You may find it easier to reposition the hook in the vise as shown in Step 4.

Step 3: *Clip, clean, and stack* (p. 32) a bundle of deer hair. Mount the hair atop the shank, tips forward, directly behind the hook eye. The tips should extend beyond the mounting wraps a distance of one shank-length.

Step 4: Bind the hair tightly atop the shank. Clip the hair butts and cover them tightly with tying thread. Return the thread to the front of the abdomen.

Step 5: *Prepare a hackle feather* (p. 39) and mount it directly ahead of the abdomen as explained in *mounting collar hackle* (p. 37)

Step 6: Take 4 to 5 turns of the hackle as shown in *wrapping dry-fly hackle* (p. 44). These wraps should all be made behind the angle that was bent in the shank in Step 1.

Step 7: Tie off and clip the hackle. Position the thread directly ahead of the last hackle wrap.

Step 8: Gather the hair in your left fingers, and draw it smoothly rearward, keeping all the hair atop the shank.

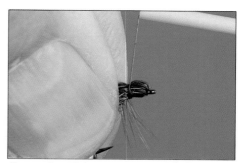

Step 9: Take several tight thread wraps over the hair, using your left fingers to keep the hair fibers positioned atop the shank.

Step 10: Whip-finish the fly over the wraps forming the wing and head.

Bullethead Midge Emerger

Hook: TMC 2487, or other light-wire scud hook, #10-#18
Thread: Brown 8/0
Shuck: White Antron
Abdomen: Olive Larva Lace
Wing/head: Deer hair
Thorax: Olive dubbing

Larva Lace gives a nice translucence to the body, which sinks below the surface film. For smaller sizes of this design, choose finely textured deer hair with short, abruptly tapering tips to maximize floatation and give definition to the wing silhouette.

Step 1: Mount the thread behind the hook eye, and lay a thread foundation to the tailing point. Secure a sparse bundle of Antron fibers atop the shank to form a shuck about one hook-gap long.

Step 2: Clip and bind the excess Antron. Mount a length of Larva Lace atop the shuck-mounting wraps. Bind the Larva Lace to the top of the shank forming smooth underbody over the rear ⅔ of the shank. Clip the excess tubing.

Step 3: Wrap the Larva Lace forward in touching turns until the front of the underbody is reached. Bind down the tubing and clip the excess. Position the thread behind the hook eye.

Step 4: *Clip, clean, and stack* (p. 32) a bundle of deer hair. Secure it atop the shank, just behind the eye, so that the tips extending a distance of one shank-length beyond the mounting wraps. Clip the hair butts and bind down with thread.

Step 5: Use the *direct dubbing* method (p. 34) to dub the thorax, moving from the hook eye to the abdomen. Position the thread at the front of the abdomen.

Step 6: Draw the hair smoothly and evenly rearward over the top of the thorax. Secure the hair atop the shank at the front of the abdomen. Whip finish the fly over these thread wraps.

GRHE Emerger

Originator: David Hunter
Hook: TMC 2487, or other light-wire scud hook, #12-#14
Thread: Tan 6/0
Tail: Partridge hackle fibers
Rib: Oval gold tinsel
Abdomen: Hare's ear dubbing
Thorax: Hare's ear dubbing
Wing: Deer hair over one olive Type 1 CDC feather over 4 strands yellow Krystal Flash

This pattern shows the possibilities of multiple materials for the bullethead. The layered wing, heavy thorax, and bullethead give this fly a block, meaty appearance. It floats low but is still visible to the angler.

Step 1: Mount the thread and position it at the tailing point. *Align and strip* (p. 30) 6-8 partridge fibers, and secure them atop the shank at the tailing position to form a tail about one-shank length long. Strip the ⅛" of the metallic coating off a length of oval tinsel, and secure it atop the tailing wraps.

Step 2: Use the *direct dubbing* method (p. 34) to dub a slightly tapered abdomen just beyond the midpoint of the shank. *Counter-rib* (p. 33) the tinsel and tie it off in front of the abdomen. Clip the excess. Position the tying thread behind the hook eye.

Step 3: *Clip, clean, and stack* (p. 32) a bundle of deer hair. Secure it tightly atop the shank behind the hook eye so that the tips extends over the hook eye a distance of two shank-lengths. Clip and bind down the hair butts.

Step 4: Mount the CDC feather atop the shank so that the feather tip is aligned with the deer-hair tips. Bind and clip the excess. Then mount the Krystal Flash atop the CDC so that the tips of all three materials are aligned. Bind and clip the excess. Position the tying thread in front of the abdomen.

Step 5: Form the thorax by dubbing a layer of hare's ear from the abdomen to the hook eye; then dub another layer rearward, producing a thick thorax and ending with the thread directly in front of the abdomen.

Step 6: Draw the stack of three wing materials smoothly rearward over the top of the shank. The Krystal Flash should be on the bottom, the CDC in the middle, the deer hair on top. Secure them tightly ahead of the abdomen with several wraps, and whip finish the fly over these wraps.

Emerging Caddis

Originator: Roman Moser
Hook: TMC 100, or equivalent dry-fly hook, #14-#20
Thread: Tan 8/0
Abdomen: Tan dubbing
Thorax: Tan dubbing
Wing: Natural light elk hair
Bullethead: Yellow ⅛" closed-cell foam

This low-floating pattern is quite easy to tie, and the yellow foam makes it easy to see. Body colors and materials can be varied—olive, gray, peacock—and deer hair can be used for the wing to imitate darker caddis species.

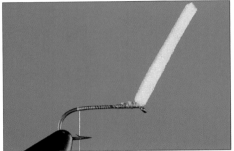

Step 1: Mount the thread behind the hook eye. Wrap rearward about ⅓ of a shank-length, then lay a thread foundation back to the eye. Cut a strip of foam about ½ the hook gap in width. Mount the foam directly behind the eye, binding down the tag as you wrap the thread to the rear of the shank.

Step 2: Use the *direct dubbing* method (p. 34) to dub an abdomen over the rear ⅔ of the shank.

Step 3: *Clip, clean, and stack* (p. 32) a sparse bundle of elk hair. Mount the hair atop the shank directly in front of the abdomen so that the hair tips extend just beyond the hook bend.

Step 4: Clip and bind the excess hair. Wrap the thread to the rear of the hook eye. Apply thorax dubbing and wrap rearward to the front of the abdomen.

Step 5: Fold the foam strip back over the top of the shank, and secure it at the front of the abdomen. Whip finish over these wraps.

Step 6: Clip the foam to form a short wing about ¼ of a shank-length long.

Foam Emerger

Hook: TMC 206BL, or other fine-wire scud hook, #14-#18
Thread: Black 8/0
Shuck: White Antron
Body: Stripped peacock quill
Hackle: Dun hen hackle
Bullethead: Gray ⅛" closed-cell foam (or 2mm foam on smaller hooks)

We've seen many patterns of this type tied for all kinds of hatches. This generic version can be fished as a midge or mayfly imitation. Colors can, of course, be substituted, but the fly rides best if the body is tied of a non-buoyant material—hackle quill, V-Rib, vinyl tubing, and so on, to sink it beneath the surface.

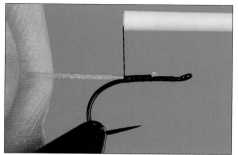

Step 1: Mount the thread behind the hook eye, and wrap rearward about ⅓ of shank-length. Take a very sparse bundle of Antron, and secure it atop the shank. Clip the front tag. With a *flattened thread* (p. 37), wrap rearward, binding the Antron to the top of the hook and forming a smooth underbody for the quill.

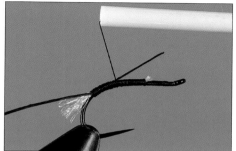

Step 2: Bind the Antron to a point just around the hook bend. Clip to form a short tail about ½ the hook gap in length. Mount the tip of stripped peacock quill atop the rearmost tailing wrap. Bind the tag of the quill atop the shank, forming a smooth underbody to the point where the shuck material was first mounted. Clip the excess.

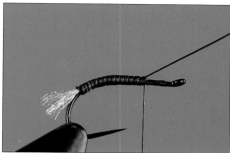

Step 3: Using the method shown in *wrapping quill bodies* (p. 47), wrap the quill forward over ⅔ of the shank. Tie off and clip the excess. Position the thread behind the hook eye.

Step 4: Cut a strip of foam ½ the hook gap in width. Mount it behind the eye, and bind down the tag. *Prepare a hackle feather* (p. 39) and mount it in front of the abdomen as explained in *mounting collar hackle* (p. 37).

Step 5: Take 3 or 4 turns of the feather as explained in *wrapping wet-fly hackle* (p. 50). Secure and clip the feather tip.

Step 6: Fold the foam rearward over the top of the shank, and secure it directly in front of the hackle. Whip finish over these wraps. Clip the foam to form a wing about ½ the length of the abdomen. Coat the quill body with head cement for durability.

Callibaetis Foam Emerger

Originator: Philip Rowley
Hook: TMC 2487, or other fine-wire scud hook, #10-#14
Thread: Light brown 8/0
Tail: Gray partridge hackle fibers
Abdomen: Tan Antron dubbing
Rib: Pearl Flashabou
Underwing: Gray Z-Lon over pearl Crystal Hair
Overwing: One Type 1 or Type 2 gray CDC feather
Thorax: Tan Antron dubbing
Wing case: Gray ⅛" closed-cell foam
Legs: Gray partridge hackle fibers

Callibaetis can vary significantly in color from one body of water to another, and the dubbing color can be adjusted accordingly. Don't treat the fly with floatant, but you can squeeze a little water into the abdomen to make it sink below the film.

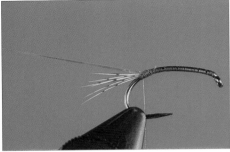

Step 1: Mount the thread and wrap to the tailing point. *Align and strip* (p. 30) 6-8 partridge fibers and mount them atop the shank to form a tail about one hook-gap in length. Mount the ribbing material atop the tailing wraps.

Step 2: Use the *direct dubbing* method (p. 34) to dub a slender abdomen over the rear half of the hook shank. Spiral the ribbing forward to the front of the abdomen. Tie off and clip the excess.

Step 3: Mount 3-5 strands of Crystal Hair at the front of the abdomen so that they extend rearward to the bend of the hook. Clip and bind the excess.

Step 4: Mount a sparse bundle of Z-Lon over the Crystal Hair, again extending rearward to the hook bend. Clip and bind the excess.

Step 5: Mount a CDC feather over the Z-Lon so that the tip is aligned with the underwing materials. Clip and bind the excess.

Step 6: Position the thread 4-5 thread-wraps' distance behind the hook eye. Cut a strip of foam about ⅓ the hook gap in width. Mount it behind the eye, and wrap rearward to bind down the tag end. Wrap the thread forward again to the hook eye.

Step 7: Apply dubbing and wrap rearward to the front of the abdomen, forming a thorax that is slightly thicker than the abdomen.

Step 8: Fold the foam rearward over the top of the shank, and bind it down in front of the abdomen. Whip finish over these wraps, and clip the thread.

Step 9: Clip the foam to form a wing about ½ the hook-gap in height.

Step 10: Re-mount the thread behind the hook eye. Use the method shown in *throat hackle* (p. 41) to mount 6-8 partridge fibers to form legs that extend just beyond the hook point. Clip and bind the excess. Whip finish.

Chapter 17: Clipped Deer-Hair Emergers

The natural buoyancy of clipped deer hair would seem to make it an obvious choice for emerger patterns, but tyers have not explored this approach much, even though one emerger pattern of this style, the Serendipity, is widely used in the Rocky Mountain states.

But there are advantages to the approach. Clipped deer-hair flies incorporate the most buoyant part of the hair, producing a fly that floats well without requiring excessive amounts of material; conversely clipped hair can, when desired, give the appearance of volume or substance to a pattern with relatively little material. Clipped hair is quite durable, and it can be trimmed to any variety of shape. Serbian tyer Goran Grubic uses a simple, tapered body on his all-purpose Deer Hair Floating Nymph, while Jim Pettis's intriguing Pulsating Caddis incorporates a more carefully manicured wing that suggests the kind of interesting possibilities that spun deer hair holds out for tying emerger patterns.

Serendipity

Hook: TMC 2487, or other fine-wire scud hook, #12-#20
Thread: Olive 6/0
Body: Olive Antron yarn
Head: Deer hair

Though this standard pattern on Western waters is often fished deep, it is an excellent midge emerger that can be fished in the film. It is simple to tie and can be altered to match the color of the natural. Treat just the deer hair with floatant so that the abdomen sinks beneath the surface. Because it can be difficult to see, the fly is often fished as a trailer behind a larger dry fly.

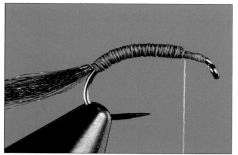

Step 1: Attach the thread. Lay a thread foundation to the rearmost point of the body. Mount a strand of Antron yarn, and bind it atop the shank, wrapping forward to a point ¼ of a shank-length behind the hook eye. Clip the excess Antron.

Step 2: Twist the yarn clockwise tightly, and wrap forward in close, tight turns to form a segmented body.

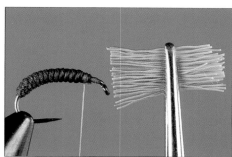

Step 3: Continue wrapping the body forward to the tying thread. Secure the yarn and clip the excess. *Clip, clean, and stack* (p. 32) a bundle of deer hair. Trim both the tips and butts of the hair so that they are even.

Step 4: Secure the hair atop the shank with 3-4 tight thread wraps. Hold the hair firmly in the left fingers so that it doesn't roll around the shank.

Step 5: Preen the hair rearward, and whip finish around the shank only, directly behind the hook eye.

Step 6: Trim the head to shape by rounding the butts that extend over the hook eye and by clipping the tip ends at an angle to form a wing about half the length of the body, as shown.

Deer Hair Floating Nymph

Originator: Goran Grubic
Hook: TMC 102Y, or equivalent dry-fly hook, #11-#15
Thread: Olive 6/0
Tail: Deer hair
Body: Deer hair
Collar: Deer hair
Head: Clipped butts from collar

Tyer Goran Grubic uses this fly as a generalized emerger pattern on his home waters in Serbia. Though it sits on the surface film, the clipped deer hair gives it excellent floatation, making it a good choice in choppy or turbulent water.

Step 1: Attach the thread and position it at the tailing point. *Clip, clean, and stack* (p. 32) a sparse bundle of deer hair. Mount it atop the shank to form a tail about ⅔ of a shank-length long. If the hair flares excessively, make a snug, but not tight, turn of thread just behind the rearmost wrap to consolidate the hair.

Step 2: Clip, clean, and stack a bundle of deer hair that is about ⅓ to ½ the hook gap in diameter. Trim off the tips. Position the hair atop the shank so that the bundle is centered over the tying thread. Take two snug thread wraps around the center of the hair, using the left fingers to keep the hair atop the shank.

Step 3: Apply tension to the thread. As the hair begins to slide around the far side of the shank, release it from the left finger. Apply more tension to the thread, and begin wrapping the thread around the hook shank.

Step 4: As the hair begins to flare and migrate around the shank, apply thread tension just below the breaking point, and continue wrapping the thread around the center of hair. After two or three wraps, enough friction will build that the hair will be fully flared and will no longer spin.

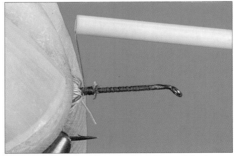

Step 5: Preen back the flared hair as shown, and take 3 or 4 thread wraps against the base of the hair.

Step 6: Repeat Steps 2-6 to spin a second bundle of hair around the shank. When the second bundle is secured, use your fingers as shown to push the flared hair inward from both sides and compress it. Compacting the hair helps create a dense, uniform body.

Step 7: Continue spinning and compressing bundles of hair until ¾ of the hook shank is covered. Take a few half-hitches ahead of the last bundle of hair, and clip the tying thread.

Step 8: Use sharp scissors to trim the hair to the block-like shape shown in this front view. Notice that the hair beneath the shank is trimmed very close to the shank to maximize the hooking gap.

Step 9: Working from front to back, trim the corners of the block and taper the body toward the tail.

Step 10: Finally, work carefully around the tail to trim away any hairs that project rearward.

Step 11: Attach the tying thread at the front edge of the body. Clip, clean and stack a bundle of deer hair. Trim the end to make the bundle as long as the hook shank. Position the hair atop the shank so that the butt ends extend to the hook eye. Take two snug, but not tight, wraps.

Step 12: Use the technique explained in Steps 3 and 4 to spin the hair around the shank to form a collar. Use heavy thread pressure. When the hair no longer spins, whip finish the fly behind the eye, in front of the hair butts.

Step 13: Trim the head to the same diameter as the body.

Pulsating Caddis Emerger—Tan

Originator: Jim Pettis
Hook: TMC 2312, or other fine-wire 2XL ring-eye hook,
 #14-#16
Thread: Olive 6/0
Lower body: Lava brown Paxton's Buggy Nymph dubbing;
 three light orange 14/0 glass beads; olive-brown
 marabou
Upper body: Pale olive-yellow Scintilla dubbing
Wing: Light tan elk hair
Legs: Mallard flank dyed wood duck

Brushed dubbing on the body gives this pattern mobility and translucence in the water, while glass beads give it some sparkle. Only the wings and legs should be dressed with floatant to ensure proper position of the fly in the water. Jim Pettis recommends a downstream-and-across presentation, alternately drifting and twitching the fly.

Step 1: Slide 3 beads onto the hook shank. Mount the tying thread, and position it at the midpoint of the shank. Wrap rearward, placing 1 or 2 thread wraps between each pair of beads, ending behind the rearmost bead, as shown.

Step 2: Use the *direct dubbing* method (p. 34) to dub a ball at the rear of the body just large enough to form a back-stop for the beads.

Step 3: With a dubbed thread, wrap forward, placing one or two wraps of dubbing between each pair of beads, ending with a wrap or two ahead of the frontmost bead.

Step 4: Use a dubbing teaser to brush out the dubbing between the beads, forming a flowing, veil-like capsule, through which the beads are visible.

Step 5: Using the method shown in *side-mounted legs* (p. 39), secure a small tuft of marabou fibers on either side of the shank just ahead of the dub-bing.

Step 6: Dub forward with the upper-body dubbing color, forming a tight, slightly tapered body to a point 6 or 7 thread-wraps' distance behind the hook eye.

Step 7: *Clip, clean, and stack* (p. 32) a sparse bundle of elk hair. Clip both the tips and the butts. Mount the bundle atop the shank, directly ahead of the thorax. Do not allow the hair to spin around the shank; it should flare upward and outward over the top half of the shank.

Step 8: Secure 6-10 mallard fibers beneath the shank and behind the hook eye, with the tips extending beyond the hook eye about ¾ the shank length. Clip the excess. Whip finish behind the eye, around the shank only.

Step 9: Trim the elk-hair wing at an angle, as shown, so that it extends rearward about half the length of the body.

Step 10: Trim the dubbed portion of the fly to the wedge shape shown in this top view.

Step 11: Trim the wings to a tent-like shape, as shown in this rear view of the fly.

Step 12: Here is a view of the fly from underneath.

Index of Pattern Types

The majority of emerger patterns are designed to represent a certain type of insect, such as caddisflies, and these are listed under the corresponding category. Other patterns, however, are productive during more than one type of emergence—both mayfly and midge hatches, for instance—and such patterns are listed under both categories. A handful of patterns have very broad applications, and these are listed in the category "All-purpose Emergers."

Index of Patterns

Index of Tyers/Originators